Great Irish Speeches

OF THE TWENTIETH CENTURY

Great Irish Speeches

Of The Twentieth Century

MICHAEL McLOUGHLIN

POOLBEG

Published 1996
by Poolbeg Press Ltd
123 Baldoyle Industrial Estate
Dublin 13, Ireland

© Michael McLoughlin 1996

The moral right of the author has been asserted.

A catalogue record for this book is available from the British Library.

ISBN 1 85371 613 8

Cover photography by The Slide File
Cover design by Poolbeg Group Services Ltd
Set by Poolbeg Group Services Ltd in Garamond 11/14
Printed by The Guernsey Press Ltd,
Vale, Guernsey, Channel Islands.

ACKNOWLEDGEMENTS

I would like to acknowledge the help of a large number of people without whom this book would not have been written.

For interest and general advice, particularly at the start of the project, I am particularly grateful to Vivienne Byrne and Sean Faughnan. I am especially appreciative of the help given to me by Anne Walsh of Trinity College Dublin Library and to the staff of the National Library of Ireland. I also received considerable support and information from Mary Cummins, Ciaron Denny and Mary McLoughlin.

The unenviable task of converting illegible copies of speeches and commentaries into a legible text was undertaken by Helen Casey, and by Marie Tully. Their enthusiasm throughout the project was crucial to its completion.

Poolbeg Press, particularly Kate Cruise O'Brien and Nicole Hodson have been supportive, patient and constructive throughout. I am grateful to them. All mistakes, of course, are my responsibility.

I must also acknowledge my debt to my family and especially to my father who unwittingly started me on this path many years ago, when he played me an old reel to reel recording of John F Kennedy's address to the Oireachtas.

Most of all my thanks to my wife Margaret, and my son Robert (who arrived somewhere between the 1916 Proclamation and John Dillon's speech to the Commons). This book is dedicated to them.

For Margaret

and Robert

CONTENTS

INTRODUCTION

The twentieth century has been a period of great change for the island of Ireland. In 1900, full independence was the distant aspiration of a minority, while the majority of nationalists seemed content to place their faith in the Irish Parliamentary Party at Westminster. For Unionists, their place in the Empire did not seem under immediate threat, Little had been heard, in political terms, of Pearse or Craig, Collins was just ten years old and Queen Victoria reigned over an Empire on which the sun never set.

Ninety-six years later, an independent Republic of Ireland assumes on a periodic basis the presidency of the European Union, a union of states that stretches from Greece and Spain in the South to the Nordic Countries and as far west as Ireland. Other countries from the former Eastern Bloc clamber for admission.

In between there has been the struggle for Irish Independence, partition, and in a wider theatre, two world wars, the collapse of established empires, and the arrival and departure of various forms of totalitarianism.

Between these two snapshots in time lies a wealth of passion and triumph, of struggle and bitterness, of creation and recreation of the modern state. With the benefit of hindsight we can see common threads, and in many ways we have come to understand each event in the context of what followed. The Treaty Debates take on a different meaning when read with the knowledge of the next seventy years. But to those whose words jump from these pages, the issues they addressed were here and now; they knew only that they were at a cross-roads – not where they would eventually be slotted in a later interpretation of history. The power of these speeches lies in the fact that they

1

are the voices of the moment; unclouded by later events or revision. Their passion may add more to our understanding of our history than much of the analysis which fed off their words and deeds.

Although much has changed much has stayed the same. In 1922, Winston Churchill decried the continued presence of the dreary steeples of Fermanagh and Tyrone. The core difficulties of Ulster remain and the dispute between nationalism and unionism seems etched in the language and line of a century ago. The twentieth century has seen only periodic reduction in emigration, and as a consequence over seventy million people globally claim Irish descent.

The compilation of a collection such as this is inevitably a personal choice and for every speech that is included, there are ten others that could be considered. The criteria for inclusion were set as broadly as possible. Speeches were defined to include Statements that were issued, by an individual or group of individuals. I have also included political statements such as Kipling's "Ulster 1912", and Connolly's "Let us Free Ireland", because they typify the case that each made for the causes in which they believed. It is also easier to select speeches for inclusion from the first decades of the century than when dealing with contemporary events, when the full impact of individual statements or speeches remains to be seen.

In terms of subject matter, "Irish" has also been left deliberately vague. The speeches that have been included may have been selected because of the fact that they were made by an Irish person, that they were made on Irish soil, or because they impacted in some way on Irish politics and life. Not all of the speeches that have been selected are examples of great oratory, but they all influenced or reflected a defining moment in Irish life.

Every effort has been made to ensure that no breach of copyright has occurred in drawing together this collection. Any oversight in this regard will be rectified. Please contact the publisher.

"A NATION . . . CAN ONLY . . . MAINTAIN SELF EXISTENCE AND INDEPENDENCE BY ITS OWN POWER AND RESOURCES"

Arthur Griffith (1871–1922) was born in Dublin and educated at Christian Brothers School, Strand Street. After spending some time as a printer, and travelling to South Africa where he worked in the gold mines, he came back to Ireland in 1898 to edit a new weekly paper, The United Irishman. *With the Irish Parliamentary Party in disarray after the fall of Parnell, Griffith argued that a new approach to the Irish question was needed – based on the development of passive resistance to English rule in Ireland, and the establishment of an alternative government. The arguments were published in 1904 as a pamphlet –* The Resurrection of Hungary. *At a conference in 1905, Griffith developed this policy under the name Sinn Féin.*

SINN FEIN ARD FHEIS, DUBLIN, DECEMBER 9, 1905

The Anglicisation of the Irish mind is best exhibited in its attitude towards economics . . . I am in economics largely a follower of the man who thwarted England's dream of the commercial conquest of the world, and who made the mighty confederation before which England has fallen commercially and is falling politically – Germany. His name is a famous one in the outside world, his works are the text books of economic science in other counties – in Ireland his name is unknown and his works unheard of – I refer to Frederick List, the real founder of the German Zollverein . . .

Brushing aside the fallacies of Adam Smith and his tribe, List points out that between the individual and humanity stands,

3

and must continue to stand, a great fact – the Nation. The Nation, with its special language and literature, with its peculiar origin and history, with its special manners and customs, laws and institutions, with the claims of all these for existence, independence, perfection, and continuance for the future, with its separate territory, a society which, united by a thousand ties of minds and interests, combines itself into one independent whole, which recognises the law of right for and within itself, and in its united character is still opposed to other societies of a similar kind in their national liberty, and consequently can, only under the existing conditions of the world, maintain self-existence and independence by its own power and resources. As the individual chiefly obtains by means of the nation and in the nation, mental culture, power of production, security and prosperity, so is the civilisation of the human race only conceivable and possible by means of the civilisation and development of individual nations. But as there are amongst men infinite differences in condition and circumstances, so there are in nations – some are strong, some are weak, some are highly civilised, some are half civilised, but in all exists as in the unit the impulse of self-preservation and the desire for improvement. It is the task of national politics to ensure existence and continuance to the nation to make the weak strong, the half civilised more civilised. It is the task of national economics to accomplish the economical development of the nation and fit it for admission into the universal society of the future . . .

We in Ireland have been taught by our British lords lieutenant, our British Educational Boards, and our Barrington Lecturers, that our destiny is to be the fruitful mother of flocks and herds – that it is not necessary for us to pay attention to our manufacturing arm, since our agricultural arm is all sufficient. The fallacy is apparent to the man who thinks – but it is a fallacy which has passed for truth in Ireland. With List I reply: a nation cannot promote and further its civilisation, its prosperity, and its social progress equally as well by exchanging

4

agricultural products for manufactured goods as by establishing a manufacturing power of its own. A merely agricultural nation can never develop to any extent a home or foreign commerce with inland means of transport and its foreign navigation, increase its population in due proportion to their well-being or make notable progress in its moral, intellectual, social and political development: it will never acquire important political power or be placed in a position to influence less advanced nations and to form colonies of its own. A mere agricultural state is infinitely less powerful than an agricultural-manufacturing state. The former is always economically and politically dependent on those foreign nations who take from it agriculture in exchange for manufactured goods . . . An agricultural nation is a man with one arm who makes use of an arm belonging to another person, but cannot, of course, be sure of having it always available. An agricultural-manufacturing nation is a man who has both arms of his own at his own disposal . . . We must offer our producers protection where protection is necessary; and let it be clearly understood what protection is. Protection does not mean the exclusion of foreign competition – it means the enabling of the native manufacturer to meet foreign competition on an equal footing. It does not mean that we shall pay a higher profit to any Irish manufacturer but we shall not stand by and see him crushed by mere weight of foreign capital. If an Irish manufacturer cannot produce an article as cheaply as an English or other foreigner, solely because his foreign competitor has had larger resources at his disposal, then it is the first duty of the Irish nation to accord protection to the Irish manufacturer. If, on the other hand, an Irish manufacturer can produce as cheaply, but charges an enhanced price, such a man deserves no support – he is in plain words a swindler. It is the duty of our public bodies in whose hands the expenditure of £4,000,000 annually is placed to pay where necessary an enhanced price for Irish manufactured articles, when the manufacturers show them they cannot produce them at the lesser price – this is protection . . .

With the development of her manufacturing arm will proceed the rise of a national middle-class in Ireland and a trained national democracy – and – I here again quote List against the charlatans who profess to see in a nation's language and tradition things of no economic value – "in every nation will the authority of national language and national literature, the civilising arts and the perfection of municipal institutions keep pace with the development of the manufacturing arm". How are we to accord protection to and procure the development of our manufacturing arm? First, by ourselves individually; secondly, through our County, Urban, and District Councils, and Poor Law Guardians; thirdly, by taking over control of those inefficient bodies known as Harbour Commissioners; fourthly, by stimulating our manufacturers and our people to industrial enterprise; and fifthly, by inviting to aid in our development, on commercial lines, Irish-American capital. In the first case, every individual knows his duty, whether he practises it or not – it is, unless where fraud is attempted, to pay if necessary an enhanced price for Irish goods, and to use whenever possible none but Irish goods. As to our public elective bodies which annually control the expenditure of our local taxation, their duty is the same. The duty of our harbour bodies is to arrange the incidence of port dues so that they shall fall most heavily on manufactured goods coming into the country, and to keep and publish a table of all goods imported and to whom consigned . . .

We propose the formation of a Council of Three Hundred, composed of members of the General Council of County Councils and representatives of the Urban Councils, Rural Councils, Poor Law Boards, and Harbour Boards of the country to sit in Dublin and form a de facto Irish Parliament. Associated and sitting and voting with this body, which might assemble in Dublin in the spring and in the autumn, could be the persons elected for Irish constituencies, who decline to confer on the affairs of Ireland with foreigners in a foreign city. On its assembly in Dublin this National Assembly should appoint committees to especially consider and report to the general assembly on all subjects appertaining to the country. On the reports of these committees the Council should deliberate and formulate workable schemes, which, once formulated, it would be the duty of all County and Urban Councils, Rural Councils, Poor Law Boards, and other bodies to give legal effect to so far as their powers permit, and where their legal powers fall short, to give it the moral force of law by inducing and instructing those whom they represent to honour and obey the recommendations of the Council of Three Hundred individually and collectively . . .

"LET US FREE IRELAND"

James Connolly (1868–1916) was a crucial formative influence on the Irish Labour movement in the early years of the century. Born in Edinburgh, he came back to Ireland in 1896 (having previously served in Ireland with the British Army) as paid organiser of the Dublin Socialist Club. Like his trade union colleague James Larkin, Connolly's influence extended beyond Ireland to Britain and the United States, where he stayed from 1903 to 1910. On his return Connolly became Ulster organiser for the Transport Workers Union.

After Larkin, the leader of the workers in the Dublin Lockout of 1913, was imprisoned, Connolly took Larkin's place at the helm. Connolly also founded the Irish Citizens' Army, which was to play a role in the Easter Rising of 1916. As one of the seven signatories of the 1916 Proclamation, he was executed on May 12, 1916.

"Let Us Free Ireland" demonstrated the twin strands of Connolly's ideology – nationalism and socialism. It was first published in the Workers' Republic *in 1899 but reprinted in* Socialism Made Easy *in Chicago 1908. Although not delivered directly as a speech, it typifies Connolly's approach, and is thus included in this collection.*

CHICAGO 1908

Let Us Free Ireland! Never mind such base carnal thoughts as concern work and wages, healthy homes, or lives unclouded by poverty.

Let Us Free Ireland! The rack-renting landlord; is he not also

8

an Irishman, and wherefore should we hate him? Nay, let us not speak harshly of our brother, yea, even when he raises our rent.

Let Us Free Ireland! The profit-grinding capitalist, who robs us of three-fourths of the fruit of our labour, who sucks the very marrow of our bones when we are young, and then throws us out in the street like a worn-out tool when we are grown prematurely old in his service, is he not an Irishman, and mayhap a patriot, and wherefore should we think harshly of him?

Let Us Free Ireland! "The land that bred and bore us." And the landlord who makes us pay for permission to live upon it. Whoop it up for liberty!

"Let us free Ireland," says the patriot who won't touch Socialism. Let us all join together, and cr-r-rush the br-r-rutal Saxon. Let us all join together, says he, all classes and creeds. And, says the town worker, after we have crushed the Saxon and freed Ireland, what will we do? Oh, then you can go back to your slums, same as before. Whoop it up for liberty!

And, says the agricultural worker, after we have freed Ireland, what then? Oh, then you can go scraping around for the landlord's rent or the money-lender's interest same as before. Whoop it up for liberty!

After Ireland is free, says the patriot who won't touch Socialism, we will protect all classes, and if you won't pay your rent you will be evicted same as now. But the evicting party, under the command of the sheriff, will wear green uniforms and the Harp without the Crown, and the warrant turning you out on the roadside will be stamped with the arms of the Irish Republic. Now isn't that worth fighting for?

And when you cannot find employment, and, giving up the struggle for life in despair, enter the poorhouse, the band of the nearest regiment of the Irish army will escort you to the poorhouse door to the tune of "St Patrick's Day". Oh! it will be nice to live in those days.

"With the Green Flag floating o'er us" and an ever-increasing army of unemployed workers walking about under the Green

Flag, wishing they had something to eat. Same as now! Whoop it up for liberty!

Now, my friend, I also am Irish, but I'm a bit more logical. The capitalist, I say, is a parasite on industry; as useless in the present stage of our industrial development as any other parasite in the animal or vegetable world is to the life of the animal or vegetable upon which it feeds.

The working class is the victim of this parasite – this human leech, and it is the duty and interest of the working class to use every means in its power to oust this parasite class from the position which enables it to thus prey upon the vitals of labour.

Therefore, I say, let us organise to meet our masters and destroy their mastership; organise to drive them from their hold upon public life through their political power; organise to wrench from their robber clutch the land and workshops on and in which they enslave us; organise to cleanse our social life from the stain of social cannibalism, from the preying of man upon his fellow man.

Organise for a full, free and happy life For All Or For None.

"ULSTER 1912"

Rudyard Kipling (1865–1936) was born in Bombay and educated in England. He returned to India in 1882 and became a journalist and short story writer. He eventually settled in England in 1896. Kipling became an extremely popular writer, and he won the Nobel Prize for Literature in 1907.

Given his background, Kipling's absolute support of the Unionist cause and of the Empire was unsurprising. His poem, "Ulster 1912", which was first published in the Morning Post, *graphically illustrates his political view of Home Rule and his call to others to support Unionism in its hour of need.*

The poem was quoted by Peter Robinson MP, deputy leader of the Democratic Unionist Party, in his November 1985 Commons speech opposing the Anglo-Irish Agreement.

Morning Post, April 9, 1912

"Ulster 1912"
  The dark eleventh hour
  Draws on and sees us sold
  To every evil power
  We fought against of old.
  Rebellion, rapine, hate,
  Oppression, wrong and greed
  Are loosed to rule our fate,
  By England's act and deed.

The faith in which we stand
The laws we made and guard,
Our honour, lives and land
Are given for reward
To murder done at night,
To treason taught by day,
To folly, sloth, and spite,
And we are thrust away.

The blood our fathers spilt
Our love, our toils, our pains,
Are counted us for guilt,
And only bind our chains.
Before an Empire's eyes,
The traitor claims his price.
What need of further lies?
We are the sacrifice.

We know the war prepared
On every peaceful home,
We know the hells declared
For such as serve not Rome –
The terror, threats, and dread
In market, hearth, and field –
We know, when all is said,
We perish if we yield.

Believe, we dare not boast,
Believe, we do not fear –
We stand to pay the cost
In all that men hold dear.
What answer from the North?
One Law, one Land, one Throne.
If England drives us forth
We shall not fall alone.

"HOLD THE PASS FOR THE EMPIRE"

Andrew Bonar Law (1858–1923) was born in New Brunswick, Canada, of Ulster Presbyterian stock. He made a considerable fortune in the steel business in Edinburgh, and entered Parliament in 1900 as Unionist MP for the Glasgow constituency of Bladkfriars.

Bonar Law was elected as leader of the Conservative Party in 1911. He regarded opposition to Irish Home Rule as one of the key tenets of his political existence. He was also prepared to settle for a scheme of partition far earlier than many of his colleagues on the Conservative and Unionist benches.

Bonar Law was a ruthless political operator. With the Conservatives out of power since 1905, he also saw Home Rule for Ireland as a political issue which could throw his party a life-line in opposition. In two speeches in 1912, he urged Unionists to go as far as necessary to defeat Home Rule.

At Balmoral near Belfast on April 9, 1912 (two days before the introduction of the Third Home Rule Bill), Bonar Law pushed the parameters of opposition to encompass far more than they had before.

BALMORAL, APRIL 9, 1912

I say it to you with all solemnity; you must trust to yourselves. Once again you hold the pass for the Empire. You are a besieged city. Does not the picture of the past, the glorious past with which you are so familiar, rise again before your eyes? The timid have left you, your Lundys have betrayed you, but you have closed your gates. The Government by their

Parliament Act have erected a boom against you, a boom to cut you off from the help of the British people. You will burst that boom. The help will come and when the crisis is over men will say of you in words not unlike those once used by Pitt, 'You have saved yourselves by your exertions, and you will save the Empire by your example'.

Three months later at Blenheim Palace, during a Conservative Party Anti-Home Rule rally, Bonar Law returned to his theme. In a remarkable speech for a constitutional politician, let alone the leader of the opposition in Westminster, he advocated rebellion if the Bill was passed, through military resistance to an Act of Parliament.

BLENHEIM PALACE, JULY 29, 1912

In our opposition to them we shall not be guided by the considerations or bound by the restraints which would influence us in an ordinary Constitutional struggle. We shall take the means, whatever means seem to us most effective, to deprive them of the despotic power which they have usurped and compel them to appeal to the people whom they have deceived. They may, perhaps they will, carry their Home Rule Bill through the House of Commons but what then? I said the other day in the House of Commons and I repeat here that there are things stronger than Parliamentary majorities . . .

Before I occupied the position which I now fill in the Party I said that, in my belief, if an attempt were made to deprive these men of their birthright – as part of a corrupt Parliamentary bargain – they would be justified in resisting such an attempt by all means in their power, including force. I said it then, and I repeat now with a full sense of the responsibility which attaches to my position, that, in my opinion, if such an attempt is made, I can imagine no length of resistance to which Ulster can go in which I should not be prepared to support them, and in which, in my belief, they would not be supported by the overwhelming majority of the British people.

THE ULSTER COVENANT

Edward Carson (1854–1935) was born in Dublin and educated at Portarlington School and Trinity College Dublin. At the age of 23 he qualified as a barrister and he quickly built up a substantial reputation and practice, including the damning cross examination of Oscar Wilde in the Queensbury libel case. In 1892, he became Solicitor-General for Ireland and MP for Trinity College. He represented Trinity until 1918 when he moved to the constituency of Duncairn in Belfast.

Carson's life's work was to oppose any weakening of the link between Ireland and Britain. He became leader of the Irish Unionists in 1910. As the prospect of Home Rule swept over the island, he refocused his energies on ensuring an opt-out for six of the counties of Ulster. He was instrumental in establishing the Ulster Volunteer Force and in the creation of the Ulster Covenant.

After his election to the leadership of Unionism in 1910, and assisted by James Craig (later Lord Craigavon), he revived the Unionist Club movement which had been dormant for twenty years. At a mass rally at Craigavon in September 1911, Carson warned that the day Home Rule passed, Unionists should be prepared to become responsible for the government of the Protestant Province of Ulster.

The Third Home Rule Bill of 1912 aimed to establish a parliament in Dublin, subservient to London. In response to this Bill, introduced by Asquith's government, the Ulster Covenant was prepared.

In September 1912, 450,000 Unionists signed a Solemn

League and Covenant, and an accompanying declaration. The Covenant was modelled on a 16th Century Scottish Covenant. It opposed Home Rule for Ireland, but gave no mention of any separate treatment for the North. It was an impressive display of Unionist unity, the organisational capabilities of the Ulster Unionists and the strength of a movement that was to frustrate the nationalist campaigns over the next decade.

BELFAST "ULSTER DAY", SEPTEMBER 28, 1912

Being convinced in our consciences that Home Rule would be disastrous to the material well-being of Ulster as well as of the whole of Ireland, subversive of our civil and religious freedom, destructive of our citizenship and perilous to the unity of the Empire, we, whose names are underwritten, men of Ulster, loyal subjects of His Gracious Majesty, King George V, humbly relying on the God whom our fathers in days of stress and trial confidently trusted, do hereby pledge ourselves in solemn Covenant throughout this our time of threatened calamity to stand by one another in defending for ourselves and our children our cherished position of equal citizenship in the United Kingdom and in using all means which may be found necessary to defeat the present conspiracy to set up a Home Rule Parliament in Ireland. And in the event of such a Parliament being forced upon us we further solemnly and mutually pledge ourselves to refuse to recognise its authority. In sure confidence that God will defend the right we hereto subscribe our names. And further, we individually declare that we have not already signed this Covenant. God Save the King.

On September 23, 1912, five hundred delegates attended a meeting of the Ulster Unionist Council in the Ulster Hall and ratified the Covenant. They also accepted the following Resolution.

16

ULSTER HALL, SEPTEMBER 23, 1912

Inasmuch as we, the duly elected delegates and members of the Ulster Unionist Council, representing all parts of Ulster, are firmly persuaded that by no law can the right to govern those whom we represent be bartered away without their consent; that although the present Government, the services and sacrifices of our race having been forgotten, may drive us forth from a Constitution which we have ever loyally upheld, they may not deliver us bound into the hands of our enemies; and that it is incompetent for any authority, party, or people to appoint as our rulers a Government dominated by men disloyal to the Empire, and to whom our faith and traditions are hateful; and inasmuch as we reverently believe that, as in times past it was given our fathers to save themselves from a like calamity, so now it may be ordered that our deliverance shall be by our own hands, to which end it is needful that we be knit together as one man, each strengthening the other, and none holding back or counting the cost – therefore, we, Loyalists of Ulster, ratify and confirm the steps so far taken by the Special Commission to carry on its work on our behalf in the past.

We enter into the Solemn Covenant appended hereto, and, knowing the greatness of the issues depending on our faithfulness, we promise each to the others that, to the uttermost of the strength and means given to us, and not regarding any selfish or private interest, our substance or our lives, we will make good the said Covenant; and we now bind ourselves in the steadfast determination that, whatever may befall, no such domination shall be thrust upon us, and in the hope that by the blessing of God our Union with Great Britain, upon which are fixed our affections and trust, may yet be maintained, and that for ourselves and for our children, for this province and for the whole of Ireland, peace, prosperity, and civil and religious liberty may be secured under the Parliament of the United Kingdom and of the King whose faithful subjects we are and will continue all our days.

"IF THEY WANT PEACE WE ARE PREPARED TO MEET THEM, BUT IF THEY WANT WAR, THEN WAR THEY WILL HAVE"

James Larkin (1878–1947) was born in Liverpool, the son of Irish immigrants. After spending his early years with his grandparents in Newry, Co. Down, he returned to Liverpool to work. After a period as a seaman, a docker and a foreman on the docks, he became an organiser for the National Union of Dockers. He played a role in the 1907 strikes in Belfast and a year later came to Dublin. His own trade union organisation, the Irish Transport and General Workers' Union, was formed in 1909, to cater for the unskilled workers of Dublin.

Larkin had a charismatic, if difficult, personality, and its appeal coupled with the effectiveness of extreme techniques led to thousands joining up. His success as a union organiser led to the organisation of an employers' federation, headed by William Martin Murphy. Murphy was of the most notable entrepreneurs of his age, a former Member of Parliament, founder of the Irish Independent *newspaper and a supporter of the cause of Home Rule. The two clashed in the great Dublin Lock-Out of 1913, when those employees who refused to leave Larkin's union were locked-out by their employers.*

In an attempt to break the impasse, a tribunal of inquiry into the dispute was formed by the government. Both sides were asked to present their cases, with Murphy, and his counsel Mr Tim Healy, acting as spokesmen for the employers. Larkin acted as spokesman for the workers. Larkin's address to the inquiry demonstrated all of his skill as an orator. This speech ironically is reconstructed from The Freeman's Journal, *owned by William Martin Murphy. The Commission of Inquiry came out on the side of the Trade Union. In spite of this, the workers were defeated.*

TRIBUNAL OF INQUIRY INTO THE DUBLIN TRADES OCTOBER 4, 1913
DISPUTE, DUBLIN CASTLE

. . . I hope you will bear with me in putting before you as plainly as possible a reply somewhat of a personal character, but which I think will cover the matters dealt with during the last few days. The first point I want to make is that the employers in this city, and throughout Ireland generally, have put forward a claim that they have a right to deal with their own; that they have a right to use and exploit individuals as they please; that they have duties which they limit, and they have responsibilities which they also limit, in their operation. They take to themselves that they have all the rights that are given to men and to societies of men, but they deny the right of the men to claim that they also have a substantial claim on the share of the produce they produce, and they further say that they want no third party interference. They want to deal with their workingmen individually. They say that they are men of such paramount intelligence and so able in their organising ability as captains of industry, who can always carry on their business in their own way, and they deny the right of the men and women who work for them to combine and try to assist one another in trying to improve their conditions of life . . .

. . . There must be fair play between man and man. There are rights on both sides, but these men opposite assume to themselves certain privileges, and they deny to the workingmen, who make their wealth and keep them in affluence, their rights.

Shakespeare it was who said that, "He who holds the means whereby I live, holds my life and controls me." That is not the exact quotation, but I can give it. [The quotation is from *The Merchant of Venice*],

"You take my house when you do take the prop,

That doth sustain my house, you take my life,
When you doth take the means whereby I live."

It means that the men who hold the means of life control our lives, and, because we workingmen have tried to get some measure of justice, some measure of betterment, they deny the right of the human being to associate with his fellow. Why, the very law of nature was mutual co-operation. Man must be associated with his fellows. The employers were not able to make their own case. Let him help them. They had had all the technique and the craftsmanship, but they have not been able to put their case in proper focus. What was the position of affairs in connection with life in industrial Ireland? Let them take the statement made by their own apologist. Take Dr Cameron's statement that there are 21,000 families – four and a half persons to a family – living in single rooms. Who are responsible? The gentlemen opposite would have to accept the responsibility. Of course they must. They said they control the means of life; then the responsibility rests upon them. Twenty-one thousand people multiplied by five, over 100,000 people huddled together in the putrid slums of Dublin, five in a room in cubic space less than 1,000 feet, though the law lays it down that every human being should have 300 cubic feet.

We are determined that this shall no longer go on; we are determined the system shall stop; we are determined that Christ will not be crucified in Dublin by these men. Mr Waldron was good enough to say yesterday that Larkin had done what was right and just in getting facilities for the workers on the Canal to be enabled to get to Mass on Sundays. Let them go further with the argument and add a little more to the picture. There were phases of the subject that he was not going to enter into in a mixed audience. The argument was used that Larkin came from Liverpool. Well, if that was so, it was time that someone came from some place in order to teach those whom he addressed their responsibilities. What about the gentlemen on the other side? Were they to be asked to produce their birth certificates? Could they all speak as men who represented the Irish race?

These men had no feeling of respect for the Dublin workman or for its development. The only purpose and desire they had was to grind out wealth from the poor men, their wives and children.

Let people who desire to know the truth go to the factories and see the maimed girls, the weak and sickly, whose eyes are being put out and their bodies scarred and their souls seared and when they were no longer able to be useful enough to gain their £1 a week, or whatever wage they earned, were thrown into the human scrap heap. These things were to be found in their midst, and yet the people who caused these conditions of wretchedness described workingmen as loafers.

True it was that Mr Murphy said that the Dublin workman was a decent man; but he would deny the right of the Dublin workmen to work in their city on terms of decency, on the streets or on the quays. He would deny their right to develop their activities and to receive proper and living wages. He was an instrument to bring down the wages. The souls of these men were steeped in the grime of profit-making. This dispute would do one thing and had already done something in that direction – it would arouse the social conscience. It had done what every man would thank God for. Let him go closer to the subject. He was out in this struggle to elevate the class he belonged to and he believed it to be his duty, and in doing it he believed he did much even to elevate those who were opposed to them.

They should all work together in a co-operative way, and they wanted to address them in a way that he hoped would not fall on barren ground. I hope that Mr. Murphy would not take anything I said in a personal light. Mr. Murphy had very strong views on the subject of the rights of property, and he is one of the strongest amongst the capitalists in this country, in Western Europe, or in America . . .

. . . Mr Murphy admitted he did not know the details of his own business, and stated that (Larkin) had no right to interfere with him to induce the men to fight him. Mr Murphy was absolutely unable to state his own case. He admitted he had no knowledge of the details of his own business. He admitted he had no strikes at any moment during his connection with industrial concerns, but (Larkin) had proved that his life had been one continuous struggle against the working classes. I give him credit, too, that in a great many cases he came out on top, because he had never been faced by a man who was able to deal with him; he had never been faced by a social conscience such as now existed, and according to which the working classes could combine to alter the present conditions of labour. There was such a thing as human thought, and no one had killed it yet, not even the theologians or the politicians, and Mr Murphy might try to realise during the later hours of his life, before "he passed hence" that those who gave him affluence and wealth deserved something to encourage them from the lower plane on which they existed to a higher plane on which they might live. He had been an able man, backed up by able men; he was backed up at that inquiry by one of the ablest counsel at the Bar, who used his power relentlessly. That could be seen up to a certain point, but there must be a break. There was a point where all that abuse would meet with its own result, and that result would be that the power wielded by such men would be smashed, and deservedly smashed . . .

. . . I am concerned in something greater, something better, and something holier – a mutual relation between those carrying on industry in Ireland. These men (the employers) with their limited intelligence cannot see that. I cannot help that. I cannot compel them to look at the thing from my point of view. Surely they have a right to realise the work in which I am engaged. It is not to our interest to have men locked-out or on strike. We don't get double wages. They say "Larkin is making £18 a week", and has made more than £18 a week, but he never got it unfortunately. I have lived among the working classes all my life. I have starved because men denied me food. I worked very hard at a very early age. I had no opportunities like the men opposite, but whatever opportunities I got I have availed of them. I am called an anti-Christ and an atheist. If I were an atheist I would not deny it. I am a Socialist and have always claimed to be a Socialist.

I believe in a co-operative commonwealth. That is a long way ahead in Ireland. Why cannot I help as you can help in working the present system in a proper, reasonable way, conducive to both sides, and I have suggested the machinery that may be put into operation . . .

Can anyone say one word against me as a man? Can they make any disparagement of my character? Have I lessened the standard of life? Have I demoralised anyone? Is there anything in my private life or my public life of which I should feel ashamed? These men denounced me from the pulpit, and say I am making £18 a week and that I have a mansion in Dublin. The men who are described as Larkin's dupes are asked to go back. All this is done two thousand years after Christ appeared in Galilee. Why, these men are making people atheists – they are making them godless. But we are going to stop that.

When the position of the workers in Dublin was taken into consideration, was it any wonder that there was necessity for a Larkin to arise, and if there was one thing more than another in my life of which I will always be proud it was the part I have taken in rescuing the workers of Dublin from the brutalising and degrading conditions under which they laboured.

We are out . . . to break down racial and sectarian barriers. My suggestion to the employers is that if they want peace we are prepared to meet them, but if they want war, then war they will have.

"IF YOU WANT ULSTER, GO AND TAKE HER,
OR GO AND WIN HER"

Edward Carson was extremely close to the conservative opposition and the political establishment in Britain and particularly to Andrew Bonar Law, the opposition leader of the Conservative Party.

Carson's response to the King's speech in 1914 attacked the government's plans for Home Rule. It fused together the anger, tenacity and doubt of the Unionist cause at the time. It was an argument for the status quo and warning of what would happen if it was tampered with.

HOUSE OF COMMONS, FEBRUARY 11, 1914

. . . I doubt if the House has yet realised, or if the country has realised, the unparalleled gravity of the statement in the Gracious Speech from the Throne. I venture to think that in the political life of no Member of this House has such a grave statement been made with reference to the domestic relations of fellow citizens of the United Kingdom. We have had in the past, no doubt, warnings of foreign complications, warnings of difficult diplomatic negotiations. When, I should like to know, has the Gracious Speech from the Throne told us that the hopes and fears of our own subjects within the limits of the United Kingdom threatened grave future difficulties; and I think the House may well remember that the Ministers who advise the Crown are not likely to put into the mouth of the Sovereign any but the very mildest terms in relation to a situation which they certainly would not like to exaggerate. What is the first lesson that we deduce or learn from this grave statement in His Majesty's Speech? We have been two years discussing this question, and I certainly have been two years trying to make the position of the loyalists of Ireland known, and now, after two years, the first lesson we learn is this, that the Bill of the Government, on their own confession, has utterly failed to find a solution of the Irish question.

. . . at a time of great tension in the north of Ireland, when men are hardening day by day in the anticipation of the dangers to which they are becoming accustomed, we were entitled to expect, and we did expect, that at this hour of the day, and having regard to the words which the Prime Minister had advised His Majesty to use in the Speech from the Throne, the Right Hon. Gentleman would have been able to give us at all events some specific outline of what it was he had in his mind, as being the methods which he was going to suggest at the earliest possible moment. But he outlined no proposals whatsoever. He did take one step forward, and I gratefully admit it, in his admission that it was now the duty of the Government to take the initiative . . .

. . . I say that the position, at all events to us Irish Unionists in this House, is an intolerable one. We are asked to sit here quietly and patiently, to vote for Estimates, to vote, I suppose, for the pay of the Army, which you are so ready to say that you will send, but which you never will send, over to Ulster. The position becomes daily more intolerable and more difficult in Ulster itself, where increasing sacrifices are made from day to day, not by great or rich men, but more and more by the democracy of the place, whose whole minds are turning practically on nothing else but this question, and for whom, at all events, you ought to have some consideration, and not tell them: "You men of Ulster, remain quiet, and be quite satisfied that when we have done our financial business we will try and see what we can do to relieve ourselves from the grave difficulties that face us in the future . . ."

They are always talking of concessions to Ulster. Ulster is not asking for concessions. Ulster is asking to be let alone. When you talk of concessions, what you really mean is, "We want to lay down what is the minimum of wrong we can do to Ulster." Let me tell you that the results of two years' delay and the treatment we have received during these two years have made your task and made our task far more difficult. You have driven these men to enter into a covenant for their mutual protection. No doubt you have laughed at their covenant. Have a good laugh at it now. Well, so far as I am concerned, I am not the kind of man who will go over to Ulster one day and say, "Enter into a covenant," and go over next day and say, "Break it." But there is something more. You have insulted them. I do not say the Prime Minister has done so. I would be wrong if I were to say that he has done so. He has treated them seriously, but the large body of his colleagues in the rank and file of his party have taken every opportunity of jeering at these men, of branding them as braggarts and bluffers and cowards, and all the rest of it. Well, do not you see that having done that, these men can ever go back, and ever will go back, and allow these gibes and insults and sneers to prove true.

The Speech from the Throne talks of the fears of these men. Yes, they have, I think, genuine fears for their civil and religious liberty under the Bill, but do not imagine that that is all that these men are fighting for. They are fighting for a great principle, and a great ideal. They are fighting to stay under the Government which they were invited to come under, under which they have flourished, and under which they are content, and to refuse to come under a Government which they loath and detest. Men do not make sacrifices or take up the attitude these men in Ulster have taken up on a question of detail or paper safeguards. I am not going to argue whether they are right or wrong in resisting. It would be useless to argue it, because they have thoroughly made up their minds, but I say this: If these men are not morally justified when they are attempted to be driven out of one Government with which they are satisfied, and put under another which they loath, I do not see how resistance ever can be justified in history at all. There was one point made by the Prime Minister yesterday, and repeated by Lord Morley in another place, which I should like to deal with for one moment, although it has been ready referred to by my Right Hon. Friend last night. The Prime Minister said, it is "as the price of peace that any suggestion we make will be put forward," and he elaborated that by saying that he did not mean the mere abandonment of resistance, but that he meant that the Bill, if these changes were made, as I understood him, should as the price of the changes be accepted generally by opponents in Ireland, and in the Unionist party, so as to give, as he hoped, a good chance and send-off to the Bill. If he means that as the condition of the changes in the Bill we are to support the Bill or take any responsibility whatever for it, I tell him we never can do it. Ulster looms very largely in this controversy, simply because Ulster has a strong right arm, but there are Unionists in the South and West who loath the Bill just as much as we Ulster people loath it, whose difficulties are far greater and who would willingly fight, as Ulster would fight, if they had the numbers.

. . . Yes, we can never support the Bill which hands these people over to the tender mercies of those who have always been their bitterest enemies. We must go on whatever happens, opposing the Bill to the end. That we are entitled to do; that we are bound to do. But I want to speak explicitly about the exclusion of Ulster. I am not at all sure that I entirely understood what the Prime Minister said yesterday in his speech on this subject. In one part of his speech I understood him to say that he did not, in making these changes, which are eventually to be put upon the Table of the House, reject the exclusion of Ulster as a possibility. In another part of his speech he said: "There is nothing we will not do, consistent with the maintenance of the fundamental principles of the Bill, in the solution of this question, to avoid the terrible calamity of civil war or bloodshed." If I take these two passages together I suppose I am entitled to say that the exclusion of Ulster is not opposed to the fundamental principles of the Bill . . . Now that is a very important matter. If the exclusion of Ulster is not shut out, and if at the same time the Prime Minister says he cannot admit anything contrary to the fundamental principles of the Bill, I think it follows that the exclusion of Ulster is not contrary to the fundamental principles of the Bill . . .

. . . Believe me, whatever way you settle the Irish question, there are only two ways to deal with Ulster. It is for statesmen to say which is the best and right one. She is not a part of the community which can be bought. She will not allow herself to be sold. You must therefore either coerce her if you go on, or you must, in the long run, by showing that good government can come under the Home Rule Bill, try and win her over to the case of the rest of Ireland. You probably can coerce her – although I doubt it. If you do, what will be the disastrous consequences not only to Ulster, but to this country and the Empire? Will my fellow countryman, the Leader of the Nationalist party, have gained anything? I will agree with him – I do not believe he wants to triumph any more than I do. But will he have gained anything if he takes over these people and then applies for what he used to call – at all events his party used to call – the enemies of the people to come in and coerce them into obedience? No, Sir, one false step taken in relation to Ulster will, in my opinion, render for ever impossible a solution of the Irish question. I say this to my Nationalist fellow countrymen, and, indeed, also to the Government: you have never tried to win over Ulster. You have never tried to understand her position. You have never alleged, and can never allege, that this Bill gives her one atom of advantage. Nay, you cannot deny that it takes away many advantages that she has as a constituent part of the United Kingdom. You cannot deny that in the past she had produced the most loyal and law-abiding part of the citizens of Ireland. After all that, for these two years, every time we came before you your only answer to us – the majority of you, at all events – was to insult us, and to make little of us. I say to the leader of the Nationalist party, if you want Ulster, go and take her, or go and win her. You have never wanted her affections; you have wanted her taxes . . .

"THE TEMPORARY EXCLUSION OF ULSTER"

Henry Asquith (1852–1928) was born in Yorkshire and educated in London and at Oxford. After a career at the Bar, he became a Liberal MP and served as Home Secretary and Chancellor of the Exchequer. He became Prime Minister of Britain in 1908, a post he held until 1915.

Next to the outbreak of the First World War, the Irish question was to dominate his premiership. He reduced the power of the House of Lords in 1911, through the abolition of its power of veto. This was intended to facilitate the introduction of Home Rule for Ireland. The Third Home Rule Bill was introduced one year later into this period of high political tension. With the differences between government and opposition on the Irish question widening, and with Unionists in Ulster preparing to rebel, Asquith put it to the Commons on March 9 1914 that individual counties might be allowed to opt out for six years, after which they would automatically come under the Irish parliament. Carson called this "a sentence of death with a stay of execution for six years".

The move to exclude Ulster, even temporarily, demonstrated the inability of the Liberal government to implement the Act of Parliament in the face of continued Conservative and Unionist resistance. From this point on, partition became an increasingly acceptable alternative for both government and opposition in London.

HOUSE OF COMMONS, MARCH 9, 1914

. . . The Question, Sir, that you are about to put from the

29

Chair is that this Bill be read a second time. But I do not conceive that I should be making an appropriate use of the occasion if I were to take advantage of it to restate the case so often presented in favour of a Bill which in successive Sessions has twice passed through the House of Commons. This, however, I will say: Those who have supported it in all its stages are as convinced to-day as they ever were of the soundness, both of its principles and its machinery. They regard it as an attempt at once sincere and considerate to base upon a solid foundation the fabric of Irish self-government, and they do not believe – none of them believe – if it were placed as it stands on the Statute Book tomorrow that its practical operation would involve injustice or oppression either to classes or to individuals in Ireland. I am obliged, in this respect, to repeat to-day with clearness and with emphasis at the outset of what I have to say to the House, what I have said many times before, both inside and outside its walls. If then, I come here to-day, as I do, with suggestions to make, which, if accepted, would require substantial modifications in or, to speak with greater accuracy, substantial additions and supplementary provisions to our plan, it is not because we are running away from it, but because we are, above all things, anxious that the changes which we believe to be inevitable in the government of Ireland should start under conditions which will secure for them, from the first, the best chance of ultimate success.

What are the dangers which lie ahead, and which, in my opinion, at any rate, it is the duty of statesmanship, if it be possible, to avert? On the one hand, if Home Rule as embodied in this Bill is carried now, there is, I regret to say it, but nobody can deny it, in Ulster the prospect of acute dissension and even of civil strife. On the other hand, if at this stage Home Rule were to be shipwrecked, or permanently mutilated, or indefinitely postponed, there is in Ireland, as a whole, at least an equally formidable outlook. The hazards in either event are such as to warrant in all quarters, I think not indeed a surrender of principles, but any practical form of accommodation and approach which would lead to an agreed settlement. It is obvious – it is no use blinking the facts – that such a settlement must involve, in the first place, on the side of our opponents the acceptance of a Home Rule Legislature and Executive in Dublin, and, on the other hand, on the side of our supporters, some form of special treatment for the Ulster minority over and above any of the safeguards which are contained in this Bill . . .

With that preface, let me now come to describe to the House the various ways in which we . . . try to meet them. By far the most serious of them, of course, is that which is presented by what is compendiously and conveniently called the question of Ulster. I have tried, and my colleagues have tried, honestly and seriously, to meet that difficulty by three different roads. In the first place – and this was the solution, or, at any rate, an expedient which I confess commended itself very much to my own judgement – we tried the road which goes by a name I think first invented by my Right Hon. Friend (Sir E. Grey) – what is called "Home Rule within Home Rule" . . . Without for a moment defining the part of Ulster to which the suggestion was to apply, leaving that over for further consideration, calling the part to which it was to apply by the name of statutory Ulster, which means that it does not include the whole province, I had first in view with a vivid memory, in all the Debates which have taken place in this House and upon this Bill, statements made from that bench by the Ulster Members, by no one, I think, with more emphasis than by the Right Hon. Gentleman (Sir E. Carson), that what they were really afraid of as the consequence of Home Rule was not so much the legislation of an Irish Parliament as the administration of an Irish Executive. That, as the House knows, has been frequently stated. It was of the essence of my proposal – what is called "Home Rule within Home Rule" – that as regards administration, Ulster . . . should be, until the Imperial Parliament otherwise decided, entirely exempt from the executive and administrative authority of the Irish Parliament in Dublin. It is not such a difficult problem as it seems. The police and everything connected with land purchase are, under the Bill as it stands, reserved services, which do not pass within the ambit or province of the Irish Executive; and as regards what was left – education and local government – it seemed to me it might very well be in the excluded area, or the protected area, because it was not to be excluded, administered by some local authority; while as regards the important province of factory and workshop administration, that would remain, as it is at present, under the Secretary of State here in Whitehall . . .

Then, as regards legislation, my proposal was this – and I am still rather wedded to it, though I am afraid I met with very little support in any quarter – that Ulster should return, like all the rest of Ireland, representatives to both the Upper and the Lower House of the Irish Legislature, but then when any law was passed by those two Houses to which in respect of its application to Ulster the majority of the representatives of Ulster were opposed, it should not come into force *quoad* Ulster, if they protested, until it received the sanction of the Imperial Parliament . . .

I now come to the second. The second was this, a suggestion that the whole of Ireland should be, in the first instance, included, both for legislative and executive purposes, in the Bill as it stands, but that an option should be given, after the lapse of a certain time, for the Ulster counties . . . to remove themselves from the jurisdiction of the Irish Legislature and Executive, and to revert to the position in which they at present stand. That is a proposal which we had considered even before it was put forward, as it has been put forward by a high authority, a very distinguished Irishman, to whom Ireland is under a very great debt of gratitude for many public services – I mean Sir Horace Plunkett. Here, again, the proposal has the great merit that it starts from the beginning with a fully representative and fully developed Irish Legislature, with no adjustments of a very complicated kind, such as are incident to any form of exclusion, to embarrass them – a practical working Irish Parliament, a Parliament for all Ireland which would in a very few years show whether the apprehensions were or were not well founded. If they were not, things would go on as they are. If they were well founded, the minority had a constitutional door of escape. I think there is a great deal to be said for that plan. There again, I must add that it would be an excellent thing if it could be made acceptable to those whom it is proposed to include, but I am afraid it cannot – or cannot, at any rate, for the moment – and compulsory inclusion at the outset, even with the option of exclusion as time goes on, has, of course, all the drawbacks and all the dangers incident to any scheme that has to be coercively enforced. Therefore, I am afraid it cannot be regarded as giving a practical answer to the demand for an agreed road to settlement.

Both these roads being blocked – I hope not permanently – for the time being, we then proceeded to explore the third. I do not say that we had not had it in view throughout, because we did not proceed in this logical manner step by step. We had to explore in detail in the third road, which goes popularly by the name of "exclusion". There are obvious and formidable objections to exclusion in whatever guise they may be clothed, and I believe they are felt quite as much by men of all parties and opinions in Ireland as they are by more detached critics outside. What are they? You start, whatever form exclusion takes, with an Irish Legislature which – in the first instance, at any rate – is not fully representative of and responsible to the whole of the Irish people. You recognise whatever form exclusion may take – and in recognising you run the risk of stereotyping and perpetuating – traditions which are inherited from the past, which we all hope, and many of us believe, the future will soften and in time obliterate. It has the further drawback that it necessarily keeps the controversy alive, and finally it involves a number of more or less complicated and difficult administrative and financial adjustments. No one is more alive than I am to the force and seriousness of these objections. The Unionists, of course, can get rid of the difficulties of exclusion by a simple denial of Home Rule. Home

Rulers can get rid of them if they are ready to start Home Rule in an atmosphere of discord and of tumult. But it appears to me that each, Unionist and Home Ruler alike, can find, in some form, provisional exclusion by a media between the surrender of principle and the application of force. Exclusion in any form must be put forward, and can only be put forward, not as a solution, but as an expedient which may pave the way in time for a final settlement . . .

. . . We have come to the conclusion that the best, and, indeed, the only practical, way – at any rate far the simplest and the fairest plan – is to allow the Ulster counties themselves to determine, in the first instance, whether or not they desire to be excluded. I will say something in a moment about two crucial points of difficulty which arise – the points of area and of time – but I would first, very briefly, describe to the House what is the plan we are putting forward. It is that any county in the province of Ulster is to be excluded for a certain period, if on a poll being taken of the Parliamentary electors in the country before the Bill comes into operation, a majority – a bare majority – vote in favour of exclusion. The poll will be taken in a county if a requisition is presented signed by, say, one-tenth of the electors, and presented, say, within three months of the date of the passing of the Bill. The poll will be taken for the county as a whole, without regard to its Parliamentary Divisions . . .

. . . The House will observe that I have used the term "county", and when I speak of the county I include as separate counties for this purpose the two great county boroughs in Ulster – Belfast and Londonderry . . .

. . . Then arises the question what ought to be the term of exclusion for a county, if it pleases it to vote for its own exclusion. We have, after much consideration, thought it ought to be a term of six years, and six years, not from the taking of the poll, but six years from the first meeting of the Irish Legislature in Dublin. Why have we adopted that period? . . . We have taken the term of six years to ensure that before the period of exclusion comes to an end there shall be, first, ample time – six years – to test by experience the actual working of the Irish Parliament. That is why we take the beginning of the six years, not from the taking of the poll, but from the first assembling of the new legislature, and, in the second place, to ensure, also, that before that period of exclusion comes to an end there shall be a full and certain opportunity for the electors of the whole of the United Kingdom, both Great Britain and Ireland, with that experience to pronounce whether or not the exclusion shall come to an end . . .

. . . We believe that that is a fair and equitable arrangement. It gives to these counties, it gives to the whole of Ulster, in the first instance, the option to say whether they will come within the Bill, and if they vote for exclusion they cannot be brought back into it unless with the assent, at a Great Election, of a majority of the electorate of the whole of the United Kingdom.

"THE INTERESTS OF IRELAND – THE WHOLE OF IRELAND ARE AT STAKE IN THIS WAR"

John Redmond (1856–1918) was educated at Clongowes Wood College and Trinity College Dublin. At the age of 25, he was elected as Irish Parliamentary Party MP for New Ross. After the O'Shea divorce case and the demise of Parnell, the Irish Parliamentary Party split into several factions. Redmond led the minority which supported Parnell. When the split was healed in 1900, he became leader of the reunited Irish Parliamentary Party. Redmond resolutely believed that the House of Commons was the means to make progress on the issue of Home Rule for Ireland.

He secured the introduction of the Third Home Rule Bill in 1912. He failed to get support from the British government for distinctive regiments for the Irish Volunteers in World War I and he turned down an opportunity to serve in Asquith's war cabinet.

Redmond nonetheless felt it right that the Irish Volunteers should enlist in support of the war effort. His famous speech at Woodenbridge in Wicklow, in which he exhorted Irish Volunteers to fight, shows how much he believed that the First World War was about the fate of small nations and in defence of liberty. It was a view that was to split the Irish Volunteers. The outbreak of war started the decline in Redmond's career which continued until his death, just prior to the electoral annihilation of his party by Sinn Fein in 1918.

SEPTEMBER 20, 1914, WOODENBRIDGE, CO. WICKLOW

Fellow-countrymen, it was fortunate chance that enabled me to be present here today. I was motoring past, and I did not know until I arrived here that this gathering of the Volunteers

36

was to take place at Woodenbridge. I could not deny myself the pleasure and honour of waiting to meet you, to meet so many of those whom I have personally known for many long years, and to see them fulfilling a high duty to their country. I have no intention of making a speech. All I desire to say to you is that I congratulate you upon the favourable beginning of the work you have made.

You have only barely made a beginning. You will yet have hard work before you can call yourselves efficient soldiers, and you will have to have in your hand – every man – as efficient weapons as I am glad to see in hands of some, at any rate, of your numbers. Looking back as I naturally do, upon the history of Wicklow, I know that you will make efficient soldiers. Efficient soldiers for what?

Wicklow Volunteers, in spite of the peaceful happiness and beauty of the scene in which we stand, remember this country at this moment is in a state of war, and your duty is a twofold duty. The duty of the manhood of Ireland is twofold. Its duty is, at all costs, to defend the shores of Ireland against foreign invasion. It is a duty more than that of taking care that Irish valour proves itself; on the field of war it has always proved itself in the past. The interests of Ireland – of the whole of Ireland – are at stake in this war. This war is undertaken in the defence of the highest principles of religion and morality and right, and it would be a disgrace for ever to our country and a reproach to her manhood and a denial of the lessons of her history if young Ireland confined their efforts to remaining at home to defend the shores of Ireland from an unlikely invasion, and to shrinking from the duty of proving on the field of battle that gallantry and courage which has distinguished our race all through its history. I say to you, therefore, your duty is twofold. I am glad to see such magnificent material for soldiers around me, and I say to you – Go on drilling and make yourself efficient for the work, and then account yourselves as men, not only for Ireland itself, but wherever the fighting line extends, in defence of right, of freedom and religion in this war.

"WHILE IRELAND HOLDS THESE GRAVES"

Padraig Pearse (1879–1916), leader of the 1916 Rising, was born in Dublin and educated at Christian Brothers School, Westland Row and the Royal University. From his early days he had an interest in the Irish language, and became editor of An Claidheamh Soluis, *the journal of the Gaelic League. His interest in Irish was complemented by an interest in education and he founded his own school – initially in Ranelagh, but latterly in St Enda's in Rathfarnham. In the Easter Rising of 1916, he was Commander in Chief of the insurgents, President of the Provisional Government and one of the signatories of the Proclamation. He was court-martialled, and executed on May 3, 1916.*

Pearse reluctantly supported the Third Home Rule Bill, introduced in 1912, but warned of the consequences if it were not passed. Pearse's belief in military solutions became increasingly evident in 1913-16, and on numerous occasions he called for military involvement for all groups on the island.

His oration over the grave of O'Donovan Rossa, a veteran of the Fenian Rising of 1867 who had been effectively deported to the USA in 1871 and who died in 1915 in New York, typified his approach – his link to the past, his use of religious analogies for the nationalist cause and his commitment to an unrelenting struggle for Irish independence.

GLASNEVIN CEMETERY, AUGUST 1, 1915

It has seemed right, before we turn away from this place in which we have laid the mortal remains of O'Donovan Rossa, that one among us should, in the name of all, speak the praise

38

of that valiant man, and endeavour to formulate the thought and the hope that are in us as we stand around his grave. And if there is anything that makes it fitting that I, rather than some other, I rather than one of the grey-haired men who were young with him and shared in his labour and in his suffering, should speak here, it is perhaps that I may be taken as speaking on behalf of a new generation that has been re-baptised in the Fenian faith, and that has accepted the responsibility of carrying out the Fenian programme. I propose to you then that, here by the grave of this unrepentant Fenian, we renew our baptismal vows; that, here by the grave of this unconquered and unconquerable man, we ask God, each one for himself, such unshakeable purpose, such high and gallant courage, such unbreakable strength of soul as belonged to O'Donovan Rossa.

Deliberately here we avow ourselves, as he avowed himself in the dock, Irishmen of one allegiance only. We of the Irish Volunteers, and you others who are associated with us in today's task and duty, are bound together and must stand together henceforth in brotherly union for the achievement of the freedom of Ireland. And we know only one definition of freedom: it is Tone's definition, it is Mitchel's definition, it is Rossa's definition. Let no man blaspheme the cause that the dead generations of Ireland served by giving it any other name and definition than their name and their definition.

We stand at Rossa's grave not in sadness but rather in exaltation of spirit that it has been given to us to come thus into so close a communion with that brave and splendid Gael. Splendid and holy causes are served by men who are themselves splendid and holy. O'Donovan Rossa was splendid in the proud manhood of him, splendid in the heroic grace of him, splendid in the Gaelic strength and clarity and truth of him. And all that splendour and pride and strength was compatible with a humility and a simplicity of devotion to Ireland, to all that was olden and beautiful and Gaelic in Ireland, the holiness and simplicity of patriotism of a Michael

O'Clery or of an Eoghan O'Growney. The clear true eyes of this man almost alone in his day visioned Ireland as we of today would surely have her: not free merely, but Gaelic as well; not Gaelic merely, but free as well.

In a closer spiritual communion with him now than ever before or perhaps ever again, in a spiritual communion with those of his day, living and dead, who suffered with him in English prisons, in communion of spirit too with our dear comrades who suffer in English prisons today, and speaking on their behalf as well as our own, we pledge to Ireland our love, and we pledge to English rule in Ireland our hate. This is a place of peace, sacred to the dead, where men should speak with all charity and with all restraints; but I hold it a Christian thing, as O'Donovan Rossa held it, to hate evil, to hate untruth, to hate oppression, and, hating them, to strive to overthrow them. Our foes are strong and wise and wary; but, strong and wise and wary as they are, they cannot undo the miracles of God who ripens in the hearts of young men the seeds sown by the young men of a former generation. And the seeds sown by the young men of '65 and '67 are coming to their miraculous ripening today. Rulers and Defenders of Realms had need to be wary if they would guard against such processes. Life springs from death; and from the graves of patriot men and women spring living nations. The Defenders of this Realm have worked well in secret and in the open. They think that they have pacified Ireland. They think that they have purchased half of us and intimidated the other half. They think that they have foreseen everything, think that they have provided against everything; but the fools, the fools, the fools! – they have left us our Fenian dead, and while Ireland holds these graves, Ireland unfree shall never be at peace.

THE 1916 PROCLAMATION

On the morning of Easter Monday 1916, Padraig Pearse stepped out of the General Post Office in O'Connell Street, Dublin and read aloud the proclamation of a Provisional Government to the sparse crowd outside. The Proclamation was signed by Thomas Clarke, Sean MacDiarmada, Thomas McDonagh, PH Pearse, Eamon Ceannt, James Connolly and Joseph Plunkett.

In Ireland Since the Famine, *FSL Lyons makes several points about the Proclamation. It is essentially historical in conception – linking 1916 to attempts in previous generations to secure independence, and particularly to the Republican tradition. The idea that the rebellion was "supported by gallant allies in Europe" was more fantasy than fact, but it left the signatories open to the charge of treason and was used as one of the justifications for their subsequent executions. Finally the influence of Connolly can be seen in the area of political, civil and social rights, where all of the nation's children were to be cherished equally.*

Like many of the events centred around the Easter Rising, the proclamation grew in importance as time passed, and after independence it became a powerful symbol of what 1916 and the war of independence had been about.

GENERAL POST OFFICE, DUBLIN, APRIL 24, 1916

Poblacht na hÉireann.

The Provisional Government of the Irish Republic to the people of Ireland.

Irishmen and Irishwomen: In the name of God and of the

41

dead generations from which she receives her old tradition of nationhood, Ireland, through us, summons her children to her flag and strikes for her freedom.

Having organised and trained her manhood through her secret revolutionary organisation, the Irish Republican Brotherhood, and through her open military organisations, the Irish Volunteers, and the Irish Citizen Army, having patiently perfected her discipline, having resolutely waited for the right moment to reveal itself, she now seizes that moment, and, supported by her exiled children in America and by gallant allies in Europe, but relying in the first on her own strength, she strikes in full confidence of victory.

We declare the right of the people of Ireland to the ownership of Ireland, and to the unfettered control of Irish destinies, to be sovereign and indefeasible. The long usurpation of that right by a foreign people and government has not extinguished the right, nor can it ever be extinguished except by the destruction of the Irish people. In every generation the Irish people have asserted their right to national freedom and sovereignty; six times during the past three hundred years they have asserted it in arms. Standing on that fundamental right and again asserting it in arms in the face of the world, we hereby proclaim the Irish Republic as a sovereign independent state, and we pledge our lives and the lives of our comrades-in-arms to the cause of its freedom, of its welfare, and of its exaltation among the nations.

The Irish Republic is entitled to, and hereby claims, the allegiance of every Irishman and Irishwoman. The Republic guarantees religious and civil liberty, equal rights and equal opportunities to all its citizens, and declares its resolve to pursue the happiness and prosperity of the whole nation and of all its parts, cherishing all the children of the nation equally, and oblivious of the differences carefully fostered by an alien government, which have divided a minority from the majority in the past.

Until our arms have brought the opportune moment for the

establishment of a permanent national government, representative of the whole people of Ireland, and elected by the suffrages of all her men and women, the Provisional Government, hereby constituted, will administer the civil and military affairs of the republic in trust for the people. We place the cause of the Irish Republic under the protection of the Most High God, whose blessing we invoke upon our arms, and we pray that no one who serves that cause will dishonour it by cowardice, inhumanity, or rapine. In this supreme hour the Irish nation must, by its valour and discipline, and by the readiness of its children to sacrifice themselves for the common good, prove itself worthy of the august destiny to which it is called.

Signed on behalf of the provisional government,

Thomas J Clarke, Sean MacDiarmada, Thomas MacDonagh, PH Pearse, Eamon Ceannt, James Connolly, Joseph Plunkett.

"I AM PROUD OF THESE MEN"

John Dillon (1851–1927) was born in Dublin, the son of the nationalist John Blake Dillon. After qualifying as a surgeon, he switched his attention to politics and became a strong Parnell supporter in the Land League. He was elected as MP for Tipperary in 1880, and five years later moved to represent East Mayo – a seat he held for over thirty years until his defeat by de Valera in 1918. He led the anti-Parnellite faction in the Irish Parliamentary Party after the O'Shea divorce case but was instrumental in ensuring Redmond's accession to the leadership of the re-united party in 1900.

During the 1916 Rising, Dillon, at home in his house in North Great Georges Street, was the only leader of the Irish Parliamentary Party in Dublin. After the surrender he came quickly to the view that there should be no executions. Despite his lobbying of the civilian and military authorities in Dublin, of Redmond and the Prime Minister, Asquith, the executions continued. When Dillon finally reached London he spoke in Parliament on May 11 with a passion and a bitterness that was to shock the House and to set him apart for evermore from many of his colleagues in the Irish Parliamentary Party. Dillon's motion on the adjournment of the House was an attempt to stop the executions, and a warning to the government of what its response to the Rising had unleashed.

HOUSE OF COMMONS, MAY 11, 1916
    . . . I go on to say a word as to the condition of Dublin itself, and of Ireland, from the point of view of military law. But

before I do so I just want to say that the primary object of my Motion is to put an absolute and final stop to these executions. You are letting loose a river of blood, and, make no mistake about it, between two races who, after three hundred years of hatred and of strife, we had nearly succeeded in bringing together . . .

It is the first rebellion that ever took place in Ireland where you had a majority on your side. It is the fruit of our life work. We have risked our lives a hundred times to bring about this result. We are held up to odium as traitors by those men who made this rebellion, and our lives have been in danger a hundred times during the last thirty years because we have endeavoured to reconcile the two things, and now you are washing out our whole life work in a sea of blood. In my opinion, at present the government of Ireland is largely in the hands of the Dublin clubs. The Prime Minister, when I asked him a question yesterday about the government of Ireland, told me that it was in the hands of the military officers, subject to the authority of British Cabinet. In my opinion, and I think I really am speaking on a matter that I know, the British Cabinet has much less power in Ireland today than the Kildare Street Club and certain other institutions. It is they who are influencing the policy of the military authorities. What is the use of telling me, as the Prime Minister told me yesterday, that the military authorities acted in close consultation with the civil executive officers of the Irish Government? That was the answer I got to my question. Who are the civil executive officers of the Irish Government? There are none; they have all disappeared. There is no Government in Ireland except Sir John Maxwell and the Dublin clubs, and I defy the Prime Minister to tell us who are the civil officers of the Irish Government with whom the military authorities are acting in consultation. Are we to be informed that Sir Robert Chalmers is the civil officer with whom the military generals are taking careful counsel, and is he so versed in Irish affairs that he can untie the tangle that has defied every British statesman for a hundred years? Everybody in

Dublin knows that before the civil officers took to flight out of Dublin the military authorities treated them with undisguised contempt, and from the day martial law was proclaimed civil government came to an absolute end . . .

The worst of the situation is that there are many men in Dublin, I know of my own knowledge, who are going about the streets today openly glorying in the revolt – I mean of the old ascendancy party. What is the talk in the clubs and certain districts in Dublin? It is that this is the best thing that has ever happened in Ireland, because they say it has brought us martial law, and real government into the country, and it will put an end for ever to this rotten Nationalist party . . .

This may horrify you, but I declare most solemnly, and I am not ashamed to say it in the House of Commons, that I am proud of these men. They were foolish; they were misled . . . I say I am proud of their courage, and, if you were not so dense and so stupid, as some of you English people are, you could have had these men fighting for you, and they are men worth having. [Hon. Members: "You stopped them."] That is an infamous falsehood. I and the men who sit around me have been doing our best to bring these men into the ranks of the Army. I say that we have been doing our best to bring these men into the ranks of the Army, and it is the blundering manner in which our country has been ruled which has deprived you of their services. These men require no Compulsory Service Bill to make them fight. Ours is a fighting race, and as I told you when I was speaking before on the Military Service Bill, "It is not a Military Service Bill that you want in Ireland." If you had passed a Military Service Bill for Ireland, it would have taken 150,000 men and three months' hard fighting to have dealt with it. It is not a Military Service Bill that you want in Ireland: it is to find a way to the hearts of the Irish people, and when you do that you will find that you have got a supply of the best troops in the whole world. How can we, in the face of these facts, accept the statement of the Prime Minister that according to the best of his knowledge no men are being secretly shot in Ireland? The fact of the matter is that what is poisoning the mind of Ireland, and rapidly poisoning it, is the secrecy of these trials and the continuance of these executions.

Compare the conduct of the Government in dealing with this rebellion with the conduct of General Botha. I say deliberately that in the whole of modern history, taking all the circumstances into account, there has been no rebellion or insurrection put down with so much blood and so much savagery as the recent insurrection in Ireland . . .

As I say, there were some very bad actions, but as regards the main body of the insurgents, their conduct was beyond reproach as fighting men. I admit they were wrong; I know they were wrong; but they fought a clean fight, and they fought with superb bravery and skill, and no act of savagery or act against the usual customs of war that I know of has been brought home to any leader or any organised body of insurgents. I have not heard of a single act, I may be wrong, but that is my impression . . .

What is happening is that thousands of people in Dublin, who ten days ago were bitterly opposed to the whole of the Sinn Féin movement and to the rebellion, are now becoming infuriated against the Government on account of these executions, and, as I am informed by letters received this morning, that feeling is spreading throughout the country in a most dangerous degree . . .

We, I think, have a right, we who speak for the vast majority of the Irish people, and we do; we who have risked a great deal to win the people to your side in this great crisis of your Empire's history: we who have endeavoured, and successfully endeavoured, to secure that the Irish in America shall not go into alliance with the Germans in that country – we, I think, were entitled to be consulted before this bloody course of executions were entered upon in Ireland. God knows the result of flouting our advice, as it has been flouted in the conduct of Irish affairs ever since the Coalition Government was formed, has not been a brilliant one. I think that in this matter we were entitled to be consulted . . .

But it is not murderers who are being executed; it is insurgents who have fought a clean fight, however misguided, and it would be a damned good thing for you if your soldiers were able to put up as good a fight as did these men in Dublin – three thousand men against twenty thousand with machine-guns and artillery. [An Hon. Member: "Evidently you wish they had succeeded."] That is an infamous falsehood. Who is it said that? It is an abominable falsehood. I say that these men, misguided as they were, have been our bitterest enemies. They have held us up to public odium as traitors to our country because we have supported you at this moment and stood by you in this great War, and the least we are entitled to is this, that in this great effort which we have made at considerable risk – an effort such as the Hon. Members who interrupted me could never have attempted – to bring the masses of the Irish people into harmony with you, in this great effort at reconciliation – I say, we were entitled to every assistance from the Members of this House and from the Government.

"IN IRELAND ALONE IN THIS TWENTIETH CENTURY IS LOYALTY HELD TO BE A CRIME"

Roger Casement (1864–1916) was born in Dublin and educated at Ballymena Academy. He went to Africa at the age of twenty, and eight years later joined the British colonial civil service. After service in Africa and South America, he was knighted in 1911 and resigned from the colonial service in 1912.

Casement joined the Irish National Volunteers in 1913. On the outbreak of World War I, he worked to obtain German assistance for Irish independence – attempting, for example, to enlist Irish prisoners of war into a brigade to fight for Irish independence. He succeeded in obtaining arms, which were sent in April 1916. The arms were discovered and captured by the British army. Casement was arrested and sent to London to stand trial. The prosecution team was led by FE Smith, later Lord Birkenhead, who three years earlier had been instrumental in founding and running the Ulster Volunteer Force. Casement was found guilty, and sentenced to death. Despite a vigorous campaign to commute the sentence, he was hanged in Pentonville prison on August 3, 1916.

Casement's speech from the dock, made on the fourth day of his trial, was the most eloquent of the speeches made by those executed after the 1916 Rising.

OLD BAILEY, JUNE 30, 1916

I may say at once, my lord, that I protest against the jurisdiction of this court in my case on this charge and the argument that I am going to read is addressed not to this court,

49

but to my own countrymen. There is an objection, possibly not good in law, but surely good on moral grounds, against the application to me here of this old English statute, 565 years old, that seeks to deprive an Irishman today of life and honour, not "for adhering to the king's enemies", but for adhering to his own people. When this statute was passed in 1351, what was the state of men's minds on the question of a far higher allegiance – that of a man to God and his kingdom? The law of that day did not permit a man to forsake his Church, or deny his God, save with his life. The "heretic" then had the same doom as the "traitor". Today, a man may forswear God and his heavenly kingdom without fear or penalty – all earlier statutes having gone the way of Nero's edicts against the Christians; but that Constitutional phantom, the "King", can still dig up from the dungeons and torture chambers of the Dark Ages law that takes a man's life and limb for an exercise of conscience.

If true religion rests on love, it is equally true that loyalty rests on love. The law I am charged under has no parentage in love, and claims the allegiance of today on the ignorance and blindness of the past. I am being tried, in truth, not by my peers of the live present, but by the peers of the dead past; not by the civilisation of the twentieth century, but the brutality of the fourteenth; not even by a statute framed in the language of an enemy land – so antiquated is the law that must be sought today to slay an Irishman, whose offence is that he puts Ireland first.

Loyalty is a sentiment, not a law. It rests on love, not on restraint. The government of Ireland by England rests on restraint and not on law; and since it demands no love it can evoke no loyalty.

But this statute is more absurd even than it is antiquated, and if it be potent to hang one Irishman, it is still more potent to gibbet all Englishmen.

Edward III was king not only of the realm of England, but also of the realm of France, and he was not King of Ireland. Yet his dead hand today may pull the noose around the Irishman's neck whose Sovereign he was not, but it can strain no strand around the Frenchman's throat whose Sovereign he was. For centuries the successors of Edward III claimed to be kings of France, and quartered the arms of France on their royal shield down to the Union with Ireland on 1st January, 1801. Throughout these hundreds of years these "Kings of France" were constantly at war with their realm of France and their French subjects, who should have gone from birth to death with an obvious fear of treason before their eyes. But did they? Did the "Kings of France" resident here at Windsor or in the Tower of London, hang, draw, and quarter as a traitor every Frenchman for 400 years who fell into their hands with arms in his hand? On the contrary, they received embassies of these traitors, presents from these traitors, even knighthood itself at the hands of these traitors, feasted with them, tilted with them, fought with them – but did not assassinate them by law.

Judicial assassination today is reserved only for one race of the King's subjects – for Irishmen; for those who cannot forget their allegiance to the realm of Ireland. The kings of England as such had no rights in Ireland up to the time of Henry VIII, have such as rested on compact and mutual obligation entered into between them and certain princes, chiefs and lords of Ireland. This form of legal right, such as it was, gave no king of England lawful power to impeach an Irishman for his high treason under the statute of King Edward III of England until an Irish Act, known as Poynings' Law, the tenth of Henry VII, was passed in 1494 at Drogheda by the Parliament of the Pale in Ireland and enacted as law in that part of Ireland. But if by Pale in Ireland an Irishman of the Pale could be indicted for high treason under this Act, he could be indicted only in one way, and before one tribunal – by the law of the realm of Ireland, and in Ireland. The very law of Poynings, which, I believe, applies his statute of Edward III to Ireland, enacted also for the Irishman's defence "all those laws by which England claims her liberty". And what is the fundamental charter of an Englishman's liberty? that he shall be tried by his peers. With all respect, I assert this court is to me, an Irishman, not a jury of my peers to try me in this vital issue; for it is patent to every man of conscience that I have an indefeasible right, if tried at all under this statute of high treason, to be tried in Ireland, before an Irish court and an Irish jury. This court, this jury, the public opinion of this country, England, cannot but be prejudiced in varying degrees against me, most of all in time of war. I did not land in England. I landed in Ireland. It was to Ireland I came; to Ireland I wanted to come; and the last place I desired to land in was England.

But, for the Attorney General of England, there is only England; there is no Ireland; there is only the law of England, no right of Ireland; the liberty of Ireland and of Irishmen is to be judged by the power of England. Yet for me, the Irish outlaw, there is a land of Ireland, a right of Ireland, and a charter for all Irishmen to appeal to, in the last resort, a charter that even the very statutes of England cannot deprive us of – nay more, a charter that Englishmen themselves assert as the fundamental bond of law that connects the two kingdoms. This charge of high treason involves a moral responsibility, as the very term of the indictment against myself recite, inasmuch as I committed the acts I am charged with to the evil example of others in the like case, and who were these others? The "evil example" charge is that I asserted the right of my own country, and "the others" to whom I appealed to aid my endeavour were my own countrymen. The example was not given to Englishmen, but to Irishmen, and "the like case" can never arise in England, but only in Ireland. To Englishmen, I set no evil example, for I made no appeal to them. I asked no Englishmen to help me. I asked Irishmen to fight for heir rights. The "evil example" was only to other Irishmen, who might come after me and "in like case" seek to do as I did. How, then, since neither my example nor my appeal was addressed to Englishmen, can I be rightly tried by them?

If I did wrong in making that appeal to Irishmen to join with me in an effort to fight for Ireland, it is by Irishmen, and by them alone, I can be rightfully judged. From the Court and its jurisdiction I appeal to those I am alleged to have wronged, and to those I am alleged to have injured by my "evil example", and claim that they alone are competent to decide my guilt or my innocence. If they find me guilty, the statute may affix the penalty, but the statute does not override or annul my right to seek judgement at their hands.

This is so fundamental a right, so natural, so obvious, that it is clear the Crown were aware of it when they brought me by force and by stealth from Ireland to this country. It was not I who landed in England, but the Crown that dragged me here, away from my own country to which I had returned with a price upon my head; away from my own countrymen whose loyalty is not in doubt, and safe from the judgement of my peers, whose judgement I do not shrink from. I admit no other judgement but theirs. I accept no verdict save at their hands. I assert from this dock that I am being tried here, not because it is just, but because it is unjust. Place me before a jury of my own country-men, be it Protestant or Catholic, Unionist or Nationalist, Sinn Feineach or Orange, and I shall accept the verdict and bow to the statute and all its penalties. But I shall accept no meaner finding against me than that of those whose loyalty I endanger by my example and to whom alone I made appeal. If they adjudge me guilty, then guilty I am. It is not I who am afraid of their verdict; it is the Crown. If this be not so, why fear the test? I fear it not. I demand it as my right.

This is the condemnation of English rule, of English-made law, of English government in Ireland, that it dare not rest on the will of the Irish people, but it exists in defiance of their will; that it is a rule derived not from right, but from conquest. But conquest, my lord, gives no title, and if it exists over the body, it fails over the mind. It can exert no empire over men's reason and judgement and affections; and it is from this law of conquest that I appeal. I would add that the generous expressions of sympathy extended to me from many quarters, particularly from America, have touched me very much. In that country, as in my own, I am sure that my motives are understood, and not misjudged, for the achievement of their liberty has been an abiding inspiration to Irishmen, and to all men elsewhere, rightly struggling to be free.

Let me pass from myself and my own fate to a more pressing, as it is a far more urgent theme – not the fate of the individual Irishman who may have tried and failed, but the claims and the fate of the country that has not failed. Ireland has outlived the failure of all her hopes – and she still hopes. Ireland has seen her sons – aye, and her daughters, too – suffer from generation to generation always for the same cause, meeting always the same fate, and always at the hands of the same power. Still always a fresh generation has passed on to withstand the same oppression. For if English authority be omnipotent – a power, as Mr Gladstone phrased it, that reaches to the very ends of the earth – Irish hope exceeds the dimensions of that power, excels its authority, and renews with each generation the claims of the last. The cause that begets this indomitable persistency, the faculty of preserving through centuries of misery the remembrance of lost liberty, this surely is the noblest cause ever man strove for, ever lived for, ever died for. If this be the case I stand here to-day indicted for, and convicted of sustaining, then I stand in a goodly company and a right noble succession.

My counsel has referred to the Ulster Volunteer movement, and I will not touch at length upon that ground save only to say this, that neither I nor any of the leaders of the Irish Volunteers who were founded in Dublin in November 1913 had quarrel with the Ulster Volunteers, as such, who were born a year earlier. Our movement was not directed against them, but against the men who misused and misdirected the courage, the sincerity, and the local patriotism of the men of the North of Ireland. On the contrary, we welcomed the coming of the Ulster Volunteers, even while we deprecated the aims and intentions of those Englishmen who sought to pervert to an English party use – to the mean purposes of their own bid for place and power in England – the armed activities of simple Irishmen. We

54

aimed at winning the Ulster Volunteers to the cause of a united Ireland. We aimed at uniting all Irishmen in a natural and national bond of cohesion based on mutual self-respect. Our hope was a natural one, and were we left to ourselves, not hard to accomplish. If external influences of disintegration would but leave us alone, we were sure that Nature itself must bring us together. It was not we, the Irish Volunteers, who broke the law, but a British party. The Government had permitted the Ulster Volunteers to be armed by Englishmen, to threaten not merely an English party in its hold on office, but to threaten that party through the lives and blood of Irishmen.

The battle was to be fought in Ireland in order that the political "outs" of today should be the "ins" of tomorrow in Great Britain. A law designed for the benefit of Ireland was to be met, not on the floor of Parliament, where the fight had indeed been won, but on the field of battle much nearer home, where the armies would be composed of Irishmen slaying each other for some English party gain; and the British Navy would be chartered "transports" that were to bring to our shores a numerous assemblage of military and ex-military experts in the congenial and profitable exercise of holding down subject populations abroad. Our choice lay in submitting to foreign lawlessness or resisting it, and we did not hesitate to choose. But while the law-breakers had armed their would-be agents openly, and had been permitted to arm them openly, we were met within a few days of the founding of our movement – that aimed at a united Ireland from within – by Government action from without, directed against our obtaining any arms at all. The manifesto of the Irish Volunteers, promulgated at a public meeting in Dublin 25th November, 1913, stated with sincerity the aims of the organisation as I have outlined them. If the aims set in that manifesto were a threat to the unity of the British Empire, then so much the worse for the Empire. An Empire that can only be held together by one section of its governing population perpetually holding down and sowing dissension among a smaller but none the less governing section, must have some canker in its heart, some ruin at its root. The Government that permitted the arming of those whose leaders declared that Irish national unity was a thing that should be opposed by force of arms, within nine days of the issue of our manifesto of good-will to Irishmen of every creed and class, took steps to nullify our effort by prohibiting the import of all arms into Ireland as if it had been a hostile and blockaded coast. And this Proclamation of the 4th December, 1913, known as the Arms Proclamation, was itself based on an illegal interpretation of the law, as the Chief Secretary has now publicly confessed. The proclamation was met by the loyalists of Great Britain with an act of still more lawless defiance – an act of widespread gun-running into Ulster that was denounced by the Lord Chancellor of England as "grossly illegal and utterly unconstitutional". How did the Irish Volunteers meet the incitements of civil war that were uttered by the party of law and order in England?

I can answer for my own acts and speeches. While one English party was responsible for preaching a doctrine of hatred designed to bring about civil war in Ireland, the other – and that the party in power – took no active steps to restrain a propaganda that found its advocates in the Army, Navy, and Privy Council – in the Houses of Parliament and in the State church – a propaganda the methods of whose expression were so "grossly illegal and utterly unconstitutional" that even the Lord Chancellor of England could find only words and no repressive action to apply to them. Since lawlessness sat in high places in England and laughed at the law as at the custodians of the law, what wonder was it that Irishmen should refuse to accept the verbal protestations of an English Lord Chancellor as a sufficient safeguard for their lives and their liberties? I know not how all my colleagues on the Volunteer Committee in Dublin received the growing menace, but those with whom I was in closest co-operation re-doubled, in face of these threats from without, our efforts to unite all Irishmen from within. Our appeals were made to Protestant and Unionist as much almost as to Catholic and Nationalist Irishmen. We hoped that by the exhibition of affection and goodwill on our part towards our political opponents in Ireland we should yet succeed in winning them from the side of an English party whose sole interest in our country lay in its oppression in the past, and in the present in its degradation to the mean and narrow needs of their political animosities.

It is true that they based their actions – so they averred – on "fears for the Empire", and on a very diffuse loyalty that took in all the peoples of the Empire, save only the Irish. That blessed word "Empire" that bears so paradoxical a resemblance to charity! For if charity begins at home, "Empire" begins in other men's homes, and both may cover a multitude of sins. I for one was determined that Ireland was much more to me than "Empire", and that if charity begins at home so must loyalty. Since arms were so necessary to make our organisation a reality, and to give to the minds of Irishmen menaced with the most outrageous threats a sense of security, it was our bounden duty to get arms before all else. I decided with this end in view, to go to America, with surely a better right to appeal to Irishmen there for help in an hour of great national trial than those envoys of "Empire" could assert for their weekend descents upon Ireland, or their appeals to Germany. If, as the right honourable gentleman, the present Attorney-General, asserted in a speech at Manchester, Nationalists would neither fight for Home Rule nor pay for it, it was our duty to show him that we knew how to do both. Within a few weeks of my arrival in the States the fund that had been opened to secure arms for the Volunteers of Ireland amounted to many thousands of pounds. In every case the money subscribed, whether it came from the purse of the wealthy man or the still readier pocket of the poor man, was Irish gold.

Then came the war which as Mr Birrell said in his evidence recently laid before the commission of inquiry into the causes of the late rebellion in Ireland, "the war upset all our calculations". It upset mine no less than Mr Birrell's, and put an end to my mission of peaceful America. War between Great

Britain and Germany meant, as I believed, ruin of all the hopes we had founded on the enrolment of the Irish Volunteers. A constitutional movement in Ireland is never very far from a breach of the constitution, as the loyalists of Ulster had been so eager to show us. The cause is not far to seek. A constitution to be maintained intact must be the achievement and the pride of the people themselves; must rest on their own free will and on their determination to sustain it, instead of being something resident in another land whose chief representative is an armed force – armed not to protect the population, but to hold it down. We had seen the working of Irish Constitution in the refusal of the army occupation at the Curragh to obey the orders of the Crown. And now that we were told the first duty of an Irishman was to enter the army, in return for a promissory note, payable after death – a scrap of paper that might or might not be redeemed, I felt over there in America that my first duty was to keep Irishmen at home in the only army that could safeguard our national existence. If small nationalities were to be the pawns in this game of embattled giants, I saw no reason why Ireland should shed her blood in any cause but her own, and if that be treason beyond the seas, I am not ashamed to avow it or to answer for it here with my life. And when we had the doctrine of Unionist loyalty at last – "Mausers and Kaisers and any King you like", and I have heard that at Hamburg, not far from Limburg on the Lahn – I felt I needed no other than these words conveyed – to go forth and do likewise. The difference between us was that the Unionist champions chose a path they felt would lead to the Woolsack; while I went a road I knew must lead to the dock.

The difference between us was that my "treason" was based on a ruthless sincerity that forced me to attempt in time and season to carry out in action what I said in words – whereas their treason lay in verbal incitements that they knew need never be made good in their bodies. And so, I am prouder to stand here today in the traitor's dock to answer this impeachment than to fill the place of my right honourable accusers.

We have been told, we have been asked to hope, that after this war Ireland will get Home Rule as a reward for the lifeblood shed in a cause which whomever else its success may benefit, can surely not benefit Ireland. And what will Home Rule be in return for what its vague promise has taken and still hopes to take from Ireland? It is not necessary to climb the painful stairs of Irish history to review the long list of British promises made only to be broken – of Irish hopes raised only to be dashed to the ground. Home Rule when it comes, if come it does, will find an Ireland drained of all that is vital to its very busy existence – unless it be that unquenchable hope that we build on the graves of the dead. We are told that if Irishmen go by the thousand to die, not for Ireland, but for Flanders, for Belgium, for a patch of sand on the deserts of Mesopotamia, or a rocky trench on the heights of Gallipoli, they are winning self-government for Ireland. But if they dare to lay down their lives on their native soil, if they dare to dream even that freedom can be won only at home by men resolved to fight for it there, then they are traitors to their country and their dream and their deaths alike are phases of a dishonourable fantasy.

But history is not so recorded in other lands. In Ireland alone in this twentieth century is loyalty held to be a crime. If loyalty be something less than love and more than law, then we have had enough of such loyalty for Ireland or Irishmen. If we are to be indicted as criminals, to be shot as murderers, to be imprisoned as convicts because our offence is that we love Ireland more than we value our lives, then I know not what virtue resides in any offer of self-government is our right, a thing born in us at birth; a thing no more to be doled out to us or withheld from us by another people than the right to life itself – than the right to feel the sun or smell the flowers, or to love our kind. It is only from the convict these things are withheld for crimes committed and proven – and, Ireland, that has wronged no man, that has injured no land, that has sought no dominion over others – Ireland is treated today among the nations of the world as if she was a convicted criminal. If it be treason to fight against such an unnatural fate as this, then I am proud to be a rebel, and shall cling to my "rebellion" with the last drop of my blood. If there be no right of rebellion against a state of things that no savage tribe would endure without resistance, then I am sure that it is better for men to fight and die without right than to live in such a state of right as this. Where all your rights become only an accumulated wrong; where men must beg with bated breath for leave to subsist in their own land, to think their own thoughts, to sing their own songs, to garner the fruits of their own labours – and, even while they beg, to see things inexorably withdrawn from them – then, surely, it is braver, a saner and a truer thing, to be a rebel in act and deed against such circumstances as these than tamely to accept it as the natural lot of men . . .

"THE LABOUR PARTY . . . IS PREPARED TO SACRIFICE PARTY IN THE INTEREST OF THE NATION"

The Irish Labour Party, the oldest of the Republic's political parties, traces its foundation to the 1912 Conference of the Irish Trade Union Congress held in Clonmel. At that point in its history Irish trade unionism was extremely militant (particularly under the leadership of Larkin and Connolly) and this militancy contrasts with the subsequent history of the Irish Labour Party.

The national question of 1916–1923 posed major problems for the Irish Labour Party. The working class was split several ways – in the north many were Unionists, some supported the Irish Parliamentary Party, while others moved towards Sinn Fein.

In dealing with the national question in the 1918 election, Labour avoided it. It has been argued that Labour's decision to avoid this "crucial" election damaged it subsequently as, by staying out, it missed the chance to gain the allegiance of many first-time voters, who instead formed an attachment to Sinn Féin. It was only with the decline of the Treaty as an issue in Irish politics that Labour began to have a more significant political impact. The statement below, outlined the reasons behind Labour's decision not to contest the 1918 general election.

DUBLIN, NOVEMBER 9, 1918

Six weeks ago, when the National Executive decided that it was for the best interest of Ireland and Labour that a number of constituencies should be fought by Labour candidates at the forthcoming General Election, there was little sign of an early peace. The prospect before us was that the election then expected would be a "war election," to be followed at the end of the war by a dissolution and second election.

The unexpected call for an armistice on the part of the Central Powers has brought us face to face with the crisis which was not expected to develop until the "peace election" was at hand.

We had hoped to use the period between the two elections for an active educational propaganda directed towards ensuring that the building of the new Ireland shall be in the hands of men and women who view the problems of political and social development from the standpoint of the working-class, to determine, as far as our means and abilities allowed, that the Irish Republic – if such were to be the form of government determined upon by a people guaranteed the right to choose its own sovereignty – should be a Worker's Republic, not an imitation of those republics of Europe and America, where political democracy is but a cloak for capitalist oligarchy.

But circumstances have decided that the election now upon us is to be the "peace election", not the "war election." The Grand Inquest about to be opened has for a jury the nations of the world. The verdict will be given according to the weight of evidence adduced, and that will depend upon the degree of unanimity marked at the polls on the demand for self-determination.

A call comes from all parts of Ireland for a demonstration of unity on this question, such as was witnessed on the Conscription issue. Your Executive believes that the workers of Ireland join earnestly in this desire, that they would willingly sacrifice for a brief period their aspirations towards political power if thereby the fortunes of the nation can be enhanced.

In the light of these new circumstances the National Executive has reviewed the position, and has decided to recommend the withdrawal from this election of all Labour candidates. They do so in the hope that the democratic demand for self determination to which the Irish Labour Party and its candidates give its unqualified adherence will thereby obtain the greatest chance of expression at the polls. We shall show by this action that while each of the other political parties is prepared to divide the people in their effort to obtain power, the Labour Party is the only party which is prepared to sacrifice party in the interest of the nation in this important crisis of the history of Ireland. We shall also thereby demonstrate to the peoples of all nations as emphatically as peaceful means allow that at this hour, when other small nations of Europe are asserting their freedom, Ireland, too, demands all the rights of a free nation.

"THE PASSING OF THE CONSCRIPTION BILL . . . MUST BE VIEWED AS A DECLARATION OF WAR"

Throughout World War I, the issue of conscription for Ireland was debated vigorously in the House of Commons, but it was not introduced. In March 1918 the launch of the German offensive meant that more and more soldiers were required for the war effort. For several weeks the cabinet struggled with the problem of how to recruit 150,000 men from Ireland without inducing the political crisis that the introduction of conscription would undoubtedly cause.

On April 10, 1918, Lloyd George introduced a Military Service Bill which gave the government the power to introduce conscription in Ireland if it was required. He attempted to link it with the introduction of Home Rule. Dillon (who had taken over the leadership of the Irish Parliamentary Party on the death of Redmond) led his colleagues out of Westminster and back to Dublin. The Irish Parliamentary Party joined with Sinn Féin and a nationalist consensus emerged, supported for the first time by the Catholic Church.

On April 18, a round table conference was called by the Lord Mayor of Dublin on the issue. Those present included Griffith, de Valera, Dillon, Joseph Devlin, Tim Healy and William O'Brien. That meeting produced a statement and a pledge that was to be taken at church doors, the following Sunday (April 21, 1918). Following a meeting in Maynooth with a delegation from the conference, the Catholic Hierarchy issued its own statement of support.

The effect of the campaign was to give Sinn Féin a legitimacy and authority prior to the 1918 election. It also linked the Church and radical nationalism in a way that had not previously happened and was to unify the nationalist community under a militant agenda, from which British government in Ireland never recovered.

MANSION HOUSE, APRIL 18, 1918

Taking our stand on Ireland's separate and distinct nationhood, and affirming the principle of liberty, that the Governments of nations derive their just powers from the consent of the governed, we deny the right of the British Government or any external authority to impose compulsory military service in Ireland against the clearly expressed will of the Irish people.

The passing of the Conscription Bill by the British House of Commons must be regarded as a declaration of war on the Irish nation. The alternative to accepting it as such is to surrender our liberties and to acknowledge ourselves slaves. It is in direct violation of the rights of small nationalities to self-determination, which even the Prime Minister of England – now preparing to employ naked militarism and force his Act upon Ireland – himself officially announced as an essential condition for peace at the Peace Congress.

The attempt to enforce it will be an unwarrantable aggression, which we call upon all Irishmen to resist by the most effective means at their disposal.

THE HIERARCHY'S STATEMENT AGAINST CONSCRIPTION

MAYNOOTH, APRIL 18, 1918

An attempt is being made to force conscription upon Ireland against the will of the Irish nation and in defiance of the protests of its leaders.

In view especially of the historic relations between the two countries from the very beginning up to the present moment, we consider that conscription forced in this way upon Ireland is an oppressive and inhuman law, which the Irish people have a right to resist by all means that are consonant with the law of God.

We wish to remind our people that there is a higher Power which controls the affairs of men. They have in their hands the means of conciliating that Power by strict adherence to the Divine Law, by more earnest attention on their religious duties, and by fervent and persevering prayer.

In order to secure the aid of the Holy Mother of God, who shielded our people in the days of their greatest trials, we have already sanctioned a National Novena in honour of Our Lady of Lourdes, commencing on the 3rd of May, to secure general and domestic peace.

We also exhort the heads of families to have the Rosary recited every evening with the intention of protecting the spiritual and temporal welfare of our beloved country, and bringing us safe through this crisis of unparalleled gravity.

"MESSAGE TO THE FREE NATIONS OF THE WORLD"

After the 1918 election, the members of Sinn Féin who had been returned as Members of Parliament carried out their pre-election promise of abstention from the House of Commons and set about establishing an alternative parliament in Dublin. Those who had been elected (from all parties) were invited to attend the first session of Dáil Éireann to be held on January 21, 1919. The Unionists and the remnants of the Irish Parliamentary Party ignored the request. Of the Sinn Féin members elected, 34 were in prison, 8 were absent for other reasons and only the remainder (27) were present.

The meeting, held in the Round Room of the Mansion House, took less than two hours. It was agreed that an executive council, consisting of a Prime Minister and four other Ministers, was to be elected.

The meeting also sent greetings to the Free Nations of the World – which was a re-affirmation of Sinn Féin's belief in Irish independence and a demand that the post-World War I Peace Conference deal with the Irish issue. The Dáil actually appointed three delegates to the Peace Conference – Griffith, de Valera and Count Plunkett. Unsurprisingly, the appeal fell on deaf ears.

MANSION HOUSE, DUBLIN, JANUARY 21, 1919

To the Nations of the World! Greeting.

The Nation of Ireland having proclaimed her national independence, calls through her elected representatives in Parliament assembled in the Irish Capital on January 21st, 1919, upon every free nation to support the Irish Republic by recognising Ireland's national status and her right to its vindication at the Peace Congress.

Nationally, the race, the language, the customs and traditions of Ireland are radically distinct from the English. Ireland is one of the most ancient nations in Europe, and she has preserved her national integrity, vigorous and intact, through seven centuries of foreign oppression: she has never relinquished her national rights, and throughout the long era of English usurpation she has in every generation defiantly proclaimed her inalienable right of nationhood down to her last glorious resort to arms in 1916.

Internationally, Ireland is the gateway of the Atlantic. Ireland is the last outpost of Europe towards the West: Ireland is the point upon which great trade routes between East and West converge: her independence is demanded by the Freedom of the Seas: her great harbours must be open to all nations, instead of being the monopoly of England. Today these harbours are empty and idle solely because English policy is determined to retain Ireland as a barren bulwark for English aggrandisement, and the unique geographical position of this island, far from being a benefit and safeguard to Europe and America, is subjected to the purposes of England's policy of world domination.

Ireland today reasserts her historic nationhood the more confidently before the new world emerging from the War, because she believes in freedom and justice as the fundamental principles of international law, because she believes in a frank co-operation between the peoples for equal rights against the vested privileges of ancient tyrannies, because the permanent peace of Europe can never be secured by perpetuating military dominion for the profit of empire but only by establishing the control of government in every land upon the basis of the free will of a free people, and the existing state of war, between Ireland and England, can never be ended until Ireland is definitely evacuated by the armed forces of England.

For these among other reasons, Ireland – resolutely and

irrevocably determined at the dawn of the promised era of self-determination and liberty that she will suffer foreign dominion no longer – calls upon every free nation to uphold her national claim to complete independence as an Irish Republic against the arrogant pretensions of England founded in fraud and sustained only by an overwhelming military occupation, and demands to be confronted publicly with England at the Congress of the Nations, in order that the civilised world having judged between English wrong and Irish right may guarantee to Ireland its permanent support for the maintenance of her national independence.

THE DEMOCRATIC PROGRAMME

The first session of the Dáil also passed the Democratic Programme. It is a radical statement which invokes the parentage of Pearse (but not Connolly). It affirmed that all rights to private property must be subordinated to the public right and welfare.

Despite its intentions, the Democratic Programme never had much influence in policy terms. In the post-independence era, consolidation and conservative economic orthodoxy became the order of the day as the new state sought to establish its bona fides. It remains, however, as testimony to the initial radicalism of the independence movement.

MANSION HOUSE, DUBLIN, JANUARY 21, 1919

We declare in the words of the Irish Republican Proclamation the right of the people of Ireland to the ownership of Ireland, and to the unfettered control of Irish destinies to be indefeasible, and in the language of our first President, Padraig MacPhiarais, we declare that the Nation's sovereignty extends not only to all men and women of the Nation, but to all its material possessions, the Nation's soil and all its resources, all the wealth and all the wealth-producing processes within the Nation, and with him we reaffirm that all right to private property must be subordinated to the public right and welfare.

We declare that we desire our country to be ruled in accordance with the principles of Liberty, Equality, and Justice for all, which alone can secure permanence of Government in the willing adhesion of the people.

We affirm the duty of every man and woman to give allegiance and service to the Commonwealth, and declare it is the duty of the Nation to assure that every citizen shall have opportunity to spend his or her strength and faculties in the service of the people. In return for willing service, we, in the name of the Republic, declare the right of every citizen to an adequate share of the produce of the Nation's labour.

It shall be the first duty of the Government of the Republic to make provision for the physical, mental and spiritual well-being of the children, to secure that no child shall suffer hunger or cold from lack of food, clothing, or shelter, but that all shall be provided with the means and facilities requisite for their proper education and training as Citizens of a Free and Gaelic Ireland.

The Irish Republic fully realises the necessity of abolishing the present odious, degrading and foreign Poor Law System, substituting therefor a sympathetic native scheme for the care of the Nation's aged and infirm, who shall not be regarded as a burden, but rather entitled to the Nation's gratitude and consideration. Likewise it shall be the duty of the Republic to take such measures as will safeguard the health of the people and ensure the physical as well as the moral well-being of the Nation.

It shall be our duty to promote the development of the Nation's resources, to increase the productivity of its soil, to exploit its mineral deposits, peat bogs, and fisheries, its waterways and harbours, in the interests and for the benefit of the Irish people.

It shall be the duty of the Republic to adopt all measures necessary for the recreation and invigoration of our Industries, and to ensure their being developed on the most beneficial and progressive co-operative and industrial lines. With the adoption of an extensive Irish Consular Service, trade with foreign Nations shall be revived on terms of mutual advantage and goodwill, and while undertaking the organisation of the Nation's trade, import and export, it shall be the duty of the

Republic to prevent the shipment from Ireland of food and other necessaries until the wants of the Irish people are fully satisfied and the future provided for.

It shall also devolve upon the National Government to seek co-operation of the Governments of other countries in determining a standard of Social and Industrial Legislation with a view to a general and lasting improvement in the conditions under which the working classes live and labour.

"WE ASK FOR NO MERCY, AND WE
WILL MAKE NO COMPROMISE"

*Terence MacSwiney (1879–1920) was born in Cork and
educated at North Monastery Christian Brothers School and the
Royal University (later University College, Cork). He was
instrumental in forming the Cork Volunteers and became its full-
time organiser in 1915. MacSwiney took no part in the 1916
Rising, but remained active in the nationalist movement and
was imprisoned briefly in both 1916 and 1917. A member of the
First Dáil, he was elected Lord Mayor of Cork following the
assassination of his predecessor Thomas MacCurtain by the
Royal Irish Constabulary. He made the speech below on his
election.*

*This speech was included in the evidence used to court
martial MacSwiney and he was sentenced to two years'
imprisonment in Brixton Gaol. After his conviction he went on
immediate hunger strike, and died 74 days later.*

CORK CITY HALL, MARCH 20, 1920

I shall be as brief as possible. This is not an occasion for
many words; least of all, a conventional exchange of
compliments and thanks. The circumstances in the vacancy in
the office of Lord Mayor governed inevitably the filling of it.
And I come here more as a soldier stepping into the breach,
than as an administrator to fill the first post in the municipality.
At a normal time it would be your duty to find for this post the
Councillor most practised and experienced in public affairs. But
the time is not normal. We see in the manner in which our late

73

Lord Mayor was murdered an attempt to terrify us all. Our first duty is to answer that threat in the only fitting manner by showing ourselves unterrified, cool and inflexible for the fulfilment of our chief purpose – the establishment of the independence and integrity of our country – the peace and happiness of our country. To that end I am here.

I was more closely associated than any other here with our late murdered friend and colleague, both before and since the events of Easter Week, in prison and out of it, in a common work of love for Ireland, down to the hour of his death. For that reason, I take his place. It is, I think, though I say it, the fitting answer to those who struck him down. Following from that, there is a further matter of importance only less great – it touches the efficient continuance of our civic administration. If this recent unbearable aggravation of our persecution by our enemies should cause us to suspend voluntarily the normal discharge of our duties, it would help them very materially in their campaign to overthrow our cause. I feel the future conduct of our affairs is in all our minds. And I think I am voicing the general view when I say that the normal functions of our Corporate body must proceed, as far as in our power lies, uninterrupted, with that efficiency and integrity of which our late civic head gave such brilliant promise.

I don't wish to sound a personal note, but this much may be permitted under the circumstances. I made myself active in the selection of our late colleague for the office of Lord Mayor. He did not seek the honour, and would not accept it as such; but, when put to him as a duty, he stepped to his place like a soldier. Before his election, we discussed together in the intimate way we discussed everything touching our common work since Easter Week – we debated together what ought to be done, and what could be done, keeping in mind, as in duty bound, not only the ideal line of action, but the practicable line of action at the moment as well. That line he followed with an ability and a success all his own. Gentlemen, you have paid tribute to him on all sides. It will be my duty and steady purpose to follow that line as faithfully as may be in my power, though no man in this company could hope to discharge its functions with his ability and his perfect grasp of public business in all its details as one harmonious whole.

I have thought it necessary to touch on this normal duty of ours, though – and it may seem strange to say it – I feel even at the moment it is a digression. For the menace of our enemies hangs over us, and the essential immediate purpose is to show the spirit that animates us, and how we face the future. Our spirit is but a more lively manifestation of the spirit in which we began the year – to work for the city with a new zeal, inspired by our initial act when we dedicated it and formally attested our allegiance, and by working for our city's advancement with constancy in all honourable ways in her new dignity as one of the first cities of Ireland to work for and, if need be, to die for.

I would recall some words of mine on the day of our first meeting after the election of Lord Mayor. I realised that most of you in the minority here would be loyal to us, if doing so did not threaten your lives; but that you lacked the spirit and the hope to join with us to complete the work of liberation so well begun. I allude to it here again, because I wish to point out again the secret of our strength and the assurance of our final victory. This contest of ours is not, on our side, a rivalry of vengeance, but one of endurance – it is not they who can inflict most, but they who can suffer most, will conquer – though we do not abrogate our function to demand and see that evil-doers and murderers are punished for their crimes. But it is conceivable that they could interrupt our course for a time; then it becomes a question simply of trust in God and endurance. Those whose faith is strong will endure to the end, and triumph. The shining hope of our time is that the great majority of our people are now strong in that faith.

To you, gentlemen of the minority here, I would address a word. I ask you again to take courage and hope. To me it seems – and I don't say it to hurt you – that you have a lively faith in the power of the devil, and but little faith in God. But

God is over us. Anyone surveying the events in Ireland for the past five years must see that it is approaching a miracle how our country has been preserved. God has permitted this to be to try our spirits, to prove us worthy of a noble line, to prepare us for a great and noble destiny. You among us who have yet no vision of the future have been led astray by false prophets. The liberty for which we to-day strive is a sacred thing – inseparably entwined, as body with soul, with that spiritual liberty for which the Saviour of men died, and which is the inspiration and foundation of all just government. Because it is sacred – and death for it is akin to the Sacrifice on Calvary, following far off but akin to that Divine Example – in every generation, our best and bravest have died.

Sometimes in our grief we cry out foolish and unthinking words: "The sacrifice is too great." But, it is because they were our best and bravest, they had to die. No lesser sacrifice would save us. Because of it our struggle is holy – our battle is sanctified by their blood, and our victory is assured by their martyrdom. We, taking up the work they left incomplete, confident in God, offer in turn sacrifice from ourselves. It is not we who take innocent blood, we but offer it, sustained by the example of our immortal dead and that Divine Example which inspires us all – for the redemption of our country. Facing our enemies, we must declare our attitude simply. We ask for no mercy, and we will make no compromise. But to the Divine Author of mercy we appeal for strength to sustain us, whatever the persecution, that we may bring our people victory in the end. The civilised world dare not continue to look on indifferent. But if the rulers of earth fail us, we have yet some succour in the Ruler of Heaven; and though to some impatient hearts his judgements seem slow, they never fail, and when they fall they are overwhelming and final.

"I CANNOT CONDEMN THOSE POLICEMEN"

Lieut-Colonel Sir Hamar Greenwood, a Canadian, was appointed Chief Secretary for Ireland in 1920, by a British government which felt that his military background and personality were strong enough to break the military campaign of the IRA.

Greenwood believed in a military solution to the Irish problem and in December 1920, he advised the government to refuse a truce – on the exact terms it was to accept in July 1921 – because of his belief that the IRA was on the verge of collapse and that the British government was supported by Irish public opinion.

In 1920 two new forces were formed to aid the Royal Irish Constabulary – the Black and Tans and the Auxiliaries. One of the law enforcement methods employed by these groups was reprisal. After the killing of an RIC officer and his brother in Balbriggan, Co. Dublin in October, the Black and Tans went to avenge their deaths. The town of Balbriggan was burnt to the ground.

The Labour MP for Paisley, Arthur Henderson, demanded an inquiry into the "Sack of Balbriggan". Sir Hamar Greenwood's reply to the House of Commons was indicative of a British government that was fast losing control of the situation in Ireland.

HOUSE OF COMMONS, OCTOBER 20, 1920
 . . . . The Right Hon. Gentleman referred to "doings in Ireland." I call it a deliberate, organised, highly-paid conspiracy to smash the British Empire.

I say "smash the British Empire" because those are the words of the Lord Mayor of Cork, an authority on Ireland whom the Hon. Gentleman will hardly dispute. My Right Hon. Friend referred to "more active elements among the Irish Nationalists." The Irish Nationalists have nothing to do with the difficulties in Ireland at the moment. There are no reprisals, or alleged reprisals, on Irish Nationalists . . .

I want it to be perfectly clear that there is no connection whatever between the Irish Nationalist party and the difficulties that we have in Ireland. First of all, I would like to ask the Right Hon. Gentleman the source of the information that he has seen fit to communicate to the House. I will tell him the source, for I am familiar with it. His information comes from the headquarters of the Irish Republican Army, which army comprises within its ranks the Irish Republican Brotherhood which supplies the assassins who have killed loyal servants of the Crown and loyal civilians during the past two years, and this House must make up its mind whether it will accept information from the headquarters of the Irish Republican Army or information from the Chief Secretary for Ireland speaking with official knowledge from this Box. There is a highly organised Propaganda Department connected with the Irish Republican movement not only in this country, but especially in the United States and in certain countries in Europe, and everything that can be said, regardless of fact, to smirch the name of the United Kingdom and of the British Empire and to smirch the names of loyal servants of the Crown is said by this Propaganda Department.

The majority of British papers decline to accept this information, but some British papers and some British politicians do accept it. Let me make clear to the House the position in reference to information from Ireland. Up till the beginning of this year Irish papers were not afraid to call the assassination of a policeman or of a civilian or of a soldier, murder. There is no Irish paper today in the south and west of Ireland that dares to refer to the most horrible assassination of a loyal servant of the Crown as murder. The reason for that is that the owners, the editors, the reporters and the linotypers either acquiesce in the non-use of the word "murder" or they are intimidated by the terrorists of the Sinn Féin Movement. There is no question about this. Every British journalist and American journalist that goes to Ireland knows it. There have been several cases of English journalists who have gone to Ireland to get the real facts and who have been threatened with their lives for the publication of those facts, and they have had to leave Ireland because of those threats.

I submit that the Right Hon. Gentleman has not put before the House one single case which justifies him and his friends in the resolution standing in their name, namely:

"That this House regrets the present state of lawlessness in Ireland, and the lack of discipline in the armed forces of the Crown, resulting in the death or injury of innocent citizens and the destruction of property."

I want to point out to the House that the Right Hon. Gentleman's reading of the recent history of Ireland will not do. The suggestion is that all these awful outrages and the disastrous and almost anarchical state of a part of Ireland is due to the sins of the Government since 1917. It will not do. It is not military repression and the suspension of all civil rights that has caused the present difficulties in Ireland. They are rooted in an unhappy and ancient past. No one regrets it more than the present Chief Secretary for Ireland. No one believes more heartily than I do that the ultimate solution must be some liberal form of Home Rule, and no one has more consistently supported measures of Home Rule in this House while I have had the honour of sitting in it. The difficulty today is not based upon a demand for Home Rule. It is based upon a demand for complete independence, and that demand is reinforced by an army equipped, organised, and working day and night. That demand is insisted upon by a policy of assassination and of burning that makes the last two years the saddest and worst in the history of Ireland.

The Right Hon. Gentleman talked about military aggression and imprisoning men on suspicion. When I had the honour of becoming the Chief Secretary of Ireland in April last, the Government, to show its goodwill, let out scores of men who were arrested on suspicion, and justifiable suspicion. Many of them have been re-arrested since for shooting policemen. The Government let out every hunger-striker. The Government let out certain convicted hunger-strikers. It may have been right or it may have been wrong – but, at any rate, it meets the argument of the Right Hon. Gentleman that the Government's policy of aggression and imprisonment without trial is the cause of this outburst, especially of the last few months. From the time of the release of those prisoners in April outrages have increased, murder has become more common, and the brutality of the murders more pronounced. Recently expanding bullets, condemned by every civilised race, have become the common weapon of revolting mutilation in carrying out this policy to smash the British Empire. I went to Ireland with high hopes of bringing peace to that country. By no word or deed did I say or do anything to revive old sores nor did I neglect to try to heal old difficulties. I am profoundly sorry to confess that my attempts at conciliation failed before a policy of assassination. Let there be no mistake. A policy of paid and organised assassination is the policy of the Irish Republican party in Ireland today. It is not a question of Home Rule, it is not a question of the ordinary Sinn Feiner, who is entitled to his political views. I have never myself arrested, or allowed anybody to be arrested, merely because of his political views in Ireland. I am speaking from this Box with authority. The point is that the difficulties of the forces of the Crown are not involved in combating opinions, but in putting down crime of the most hideous and revolting nature . . .

We have another source from which we draw reinforcements for the Royal Irish Constabulary, namely, ex-officers. This is called the auxiliary division and is composed entirely of ex-officers, ranking from Brigadier-General to subalterns, men who have served this noble country and Empire well on every field of battle in the late War. This force is put into the most disturbed areas and runs the greatest dangers, and I have yet to find one authenticated case of a member of this auxiliary division being accused of anything but the highest conduct characteristic of them. All this wild criticism of these gallant men comes from the same tainted source from which the Right Hon. Gentleman draws his indictment of His Majesty's Government . . .

It is only the British Government, acting through the forces in Ireland, that can break this terror. The Irish people are helpless under it, admittedly helpless under it. The Roman Catholic Church is admittedly impotent to break the terror in Ireland. I should consider the British Government unworthy of the name "British" or "Government" if it failed to assume this burden, not only of government, but of civilisation, to break a terror based upon the revolver and the assassin. We are breaking it; North, South, East and West it is coming to an end, and with the support of this House I foresee at no distant date an end of the rule of the assassin in Ireland . . .

I regret reprisals; nobody regrets them more. I do not want men to get out of hand, because it hurts the discipline of an organised force. I do not want reprisals even on notorious Sinn Feiners. I want them to be arrested, and, if guilty of crime, to be tried. I want no reprisals. I have a right to complain of reprisals, because I am responsible for the discipline of the Irish Constabulary. The Commander-in-Chief has a right to complain of reprisals, because he is responsible for the discipline of the British Army in Ireland. But those men who acquiesced in, connived at, condoned or supported the murder of District Inspector Brady, or members of the Royal Irish Constabulary, have no right to complain of reprisals. They are members of the Irish Republican Army that is pledged by force of arms to set up an independent republic in Ireland, to defy the authority of this House and to claim the right to assassinate the officers of the Crown. I could give many cases of an equally horrible character to this House. I will give one more. To me it is a painful business to think that anyone would stoop so low as to use expanding bullets and carry on a system of assassination that has characterised some of the counties in Ireland . . .

Head Constable Burke was not only a man of great courage but a very popular man with the police. In two depots miles away from Balbriggan when they heard of this murder they came in lorries to Balbriggan. When they saw the body of Burke and of his brother they – I admit it – they saw red! I admit it with regret. I always view these actions with the profoundest regret. In Balbriggan that night, 19 houses of Sinn Féiners were destroyed or damaged, and one hosiery factory which employed 200 hands, was also destroyed. I admit at once that it is difficult to defend the destruction of that factory. And two men were killed.

If the Right Hon. Gentleman the Member of Paisley gets any satisfaction out of it, I will say "murdered". I myself have had the fullest inquiry made into the case. I will tell the House what I found. I found that from 100 to 150 men went to Balbriggan determined to revenge the death of a popular comrade shot at and murdered in cold blood. I find it is impossible out of that 150 to find the men who did the deed, who did the burning. I have had the most searching inquiry made. I have laid down a code of still more severe discipline for the Royal Irish Constabulary, and I shall be glad to know that it will meet with approval. I myself had a parade of a large number of the Royal Irish Constabulary. I addressed them. I saw that what I said was published in nearly every paper in Ireland. I do not want to weary the House with a repetition of my speech, but I put the matter in as strong words as I could command that their business, and mine, was to prevent crime and to detect criminals, and when there was great provocation they must not give way. But I cannot in my heart of hearts – and, Mr Speaker, I say this – it may be right or it may be wrong – I cannot condemn in the same way those policeman who lost their heads as I condemn the assassins who provoked this outrage. My quarrel with the Right Hon. Gentleman the Member of Paisley and his friends is that they put all the emphasis on reprisals in Ireland: I put it on the provocation.

"IT IS A TREATY HONOURABLE TO IRELAND"

The signing of the Anglo-Irish Treaty in December 1921 was to etch the lines of political division in Ireland for the twentieth century. The issues and participants in the Treaty Debate have been examined in great detail elsewhere. The issues debated included the oath of allegiance to the British Crown, the actual level of independence that was on offer, partition, as well as the individuals involved on the pro- and anti- Treaty side. What is interesting about the speeches selected is the emphasis that each speaker places on the different issues. There is no mention from Griffith, de Valera or Collins of partition. Griffith's speech was a justification of what they achieved, de Valera's focused on the links that remained with the Empire. Collin's speech focused on what he felt was feasible, while Childers took a strong stance against the concept of the Oath and the level of freedom that was on offer.

Council Chamber, University College, Dublin, December 19, 1921
   Arthur Griffith, Minister for Foreign Affairs
   I move the motion standing in my name –
   "That Dáil Éireann approves of the Treaty between Great Britain and Ireland, signed in London on December 6, 1921."
   Nearly three months ago Dáil Éireann appointed plenipotentiaries to go to London to treat with the British Government and to make a bargain with them. We have made a bargain. We have brought it back. We were to go there to reconcile our aspirations with the association of the community of nations known as the British Empire. That task which was

83

given to us was as hard as was ever placed on the shoulders of men. We faced that task; we knew that whatever happened we would have our critics, and we made up our minds to do whatever was right and disregard whatever criticism might occur. We could have shirked the responsibility. We did not seek to act as the plenipotentiaries; other men were asked and other men refused. We went. The responsibility is on our shoulders; we took the responsibility in London and we take the responsibility in Dublin. I signed that Treaty not as the ideal thing, but fully believing, as I believe now, it is a treaty honourable to Ireland, and safeguards the vital interests of Ireland.

And now by that Treaty I am going to stand, and every man with a scrap of honour who signed it is going to stand. It is for the Irish people – who are our masters, not our servants as some think – it is for the Irish people to say whether it is good enough. I hold that it is, and I hold that the Irish people – that 95 per cent. of them believe it to be good enough. We are here, not as the dictators of the Irish people, but as the representatives of the Irish people, and if we misrepresent the Irish people, then the moral authority of Dáil Éireann, the strength behind it, and the fact that Dáil Éireann spoke the voice of the Irish people, is gone, and gone forever. Now, the President – and I am in a difficult position – does not wish a certain document referred to read. But I must refer to the substance of it. An effort has been made outside to represent that a certain number of men stood uncompromisingly on the rock of the Republic – the Republic, and nothing but the Republic.

It has been stated also here that the man who made this position, the man who won the war – Michael Collins – compromised Ireland's rights. In the letters that preceded the negotiations not once was a demand made for recognition of the Irish Republic. If it had been made we knew it would have been refused. We went there to see how to reconcile the two positions, and I hold we have done it. The President does not wish this document to be read. What am I to do? What am I to say? Am I to keep my mouth shut and let the Irish people think about this uncompromising rock? . . .

What we have to say is this, that the difference in this Cabinet and in this House is between half-recognising the British King and the British Empire, and between marching in, as one of the speakers said, with our heads up. The gentlemen on the other side are prepared to recognise the King of England as head of the British Commonwealth. They are prepared to go half in the Empire and half out. They are prepared to go into the Empire for war and peace and treaties, and to keep out for other matters, and that is what the Irish people have got to know is the difference. Does all this quibble of words – because it is merely a quibble of words – mean that Ireland is asked to throw away this Treaty and go back to war? So far as my power or voice extends, not one young Irishman's life shall be lost on that quibble. We owe responsibility to the Irish people. I feel my responsibility to the Irish people, and the Irish people must know, and know in every detail, the difference that exists between us, and the Irish people must be our judges. When the plenipotentiaries came back they were sought to be put in the dock. Well, if I am going to be tried, I am going to be tried by the people of Ireland. Now this Treaty has been attacked. It has been examined with a microscope to find its defects, and this little thing and that little thing has been pointed out, and the people are told – one of the gentlemen said it here – that it was less even than the proposals of July. It is the first Treaty between the representatives of the Irish Government and the representatives of the English Government since 1172 signed on equal footing. It is the first Treaty that admits the equality of Ireland. It is a Treaty of equality, and because of that I am standing by it. We have come back from London with that Treaty – Saorstat na hÉireann recognised – the Free State of Ireland. We have brought back the flag; we have brought back the evacuation of Ireland after 700 years by British troops and the formation of an Irish army. We have brought back to Ireland her full rights and powers of fiscal control. We have brought back to Ireland equality with England, equality with all nations which form that Commonwealth, and an equal voice in the direction of foreign affairs in peace and war. Well, we are told that that Treaty is a derogation from our status; that it is a Treaty not to be accepted, that it is a poor thing, and that the Irish people ought to go back and fight for something more, and that something more is what I describe as a quibble of words. Now, I shall have an opportunity later on of replying to the very formidably arranged criticism that is going to be levelled at the Treaty to show its defects. At all events, the Irish people are a people of great common sense. They know that a Treaty that gives them their flag and their Free State and their Army is not a sham Treaty, and the sophists and the men of words will not mislead them, I tell you.

Various different methods of attack on this Treaty have been made. One of them was they did not mean to keep it. Well, they have ratified it, and it can come into operation inside a fortnight. We think they do mean to keep it if we keep it. They are pledged now before the world, pledged by their signature, and if they depart from it they will be disgraced and we will be stronger in the world's eyes than we are today. During the last few years a war was waged on the Irish people, and the Irish people defended themselves, and for a portion of that time, when President de Valera was in America, I had at least the responsibility on my shoulders of standing for all that was done in that defence, and I stood for it. I would stand for it again under similar conditions. Ireland was fighting then against an enemy that was striking at her life, and was denying her liberty, but in any contest that would follow the rejection of this offer Ireland would be fighting with the sympathy of the world against her, and with all the Dominions – all the nations that comprise the British Commonwealth – against her.

The position would be such that I believe no conscientious Irishman could take the responsibility for a single Irishman's life in that futile war. Now, many criticisms, I know, will be levelled against this Treaty; one in particular, one that is in many instances quite honest, it is the question of the oath. I ask the members to see what the oath is, to read it, not to misunderstand or misrepresent it. It is an oath of allegiance to the Constitution of the Free State of Ireland and of faithfulness to King George V in his capacity as head and in virtue of the common citizenship of Ireland with Great Britain and the other nations comprising the British Commonwealth. That is an oath, I say, that any Irishman could take with honour. He pledges his allegiance to his country and to be faithful to this Treaty, and faithfulness after to the head of the British Commonwealth of Nations. If his country were unjustly used by any of the nations of that Commonwealth, or its head, then his allegiance is to his own country and his allegiance bids him to resist.

We took an oath to the Irish Republic, but, as President de Valera himself said, he understood that oath to bind him to do the best he could for Ireland. So do we. We have done the best we could for Ireland. If the Irish people say "We have got everything else but the name Republic, and we will fight for it," I would say to them that they are fools, but I will follow in the ranks. I will take no responsibility. But the Irish people will not do that. Now it has become rather a custom for men to speak of what they did, and did not do, in the past. I am not going to speak of that aspect, except one thing. It is this. The prophet I followed throughout my life, the man whose words and teachings I tried to translate into practice in politics, the man whom I revered above all Irish patriots was Thomas Davis. In the hard way of fitting practical affairs into idealism I have made Thomas Davis my guide. I have never departed in my life one inch from the principles of Thomas Davis, and in signing this Treaty and bringing it here and asking Ireland to ratify it I am following Thomas Davis still.

Later on, when coming to reply to criticism, I will deal with the other matters. Thomas Davis said:

"Peace with England, alliance with England to some extent, and, under certain circumstances, confederation with England;

but an Irish ambition, Irish hopes, strength, virtue, and rewards for the Irish."

That is what we have brought back, peace with England, alliance with England, confederation with England, an Ireland developing her own life, carving out her own way of existence, and rebuilding the Gaelic civilisation broken down at the battle of Kinsale. I say we have brought you that. I say we have translated Thomas Davis into the practical politics of the day. I ask then this Dáil to pass this resolution, and I ask the people of Ireland, and the Irish people everywhere, to ratify this Treaty, to end this bitter conflict of centuries, to end it for ever, to take away that poison that has been rankling in the two countries and ruining the relationship of good neighbours. Let us stand as free partners, equal with England, and make after 700 years the greatest revolution that has ever been made in the history of the world – a revolution of seeing the two countries standing not apart as enemies, but standing together as equals and as friends. I ask you, therefore, to pass this resolution.

"I AM AGAINST THIS TREATY BECAUSE IT WILL NOT END THE CENTURIES OF CONFLICT BETWEEN THE TWO NATIONS OF GREAT BRITAIN AND IRELAND"

Eamon de Valera (1882–1975) was born in America, but reared by his grandmother and uncle near Bruree in Co. Limerick. He was educated locally, at Christian Brothers School, Charleville and later at Blackrock College, Dublin. He excelled at Mathematics and became Professor of Mathematics at Carysfort Teacher Training College in Blackrock, Co. Dublin.

De Valera was an active participant in the 1916 Rising and served as Commandant at Boland's Mills. After the surrender he was sentenced to death but this sentence was commuted to life imprisonment. Shortly after his release from prison in 1917, he was elected to the House of Commons at a by-election for the constituency of East Clare. He did not take his seat.

At a convention in October 1917, de Valera was elected President of the "new" Sinn Féin. On April 1, 1919 he was elected as Príomh Aire (President) of the First Dáil and in that position he went to America to raise support for the Irish cause. He returned to Ireland in December 1920.

De Valera did not participate directly in the Treaty negotiations with Britain and opposed the terms agreed. After defeat on the Treaty in the Dáil, de Valera resigned as President and was replaced by Arthur Griffith. He was interned during the Civil War and re-emerged in 1924 to a political career that was to span the next fifty years.

De Valera opposed the treaty primarily on the grounds of the Oath of Allegiance. His opposition to the Oath became a corner-

stone of his politics and policies, until he succeeded in removing it during Fianna Fáil's period in government after 1932.

COUNCIL CHAMBER, UNIVERSITY COLLEGE DUBLIN, DECEMBER 19, 1921

. . . We were elected by the Irish people, and did the Irish people think we were liars when we said that we meant to uphold the Republic, which was ratified by the vote of the people three years ago, and was further ratified – expressly ratified – by the vote of the people at the elections last May? When the proposal for negotiation came from the British Government asking that we should try by negotiation to reconcile Irish national aspirations with the association of nations forming the British Empire, there was no one here as strong as I was to make sure that every human attempt should be made to find whether such reconciliation was possible. I am against this Treaty because it does not reconcile Irish national aspirations with association with the British Government. I am against this Treaty, not because I am a man of war, but a man of peace. I am against this Treaty because it will not end the centuries of conflict between the two nations of Great Britain and Ireland.

We went out to effect such a reconciliation and we have brought back a thing which will not even reconcile our own people much less reconcile Britain and Ireland.

If there was to be reconciliation, it is obvious that the party in Ireland which typifies national aspirations for centuries should be satisfied, and test of every agreement would be the test of whether the people were satisfied or not. A war-weary people will take things which are not in accordance with their aspirations. You may have a snatch election now, and you may get a vote of the people, but I will tell you that Treaty will renew the contest that is going to begin the same history that the Union began, and Lloyd George is going to have the same fruit for his labours as Pitt had. When in Downing Street the proposals to which we could unanimously assent in the Cabinet were practically turned down at the point of the pistol and

90

immediate war was threatened upon our people. It was only then that this document was signed, and the document has been signed by plenipotentiaries, not perhaps individually under duress, but it has been signed, and would only affect this nation as a document signed under duress, and this nation would not respect it.

I wanted, and the Cabinet wanted, to get a document we could stand by, a document that could enable Irishmen to meet Englishmen and shake hands with them as fellow-citizens of the world. That document makes British authority our masters in Ireland. It was said that they had only an oath to the British King in virtue of common citizenship, but you have an oath to the Irish Constitution, and the Constitution will be a Constitution which will have the King of Great Britain as head of Ireland. You will swear allegiance to that Constitution and to the King; and if the representatives of the Republic should ask the people of Ireland to do that which is inconsistent with the Republic, I say they are subverting the Republic. It would be a surrender which was never heard of in Ireland since the days of Henry II; and are we in this generation, which has made Irishmen famous throughout the world, to sign our names to the most ignoble document that could be signed.

When I was in prison in solitary confinement our warders told us that we could go from our cells into the hall, which was about fifty feet by forty. We did go out from our cells to the hall, but we did not give our word to the British jailer that he had the right to detain us in prison because we got that privilege. Again on another occasion we were told that we could get out to a garden party, where we could see the flowers and the hills, but we did not for the privilege of going out to garden parties sign a document handing over our souls and bodies to the jailers. Rather than sign a document which would give British authority in Ireland they should be ready to go into slavery until the Almighty had blotted out their tyrants. If the British Government passed a Home Rule Act or something of that kind I would not have said to the Irish people, "Do not take it." I would have said, "Very well; this is a case of the jailer leading you from the cell to the hall," but by getting that we did not sign away our right to whatever form of government we pleased. It was said that an uncompromising stand for a Republic was not made. The stand made by some of them was to try and reconcile a Republic with an association. There was a document presented to this House to try to get unanimity, to see whether the views which I hold could be reconciled to that party which typified the national aspirations of Ireland for centuries. The document was put there for that purpose, and I defy anybody in the House to say otherwise than that I was trying to bring forward before this assembly a document which would bring real peace between Britain and Ireland – a sort of document which we would have tried to get and would not have agreed if we did not get. It would be a document that would give real peace to the people of Great Britain and Ireland and not the officials. I know it would not be a politicians' peace. I know the politician in England who would not take it would risk his political future, but it would be a peace between people, and would be consistent with the Irish people being full masters of everything within their own shores. Criticism of this Treaty is scarcely necessary from this point of view, that it could not be ratified because it would not be legal for this assembly to ratify it, because it would be inconsistent with our position. We were elected here to be the guardians of an independent Irish State – a State that had declared its independence – and this House could no more than the ignominious House that voted away the Colonial Parliament that was in Ireland in 1800 unless we wished to follow the example of that House and vote away the independence of our people. We could not ratify that instrument if it were brought before us for ratification. It is, therefore, to be brought before us not for ratification, because it would be inconsistent, and the very fact that it is inconsistent shows that it could not be reconciled with Irish aspirations, because the aspirations of the Irish people have been crystallised into the form of Government they have at the present time. As far as I was concerned, I am probably the freest man here to express my opinion. Before I was elected President at the Private Session, I said, "Remember I do not take, as far as I am concerned, oaths as regards forms of Government. I regard myself here to maintain the independence of Ireland and to do the best for the Irish people," and it is to do the best for the Irish people that I ask you not to approve but to reject this Treaty.

You will be asked in the best interests of Ireland, if you pretend to the world that this will lay the foundation of a lasting peace, and you know perfectly well that even if Mr Griffith and Mr Collins set up a Provisional Government in Dublin Castle, until the Irish people would have voted upon it the Government would be looked upon as a usurpation equally with Dublin Castle in the past. We know perfectly well there is nobody here who has expressed more strongly dissent from any attacks of any kind upon the delegates that went to London than I did.

There is no one who knew better than I did how difficult is the task they had to perform. I appealed to the Dáil, telling them the delegates had to do something a mighty army or a mighty navy would not be able to do. I hold that, and I hold that it was in their excessive love for Ireland they have done what they have. I am as anxious as anyone for the material prosperity of Ireland and the Irish people, but I cannot do anything that would make the Irish people hang their heads. I would rather see the same thing over again than that Irishmen should have to hang their heads in shame for having signed and put their hands to a document handing over their authority to a foreign country. The Irish people would not want me to save them materially at the expense of their national honour. I say it is quite within the competence of the Irish people if they wished to enter into an association with other peoples, to enter into the British Empire; it is within their competence if they want to choose the British monarch as their King, but does this assembly think the Irish people have changed so much within the past year or two that they now want to get into the British Empire after seven centuries of fighting? Have they so changed that they now want to choose the person of the British monarch, whose forces they have been fighting against, and who have been associated with all the barbarities of the past couple of years; have they changed so much that they want to choose the King as their monarch? It is not King George as a monarch they choose: it is Lloyd George, because it is not the personal monarch they are choosing, it is British power and authority as sovereign authority in this country. The sad part of it, as I was saying, is that a grand peace could at this moment be made, and to see the difference. I say for instance, if approved by the Irish people, and if Mr Griffith, or whoever might be in his place, thought it wise to ask King George over to open Parliament he would see black flags in the streets of Dublin. Do you think that that would make for harmony between the two peoples? What would the people of Great Britain say when they saw the King accepted by the Irish people greeted in Dublin with black flags? If a Treaty was entered into, if it was a right Treaty, he could have been brought here . . . I say if a proper peace had been made you could bring, for instance, the President of France, the King of Spain, or the President of America here, or the head of any other friendly nation here in the name of the Irish State, and the Irish people would extend to them in a very different way a welcome as the head of a friendly nation coming on a friendly visit to their country, and not as a monarch who came to call Ireland his legitimate possession. In one case the Irish people would regard him as a usurper, in the other case it would be the same as a distinguished visitor to their country. Therefore, I am against the Treaty, because it does not do the fundamental thing and bring us peace. The Treaty leaves us a country going through a period of internal strife just as the Act of Union did.

One of the great misfortunes in Ireland for past centuries has been the fact that our internal problems and our internal domestic questions could not be gone into because of the relationship between Ireland and Great Britain. Just as in America during the last Presidential election, it was not the internal affairs of the country were uppermost; it was other matters. It was the big international question. That was the misfortune for America at the time, and it was the great misfortune for Ireland for 120 years, and if the present Pact is agreed on that will continue. I am against it because it is inconsistent with our position, because if we are to say the Irish people don't mean it, then they should have told us that they didn't mean it.

Had the Chairman of the delegation said he did not stand for the things they had said they stood for, he would not have been elected. The Irish people can change their minds if they wish to. The Irish people are our masters, and they can do as they like, but only the Irish people can do that, and we should give the people the credit that they meant what they said just as we mean what we say.

I do not think I should continue any further on this matter. I have spoken generally, and if you wish we can take these documents up, article by article, but they have been discussed in Private Session, and I do not think there is any necessity for doing so.

Therefore, I am once more asking you to reject the Treaty for two main reasons, that, as every Teachta knows, it is absolutely inconsistent with our position; it gives away Irish independence; it brings us into the British Empire; it acknowledges the head of the British Empire, not merely as the head of an association, but as the direct monarch of Ireland, as the source of executive authority in Ireland.

The Ministers of Ireland will be His Majesty's Ministers, the Army that Commandant MacKeon spoke of will be His Majesty's Army. You may sneer at words, but I say words mean, and I say in a Treaty words do mean something, else why should they be put down? They have meanings and they have facts, great realities that you cannot close your eyes to. This Treaty means that the Ministers of the Irish Free State will be His Majesty's

Ministers and the Irish Forces will be His Majesty's Forces. Well, time will tell, and I hope it won't have a chance, because you will throw this out. If you accept it, time will tell; it cannot be one way in this assembly and another way in the British House of Commons. The Treaty is an agreed document, and there ought to be pretty fairly common interpretation of it. If there are differences of interpretation we know who will get the best of them.

I hold, and I don't mind my words being on record, that the chief executive authority in Ireland is the British Monarch – the British authority. It is in virtue of that authority the Irish Ministers will function. It is to the Commander-in-Chief of the Irish Army, who will be the English Monarch, they will swear allegiance, these soldiers of Ireland. It is on these grounds as being inconsistent with our position, and with the whole national tradition for 750 years, that it cannot bring peace. Do you think that because you sign documents like this you can change the current of tradition? You cannot. Some of you are relying on that "cannot" to sign this Treaty. But don't put a barrier in the way of future generations.

Parnell was asked to do something like this – to say it was a final settlement. But he said, "No man has a right to set." No man "can" is a different thing. "No man has a right" – take the context and you know the meaning. Parnell said practically, "You have no right to ask me, because I have no right to say that any man can set boundaries to the march of a nation." As far as you can, if you take this you are presuming to set bounds to the onward march of a nation.

"ARE WE SIMPLY GOING TO GO ON KEEPING OURSELVES IN SLAVERY AND SUBJECTION?"

Michael Collins (1890–1922) was born in Clonakilty, Co. Cork, where he was educated at the local national school. He worked in London as a clerk, but returned to fight in the 1916 Rising. After his election in 1918 as MP for Armagh, he was appointed Minister for Home Affairs and later Minister for Finance by the First Dáil. At the same time he directed the military effort for independence.

Somewhat reluctantly he agreed to become a member of the Treaty negotiation team and, after its signing, became a member of the Provisional Government formed to implement it. With the outbreak of Civil War in June 1922 he became Commander in Chief of the Army and was shot dead two months later by anti-Treaty forces at Béal na Bláth in Cork.

Collins's approach to the Treaty was a pragmatic one – he spoke as a soldier, with the knowledge of the capacity of his own side and the enemy. His approach contrasted with that of de Valera, and Collins's speech was more pragmatic and less concerned than that of de Valera with the theory of constitutional relations.

COUNCIL CHAMBER, UNIVERSITY COLLEGE DUBLIN, DECEMBER 19, 1921

. . . A Deputy has stated that the delegation should introduce this Treaty not, he describes, as bagmen for England, but with an apology for its introduction. I cannot imagine anything more mean, anything more despicable, anything more unmanly than this dishonouring of one's signature. Rightly or wrongly when you make a bargain you cannot alter it, you cannot go back and get sorry for it and say "I ought to have made a better bargain." Business cannot be done on those bases. I must make reference to the signing of the Treaty. This Treaty was not signed under personal intimidation. If personal intimidation had been attempted no member of the delegation would have signed it.

At a fateful moment I was called upon to make a decision, and if I were called upon at the present moment for a decision on the same question my decision would be the same. Let there be no mistake and no misunderstanding about that.

I have used the word "intimidation." The whole attitude of Britain towards Ireland in the past was an attitude of intimidation, and we, as negotiators, were not in the position of conquerors dictating terms of peace to a vanquished foe. We had not beaten the enemy out of our country by force of arms.

To return to the Treaty, hardly anyone, even those who support it, really understands it, and it is necessary to explain it, and the immense powers and liberties it secures. This is my justification for having signed it, and for recommending it to the nation. Should the Dáil reject it, I am, as I said, no longer responsible. But I am responsible for making the nation fully understand what it gains by accepting it, and what is involved in its rejection. So long as I have made that clear I am perfectly happy and satisfied. Now we must look facts in the face. For our continued national and spiritual existence two things are necessary – security and freedom. If the Treaty gives us these or helps us to get at these, then I maintain that it satisfies our national aspirations. The history of this nation has not been, as is so often said, the history of a military struggle of 750 years; it has been much more a history of peaceful penetration of 750 years. It has not been a struggle for the ideal of freedom for 750 years symbolised in the name Republic. It has been a story of slow, steady, economic encroach by England. It has been a struggle on our part to prevent that, a struggle against exploitation, a struggle against the cancer that was eating up our lives, and it was only after discovering that, that it was economic penetration, that we discovered that political freedom was necessary in order that that should be stopped. Our aspirations, by whatever term they may be symbolised, had one thing in front all the time, that was to rid the country of the enemy strength. Now it was not by any form of communication except through their military strength that the English held this country. That is simply a plain fact which, I think, nobody will deny. It wasn't by any forms of government, it wasn't by their judiciary or anything of that kind. These people could not operate except for the military strength that was always there. Now, starting from that, I maintain that the disappearance of that military strength gives us the chief proof that our national liberties are established. And as to what has been said about guarantees of the withdrawal of that military strength, no guarantees, I say, can alter the fact of their withdrawal, because we are a weaker nation, and we shall be a weaker nation for a long time to come. But certain things do give us a certain guarantee. We are defined as having the constitutional status of Canada, Australia, New Zealand, South Africa. If the English do not withdraw the military strength, our association with those places do give us, to some extent, a guarantee that they must withdraw them. I know that it would be finer to stand alone, but if it is necessary to our security, if it is necessary to the development of our own life, and if we find we can stand alone, what can we do but enter into some association? . . .

If there was no association, if we stood alone, the occupation of the ports might probably be a danger to us. Associated in a free partnership with these other nations it is not a danger, for their association is a guarantee that it won't be used as a jumping-off ground against us. And that same person tells us that we haven't Dominion status because of the occupation of these ports, but that South Africa had even when Simonstown was occupied. I cannot accept that argument. I am not an apologist for this Treaty. We have got rid of the word "Empire." For the first time in an official document the former Empire is styled "The Community of Nations known as the

British Empire." Common citizenship has been mentioned. Common citizenship is the substitution for the subjection of Ireland. It is an admission by them that they no longer can dominate Ireland . . .

. . . The Treaty was signed by me, not because they held up the alternative of immediate war. I signed it because I would not be one of those to commit the Irish people to war without the Irish people committing themselves to war. If my constituents send me to represent them in war, I will do my best to represent them in war. Now I was not going to refer to anything that had been said by the speakers of the Coalition side today. I do want to say this in regard to the President's remark about Pitt, a remark, it will be admitted, which was not very flattering to us. Well, now, what happened at the time of the Union? Grattan's Parliament was thrown away without reference to the people and against their wishes. Is the Parliament which this Treaty offers us to be similarly treated? Is it to be thrown away without reference to the people and against their wishes?

Now I have gone into more or less a general survey of the Treaty, apart from one section of it, the section dealing with North-East Ulster. Again I am as anxious to face facts in that case as I am in any other case. We have stated that we will not coerce the North-East. We have stated it officially in our correspondence. I stated it publicly in Armagh and nobody has found fault with it. What did we mean? Did we mean we were going to coerce them or we were not going to coerce them? What was the use of talking big phrases about not agreeing to the partition of our country. Surely we recognise that the North-East corner does exist, and surely our intention was that we should take such steps as would sooner or later lead to greater understanding. The Treaty has made an effort to deal with it, and has made an effort, in my opinion, on lines that will lead very rapidly to goodwill, and the entry of the North-East under the Irish Parliament. I do not say it is an ideal arrangement, but if our policy is, as has been stated, a policy of non-coercion, then let somebody else get a better way out of it.

I say that this Treaty gives us, not recognition of the Irish Republic, but it gives us more recognition on the part of Great Britain and the associated States than we have got from any other nation. Again I want to speak plainly. America did not recognise the Irish Republic. As things in London were coming to a close I received cablegrams from America. I understand that my name is pretty well known in America, and what I am going to say now will make me unpopular there for the rest of my life, but I am not going to say anything or hide anything for the sake of American popularity. I received a cablegram from San Francisco, saying, "Stand fast, we will send you a million dollars a month." Well, my reply to that is, "Send us half-a-million and send us a thousand men fully equipped." I received another cablegram from a branch of the American Association for the Recognition of the Irish Republic and they said to me, "Don't weaken now, stand with de Valera." Well, let that branch come over and stand with us both. The question before me was were we going to go on with this fight, without referring it to the Irish people, for the sake of propaganda in America? I was not going to take that responsibility. And as this may be the last opportunity I shall ever have of speaking publicly to the Dáil, I want to say that there was never an Irish man placed in such a position as I was by reason of these negotiations. I had got a certain name, whether I deserved it or not, and I knew when I was going over there that I was being placed in a position that I could not reconcile, and that could not in the public mind be reconciled with what they thought I stood for, no matter what we brought back, – and if we brought back the recognition of the Republic – but I knew that the English would make a greater effort if I were there than they would if I were not there, and I didn't care if my popularity was sacrificed or not. I should have been unfair to my own country if I did not go there. Members of the Dáil well remember that I protested against being selected. I want to say another thing. It will be remembered that a certain incident occurred in the South of Ireland, an incident which led to the excommunication of the whole population of that district. At the time I took responsibility for that in our private councils. I take responsibility for it now publicly. I only want to say that I stand for every action as an individual member of the Cabinet, which I suppose I shall be no longer; I stand for every action, no matter how it looked publicly, and I shall always like the men to remember me like that. In coming to the decision I did I tried to weigh what my own responsibility was. Deputies have spoken about whether dead men would approve of it, and they have spoken as to whether children yet unborn will approve of it, but few of them have spoken as to whether the living approve of it. In my own small way I tried to have before my mind what the whole lot of them would think of it. And the proper way for us to look at it is in that way. There is no man here who has more regard for the dead men than I have. I don't think it is fair to be quoting them against us. I think the decision ought to be a clear decision on the documents as they are before us – on the Treaty as it is before us. On that we shall be judged, as to whether we have done the right thing in our own conscience or not. Don't let us put the responsibility, the individual responsibility, upon anybody else. Let us take the responsibility ourselves and let us in God's name abide by the decision.

"IT IS THE QUESTION OF WHAT THE DELEGATION WAS ENTITLED TO DO"

Erskine Childers (1870–1922) was born in London and educated at Cambridge. After university, he spent fifteen years working as a clerk in the House of Commons. He became interested in Irish politics and resigned his job in the Commons. In July 1914 he sailed the Asgard into Howth with arms from Germany for the Irish Volunteers. With the outbreak of World War I, he enlisted in the British Navy believing the allies would aid the cause of Ireland. On demobilisation he became ever more involved in the campaign for Irish independence. He was elected to the Dáil in 1921, served as Minister for Propaganda and later as principal secretary to the Irish delegation in the Treaty negotiations. He opposed the Treaty, joined the Republican forces in the Civil War, was arrested for possession of a hand-gun (which had been given to him by Collins), and was court martialled. He was executed on November 24, 1922.

In his speech opposing the Treaty, Childers, like de Valera, focused on the links that remained with Britain and the Empire on why the Irish situation could not be the status of Canada. He also focused on clauses 7 and 8, which gave Britain the right to use named ports in times of war and peace.

COUNCIL CHAMBER, UNIVERSITY COLLEGE DUBLIN, DECEMBER 19, 1921

I wish to recall this assembly to the immediate subject before us, one side of which was hardly touched upon, indeed if it was touched upon at all, by the Minister for Finance, the question whether Dáil Éireann, the national assembly of the

103

people of Ireland, having declared its independence, shall approve of and ratify a Treaty relinquishing deliberately and abandoning that independence. I must say for my own part that I missed in the speeches both of the Minister for Foreign Affairs and the Minister for Finance some note, however distant, of regret for the effect in significance of the step they were taking, and had taken, in London, that is, they were asking this assembly, Dáil Éireann, to vote its own extinction in history, which they more perhaps than anybody else had done so much to make honourable and noble. There is one thing more I would like to say, because I think the two speeches delivered by the leading members of the delegation have left it still obscure. I hardly know, indeed, what impression is left upon the minds of the delegates as a result of their speeches. It is the question of what the delegation was entitled to do and set out to do when it went to London as compared with what it has done. The Minister for Finance spoke of an isolated Republic and said quite rightly that there was no question when the delegation went to London of an isolated Republic standing alone without tie or association with any other association in the world. No such question was before Dáil Éireann or the nation. The sole question before the nation, Dáil Éireann, and the delegation was how is it possible to effect an association with the British Commonwealth which would be honourable to the Irish nation? And it ought to be known and understood, for certainly the speech of the Minister for Foreign Affairs was misleading, in my opinion, on the point. It ought to be understood that that object was held before the delegation to the last, except that last terrible hour, and that the counter proposals put up to the British Government did, on the face of them, and in their text, preserve the independence of Ireland while arranging to associate it with the British Commonwealth. Until the last moment that proposal was before the British Government. That should be understood by Dáil Éireann, and I hope other members of the delegation will confirm what I have said.

There was no question in the action of the delegation in

London of acting on some sub-conscious or unadmitted resolve to betray the Republic and to commit Ireland to an association which would forfeit her independence, none to my knowledge, at any rate, and I was secretary to the delegation. The proposals on our side were honourable proposals. They stated in explicit terms that they demanded the preservation of the independence of our country, to exclude the King of England and British authority wholly from our country, and only when that was done, and Ireland was absolutely free in Irish affairs, to enter an association on free and honourable terms with Britain.

That, alas! was lost in the last hour of the time the delegation spent in London and the result was the Treaty . . .

What is the position of Ireland? After 750 years of war, lying close up against the shores of her great neighbour, what guarantee has she, what equal voice can she have in the decisions of these questions, with England actually occupying her shores, committing her inevitably, legally, constitutionally and in every other way to all her foreign policies and to all her wars? That governing condition England has, that Ireland under this Treaty would have no real power to free action, independent action. Where English interests are concerned they will govern and limit every condition and clause in that Treaty now before you . . .

Now I do seriously wish to warn the members of the Dáil if they are going to take this tremendous and momentous step of ratifying this Treaty, not to do it under any foolish and idle illusions as to the meaning of what they are doing. Does the Deputy really suggest that Ireland is really going to have freedom to form any Constitution she pleases – "subject to the terms of this agreement" and every limitation, and there are a hundred of them, that are in this Constitution of Canada under the British Act of 1867, all the fundamental limitations as to the authority of the Crown, and the authority of the British Government will inevitably appear in the Irish Constitution if it is framed under the terms of this Treaty. What will appear? The first thing that will appear will be that the legislature of Ireland will be no longer Dáil Éireann, the body I am addressing; it will consist of King and Commons and Senate of Ireland. The King will be part of the legislature of this island, and the King will have powers there. If not the King himself, there would be the King's representative in Ireland, the Governor-General, or whatever he may be. The King, representing the British Government, or the Governor-General, will have power to give or refuse assent to Irish legislation. Now I know very well – no one better than I do – I may just say in passing, I, like all lovers of freedom, have watched and followed the development of freedom in British Dominions, and Canada with intense interest. No one knows better than I do that power is virtually obsolete in Canada. Do you suppose that power is going to be obsolete in Ireland? How can it be?

If Ireland's destiny is to be irrevocably linked with England in this Treaty, if the association with her is that of a bond slave, as it is, under these Clauses 6 and 7, do you suppose that that supremacy of England is going to be an idle phrase in the case of Ireland? Do you? Don't you see every act and deed of the Irish Parliament is going to be jealously watched from over the water, and that every act of legislation done by Ireland will be read in the light of that inflexible condition that Ireland is virtually a protectorate of England, for under this Treaty she is nothing more. "Under the Constitution of Canada, the Executive Government and authority of, and over, Canada, is hereby declared to continue, and be vested in the Queen"; that is to say now, the King. That clause, or something corresponding to it, will appear in the Constitution of Ireland without question. And here again what does the King mean? The functions of the King as an individual are very small indeed. What the King means is the British Government, and let there be no mistake, under the terms of this Treaty the British Government is going to be supreme in Ireland. It is useless again to refer to Canada. Canada is 3,000 miles away.

I know we cannot help it, but there was one way of helping it. That was to have stood by the proposals that were made in London by the Irish Delegation to the British Government, until the last moment. That was the way to avoid it, and to declare, as they declared, that authority in Ireland – legislative, executive, and judicial – shall be derived solely from the people of Ireland. That was a way out of it, and I hope and believe it remains a way out of it still. Establish that principle that authority in Ireland belongs solely to the Irish people, then make your association, and the rights of Ireland are safe. Pass that Treaty admitting the King to Ireland, or rather retaining him as he is in Ireland now, retain him while recognising him, recognise the British Government in Ireland, and your rights and independence are lost for ever. It should be remembered, too, that the King's representative in Ireland, the Governor-General, will be there definitely as the centre of British Government in Ireland. I do not know if it is realised what the full significance the proximity of Ireland to England means. But you cannot have it both ways. It is useless for the Minister for Finance to say certain things are necessary because Ireland is nearer England, and at the same time to say that Ireland would get all the powers of Canada which is 3,000 miles away. These two proposals are contradictory. The Governor-General in Ireland will be close to Downing Street. He can communicate by telephone to Downing Street. He will be in close and intimate touch with British Ministers. Irish Ministers will be the King's Ministers; the Irish Provisional Government that under this Treaty is going to be set up, within a month would be the King's Provisional Government. Every executive Act in Ireland, every administrative function in Ireland, would be performed – you cannot get away from it – in the name of the King. And the King and the Government behind the King would be barely 200 miles away, and capable of exercising immediate control over what is done in Ireland. And if anyone were to raise in any particular matter the status of Canada in connection with the Government of Ireland, what would he be told? Canadian status? Why, the King's Government is not only here in the person of the Governor-General exercising it on his behalf, but the King and the King's forces are in actual occupation of Ireland. It is useless for you to pretend that the King's authoritative and British authority are not operative in Ireland, when it is actually occupied by British Forces and you are forbidden to have Irish defensive naval forces of your own. Follow on that point a little. The Treaty promises Ireland to have an army, and a letter of Mr Lloyd George's says the British Army is to evacuate Ireland if this Treaty is passed within a short time. But do you suppose under this Treaty, your Irish Army is going to be an independent army? Do you really suppose if British troops are evacuated from the country in a short period, there is anything to prevent them returning under full legal power? Constitutional usage would have nothing to do with the matter. It has in Canada. The British Government would never dare to land a British regiment in Canada without the consent of the Canadian Government. Do you suppose that would be so in Ireland? I will tell you why not. Under Clause 6 and 7 you abandon altogether and hand over to the British Government responsibility for the defence of Ireland. There is something about a local military defence force. If you place under a foreign Power responsibility for the defence of the coasts of Ireland, inevitably and naturally you place responsibility for the defence of the whole island on that foreign Government. How can you separate the coastal defences of an island from its internal defences? Are you to have two authorities? One saying what garrisons are to be here, and the other saying what garrisons are to be there along the coast, and how they are to be co-ordinated with some central armed military body. Those matters can only be settled by one authority – Army and Navy matters both – and that one authority will be obviously, and on the very terms of the Treaty, the British authority. Then you will find the letter of the law, the legal conditions, stepping in. What will be the Irish Army? It will be His Majesty's Army, and, whether or not or whatever character the Irish flag takes, His Majesty's flag will fly in Ireland . . .

Parnell once said that no man has the right to set a boundary to the onward march of a nation. Parnell was right. Parnell spoke in a moment when Ireland was still in a subordinate position in the British Empire. Since that time Ireland has taken a step from which she can never withdraw by declaring her

108

independence. This Treaty is a step backward, and I, for my part, would be inclined to say he would be a bold man who would dare set a boundary to the backward march of a nation which, of its own free will, has deliberately relinquished its own independence. I do not believe there is any need. I profoundly regret this Treaty was signed. I profoundly regret it was signed and that the alternative proposals of the Irish Delegation were not adhered to. There should be no question now of any hopeless dilemma in which the nation is placed. There should be no question now that it is possible to associate Ireland with the British Commonwealth on terms honourable to Ireland. I am glad to know that the specific proposals prepared by the President will at a future time have your consideration. It will be disastrous, I think, if now this assembly were to declare that there is no chance of making peace with England. There is a chance. There was a chance; there is a chance. And it rests with England to understand that Ireland is genuinely anxious to hold out the hand of friendship if only that hand can be grasped on terms that will leave Ireland standing as a free nation and England honourably recognising that freedom, not treating Ireland with suspicion and distrust, occupying her ports, refusing her powers of defence, and so on. England has but to say frankly, "You desire to be free, we recognise you must be," in order to enter into a friendship that shall be truly lasting with us. That, I hope, can still be done. But any case, in the last resort, everyone one of us here, when we have done with considering the Treaty before you, and when we have considered the other question of an accommodation with England on honourable terms, beyond and above all these questions there lies the paramount and over-mastering consideration of all . . . by our own act, to abandon independence. I hold this assembly neither will nor can do that. No such act was ever performed before, so far as I know, in the history of the world or since the world became a body of democratic nations. Certainly no such act was ever taken before in the history of Ireland, and I, for my part, believe you here will inflexibly refuse to take that step.

"DREARY STEEPLES OF FERMANAGH AND TYRONE"

Winston Spencer Churchill (1874–1965) was born in Blenheim Palace, the eldest son of Lord Randoph Churchill, who had played a key role in defeating Home Rule for Ireland in the late nineteenth century. After a brief sojourn in the army, Winston Churchill entered the Commons as a Tory, but crossed the floor to the Liberal Party in 1906, opposing Chamberlain's tariff reform. He entered the cabinet in 1906, was appointed President of the Board of Trade in 1908, and Home Secretary in 1910, where his previous reputation for radicalism lost much of its gloss. In 1911 he was made first Lord of the Admiralty, where his preparation of the fleet was crucial to Britain's success in the naval battle of World War I.

After the disaster of the Dardanelles in 1915, Churchill left the Cabinet. He returned after the accession of Lloyd George to the premiership in 1917 and served as Secretary of State for War from 1917 until 1921. It was in this role that he played a key part in developing British policy on Ireland during the War of Independence. He was part of the British negotiating team in the Anglo-Irish negotiations of 1921.

Churchill's speech to the Commons was part of the government's campaign to turn the Anglo-Irish Treaty into law. He was speaking in the Commons during the second reading of the Irish Free State Bill, at a time when the Treaty had already split the Irish nationalist movement in two. Churchill predictably was supporting Griffith's provisional government in Dublin.

House of Commons, February 16, 1922

. . . The importance and urgency of this Bill are plain. Take,

110

for instance, the object of clothing the Irish Provisional Government with law. Is it not fatal to peace, social order and good Government to have power wielded by men who have no legal authority? Every day it continues is a reproach to the administration of the Empire. Every day tends to bring into contempt those solemn forms of procedure on the observance of which in every country the structure of civilised society depends. Only three days ago I spoke about some criminals, murderous criminals, who had been caught by the Irish Provisional Government in Southern Ireland, accused of murdering and robbing a British Officer, and I said that I presumed that they would be handed over to be dealt with the full rigour of the law . . .

A Provisional Government, unsanctified by law, yet recognised by the Crown, by His Majesty's Ministers, is an anomaly, unprecedented in the history of the British Empire. Its continuance one day longer than is necessary is derogatory to Parliament, to the Nation, and to the Crown. We must legalise and regularise our action. Contempt of law is one of the great evils manifesting themselves in many parts of the world at the present time, and it is disastrous for the Imperial Parliament to connive at or countenance such a situation in Ireland for one day longer than is absolutely necessary . . .

The first of these objects is a National decision upon the Treaty by the Irish people. I am asked every day by my Hon. Friends below the Gangway questions about the Irish Republican Army. I will explain the view of the Irish Government on that point. It is very important we should understand the different points of view. Whether we agree with them, or sympathise with them, is quite another matter, but it is important we should understand them. This is the view of the Irish Government, the Irish signatories of the Treaty. Their view is that the Irish Republic was set up by the Irish people at the elections which took place during the Conference, and that this Irish Republic can only be converted into an Irish Free State by the decision of the Irish people. That is not our view. We do not recognise the Irish Republic. We have never recognised it, and never will recognise it. I am explaining their view and they say that they were elected by the Irish people on a certain basis, and that only the Irish people can release them. They are determined to stand by the Treaty and to use their utmost influence with the Irish people to procure their adhesion to the Treaty, and that will, from the Irish point of view, be the act which will disestablish finally the Republic.

. . . This Parliament was made out of men who hated this country most in Ireland. It is obvious that if any progress is to be made, we must get, or there ought to be – for after all, it is not for us finally to decide – a Parliament which represents the hope of the future rather than the hate of the past.

Lastly, it is a bad thing for any body of Ministers to continue in a position of power without being supported in that position by a national mandate . . .

The sooner that election comes in Ireland the better. I am anxious to deal with every aspect. I shall be asked: "Supposing Mr de Valera and his friends win this election in Ireland, what is to happen then?" If I do not deal with this now, I shall be blamed for leaving it out. Let me say, I do not think that there is any advantage in speculating upon these ugly hypotheses. It is perfectly clear that the repudiation by Ireland of the Treaty would free all parties from their engagements, and that the position of Great Britain, standing on the Treaty, ready to carry out the Treaty, if others could be found, on behalf of the Irish nation, to do their part, that that position would be one of great moral as well as undoubted material strength. The position of Southern Ireland, on the other hand, would be one of the greatest weakness and division – absolutely isolated from the sympathy of the world, bitterly divided in herself. The position of Northern Ireland would also be quite unaffected . . .

But it would be a pity for us to go threatening and blustering at this stage and to give the impression that the Irish people are being made to vote under duress or at the point of the bayonet. All such language and suggestions would be very unhelpful at the present time, and if such language were indulged in, the fact that it could be stated that the votes had been given under duress would tend to impair the authority of the decision at a subsequent date. That is what I have to say on a perfectly fair point which may be made as to who would win the Irish election . . .

There are those who think that the present Irish Government may be overturned by a coup d'état and that a red Soviet-Republic may be set up. We do not think that is at all likely, but it is quite clear that a Soviet Republic in Ireland would ruin the Irish cause for 100 years, but would not in any respect impair the foundations of the British Empire or the security of Ulster. No people in the world are really less likely to turn Bolshevik than the Irish. Their strong sense of personal possession, their respect for the position of women, their love of country and their religious convictions constitute them in a peculiar sense the most sure and unyielding opponents of the withering and levelling doctrines of Russia. What we know of the characters and personalities at the head of the Provisional Government in Ireland leads us also to believe that they are not the men who would tamely sit still and suffer the fate of a Kerensky. Therefore I do not think this second evil alternative is one which we need allow to embarrass us or obstruct our thoughts and decisions at the present time. But this Irish Government, this Irish Ministry, ought not to be left in the position in which even the most necessary measures which they take for their own defence or for the enforcement of authority, or even for the maintenance of law and the suppression of brigandage or mutiny, are devoid of formal sanction.

If you want to see Ireland degenerate into a meaningless welter of lawless chaos and confusion, delay this Bill. If you wish to see increasingly serious bloodshed all along the borders of Ulster, delay this Bill. If you want this House to have on its hands, as it now has, the responsibility for peace and order in Southern Ireland, without the means of enforcing it, if you want to impose those same evil conditions upon the Irish Provisional

Government, delay this Bill. If you want to enable dangerous and extreme men, working out schemes of hatred in subterranean secrecy, to undermine and overturn a Government which is faithfully doing its best to keep its word with us and enabling us to keep our word with it, delay this Bill. If you want to proclaim to all the world, week after week, that the British Empire can get on just as well without law as with it, then you will delay this Bill. But if you wish to give a fair chance to a policy to which Parliament has pledged itself, and to Irish Ministers to whom you are bound in good faith, so long as they act faithfully with you, to give fair play and a fair chance, if you wish to see Ireland brought back from the confusion of tyranny to a reign of law, if you wish to give logical and coherent effect to the policy and experiment to which we are committed, you will not impede, even for a single unnecessary week, the passage of this Bill . . .

It appears to me as if the tables were turned. Ireland, not Britain, is on her trial before the nations of the world. Six months ago it was we who had to justify ourselves against every form of attack. Now it is the Irish people, who as they tell us, after 700 years of oppression, have at last an opportunity to show the kind of government that they can give to their country and the position which they can occupy amongst the nations of the world. An enormous improvement in the situation, as I see it, has been effected in the last six months. Take the position of Ulster. The position of Ulster is one of great and unshakeable strength, not only material strength, but moral strength. There was a time when, as is well known, I and others with whom I was then associated thought that Ulster was not securing her own position, but was barring the way to the rest of Ireland to obtain what they wanted. Those days are done. Ulster, by a sacrifice and by an effort, has definitely stood out of the path of the rest of Ireland, and claims only those liberties and securities which are her own, and standing on her own rights, supported as she is and as she will be by the whole force and power, if necessary, of the British Empire, I am entitled to say that she is

114

in a position of great moral and material strength at the present time . . .

But the position of Ireland is one which deserves a much greater measure of sympathy. The position of Southern Ireland is one of great difficulty and danger. The trials and responsibilities of the new Government are most serious. I have explained the weakness of their present position. I have explained how urgent it is that we should come with this Bill and clothe them with greater authority and strength. We see the efforts they are making. We cannot tell how far they will be successful. All the world is looking on at their performance. They are the people at the present time, not Ulster, not Great Britain, whose difficulties and whose task deserve sympathy and support.

Take the case of the signatories of the Treaty, the men who put their names to that document in Downing Street in December. They go back to their own comrades or colleagues in Ireland, with whom they were working. They are practically put on their trial for having betrayed the Irish Republic. These men who, whatever you may think of them, at any rate from their own country's point of view were the most vigorous and effective fighting men, were absolutely put on their trial and condemned by the more talkative section, largely composed of people whom the British Government all through regarded as perfectly harmless, and some of whom we gave the strictest instructions, should not be arrested, and when on some occasions they were arrested by mistake, they were let loose again, as you return under-sized fish to the water. These men, I say, standing by the Treaty against this kind of unfair attack, as long as they stand by the Treaty and we have confidence in them, deserve our help and deserve to be given the means of making good.

The situation on the frontier of Northern Ireland has, I think, been a little improved by the agreement of both Governments to the establishment of a Border Commission to make sure that there is no hostile attack on a large scale being organised on the one side or the other. It has also been improved, I think, by the agreement of both Governments to an impartial Commission of Inquiry into the Clones affair; and it has been, I think, generally improved by the control which has been enforced. I hope that the releases of the kidnapped men will continue. Twenty-six have already been released, and I hope the releases will continue in the next few days until the matter is completely cleared out of the way. The position in Belfast is terrible. Things are being done there of a most awful character, and I know the efforts that are being made by the Northern Government to calm things there, and to control the people and the furious and inhuman passions that are alive amongst certain sections of the population, Catholic and Protestant. I do trust that in the near future, whatever may have occurred since their last meeting there will be some form of parley between the heads of the two Governments, or representatives of the two Governments. I would point out that the Southern Government has definitely, formally, asked for such a meeting. I do trust it may be possible to bring it about in the course of the next few days or weeks. It is most desirable, from every point of view, to arrive at some method of calming the terrible vendettas and the counter-vendettas which are rife in the streets and in the alleys of Belfast . . .

Of course, all this trouble in regard to the boundaries surrounds the boundaries of Fermanagh and Tyrone. I remember on the eve of the Great War we were gathered together at a Cabinet meeting in Downing Street, and for a long time, an hour or an hour and a half, after the failure of the Buckingham Place Conference, we discussed the boundaries of Fermanagh and Tyrone. Both of the great political parties were at each other's throats. The air was full of talk of civil war. Every effort was made to settle the matter and bring them together. The differences had been narrowed down, not merely to the counties of Fermanagh and Tyrone, but to parishes and groups of parishes inside the area of Fermanagh and Tyrone, and yet, even when the differences had been so narrowed down, the problem appeared to be as insuperable as ever, and neither side would agree to reach any conclusion . . .

Then came the Great War. Every institution, almost, in the world was strained. Great Empires have been overturned. The whole map of Europe has been changed. The position of countries has been violently altered. The modes of thought of men, the whole outlook on affairs, the grouping of parties, all have encountered violent and tremendous changes in the deluge of the world, but as the deluge subsides and the waters fall short we see the dreary steeples of Fermanagh and Tyrone emerging once again. The integrity of their quarrel is one of the few institutions that has been unaltered in the cataclysm which has swept the world. That says a lot for the persistency with which Irish men on the one side or the other are able to pursue their controversies. It says a great deal for the power which Ireland has, both Nationalist and Orange, to lay their hands upon the vital strings of British life and politics, and to hold, dominate, and convulse, year after year, generation after generation, the politics of this powerful country.

I am going to speak plainly, and if I say anything which my Hon. Friends below the Gangway who represent Ulster do not approve of, do not let them think that I am expecting them to agree. I am trying to show them the outlook upon the subject which we have at the present time, and to put them in a position to do what they think is their duty, without any chance of misunderstanding or misconception. I was speaking just now of the great strength of the Ulster position at the present time, morally and materially. In that position there is, it seems to me, only one weak point and it is this: certain of these districts in Fermanagh and Tyrone, even in the county boundary, may be districts in which – I am not pre-judging – the majority of the inhabitants will prefer to join the Irish Free State. If that be true, and to the extent to which that is true, one feels that the tremendous arguments which protect the freedom of Protestant Ulster have, in those districts, lost their application and have, possibly, an opposite application. There is also one weak point

117

in the position of His Majesty's Government in respect to Ulster and in the position of the Ministers who signed the Treaty in respect to Ulster. I am not concealing it for a moment. I am locating it, defining it and exposing it. This is the weak point: The Boundary Commission to be set up under Article 12 affects the existing frontiers of the Ulster Government and may conceivably affect them prejudicially. It is far better to face facts and not to gloss them over. To that extent, Ulster may have a ground of complaint against the Government. What is the answer which the Government will make? I cannot do better than quote the words of my Right Hon. Friend the Member for Central Glasgow (Mr Bonar Law), the late Leader of the House. That Right Hon. Gentleman, whose re-appearance in the winter Session gave so much pleasure to the House, in speaking on this subject, in his cool, judicial, and fair-minded way, said: "very likely the Government felt that if they did not conclude the negotiations right away they might not conclude them at all. If so, I think that that is a defence which ought to be seriously taken into account."

I think today also it ought seriously to be taken into account. We were bound, we considered ourselves bound, to try to reach a settlement. Had we waited to refer the details of that settlement at the last moment to the Northern Government it is quite evident by what occurred in the Dáil, and by the violent opposition encountered there, that no settlement would have been achieved at all. Therefore, we agreed to the Boundary Commission. We agreed to it with, no doubt, a feeling that the argumentative position of this country in regard to some of those districts in Fermanagh and Tyrone was not as strong as in regard to what is characteristically the Protestant part. We agreed, knowing well that outside the limits of those counties there are also Protestant districts of great importance and considerable population and dimensions which it seemed to us must be taken into account and consideration in the general question of rectifying the boundaries which is entrusted to the Boundary Commission. There is no doubt whatever that we felt the difficulty in this matter.

Is it not in the interests of the North to see what sort of Parliament and Government will emerge from the elections in the South? May not that Parliament and Government be in a far stronger position and be of a far more reasonable complexion than the present Dáil Éireann? Is it not better to discuss passionate questions like the boundary question after the election than when everyone is preparing for it, and when the supporters of the Treaty are constantly exposed to the bitter reproaches of Mr de Valera and his extreme Republic sect, and when a renegade Englishman like Mr Erskine Childers is doing his best to poison the relations between the Irish people and their chosen leaders? Will it not be very much better to take up the difficult question of the boundary after the Irish elections have been held than before? After the election let us see what comes of it and let us then make up our mind what is best to do. Let us now see what is the interest of Southern Ireland in this matter . . .

A Republic is an idea most foreign to the Irish mind, associated with the butcheries of Cromwell in their minds and foreign to all the native genius of the Irish race, which is essentially monarchical . . .

I say really what the Southern Irish most desire and what Irishmen all over the world most desire is not hostility against this country, but the unity of their own. They can never attain that unity by force. That they are at last compelled to recognise and admit . . .

For generations we have been wandering and floundering in the Irish bog, but at last we think that in this Treaty we have set our feet upon a pathway, which has already become a causeway – narrow, but firm and far-reaching. Let us march along this causeway with determination and circumspection, without losing heart and without losing faith. If Britain continues to march forward along that path, the day may come – it may not be so distant as we expect – when, turning around, Britain will find at her side Ireland united, a nation, and a friend.

"THE NATION . . . WILL NOT SUBMIT
TO AN ARMED MINORITY"

*WT Cosgrave (1880–1965) was born in James's Street in Dublin
and educated at the local Christian Brothers School. Cosgrave
was involved with Sinn Féin from its inception in 1905, served
as a member of Dublin Corporation and participated in the
1916 Rising. He was elected MP for Sinn Féin in Kilkenny in a
by-election and later in the 1918 General Election. He was
appointed Minister for Local Government by the First Dáil and
established the alternative government system around which
much of the Sinn Féin campaign for independence was built.
After the deaths of Griffith and Collins in August 1922, Cosgrave
became head of the Provisional Government. He was President
of the Executive Council from 1922–32 and leader of Fine Gael
in the Dáil until his retirement in 1944.*

*With the death of Collins and Griffith, the Civil War became
increasingly bitter. Cosgrave and Kevin O'Higgins (Minister for
Home Affairs) asserted the right of the new state to authority, and
the reputation of Cumann na nGaedhael as the conservative
party of law and order and of the establishment was built.*

*Cosgrave's speech at the opening of the Parliament embodied
much of what was to become government policy over the next
decade; the priority given to law and order, no concessions to
those opposing the Treaty and the need for the nation to take on
the responsibilities and duties of independence.*

DAIL ÉIREANN, SEPTEMBER 11, 1922

. . . The Nation which has struggled so long against the most powerful foreign aggression will not submit to an armed minority which makes war upon its liberties, its institutions, its representation and its honour. During its long and bitter struggle Irish honour was bright and resplendent. An Irishman's word of honour was dearer than his life, and no political advantage can have any respect without honour. There must be clear thinking on this subject of peace. We demand no concessions which cannot be given without honour. We insist upon the people's rights. We are the custodians of the rights of the people and we shall not hesitate to shoulder them. We are willing to come to a peaceful understanding with those in arms, but it must be on a definite basis. We want peace with England on the terms agreed to by the country. Apart from the question of the honour of the Nation we are satisfied that the Nation stands to lose incomparably less from the armed internal opposition than from a reconquest. The National Army is prepared to pay the price, and so are we. Last December Ireland was in a position of power and of influence of great promise for the country. Foreign Nations expressed their appreciation of the settlement, and for a short period there was a boom in business. The action of the opposition destroyed that boom, lessened that power and damaged the reputation of the Nation. These potentialities must be restored. Great material loss has been inflicted on the Nation. It is impossible to estimate the extent of this loss, but it is easy to appreciate how much was needed to restore the country after the war with the English; war with English in this sense meaning not the last 3 or 4 or 5 years, but the war which restricted National development, which left us a poor Nation, which left us industrially and politically on the same level with the smaller Nations of Europe, and the education of the country fashioned as if Ireland were a Province and not a Nation. Hard work lies before the Parliament of the Nation, and with the active and cordial co-operation of both and of the various sections making up the community it will be possible to restore the Irish Nation not alone to the position in which it was at the time the Treaty was signed but to the potentialities which the Treaty offered and which it is possible to get out of the Treaty. There is now no reason why blame should be shifted on the British or any other Government blamed if we do not succeed. This Parliament and this Government is of the people and expects to get that support which is essential to a Government and a Parliament. We must realise our responsibilities not to one section or to one order of the community, and we must seek to make the administration of this country and the business of the Parliament something worthy of the people. Our Army and Police Force must be efficient; the Courts must command the confidence of the people, and the Parliament must resuscitate the Gaelic spirit and the Gaelic civilisation for which we have been fighting through the ages and all but lost. The Nation is still full of vigour and is conscious that a mere handful of violent persons is for the moment standing athwart its upward and onward march towards the achievement of its highest hopes.

"IF SOUTHERN IRELAND IS GOING TO BE GOVERNED BY CATHOLIC IDEAS AND BY CATHOLIC IDEAS ALONE, YOU WILL NEVER GET THE NORTH"

As well as being Ireland's most renowned poet, WB Yeats (1865–1939) also spent time in the Senate, nominated by President Cosgrave. In the Senate, Yeats often spoke as a member of the minority Protestant community.

Under the 1922 Constitution divorce was permissible, if difficult and cumbersome to obtain Cosgrave, a devout Catholic, sought to eliminate its availability. Yeats opposed the move and in a short speech to the Senate, gave the reasons for his opposition.

IRISH SENATE, JUNE 11, 1925

. . . It is perhaps the deepest political passion with this nation that North and South be united into one nation. If it ever comes that North and South unite the North will not give up any liberty which she already possesses under her constitution. You will then have to grant to another people what you refuse to grant to those within your borders. If you show that this country, Southern Ireland, is going to be governed by Catholic ideas and by Catholic ideas alone, you will never get the North. You will create an impassable barrier between South and North, and you will pass more and more Catholic laws, while the North will, gradually, assimilate its divorce and other laws to those of England. You will put a wedge into the midst of this nation. I do not think this House has ever made a more serious decision than the decision which, I believe, it is about to make

123

on this question. You will not get the North if you impose on the minority what the minority consider to be oppressive legislation. I have no doubt whatever that in the next few years the minority will make it perfectly plain that it does consider it exceedingly oppressive legislation to deprive it of rights which it has held since the 17th century.

In the long warfare of this country with England the Catholic clergy took the side of the people, and owing to that they possess here an influence that they do not possess anywhere else in Europe . . .

It is not a question of finding it legally difficult or impossible to grant to a minority what the majority does not wish for itself. You are to insist upon members of the Church of Ireland or members of no church taking a certain view of Biblical criticism, or of that authority of the text upon which that criticism is exercised, a view that they notoriously do not take . . .

You are going to have indissoluble marriage, but you are going to permit separation. You cannot help yourself there. You are going to permit young people who cannot live together, because of some intolerable wrong, to separate. You are going to invite men and women in the prime of life to accept for the rest of their existence the law of the cloisters. Do you think you are going to succeed in what the entire Europe has failed to do for the last 2,000 years? Are you going to impose the law of the cloisters on those young people? If not, you are not going to raise the morality of this country by indissoluble marriage.

I wish to close more seriously; this is a matter of very great seriousness. I think it is tragic that within three years of this country gaining its independence we should be discussing a measure which a minority of this nation considers to be grossly oppressive. I am proud to consider myself a typical man of that minority. We, against whom you have done this thing, are no petty people. We are one of the great stocks of Europe. We are the people of Burke; we are the people of Grattan; we are the people of Swift, the people of Emmet, the people of Parnell. We have created the most of the modern literature of this country. We have created the best of its political intelligence. Yet I do not altogether regret what has happened. I shall be able to find out, if not I, my children will be able to find out whether we have lost our stamina or not. You have defined our position and have given us a popular following. If we have not lost our stamina then your victory will be brief, and your defeat final, and when it comes this nation may be transformed.

"THE QUESTION . . . IS . . . WHETHER THIS
OATH . . . IS REALLY AN OATH AT ALL?"

After the passing of the Treaty, and the onset of Civil War, de Valera took a background role in the anti-Treaty military campaign. The report of the Boundary Commission, which consolidated Partition, gave him the political raison d'être to reassert his dominance over anti-Treaty politics and to move back into the political mainstream.

At the Sinn Féin Ard Fheis of 1926, de Valera proposed that provided the Oath of Allegiance was abolished, Sinn Féin should regard participation in Dáil Éireann as a matter of tactics rather than of principle. When this proposal was defeated, de Valera and his supporters left Sinn Féin and formed Fianna Fáil.

The first meeting of Fianna Fáil was held at the La Scala Theatre in Dublin on May 16, 1926. In it, de Valera sketched his hopes for the future and Fianna Fáil. He also slanted the emphasis of his opposition to the Treaty away from the Oath of Allegiance and onto partition, while at the same time moving those who opposed the Treaty towards accepting full participation in the structures of the Free State.

LA SCALA THEATRE, MAY 16, 1926

. . . The freeing of our country is not an easy task. It is a task that can never be performed except with the enthusiasm and energy that spring from the passionate feeling of the people, and such passionate feeling cannot be aroused if we move away from the realities that affect their daily lives.

When a military commander is given a task, he feels it his first duty to "appreciate", or judge, the situation correctly. He will take pains to make sure that he knows exactly where the enemy is placed and what his strength is. He will try, likewise, to know all about the condition of his own forces. Can we, in face of the magnitude of our task, afford to do less? What would you think of the military commander who would be indifferent to the facts of the situation or wilfully turn his eyes away from them? . . .

We must act similarly in our political task. We must not allow ourselves to be hypnotised by our own prejudices and feelings on the one hand or by our opponents' propaganda on the other. To underestimate our strength is even a worse fault than to overestimate it. We must not let our opponents dissuade us from attempting a task that is well within our power by suggesting that it is impossible . . . We must, if we really want to succeed, endeavour to judge the situation just as it is, measure our own strength against it, lay our plans, and then act with courage and tenacity.

You all know the political conditions at the present moment. You know the fundamental fact is that the majority of the Irish people are at heart as anxious for national independence today as they were eight or ten years ago. The problem is how to reunite them and make their desire for independence effective. Can the people be brought together again for a great national advance? Merely to shout unity will not, we know, be enough. An adequate national policy must be found.

Cut in two, as the national forces are now, one section pulling one way and the other the opposite way, it is vain to expect progress. The imperial forces are certain of easy triumph. They defeat one section of nationalism within the Free State assembly. Then they combine with that section to defeat us, the other section, outside. Victory for nationalism cannot come like that. Means must be found to bring the national forces together – together at least to this extent, that the two sections will in the main proceed along parallel lines and in a common direction so that the resultant of their combined efforts may be the greatest possible.

The duty of Republicans to my mind is clear. They must do

their part to secure common action by getting into position along the most likely line of the nation's advance. I you want to know what the direction of that line of advance at this moment is, ask yourselves what line a young man would be likely to take – a young man, let us say, with strong national feeling, honest and courageous, but without set prejudices or any commitments of his past to hamper him – who aimed solely at serving the national cause and bringing it to a successful issue.

Such a young man examining the situation would see, to begin with, the country partitioned – North separated from South. Here in the Twenty-six Counties he would see an assembly of elected representatives in control of the actual powers of government and claiming to rule by the authority and with the sanction of the majority of the people. Yet he would know that nearly one-half of the electorate was shut out from having an effective voice in determining its rulers, and that fully two-thirds was opposed in spirit to the existing regime. He would have no difficulty in tracing the anomaly to its source, the oath of allegiance to a foreign power acquiesced in by the majority under the duress of an external threat of war. The pretence at democracy, and the misrepresentation of the real wishes of the people which that pretence covered, he would recognise as the immediate obstacle to a unified national effort at home, the barrier to any enthusiastic support from the friends of Ireland abroad and the screen by which England's controlling hand was effectively concealed from a great many of the Irish people themselves and from the outside world. He would see that by isolating the oath for attack, the whole situation, and England's ultimate control, would be exposed. He could scarcely doubt that, the real feeling of the people being what it is, the oath would fall before a determined assault, and he would set out to attack it as being the most vital and, at the same time, the part most easily destroyed of the entire entrenchments of the foreign enemy. He could see ahead, once the oath was destroyed, promising lines for a further advance, with the nation moving as a whole, cutting the bonds of foreign interference one by one until the full internal sovereignty of the

Twenty-six Counties was established beyond question. Finally, with a united sovereign Twenty-six Counties, the position would be reached in which the solution of the problem of successfully bringing in the North could be confidently undertaken. Were he a young man who believed that only by force would freedom ultimately be won, he would be confirmed still more in his belief in the accuracy of this analysis. He would realise that a successful uprising in arms of a subject people is made almost impossible whilst an elected native government under contract with the enemy to maintain his overlordship stands in the way, with a native army at its command. The prospective horrors of a civil war alone are a sufficient initial deterrent to prevent any effective organisation for such an uprising. He would conclude, therefore, that the necessary condition for a successful national advance in any direction was the removal of a government subservient to the foreign master from de facto control here in the Twenty-six Counties, and that the removal of the test oath was the essential preliminary.

The conclusions of this young man indicate, I am certain, the line the nation will take ultimately. My advice to Republicans, and to all true Irish men and women, is to take it now and save, perhaps, decades of misery and futility.

What man or woman in this country who believes in the Irish nation desires to take an oath of allegiance to a foreign king or to a foreign-made constitution? Why should it not be well within our power, then, to get the majority of the people, here in the South at any rate, to say that whoever their representatives may be, they shall not degrade themselves or the nation by taking such an oath?

The question is raised whether this oath is really an oath at all in the theological sense. I am not going to answer, or pretend to answer, that question. For me it is enough that it is called an oath officially and that it begins with "I do solemnly swear" and that, whenever it suits, it will be held to be an oath by those who impose it and will be so understood by the world. I say, if it is not an oath, why not away with the mockery? Why not end the whole of this abominable prevarication at once? Why retain it as an instrument for our national and moral degradation and set it as a headline for lying and perjury for the whole country?

I want to make it clear, however, that if it were not an oath, or in the form of an oath at all – if it were no more than a simple declaration owning allegiance to a foreign power – my opposition to it would not cease. The aspect of the oath that I am concerned with is the national, not the religious one. It is a formal admission by the Irish people, through their representatives, that a foreign power has a right to rule them. It is a denial of their right, as a nation, to independence. That is the objection to it. It must go. I have enough confidence in the Irish people to believe that they will have the courage to take this first step to right themselves. I believe they can do it, and I believe they will do it. It was that we might mass them for the successful taking of this first step that I proposed to the Sinn Féin organisation that it should give to the people at the next elections a promise that, once the oath were removed and Republican representatives were free to enter, retaining their opinions and principles without compromise, they would join the other representatives of the people in a common assembly. Through that common assembly the final welding of the national forces would ultimately come, and through it, backed by the people, the reassertion of the nation's sovereignty.

Unfortunately there are Republicans who feel that the step I have indicated cannot be taken by them. I need hardly say that I am sorry that that is so, because naturally, when one's object is to unite, it is regrettable that at the start there should be division and separation from friends with whom we have worked for so long. I believe that the initial separation has, however reluctantly, to be faced, if we are not to throw away the chance of victory – victory in which we are sure to be reunited.

I see no departure from principle in declaring my readiness to meet other elected representatives of the people. I cannot see how I can consistently claim the right of veto over those whom the people may select to represent them. If I claim my right as the duly elected representative of the people of Clare to have my voice heard, and my vote cast, in any assembly where regulations that affect and govern the daily lives of the people are made, I cannot see how I can deny a similar right to whomsoever the people of Kilkenny or any other country may elect as their representative.

This ought not to be made a matter of personalities. In Dáil Éireann we were careful not to speak of members as Mr A. or Mr B. We referred to each other as the deputies and representatives from the constituencies that sent us there. That is the proper attitude, and we must not depart from it. For my part, I want freedom to hold my own opinions without compromise, freedom to give my allegiance to where I have always given it, to where only it is due – to the Irish nation. If I can secure that freedom in the common assembly, and can consequently effectively represent there the electorate that chose me because of the opinions I hold, I cannot deny a similar freedom to those who hold contrary opinions . . .

I have been asked what we would do if we secured a majority. My answer is the same – we would ignore the Lloyd George Constitution, with its foreign-made articles, and deal with them exactly as with the oath. The fundamental, the supreme, constitution is the natural right of the Irish people to rule themselves, free from foreign interference. The only authority that I recognise, or will ever recognise, in this island is the rightful authority of the people of this island expressed through their free democratic institutions. The only hope I see of ever getting unity with ordered and stable government here is through acceptance of this principle. The natural law of right and justice is the fundamental law . . .

Today we are making a new start for another attempt to get the nation out of the paralysing "Treaty" dilemma. The abolition of all political tests is still the sine qua non. Further delay on our part would be senseless. Some who oppose the policy I suggest say that it is being brought forward too soon, whilst others hold that it is being brought forward too late. The vote at the Ard-Fheis is itself sufficient answer to both these criticisms. If even now, when so many things have happened which should incline Republicans to go the greatest lengths to rescue the nation from the position to which it has been brought, one-half the official body of Sinn Féin will not accept the policy, even though there is no substitute Republican policy in the field to meet the conditions with which we have to deal, what is the ground for supposing that my proposals would have had a more favourable reception at an earlier period? As for the view of those who think that I should wait longer and set about converting the Sinn Féin organisation from within, I ask what hope of success there is in that direction, seeing that the objection that is being made by many to the proposals is that they are contrary to Republican principle? Wherein they are contrary has nowhere been set out or explained, but I must take it that there is no use arguing with those who based their objections on this ground. We can only agree to go our different ways. If it should happen that, as somebody has said, we are both but attacking a tunnel at different ends, there will certainly be great rejoicing when we meet together at the centre.

For my part, I am convinced that principle is not involved, and in that at least I am supported by the majority view of the Republican deputies and by the fact that the Ard-Fheis itself did not pronounce otherwise. If my brother and I inherit a farm, and if one stronger than either of us takes it from us, and if my brother accepts it back under lease from the robber in spite of my protest, must I refrain from exercising my own right to cultivate that land and harvest the fruit of it simply because my brother has been weak enough or mean enough to admit the robber's claim? How does his having surrendered deprive me of my right when I have not abandoned it, and how would I be compromising myself if I found it convenient or expedient to work with him? I might, of course, choose not to work with him, but then my abstention would be dictated by some consideration of policy, or resentment, and not on any real ground of principle. So, too, Republican deputies might or might not join with the Free State deputies in a common assembly. If they decided to join, and nowhere explicitly surrendered their right, they could claim to speak in that assembly as the free representatives of a sovereign people without any actual compromise.

Another objection raised is that entering a Twenty-six Counties assembly would be an acceptance of partition. I deny that. To recognise the existence of facts, as we must, is not to acquiesce in them. We have been in no way a party to the partition of our country. It has been brought about unjustly and against our will. We have not agreed to it and do not agree to it. We have not accepted it and do not accept it. We shall at all times be morally free to use any means that God give us to reunite the country and win back the part of our Ulster province that has been taken away from us. So far from the course which I propose being an acceptance of partition, it is the only line of action that I can see which gives a hope for the undoing of partition within any reasonable time – unless, indeed, it is proposed to revert to the Union! The right way to proceed is obvious. We must first make good the internal sovereignty of the people over the Twenty-six Counties. That is a task well within our power, for the nationalists in these counties are in an overwhelming majority and need only stand together to make good their will. When we have established our right and strengthened our position in the Twenty-six Counties, then we shall be in a position to attack the problem of the Six with some chance of success. Meanwhile, we must make it quite clear that we are no parties to partition and that there will be no active co-operation between us and the foreign power that has been guilty of this outrage upon our country until partition is ended . . .

I think I am right also in believing that independence – political freedom – is regarded by most of you, as it is regarded by me, simply as a means to a greater end and purpose beyond it. The purpose beyond is the right use of our freedom, and that use must surely include making provision so that every man and woman in the country shall have the opportunity of living the fullest lives that God intended them to live. It is only since I have found how neglectful of this purpose many of us are inclined to become that I have been able to sympathise fully with James Connolly's passionate protest:

"Ireland, as distinct from her people, is nothing to me; and the man who is bubbling over with love and enthusiasm for 'Ireland' and can yet pass unmoved through our streets and witness all the wrong and the suffering, the shame and the degradation brought upon the people of Ireland – aye, brought by Irishmen upon Irish men and women – without burning to end it, is, in my opinion, a fraud and a liar in his heart, no matter how he loves that combination of chemical elements he is pleased to call 'Ireland'".

Freedom that our people may live happily and rightly, freedom to make this nation of ours great in well-being and noble doing, that is what political independence must mean, if it is to be at all worthy of the efforts and sacrifices that have been made to secure it; and it is in no small measure that we might be in a position to get as close as possible, and as soon as possible, to that side of our work that I am so urgent that we should follow the line of political action which I have outlined. Whilst waiting for the achievement of the full political independence we aspire to, the Republican deputies would be able to take an effective part in improving the social and material conditions of the people and in building up the strength and morale of the nation as a whole . . .

We are being bled by an emigration worse today than almost at any time since the great exodus that followed the Famine. That must be stopped. And then, go out into the city or into one of our country towns, or even into the heart of the country itself, and see the condition of the unemployed there! I have said it before, and I repeat here, and I believe most right-thinking men will agree with me, that it is a primary duty for any government in any civilised country to see that men and women will not starve and that little children will not starve through opportunity for useful work being denied to the breadwinner. I, for one, would feel that I was not acting according to my best feelings and to the light of my reason if I held back when I might take an effective part in the fight to make good that view. There is an opportunity immediately at our hand for doing great uplifting social work in Ireland. Had our nation secured its complete freedom, it would, I believe, be now leading the way for the world in solving peacefully some of the problems that are likely to be solved elsewhere only by violent revolution. As a nation we have a wonderful opportunity, and as Republicans we have a glorious mission, if only we will rise to it . . .

To free a nation situated as ours is, in relation to its enemy, is, as I said at the outset, not any easy task. I am not one of those who believe, and I will not suggest that I believe, that somehow the task can be performed by magic overnight whilst the people are asleep. It can be done only by the conscious effort and action of the people themselves. The people themselves must make up their minds that they want their freedom and then pursue it resolutely in the manner best calculated to secure it. I am not going to pretend to the people that they can do this without running any risks. I believe that there are risks but that the people should take them – and the very courage to take the risks will itself minimise them.

Besides, the danger that is run in facing these risks is, to my mind, far less than the danger that is being run in refusing to face them. There is no use in talking of stability when everyone knows we are standing on a volcano – a volcano which may become active at any time so long as the claim of a foreign power to rule this country is admitted. The ferment in the hearts and souls of the young and old who love their country is ever going on.

Irishmen know that it is as good and as holy for them to strive to free their country from the power of the foreigner as it is for the Englishman or the Belgian or the Frenchman to free his country. Patriotism which is a virtue elsewhere cannot be a sin in Ireland; and if one section of the community arrogates to itself the right to make it so, is it to be believed that those who are thus wrongly outlawed will meekly submit and will not strive day and night to free themselves from the injustice? To sit on the safety valve is a notoriously dangerous expedient. It is in the end, then, a choice of risks, and there ought not to be much hesitation as to which should be taken . . .

I shall be satisfied if I have convinced you that Republicans have before them a great opportunity for useful national work if they will grasp it. I wish to face boldly the facts of the present situation, because I know that it is only by facing them that we can hope to overcome them.

"Is mó epert i ceach ré
  Airle Dé frí hÉirinn uill" *

* ["God's counsel concerning virgin Éire
  Is greater than can at any time be told"]

"AN EMPTY POLITICAL FORMULA"

After the assassination of Kevin O'Higgins in July 1927, the Cosgrave administration introduced the Electoral Amendment Act which required parliamentary candidates to pledge that, if elected, they would take the Oath of Allegiance. De Valera, forced into action for which he had little choice, developed a solution which was built around the concept of the oath being an empty political formula. From this point on, Fianna Fáil became a full part of the political establishment.

On August 10, 1927, as Fianna Fáil deputies entered the Dáil for the first time, Fianna Fáil issued a statement to the press to assure their supporters of continued adherence to the anti-Treaty ideals.

DUBLIN, AUGUST 10, 1927

The Fianna Fáil deputies have met and given careful consideration to the position of national emergency which has been created by the legislation now being pressed through the Free State Parliament. They recognise that this legislation may imperil the general peace and cause widespread suffering; that it disfranchises and precludes from engaging in any effective peaceful political movement towards independence, all Irish Republicans who will not acknowledge that any allegiance is due to the English Crown. Nevertheless, they have come unanimously to the decision that, even under these circumstances, it is not competent for them, as pledged Republicans and as elected representatives of the Republican section of the community, to transfer their allegiance.

137

It has, however, been repeatedly stated, and it is not uncommonly believed, that the required declaration is not an oath; that the signing of it implies no contractual obligation, and that it has no binding significance in conscience or in law; that, in short, it is merely an empty political formula which deputies could conscientiously sign without becoming involved, or without involving their nation, in obligations of loyalty to the English Crown.

The Fianna Fáil deputies would certainly not wish to have the feeling that they are allowing themselves to be debarred by nothing more than an empty formula from exercising their functions as public representatives, particularly at a moment like this. They intend, therefore, to present themselves at the Clerk's office of the Free State Dáil "for the purpose of complying with the provisions of Article 17 of the Constitution" by inscribing their names in the book kept for the purpose, among other signatures appended to the required formula. But, so that there may be no doubt as to their attitude and no misunderstanding of their action, the Fianna Fáil deputies hereby give public notice in advance to the Irish people, and to all whom it may concern, that they propose to regard the declaration as an empty formality, and repeat that their only allegiance is to the Irish nation and that it will be given to no other power or authority.

"I DO NOT PROPOSE TO HARK BACK TO THE
TRAGEDIES OF THE LAST FIVE YEARS"

Sean T O'Kelly (1882–1966) had a career in Irish politics that was almost as long as that of Eamon de Valera. A founder member of Sinn Féin, he was also prominent in the Gaelic League and fought in the GPO with Pearse in 1916. Elected as a Sinn Féin MP in 1918, he held the position of Ceann Comhairle of the First Dáil. He opposed the Treaty in 1921 and in 1926 left Sinn Fein with de Valera and was one of the founders of Fianna Fáil. After the election of 1932, he became Vice President of the Executive Council and Minister for Local Government and Public Health. In 1945 he was elected as the second President of Ireland. He retired from public life in 1959.

O'Kelly entered the Dáil in 1927 with de Valera. His first speech in the new Dáil was on the motion that WT Cosgrave be elected President of the Executive Council. It demonstrated the bitterness of politics, the depth of the splits caused by the Civil War, and Fianna Fáil's increased focus on partition.

DAIL ÉIREANN, OCTOBER 11, 1927

. . . The Deputy who has been nominated, to my knowledge, did a good deal in these early days to preach the gospel of Irish independence as Irish patriots know it, and to instil into young and old the necessity for standing faithfully by the old traditional gospel of Irish freedom. He did his share, as I say and as I acknowledge, for some years to get that policy and that gospel understood and accepted by the people. To such an extent did that gospel which he preached, in company with others, get accepted at one time that those who stood for a different political ideal, the ideal of an Ireland subordinate to the British Empire, were swept out of political existence. He preached the gospel of Ireland independent, Ireland free, Ireland united, Ireland one nation, and that free and Gaelic – the gospel of Pearse, the gospel of independence as preached by Tone.

That is what he stood for then. If he stood for the same gospel now, or if there was anyone here offered to us as President who stood for that gospel, I would be the first to record my vote for him if he were fitted in other respects for the post. Primarily, on the ground that the gentlemen nominated does not stand for the gospel, I ask Deputies not to vote for him, and not to assist his election as President . . .

I could recount for you the awful havoc that his policy has wrought by driving, as it has done, a quarter of a million of our best out of the country, most of them, probably all, belonging to one political section – those who stood faithfully by the Irish Republic. They are the ones that have been forced to emigrate. They are the ones who have been forced to find a living elsewhere and whom the policy of the gentleman proposed and his party have driven out of the country.

The sorrow and anguish of mind that he and his political policy have been responsible for can never be known. But there is a bitterness in the hearts of those people who have gone abroad, and of their relatives left at home, their fathers and mothers, arising out of a policy pursued in the last five years, of which this Deputy is the symbol, that will take many generations to outlive. I do not propose to evoke these memories further. I do not propose to hark back to the tragedies of the last five years. I would rather that we could forget them, that we should try to pour all the oil we can on and calm the waters of life, and help to make things smoother and easier, not for us individually – individually we do not matter – but for Ireland in the days to come. Therefore, I will not hark back on these things further than to say that I personally take this, the first opportunity that is given to me in an Assembly of this kind, representative of part of Ireland, to say that I would do all I could to drive out of political power and office the gentleman and the Party associated with him who have the primary, if not complete, responsibility for the tragedies, sorrows, misdeeds, poverty and suffering that make up Ireland's history in the last five years. Some gentlemen can afford to smile. They are safe now, and I hope they will continue to be so. Things were not so safe a few years ago, when you and the like of you were behind those whom even in those days the gentleman nominated was fighting, with his comrades of the Republican Army, in an effort to liberate Ireland from her thralldom.

I do not want to evoke these things. As I said, I do not want to start on a bitter note, though God knows I could, and God knows I would justification in thinking of those who live in cold graves – seventy-seven of my comrades – who lie in cold graves today – and the fathers and mothers, and the sons and daughters of these people expect us and look to us to vindicate them in some way. All we can do, and all we can hope to do, is to try and assuage their feelings – smile at it how you will – to try and make them forget the bitterness of the past by standing up for the cause for which these young men and boys were put to death, and to try and win out what they gave up their lives for, and thus vindicate them and honour their memory.

It would, I believe, be an unfortunate message to go out to the world from this Assembly that this meeting of a practically completely new body, representative of the greater part of Ireland, stands for a partitioned Ireland, stands for an Ireland not as an Irish nation, one, united, independent and free, but for a partitioned nation, a conquered nation, a nation no longer in fact, but a so-called Dominion subject to the British Empire. The gentleman who has been nominated came into public life, as you, a Chinn Comhairle, and many others here know, pledged to work for and to devote his life to achieve an Ireland free and independent. That is my recollection of the political gospel he preached when I used to stand on platforms with him – thanks be to God, I do not now – and that is the gospel that some of those alongside him now who laugh at the idea of Ireland free and independent used to preach. They did, many

141

and many a time, preach that gospel, and not alone preached it, but went around the country organising Irish societies to promote that object, swearing young men into the Irish Republican Brotherhood, if you please, the very same young men that some of them took out later and put their backs against the wall and shot, because they were true to the gospel that these men preached. That is what they did . . .

One more word. If there is one particular item more than another in the last five years which seems to have brought a curse on our country it has been the partitioning of our ancient nation. There are some in this assembly who will remember that one of the main reasons why the party of the late Mr John Redmond was driven out of power in 1918 by the party with which Deputy Cosgrave was then associated, one of the main reasons why Sinn Fein got into political control, was because Sinn Fein preached that if Redmond's party were left in control they threatened to bring partition into operation in Ireland. Not alone did Deputy Cosgrave when he got into office and power, for that amongst other reasons, not threaten to bring partition into Ireland, but he brought it into full and complete operation for the first time in the history of our country. For the first time a political party under his leadership asked for and got from this Assembly, constituted as it then was, power to partition the country and bring into practical operation in Ireland the old British policy of "divide and conquer" which they had tried for many years to put into operation with other political parties, but which it remained for the erstwhile Irish Nationalist, the erstwhile follower of Wolfe Tone, Thomas Davis, Robert Emmet and Padraic Pearse, to stand up in an Irish assembly and propose and carry and acclaim as being one of the greatest victories in Irish history. If there were no other reason why the gentleman named should not be approved of and accepted in this Assembly, that one reason alone should suffice. I, at any rate, hope that this Assembly will today rid itself of those who have remained in power for the last five years, standing for the policy of an Ireland subservient to the British Empire, an Ireland partitioned, an Ireland impoverished, an Ireland where emigration is our greatest industry. If Deputies are satisfied that these conditions ought to continue and that they cannot be bettered, then they have nobody more fitted to run Ireland on those lines than Deputy Cosgrave and his colleagues, and they ought to vote for him. If, however, they want to give Ireland half a chance to get back on its feet, to undo the harm that has been done politically and economically, they will try to find, and no doubt will find, the means of putting in power those who hope for Ireland and who stand by the old gospel that has always inspired Ireland with hope and enthusiasm, and who are prepared to back these political principles and these economic ideas – the only ones that will bring Ireland back to any shadow of prosperity, politically or materially, in our time.

"FIANNA FAIL IS A SLIGHTLY
CONSTITUTIONAL PARTY"

Sean Lemass (1899–1971) was born in Dublin and educated at O'Connell Schools, Dublin. After school he worked in his father's drapery shop in Dublin. He joined the Irish Volunteers in 1915, was in the General Post Office in 1916 escaped deportation and went back to school. After working in his father's business, he joined the Irish Volunteers on a full-time basis and was interned for a year over 1920–21.

After the signing of the Treaty, Lemass participated in the anti-Treaty campaign and was interned once more between 1922 and 1923. He was elected as a TD for Dublin City in the General Election of 1925. When de Valera resigned from Sinn Féin to form Fianna Fáil, Lemass was alongside him, and played a crucial organisational role in the party in its early years. Lemass was appointed to government in 1932, and served in every Fianna Fáil administration until his retirement in 1966. He had a long and distinguished career in government culminating in his election as Taoiseach in 1959, a post he held until his retirement.

The tensions between government and opposition after Fianna Fáil entered the Dáil have already been seen in Sean T O'Kelly's speech. The following speech, in a debate on the treatment of republican prisoners in 1928, further demonstrated that tension and bitterness. It also provided some background to the evolution of anti-Treaty thinking between 1922–1928.

DAIL ÉIREANN, MARCH 21, 1928

I think it would be right to inform Deputy Davin that Fianna

144

Fáil is a slightly constitutional party. We are perhaps open to the definition of a constitutional party, but before anything we are a Republican party. We have adopted the method of political agitation to achieve our end, because we believe, in the present circumstances, that method is best in the interests of the nation and of the Republican movement, and for no other reason . . .

Five years ago the methods we adopted were not the methods we have adopted now. Five years ago, we were on the defensive, and perhaps in time we may recoup our strength sufficiently to go on the offensive. Our object is to establish a Republican Government in Ireland. If that can be done by the present methods we have we will be very pleased, but if not we would not confine ourselves to them. The attitude the Minister has taken up on this is one which I regard more in sorrow than in anger. They have taken a narrow view and adopted the attitude that if they can justify their detention of the prisoners in jail and their chase of the men on the run in a manner sufficiently glib to convince the majority in this House their duty is done. Their attitude on the concrete facts of the prisoners is in direct variance with the words they used on other occasions when they asked us to forget the past and co-operate with them in building up the economic strength of the nation. Are we to take it that the speeches we have listened to from President Cosgrave and other members on the Government Benches were just cute devices to get the Government out of an awkward situation, to avoid discussion on matters that were unpleasant to the Government, that there was no meaning behind what they said, but that they were just giving a demonstration of general hypocrisy?

Are we to take it that when President Cosgrave was speaking on the Army Vote, speaking in the manner which Deputy Boland has mentioned, when he asked us to let these bitter memories die out, if we could, that he did not mean it, that they were only words he was speaking, and that when he is given an opportunity of putting these sentiments into practice he immediately tears off the mask and shows himself to be unchanged and in the same position which he always occupied? The Minister for Justice has given us a number of details with reference to prisoners. He has mentioned why such-and-such a man is kept in, and why somebody else is let out. He told us, for instance, that McPeake, who deserted from the Free State Army with an armoured car, was unworthy of our consideration because he was a deserter. In the years we have passed through, there have been many deserters from the Free State Army, and quite a number of deserters from the Republican Army. The deserters from the Republican Army were, in fact, unique in number, and many of these deserters are occupying seats in this House. There were, as I say, a number of deserters from the Free State Army to the Republican Army. After the attack on the Four Courts – I was on active service then – I remember one night there came out of the town of Carlow three Crossley tenders packed with deserters from the Free State Army. They brought their tenders and arms with them, and many, after participating in the campaign, were arrested and afterwards released. The amnesty seemed to apply to them. There were many other cases. Some of those who deserted were executed, but others were not executed and were released. Why was exception made in the case of McPeake? After all, what he did was done by hundreds of others. He deserted with an armoured car. That may be particularly galling to members opposite, but it only in a degree affects the case.

The men who deserted in Carlow did not desert with an armoured car, because they could not get it. They took what they could, and if they could have thrown in an armoured car they would have done so, and we would have been very glad to receive it. These men were released, but McPeake is in jail. Is it necessary for the maintenance of the State, the maintenance of the Treaty position, that he should still be in jail? Is it necessary in the interests of the nation – if we may refer to the nation here – that this particular case should be picked out from thousands of others and that this man should be retained in prison? There was the case of the men who escaped from

Mountjoy. There was a rescue of prisoners from Mountjoy. The operation was carried out successfully, and nobody was injured. I am sure that the Minister for Local Government, who has some experience in this these matters, will admit that it was a nice job neatly carried out. The men escaped. Did the incident shake the foundations of the State so severely that it was necessary to inflict punishment at any cost on everyone connected with it?

Was the incident of such a nature that today, three years after it occurred, if the officers of the law put their hands on any of the men who escaped, they must be sent to jail and sentenced to months of imprisonment for having anything to do with it? When the Public Safety Bill was going through this House I remember reading in the Press – the Press may have as usual misreported the speech – a statement by President Cosgrave that at that particular time, towards the end of 1925, I was Minister for Defence in the Republican Army, and Mr Aiken was Chief of Staff. I do not know where President Cosgrave got his information. A number of these sensational disclosures which were made here were wrong and were founded on false information, and possibly, this information was of the same kind. But if the information was correct, then Deputy Aiken and myself must have had knowledge of the Mountjoy incident and have sanctioned it, and, if the incident was of such a nature that three years after the event everyone connected with it must be punished to save the prestige of the State, it is strange that Deputy Aiken and I are here if we had anything to do with it, while those who were actually engaged in it are prisoners in Mountjoy.

Either it is not correct to inflict this severe punishment or else President Cosgrave's statement is not correct. I do not want to go to prison. I am not inviting the Government to arrest me and put me on trial. Surely in this year, 1928, it is possible to draw a veil over events that happened in 1925. A lot of water has flown under the Liffey bridges since then. Many developments occurred in the political life of this country since then, and the situation which now exists bears no resemblance to the situation in 1925. I think if those on the Government Benches, who spoke of the need of co-operation and the need for unity of effort amongst all parties, meant one iota of what they said they would see the advisability of that incident, at any rate, being forgotten and of those connected with it, either members of the rescue party or prisoners rescued, being allowed to return to their homes. If it is punishment you want I think that those who took part in it have been punished enough. A man cannot be three years on the run, away from his home and family, living from hand to mouth on the countryside, without meeting considerable hardship. If it is merely a desire to punish which is animating the Government, they can rest assured that that desire has been gratified. If they want to make unity of effort possible they must remember that the men on the run are a constant source of danger to that achievement. They are desperate. They are being hunted down like madmen, like lunatics at large, preaching the gospel of desperation. They are carrying the creed of violence into the homes they visit and amongst the people they meet and finally, sooner or later, if the Government persist in their present policy that creed of violence, that spark of violence which they are fanning to flame, will burst into flame, and this country will be driven back to the position it was in a few years ago. I move the adjournment of the debate until Friday next.

"VOTING FOR DE VALERA"

James Dillon (1902–1986) was the son of John Dillon, the last leader of the Irish Parliamentary Party. He was educated at University College Dublin. He entered the Dáil in 1932 as an independent representative for the constituency of Donegal. He later formed the National Centre Party, which in turn joined with Cumann na nGaedheal and General O'Duffy's National Guard to form Fine Gael in 1933 Dillon left Fine Gael over the party's support for Irish neutrality in the Second World War.

He served as a Minister in the Inter-Party governments (as an independent in 1948–51), rejoined Fine Gael and became its leader in 1959. In a colourful career, he contested 12 general elections but only half of them representing the party he was ultimately to lead.

Dillon's first speech in the Dáil related to the nomination of de Valera as President of the Executive Council, which he supported. In view of the shape that both careers were to take, his decision to support de Valera has a certain touch of irony.

DAIL ÉIREANN, MARCH 9, 1932

I intend to vote for Deputy de Valera as President of the Executive Council. As a Nationalist Teachta, representing the Nationalists of Donegal, I recognise that the Party which Deputy de Valera leads has received the largest number of first preference votes in the recent election, and I take that as meaning that the people have accepted his policy and desire him to do his best for Ireland as President of the Executive Council. He has not, as Deputy O'Hanlon has just said, opened

149

that policy to the Dáil as yet, but I believe it to be the duty of any Teachta, who is not bound to do what his Party leaders tell him, to do his utmost to see that the will of the people is carried out, and as I believe it is the will of the people that Deputy de Valera should have an opportunity of trying his policy for the welfare of this country, I propose to help him towards that end in so far as in me lies. I may be pardoned for saying another word. If it is the will of the people that Deputy de Valera should press forward with his policy, I believe also it is the will of the people that Deputy de Valera should ensure that the peace will be kept both at home and abroad.

THE UNITED IRELAND PARTY

Following electoral defeats in 1932 and 1933, the main pro-Treaty parties (Cumann na nGaedheal and the Centre Party) began discussions on the development of a new united party. After negotiations a new party, The United Ireland Party (or Fine Gael) was launched in the Mansion House on September 8, 1933.

The new party adopted the following aims: the voluntary reunion of the Irish nation, the maintenance of the right of the Irish people to decide for themselves their constitutional status, restoration and extension of farmers' principal markets, assistance for industries, reduction of unemployment through the development of the buying power of the community, protection of individual liberty and the securing of peace and goodwill between all classes and creeds.

The new party elected Eoin O'Duffy, the former Commissioner of the Garda Siochana, as its first president, with WT Cosgrave as its parliamentary leader. O'Duffy had established the National Guard (the Blueshirts) following his sacking as Garda Commissioner by the new Fianna Fáil government early in 1933. The National Guard was proclaimed by the government in August 1933, and O'Duffy's emergence as leader of the main opposition party was the cause of much controversy. O'Duffy's relationship with Fine Gael was intense and ultimately short-lived. He resigned abruptly as party leader in September 1934 and went on to form a new political party, The National Corporate Party, with Cosgrave replacing him as leader of Fine Gael.

1. The United Ireland Party stands for the voluntary reunion of the Irish nation as the paramount constitutional issue in Irish politics, and considers that to achieve this end the first essential is solidarity of purpose among the citizens of the Free State.

2. It maintains the fundamental right of the Irish people to decide for themselves at all times their own constitutional status. It rejects as fatal to Irish unity and in every way disastrous the Government's double-faced policy of retaining the present constitutional position and at the same time discarding its advantages. The people are being brought to beggary and defrauded of all hope of getting rid of partition by a sham republicanism which only uses the name republic as a pretext for self-glorification, for claiming a monopoly of patriotism, and for perpetuating discord.

3. The present Government gained power by reckless and impossible promises. They have not merely failed to fulfil these promises, but have sunk the country into a state of degradation from which they are wholly incompetent to raise it.

4. United Ireland has been founded to enable all patriotic citizens to co-operate in remedying the situation so created, to save the farmers by restoring and extending their principal market; to help industries to reduce unemployment by developing instead of destroying the buying power of the community, to give the workers not merely an uncertain subsistence, but secure employment and a reasonable measure of comforts and amenities, to protect individual liberty and the rights of citizenship, to work constantly for peace and good-will between all creeds and classes, and to build up for the whole of Ireland a worthy and distinctively Irish civilisation.

5. With these aims two political parties have decided to combine and with them is joined a youth movement which the Government revived the Public Safety Act to proscribe. Having tolerated violence, intimidation and military parades by their own associates, they were not ashamed to pretend danger to the State from a body which had neither interfered nor

threatened to interfere with the liberty of anyone and which will now renew a vigorous existence as an element in the United Ireland Party, inspiring our young men with love of their country and the spirit of voluntary and disciplined public service. Upon that spirit more than upon Government action depends the emergence of our country as a nation with its own language, taking pride in the past and neglecting no opportunity in the present.

6. United Ireland looking to the future while rooted in the best traditions of the past will stand for the wiping out of party animosities arising either from the Anglo-Irish War or from civil conflict.

7. The nation is in danger. To avert that danger we call upon all men and women who love their country, and who desire to work for Ireland's honour and well-being, to do their part in helping us to end the present policy of ruin and to build up an Ireland – one, prosperous and great in spirit and achievement.

"NINETY-SEVEN PERCENT OF THE ROMAN CATHOLICS OF NORTHERN IRELAND ARE DISLOYAL AND DISRUPTIVE"

Basil Brooke, (1888–1973), the third Prime Minister of Northern Ireland, was born in Fermanagh and educated at Winchester public school. After an army career which included service in World War I, he resigned his regular commission to farm his estate in Colebrook. He was elected to the Northern Ireland Senate in 1921, but resigned in 1922 to become commandant of the Ulster Special Constabulary in their fight against the IRA. He was elected as Unionist MP for the Lisnaskea division of Co. Fermanagh in 1929. He was appointed Minister for Agriculture for Northern Ireland by James Craig – the first Prime Minister of Northern Ireland – and promptly dismissed the 125 Roman Catholic workers on his estates (a quarter of the total workforce) to set an example for other landowners. He succeeded John Andrews as Prime Minister in 1943, a position he held for the next twenty years. He played a key role in linking the Orange Order, of which he was a member, with the government.

The speech is quoted from the Fermanagh Times. *For many on both sides of the political divide in Northern Ireland, it described the entrenched divisions between the two communities.*

NEWTOWNBUTLER, JULY 12, 1933
Sir Basil Brooke, Bart, MP . . . said that on July 12, when addressing a meeting at Newtownbutler, he had made certain remarks regarding the employment of Roman Catholics which

had created a certain amount of controversy. He now wished to say that he did not intend to withdraw a simple word of what he then said. (Applause). On this subject a letter had appeared in the Press from a Rev. Mr Mitchell who maintained that Protestants in the Free State were getting a square deal. (Voice – It's a lie!). He would be the last man to make the lot of Protestants or Loyalists in the Free State any harder than what is was at present, but the position there and in Northern Ireland was quite different. In the Free State Protestants were in a minority and Roman Catholics know that they could do with them what they liked. What was happening there was evidenced by the fact that the number of Protestants was decreasing yearly while, on the other hand, the number of Protestants in Northern Ireland was steadily increasing . . . He had travelled over a good part of the world and had met men professing all sorts of religions and amongst them he had met Roman Catholics who were as loyal as any of those present at the demonstration. The fact must be faced, however, that ninety-seven, if not one hundred, per cent of the Roman Catholics of Northern Ireland were disloyal and disruptive. That just made all the difference. He was not speaking against these people because they went to a different place of worship, that was their own concern only so long as they did not attempt to interfere with or injure the good Protestant faith for which the men of Derry had fought and died.

When dealing with this subject of employment he was not speaking from the religious point of view, but because he knew that the vast majority of Roman Catholics in Ireland were disloyal and that the infiltration of these disloyal men and women into Northern Ireland, if allowed to continue unchecked, would result, in a few years, in them becoming so numerous that they would be able to vote Ulster into the Free State. That was his sole reason for asking the Protestants and loyalists of the North not to employ Roman Catholics if they could get good Protestant boys and girls to take their place. (Cheers). If these Roman Catholics were prepared to back the constitution of Ulster and to support the Empire and desired to reside in it, he would not say one word against them, but so far from this being the case practically every one of them gloried in the fact that they were out to destroy Ulster and to injure the British Empire. (Hear, hear). His statements on this subject might produce ill-will in certain quarters, but unless every loyalist made up his mind to keep Ulster as it was, and to take steps to that end, it would go down in a few years.

"THE CAMPAIGN AGAINST THE EMPLOYMENT OF CATHOLICS . . . IS A GRAVE VIOLATION OF THE RIGHTS OF THE MINORITY"

Cahir Healy (1877–1970) was born in Donegal and lived in Enniskillen for most of his life. A journalist, he joined Sinn Féin, worked in various election campaigns and was eventually arrested and interned in May 1922. He was elected as Sinn Fein MP for the Westminster constituency of Fermanagh and Tyrone in November 1922, but was in prison until the general release of prisoners in 1924. He was elected as nationalist MP at Stormont for South Fermanagh in 1925, a position he held until his retirement in 1965.

In April 1934, in response to the statements of a number of cabinet ministers in Northern Ireland, Healy spoke in Stormont of the position of Northern nationalists in the Province.

STORMONT, APRIL 24, 1934

I beg to move, that in the opinion of this House the campaign against the employment of Catholics promulgated by the Minister of Agriculture and expressly sanctioned by the Prime Minister is a grave violation of the rights and liberties of the minority placed under the rule of the Northern Government.

We have put down this Motion not to elicit what the Government policy on the matter is, because we know that already, but rather to give supporters of the Government in this House and outside an opportunity of saying whether they approve of the declaration of the Minister of Agriculture who has advised audiences on more than one occasion not to

157

employ Catholics. We have been told that these statements, as well as the declaration of the Prime Minister, have shocked many Protestants both inside and outside this House and they have failed to find any justification for the practice either in the New Testament or in present day conditions here. These statements are not merely anti-Catholic, they are anti-Christian. Some supporters of the Government in this House have told us that they employ Catholics and that they will continue to do so notwithstanding the slogan of the Minister of Agriculture, "No Catholic need apply". Those Hon. Members live on terms of neighbourly friendship with Catholics and I trust that despite the interference of the Prime Minister they will continue to do so.

The policy is not a new one. The Right Hon. Member for Enniskillen (Sir Edward Archdale), who was then Minister for Agriculture, declared on the 31st March, 1925 that out of 109 officials in his Department only four were Roman Catholics, and he apologised for even having four in the service of the Government on the plea that three of them were civil servants turned over to him, "whom I had to take when we began". Some of those four have since gone, so I assume he can now breathe in peace.

The Prime Minister was not slow in making clear his own position in this matter. At Drumbanagher on 12th of July, 1932, he said:

"Ours is a Protestant Government, and I am an Orangeman".

At Belfast on 3rd of September, 1932, he said:

"I do not care a snap of my fingers so long as I have the staunch, loyal, and Protestant majority at my back. I will carry on as I have begun".

We know how he began. He began by interning 500 Nationalists, many of them from the most peaceful parts of the Six Counties, but not a single man of his own gunmen in Belfast was interned. He began by gerrymandering local government areas, even in places where the Nationalists in relation to the Protestants were as $2^{1/4}$ to 1. They were left

158

without any control of the local councils. He drove the Nationalists out of every public position where it was possible to do so, and he made, and continues to make, public appointments on sectarian and political grounds, totally ignoring merit. That is how he began, and that is how he continues.

Like attracts like. The present Minister of Agriculture, like his predecessor, was not slow to take the hint. The more intolerant the policy the better apparently it would please the Prime Minister, and so on 12th July last when he saw his present post in sight he went on a public platform at Newtownbutler and set about stirring up sectarian and political bias in a district that to my knowledge was hitherto free from any taint of these things. This is what he said.

"Many in the audience employ Catholics, but I have not one about my place."

One would think he was describing vermin of some kind.

"Catholics are out to destroy Ulster with all their might and power. They want to nullify the Protestant vote, take all they can out of Ulster and then see it to go to hell."

You will note he makes no distinction between Catholics in this declaration. The ex-Service man who risked his life in the Great War is put on a level with people like myself, who believe that the best thing for all Irishmen is a united Ireland, and that it would be a better place for all than a divided Ireland can ever be. People whose ancestors were in this country before the first of the planters proceeded to drive out the inhabitants, are to be on the same level and to be treated alike. Notwithstanding the plain precepts of the New Testament this godly Churchman's plan is plainly to extirpate his fellow Christians and to starve them to death, if, indeed, theirs is not going to be a sadder fate.

The Right Hon. Gentleman returned to the congenial task on 12th August last in Enniskillen. This time, however, he made a distinction which, in practice, leaves it exactly as it stood. He said:

"In Northern Ireland the Catholic population is increasing to a great extent . . . 97 per cent of Roman Catholics in Ireland are disloyal and disruptive."

You will notice his statistics.

"If they, in Ulster, allow Roman Catholics to work on their farms they are traitors to Ulster."

By the way, the cry about people coming across the Border is flatly contradicted by the Hon. Baronet's own organisation which met in Enniskillen on 10th April last. It is reported there that the Unionist majority shows some increase since the previous revision, notwithstanding which, you will be surprised to hear, the association reported a small debit balance, which hardly looks as if the loyalists of Fermanagh were so enthusiastically behind the Right Hon. Gentleman as he makes out. A debit balance remains. That cuts plainly across the declaration and the statements made in this Parliament recently, when the Representation of the People Bill was introduced. I fear that neither fact nor consistency will trouble the people at the back of this anti-Christian crusade.

I confess I did expect that when the Member for Lisnaskea received his portfolio as Minister he would have recognised the obligations of a Minister of the Crown. But in common with others, I did not reckon on the degree of anti-Catholic hate which seems to boil up in him periodically like a spring. At Derry, on 19th March, he confirmed his pre-Ministerial, anti-Christian, and anti-Catholic programme, as follows:

"When I made that declaration" – that is, the declaration of Newtownbutler – "I did so after careful consideration. What I said was justified. I recommend people not to employ Roman Catholics, who are 99 per cent disloyal."

You will notice that in Newtownbutler it was 97 per cent. They had increased by 2 per cent so that this extraordinary Minister of Agriculture seems to have had a new census made of the whole of the Catholics in the Six Counties. He proceeded:

"One paper admitted that 100 per cent of the Roman Catholics were Nationalists and, therefore, out for the destruction of the Ulster Constitution. What I said had nothing to do with a man's method of religion. That is no concern of anybody's, but when that religion is so politically minded and is out to destroy us as a body, it does concern us then. I will continue to criticise and to take what action I can. What astonishes me is that these people are rather hurt because of my utterance".

It is interesting to see that the Hon. Baronet is now prepared to allow Catholics to practise their religion. I am sure we are all obliged to him for that concession. In fact, we are not to be molested if we are found going to Mass. In that respect it resembles Cromwell's boast after Drogheda – that he had left two friars alive out of the thousand people massacred. But in other respects there is no difference in the policy of "to Hell or Connaught" practised by the leader of the Ironsides and the Lisnaskea Cromwell, whose slogan is – "Don't employ Catholics – starve them".

Let me draw the attention of the House to the British Act of 1920, under which it receives its authority. There was some fear at the time that the minorities in the North and South might be subject to penalties indirectly on account of religion. So Section 5 of the Government of Ireland Act, 1920, expressly stipulated that:

"In the exercise of their power to make laws under this Act the Parliament of Northern Ireland shall not make a law so as directly or indirectly to establish or endow any religion or prohibit or restrict the free exercise thereof, or give a preference, privilege or advantage, or impose any disability or disadvantage on account of religious belief or religious or ecclesiastical status".

This House has already legislated in the matter of education, so as directly to penalise Catholics.

It is true the Prime Minister claims that if Catholics transfer their schools to the secular Protestant authority they can secure the terms which are now available to the members of every other creed. He knows perfectly well that course is impossible.

Catholics cannot conscientiously transfer the religious teaching of the young to any secular authority, even if it were one without religious or political bias, which cannot be found in the Six Counties. The Minister for Agriculture, seeing the prime Minister break the undertaking he accepted under the 1920 Act, thought he would go one better. Not only would he penalise Catholics, but he would extirpate them by denying them the right to work. It is quite clear that the Government has, therefore decided, in practice, to drive a coach and four through the undertaking which the British Government gave the Irish minorities.

There is no Catholic on the Bench in Northern Ireland, where the Catholics are in a majority over any other creed. When Catholics holding public positions die or resign they are being replaced by Protestants. I have no objection to the appointment of a person of any creed, provided it is made on merit, but I do protest against this disgraceful discrimination which the Government has been persuing for a considerable time.

The Right Hon. Gentleman claims that Catholics are not loyal. Loyal to what? I will show later that the only type of loyalty which this Government recognises is that which helps them to remain upon the Treasury Bench. When they speak of loyalty they mean loyalty to His Majesty the Prime Minister. The King governs through his Ministers, and the Administration here does not know the day when a Socialist Government may replace the National one, so they stipulate for a conditional loyalty to the Throne, just so long as it suits. We have not forgotten 1914 and the Provisional Government set up here. We may live to see the praters about loyalty to the Constitution take their guns again and go out to attack the King's troops.

The Orange Order, which is the shadow and power behind the Government, was born to stir up strife amongst neighbours and has, unwittingly perhaps, carried out that policy at intervals since. Its loyalty can be judged from the fact that a Commission held that it was responsible for the attempt to oust Queen

Victoria from the Throne, and to set its own nominee – the Duke of Cumberland, in her place. The riots which disgraced the cities of Derry and Belfast from 1813 to 1886 were traced to that Order by the successive Royal Commissions which sat to take evidence. It had to be suppressed by a British Statute not less than four times in that interval.

When I spoke of the Orange mob recently to describe the rather rowdy elements which mainly made up the processions following the Member for Derry City, he protested. I would point out, however, that it was a Royal Commissioner who first used the term "mob" to describe the drum-beating brethren, not I. I gladly admit that there are many decent men in the Order, but they are not allowed to think for themselves; they are being saturated with anti-Catholic dope and then used as the vocal tools of better-informed people, who have their own axes to grind.

The Minister of Agriculture objects to our changing the Government by the vote. That is the primary purpose of the Representation of the People Bill recently introduced. Nationalists are described as disloyal because they would change the Government by constitutional means. The Right Hon. Member for Lisnaskea (Sir Basil Brooke) has a particular grievance against myself, because he says I would do my best to bring Ulster into a united Ireland by the power of the vote or by peaceful penetration. I have never used the term peaceful penetration, but I see no objection to it. If Nationalists are not permitted to work for a united Ireland by the vote, I ask you what other means are left to them? You are coming to the time when Nationalist exercise of the franchise anywhere will almost seem a wasted effort.

I warn you now that you are moulding a policy that may soon drive Nationalists out of this house altogether. At the moment they see little use in playing politics with people who do not possess even the most elementary notion of justice or fair play. They are indeed beginning to ask themselves if it is worth while keeping representatives here. They might achieve their desire for a united Ireland more readily by encouraging the rise of an independent Unionist party. There are not many constituencies in the North and the Nationalists holding the balance of power might occupy here in a few years the strong position which Parnell occupied in British politics in the eighties. You are preparing for that position now.

Whatever may be their views of the Government or laws, however much they may long for the day when they will see an end to such an intolerant and sectarian administration, and have a united government for the whole country, Nationalists are at the moment observing the law as well as any other class in the Six Counties. And therefore they ought to be treated as good citizens are treated in every country in the world. Hitler has not prosecuted the Jews nearly so much nor so subtly nor so long as you have persecuted the Catholics in the Six Counties. The world's Press proclaim his crime; it is still silent as to yours. But on this question of loyalty I think you have the slenderest right to speak. Your past belies your present professions of loyalty. On the Treasury Bench I see some of the men who in 1914 set up an illegal Provisional Government in opposition to the King's Government. One of the military chiefs of the time described the present residence of the Prime Minister as a veritable arsenal from which armed men marched to the Liverpool boat to meet Sir Edward Carson . . .

. . . The whole case made before now and up to this moment is this, that the Nationalists are not loyal, and surely I am entitled to meet that case in this way, by showing that the people who make that charge are themselves not loyal, and have no right to make it. My memory goes back to the 1914 episode out of which this whole Parliament arose, and I remember the importation of arms into the ports of Larne and Bangor. I remember the gun-running. I remember the declarations made by Right Hon. and Hon. Members of this House as to the degree of their loyalty, and I want to put those declarations in contrast with the position of Nationalists, some thousands of whom in the Great War gave up their lives hoping that it was a war in defence of small nationalities. I should like for one minute to quote here some of the declarations that were made at that time. Mr Gerard, who was the American Ambassador to Germany, said in "My Four Years in Germany":

"The raising of the Ulster Army by Sir Edward Carson . . . was reported by the German spies as a real and serious revolutionary movement, and of course it was believed by the Germans that Ireland would rise in rebellion the moment war was declared".

The *Belfast Evening Telegraph* on 27th August, 1913, stated:

"Sir Edward Carson had the honour of receiving an invitation to dine with the Kaiser last week at Hamburg."

That is an interesting thing in view of the challenge of Nationalist disloyalty.

Captain Craig, MP is reported in the *Morning Post* of 9th January, 1911 to have said:

"There is a spirit spreading, which I can testify to from my personal knowledge, that Germany and the German Emperor would be preferred to the rule of John Redmond."

Then Mr Robert Thompson, MP, chairman of the Belfast Harbour Board, on 8th April, 1912, said:

"We are promised a large measure of support from Canada . . . Germany has been looking after Ulster developments. She has the drawings completed of every dock we have in the Harbour . . . still more, she has an officer named to carry out the necessary campaign."

And this is from a report of a speech made by Sir Edward Carson in the Criterion Restaurant, London, on 24th June, 1912:

"It has been said he ought to be sent to gaol . . . he intended when he went over to Ulster to break every law that was possible."

Again at Blenheim, on 23rd July, 1912, Sir Edward Carson said:

"They may tell us if they like that that is treason. It is not for men who have such stakes as we have at issue to trouble about the cost."

At Derry, on 20th September, 1912, Sir Edward Carson said:

"Let no man make light of signing the Covenant. It was

signed by soldiers in uniform, policemen and great lawyers . . .
Any man who having made this pledge goes back on it, or fails
at the critical moment, let him beware. He is a betrayer of his
brother."

In an interview with a representative of the *Daily Telegraph*
on 20th April, 1914, Sir Edward Carson, said:

"Had the operations started by the Constabulary of seizing
the Old Town Hall the Unionist Headquarters proceeded . . . as
a high percentage of Belfast's male population carry revolvers
. . . long before the police could have arrived the streets would
have been running in blood."

Mr William Moore, KC, MP, speaking at Birkenhead on 10th
March, 1913 said:

"I have no doubt, if Home Rule is carried, its baptism in
Ireland will be a baptism in blood."

This is from an open letter which appeared in the *Coleraine
Constitution* in July, 1913:

"Can King George sign the Home Rule Bill? Let him do so
and his Empire shall perish as true as God rules heaven . . .
Therefore, let King George sign the Home Rule Bill; he is no
longer my King."

Sir Edward Carson at Belfast on 12th July, 1913, declared:

"The Army are with us."

The Irish Churchman, 14th November, 1913, stated:

"It may not be known to the rank and file of Unionists that
we have the offer of aid from a powerful continental monarch,
who, if Home Rule is forced on the Protestants of Ireland, is
prepared to send an army sufficient to relieve England of any
further trouble in Ireland by attaching it to his dominion . . .
The Protestants of Ireland will welcome this continental
deliverer as their forefathers, under similar circumstances, did
once before."

Sir William Johnson-Hicks, speaking on 6th December, 1913,
said:

"The people of Ulster have behind them the Unionist Party
. . . In God's name they said to the Prime Minister; 'Let your

armies and batteries fire. Fire if you dare! Fire and be damned.'"

My last quotation is from a speech delivered by Sir Edward Carson in Armagh on 4th October, 1913. He said:

"If anything could add to the gratification which I feel at the present moment it is that there should stand beside me here the Lord Primate of Ireland, a very good specimen, if I may say so, of a brother rebel."

Mr Speaker, I ask the Prime Minister a question through you. Who was it that first imported arms into this country? Did not the Irish Republican Army merely march in the footsteps of the gentleman who is now the King's Prime Minister in Northern Ireland? I shall be told that your treason was of the conditional type. You knew and Sir Edward Carson knew you would never be obliged to make good in the flesh your promises to the mob. And you were right in that. For you, the ringleaders in rebellion, there was to be the Government Bench and the profitable post of a law lord. For Casement, Pearse, Connolly and the rest there was to be a bullet at dawn and a grave in quick lime. That is how Justice is administered.

The old proverb has it: "Treason never does prosper". Why? When treason prospers men do not call it treason. Treason has prospered with you. You have achieved place and power by treason. There can be no better authority upon disloyalty than the Prime Minister and his pale shadows, the Ministers for Home Affairs and Agriculture.

Nationalists, whom you twit with disloyalty, never said they would prefer the Kaiser to the King in the days when war was in sight. No, instead, they sent out their sons to die for an ideal. They have been disillusioned by you. When someone said it was a war to make the world safe for democracy, he was merely telling a lie. They have read the declaration of the Minister for Agriculture. "I have not a Catholic about my place", and they know that whatever proof of loyalty they could give would not secure them the humble position of a rate collector in any County of the North. If the sons of some of them turn away from Constitutionalism, can you wonder? They look at you and they see that the only way to succeed is by treason and physical force. You may reply that because we tried to upset the Government in 1921 and 1922 that is your justification for anything and everything. In so far as it went we merely imitated your own policy and methods.

Hon. Members opposite may ask me what about Mr O'Kelly. The rather loose statement of the Vice-President of the Free State recently has caused quite a sensation up here. The people remember 1914 and since, and know that if he meant his threat which he probably did not he would be merely adopting the means you used to climb to power and partition this country. You have not the least fear of anyone in the Free State deposing you by physical force so long as the British Army is intact. It may suit your policy of stirring up sectarian strife to use such threats with which to frighten every independently minded Protestant up here and cause him to fall in behind the Orange Order, which calls the tune to which you all must dance every time.

The leaders of the Orange Order talk big of "civil and religious liberty" once or twice a year, but in practice this only means liberty for themselves. The extent of the liberty of thought the Orange Order are prepared to give anyone can be gauged by their outlawing Senator Gyle for being present in the room of the late Mr Devlin when some friend was making a prayer. I must offer my sympathy to certain members here who find themselves in an organisation so devoid of Christian charity and lacking in any knowledge of Christianity. I wish they had the courage to step outside its darkened wall into the light of liberty, of real Christianity.

In these circumstances it is now clear that the Prime Minister desires Nationalists to have votes only on condition that he has an assurance that they are always going to remain a minority. Because they aim at changing the Government itself, or the form of the Government, by constitutional means, he gets angry and says their voting power must be reduced to a minimum. If gerrymandering will not do it – where one Unionist vote is equal to 2.25 Nationalist votes – he will resort to everything calculated to prevent Nationalists getting any votes. He wants to secure that opposition must never be able to get a majority at all.

The Representation of the People Bill is the beginning; it is by no means the end of the chapter of rebellion opened by the Prime Minister in 1914. In pursuance of this policy, should there be such a landslide from the supporters of the Government, as we believe possible in a reasonable time, the Prime Minister will not hesitate to trample upon the British Constitution again, take up the gun, and set up a dictatorship. The man who says that a Catholic must not get work because he is desirous of getting rid of a Government which made rebellion fashionable in 1914, will not hesitate to substitute once more the rule of the gun for the will of the people.

Nationalists now see whither they are drifting. The Prime Minister desires them to clear out of politics altogether. His opponents may regard his opinion in that respect as carrying more wisdom than he suspects. We accept it partially. We will not allow ourselves to become an official Opposition in this House. We will only intervene when we feel that we can expose injustice. But we reserve the right to come in or stay outside, as and when our people may decide. If bad feelings develop in the North, to the loss of trade, the business people will know where the scheme originated.

Nationalists have been anxious, while reserving their right as to the form of Government under which they live, to do their best to promote the welfare of the Six Counties. They have been desirous of forgetting old sectarian animosities and cultivating friendship with all creeds and classes. The Prime Minister is afraid that such a policy – the uniting of Orange and Green – might eventually lead to a new political orientation in the North, so he has called out the dogs of war in the persons of the Hon. and learned Member for Derry (Mr Murphy) and the Minister of Agriculture, who sees a long period in his profitable office if he can only keep up the old hates, the old sectarian strife. I am glad that I was born poor, so that I can live without such spoils of office. I would rather go out on the roadside and break stones in all sorts of weather than hold any office by such degrading tactics.

We rejoice that the mass of the Northern Protestants are not likely to heed such an unChristian lead. They realise that a policy of that sort would be a great set-back to their own business or trade. Even the Members behind the Government, who employ many Catholics, are not likely to dismiss one merely because the Minister for Agriculture desires it. No political party in Great Britain would exist for a year if it advocated the restriction to its public services of people of a particular Christian church. It would be regarded as a scandal and would bring down any Government which attempted it. We know there is today no place for a Catholic in any public office. They are banned more effectively by the bigotry, secret and open, of the Northern Ministers, than they were in the days before the passing of Catholic Emancipation. But for all that, we are far from despairing. We have assurances from many Protestants that they abhor your policy and have no intention of paying the least heed to it.

We believe the justice of our case will triumph over your intolerance. The mass of the Protestant people, after all, get nothing more from you than we. It is only the select few, the friends and associates of the members of the Government, who share the plums of office. And whatever you may do by legislation we tell you now that we are not to be driven from the Six Counties. Like the Jews, we were born to suffering and persecution, and we love the land and its associations. What Elizabethans failed in doing you cannot accomplish. What Cromwell attempted in vain you will also attempt in vain. God and right are with us and these will prevail over all your machinations. This is not the last generation. Neither will your threats cause us to change our ideals, of a united and free Ireland.

"TODAY, THE CYNIC IS OUR TEACHER"

In September 1935 Italy invaded Abyssinia. De Valera, who had taken an ever-increasing role in the League of Nations, spoke to the assembly on September 16. He spoke passionately about the need to avoid war and for a strengthened role for the League. It was a bold speech, given that he was criticising Catholic Italy, a country with which Ireland had strong religious links.

His commitment to the concept of the League was rewarded by his election as President of its General Assembly in 1938. His election was vigorously supported by Britain.

LEAGUE OF NATIONS, GENEVA, SEPTEMBER 16, 1935

I come to this tribune with a feeling of deep sadness. The speakers who preceded me doubtless have had the same feeling, for no one can avoid being affected by the contrast between the high ideals and lofty purposes enunciated from this platform in former years and the atmosphere of despair which surrounds it today. From this tribune representative statesmen of successive Governments have spoken to the listening peoples, holding up to them the vision of a better world, inspiring them and leading them on to noble effort; telling them that the highest aspirations of their souls could be reached; urging that old animosities and egoistic selfishness should be laid aside; promising that by loyal co-operation, first in the smaller things, the nations would be led to realise that the highest good of each was best secured by devoted service to the common interests of all.

Today, however, the cynic is our teacher; he is whispering to

171

each of us, telling us that man in the long run is only a beast; that his duty is determined and his destiny ruled by selfishness and passion; that force is his weapon; that victory rests with the most brutal, and that it is only the fool who credits such dreams as were uttered here.

Yesterday, believing that war, as an instrument of aggressive national policy, had been outlawed, our thoughts were busy with the possibility of a Union of Europe. Today, before the mangled bodies of the youth of this continent have yet been mercifully assimilated with the clay, before the anguished hearts of countless mothers have even had a respite, we are here awaiting the result of an eleventh-hour attempt to postpone the opening of a conflict which may set the peoples of the world mutilating and destroying each other again – waiting – and expecting little but the relief that must come in exchanging the piteous, melancholy uncertainty of today for the steady resolve and active purpose of tomorrow.

To be thrown into a position of enmity with those whom we admire and would welcome an occasion to serve – what more heart-rending alternative can there be to the abandonment of duty and the betrayal of our deepest convictions and of our word solemnly given? That is, however, the alternative before us, and that is the price we may be called upon to pay for that common security without which the peace we need can never be realised.

It is a hard price, but harder still and more terrible is the future in store for us if we should fail to be ready to pay it. The final test of the League and all that it stands for has come. Our conduct in this crisis will determine whether the League of Nations is worthy to survive, or whether it is better to let it lapse and disappear and be forgotten. Make no mistake, if on any pretext whatever we were to permit the sovereignty of even the weakest State amongst us to be unjustly taken away, the whole foundation of the League would crumble into dust. If the pledge of security is not universal, if it is not to apply to all impartially, if there be picking and choosing and jockeying and

172

favouritism, if one aggressor is to be given a free hand while another is restrained, then it is far better that the old system of alliance should return and that each nation should do what it can to prepare for its own defence. Without universality, the League can be only a snare. If the Covenant is not observed as a whole for all and by all, then there is no Covenant.

I have to speak of the attitude of my own nation in this crisis. The Irish nation has no imperialistic ambitions. Though a mother-country, we covet no colonies and desire no dominions. Our sole claim is that the ancestral home of our people, unmistakably delimited by the ocean, should belong to us. We make no demands but those founded upon justice. We claim the right to order our own life in our own way and select our own governmental institutions without interference, prepared to admit for all other nations in their respective territories the same rights which we claim for ourselves in ours.

One of the oldest of the European nations, it is with feelings of intense joy that, after several centuries of attempted assimilation by a neighbouring people, we find ourselves restored again as a separate recognised member of the European family to which we belong. By our own choice and without compulsion we entered into the obligations of the Covenant. We shall fulfil these obligations in the letter and in the spirit. We have given our word and we shall keep it. For few nations will the test which may confront us tomorrow be more severe. May the good God keep this cup of bitterness from all of us.

Why cannot the nations put into the enterprises of peace the energy they are prepared to squander in the futility and frightfulness of war? Yesterday there were no finances to give the workless the opportunity of earning their bread; tomorrow, money unlimited will be found to provide for the manufacture of instruments of destruction.

Why can we not, in the spirit of justice, deal with wrongs when we perceive them? Not every demand for change deserves to be listened to, it is true, but must we wait until the wronged has risen up in armed revolt before we grant him the redress to which we know he is entitled? Why, if the problems are economic, and it is the fear of the withholding of essential raw materials that is causing alarm – why cannot these questions and their relation to colonial possessions be discussed now? Or will our conservatism, the natural philosophy of those who have and are concerned only to retain – will this conservatism give its consent and deem the time ripe only when the slaughter has begun? Are adjustments never to be made but at the expense of the weak?

Why cannot the Peace Conference which will meet in Europe when the next conflict has decimated the nations, and disaster and exhaustion have tamed some of them into temporary submission – why cannot this Conference be convened now, when calm reason might have a chance to bring the nations into friendly co-operation and a lasting association of mutual help?

Why can we not at least place this League of Nations on a stable foundation? Why can we not free the fundamental instrument of the League from its association with political arrangements which are universally recognised as unjust? Why can we not endeavour to forge an international instrument, not merely for settling international disputes when they arise, but for removing in advance the causes of those disputes?

The solidarity of which we have had, happily, such a manifestation within the past few days is an earnest that the goodwill of the nations can in the last resort be depended upon for the fulfilment of the obligations into which they have freely entered. Would that goodwill not be all the more active and effective in a system of collective security in which the legitimate national requirements of States are provided for, and their loyalty to the system thereby doubly assured? Such goodwill would have given us the Protocol ten years ago. But ten years ago there was no sense of impending calamity, no crisis, in the intensity of which we could be welded to a common purpose of self-preservation. Such a crisis is here now. God grant us the will and the wisdom to avail ourselves of it.

"THE WAR IN SPAIN IS A WAR FOR THE
VICTORY OR DEFEAT OF COMMUNISM"

*After the resignation of O'Duffy from the leadership of Fine Gael
and the launch of his new party, the National Corporate Party,
the bulk of those who supported the Blueshirts remained
supporters of Fine Gael.*

*When the Spanish Civil War broke out in July 1936, O'Duffy
organised an Irish Brigade to fight for the nationalists under
Franco. The Irish government, pursuing a neutral policy, passed
legislation which made participation in the war illegal. O'Duffy
led 700 volunteers to the Spanish front in 1936 and 1937.*

*In November 1937, Cosgrave sought to obtain Irish
government recognition for Franco's government. In his speech
Cosgrave placed the Spanish Civil War at the core of the battle
between Soviet Communism and Western Civilisation. His
motion was defeated.*

DAIL ÉIREANN, NOVEMBER 27, 1937

. . . Many a statesman in Europe has probably solaced
himself in recent years with the assumption that the Soviet
Union has, apparently, finally settled down, within its own
borders, content to take its place in a normal fashion amid the
other States of Europe. Those statesmen and nations who have
founded on that assumption a sense of security have paid no
attention to the two-fold voice with which in recent years
Moscow has been wont to speak. The Russian Foreign Office
tries to attune its voice to the accustomed language of the
Chancelleries of Europe, but the work of spreading the gospel

has been ceaselessly prosecuted by the other voice, the Comintern, the Communist International, with its Headquarters in Moscow and under the domination of the party which controls the Russian Government.

Twelve months ago it was possible for people to be misled by that apparent change of policy on the part of the Russian Foreign Office, but the events of the last year and, especially recent happenings in Spain, should tear the bandage from the eyes of everybody who has any interest in the higher aspects of our present complex social organisation. Whatever pretence there may have been in the beginning it must surely now be clear to everyone that the cause of the Caballero Government and the cause of the Communist International are identical. Moscow, Barcelona and Madrid form a common front. We have only to ask ourselves do we wish for victory for the cause for which these comrades stand. Let there be no mistake about it, the victory of the Communist cause in Spain would probably be a deciding factor for the fate of Europe. It is not a question which any person with a vision which extends beyond his own parish can regard as something in which he has no interest. The war in Spain is a war for the victory or defeat of Communism and all it stands for, with its denial of Christian principles, individual liberty, and democracy.

I do not see how a country with our history, our beliefs, our traditions and our ideals, moral, religious and political, can fail to withdraw recognition from a Government standing for everything we abhor and accord it to a Government that is fighting enemies that are the greatest we have to combat in Europe now or in the future. I am not suggesting that we abandon the policy of non-intervention. I am bringing forward this amendment, not for the purpose of criticising the Government for having adopted that policy. Of that policy we on this side of the House fully approve. I believe that the intervention of outside Powers would, as far as our human intelligence can judge, almost certainly lead to a general conflagration, a conflagration that might bring upon us at once these disastrous consequences that would follow inevitably but at a slower pace on the victory of the Red Forces in Spain. Considering the present position in international affairs, and considering any other machinery that might possibly be called in to preserve the peace, I can see no better method than the policy of non-intervention to prevent such a catastrophe.

Whole-heartedly desiring as I do the defeat of Communism and all it stands for in Spain and elsewhere, I do not believe that the policy of intervention could accomplish that defeat. Intervention might do irreparable damage in that respect, too. But what I advocate connotes in no way the abandonment of the policy of non-intervention. The recognition of General Franco's Government does not, it is clear, run contrary to that policy of non-intervention to which the Government is rightly committed. We, I am quite willing to admit, are but a small State. Our material resources are comparatively slight. We cannot sway the counsels of the European States, but against this I put certain considerations before the house. I do not believe that our influence in world affairs can be measured at all adequately by our material strength. There is another consideration of perhaps even greater importance. It would indeed be a pity, in this present struggle for and against Communism, in which all Europe seems determined to take sides, that it should seem to be left to those States that boast their non-democratic character to take the step of recognising as a Government that Party in Spain which is fighting our most deadly foe. I believe that Communism is in the end not only destructive of our civilisation but is more injurious to democracies than to dictatorships. It is fitting and necessary that a Christian and democratic State such as ours should give a clear and clean lead in this matter which involves a life and death struggle against the enemies of our common civilisation.

I have confined myself to the essential issues in the case. I have not dwelt on the sacrileges, the destruction, the atrocities, that have shaken our people to the very core, because I was anxious that the main issue at stake should be clearly put before the Dáil. I believe that a step of such paramount importance as this should transcend all party issues, that our national honour and more than our national honour is involved. It is of importance that the nation here should speak with one voice on this issue, and it does appear to me that the plain facts as they appear to all men indicate that whatever may have been the beginnings of the history of the struggle at present being waged in Spain, that struggle has now assumed a character of European and of world importance. It is not fitting that even by passive taking of sides we should as a nation interest ourselves in domestic quarrels between two sections of any people. The war in Spain, as I have said, has ceased to have that character. Ranged behind the Madrid Government are all the forces whose aims we, as Christians and as Irishmen, abhor. What I am asking the Government to do involves no military operations, no breach in the policy of non-intervention. It seems to me to involve merely the taking of a simple action which will bring this generation of Irishmen into line and into harmony with those who have gone before us and left to us a great tradition.

I think, and I hope the House will agree with me, that the Government of General Franco in Spain should be recognised and that recognition should be withdrawn from the combination which opposes him.

"THE PORTS ARE HANDED OVER UNCONDITIONALLY"

The Anglo-Irish economic war, which had commenced in 1932, caused significant hardship and damage to Ireland's agricultural and manufacturing economy in the 1930s. The dispute was over the issue of land annuities payable to the British government as a result of the Land Acts of the late nineteenth and early twentieth centuries. The dispute was brought to a close by an agreement between the two governments signed in April, 1938.

The agreement covered issues broader than just annuities, in particular defence and trade. The ports which Britain still possessed after the signing of the Treaty in 1921 were handed back to the Irish government. As a consequence, a policy of neutrality was made feasible for World War II. As Taoiseach, Eamon de Valera addressed the Dáil on the outcome of the negotiations.

DAIL ÉIREANN, APRIL 27, 1938

. . . The effect of that agreement is to hand over to the Irish State complete control of those defences; and it recognises and finally establishes Irish Sovereignty over the Twenty-six Counties and the territorial seas. I do not think it is necessary for me to stress to anybody who has desired the independence of this country the importance of that agreement from the point of view of Irish Sovereignty. The ports are handed over unconditionally. They belong to us as a matter of right, we have always held. We are glad that that right has been recognised and that now we are to have them. Among the articles of the

179

Treaty of 1921 that gave most offence to national sentiment were these, because they meant that part of our territory was still in British occupation. Unfortunately we cannot say today that Irish sovereignty is effective over more than Twenty-six Counties. I am confident that, having got to that point, it is only a matter of time – and, I hope and believe, a short time – before somebody speaking from this bench will be able to announce to the whole Irish race that at last the British people have been wise and the British Government has been wise; and that our people here in Ireland, of all sections, have been wise; and that Ireland at last is a completely independent sovereign state.

Whatever person may have the good fortune to be able to make that announcement, it will, for him at any rate and for the Irish nation also, be a proud moment. It will mark the end of one of the greatest struggles in history by a small nation to maintain its separate nationality and its rights as a separate nation. Unfortunately we have not yet got to this point; and if I thought for one moment that the agreements which we have here and which I am asking you to approve of would put an obstacle to, or delay for any time, the final securing of those aspirations, then I would not be found here asking you to approve of them. I am asking you to approve of them, however, because I believe, not merely that they put no obstacle in the way, but that they do in a variety of ways constitute a positive advance towards that final goal.

These agreements, as a whole, will remove from the field of dispute between Great Britain and ourselves all the major items now, except that one. The whole Irish race can now concentrate upon that one; and, with a united effort, I believe, as I have said already, that a completely independent sovereign Ireland will be achieved; and it is a matter of great satisfaction to me to know that henceforth, whatever differences may have divided us here on questions of national policy, once these agreements are passed, the vast bulk of the Irish nation will be reunited and all marching together towards the same goal.

This achievement appears to some people to be so great that

they can hardly believe that it is true. They are looking for the snag somewhere. Their attitude is: "Do we believe our eyes when we read this?"; and I have been challenged to say that, if we wanted to, we could destroy the defences of these ports. I have said, and I repeat, that we have got these defences unconditionally. What we do with them is a matter for Irish policy. So far as this Government is concerned, we have long ago indicated our policy. This Government has made it quite clear that, in looking for sovereignty over our own territory, we meant to defend that sovereignty, we meant to do what other nations have had to do, and this is defend our interests and our rights. If, then, those who talk like that simply want to confuse issues, I make them a present of it. If they want to confuse the steps which an Irish Government has to take – in its independence, in its full sovereignty – to defend its territory, with some suggestion that there has been a bargain or something of that sort, they can do it. There has been no bargain. There are no conditions. There is no secret understanding. But there is a belief, I am certain – a belief which I have tried, over twenty years, to get into the minds of British Governments and of the British people, in so far as I could – that it is far better for Britain, far more advantageous for Britain, to have a free Ireland by its side than an Ireland that would be unfriendly because of liberties which Britain denied.

I have said that the Irish Government – that this Government anyhow, and that has been our policy and will remain our policy – is not going to permit its territory to be used as a base of attack against Britain. I have said that for many years now. I indicated the policy which is behind it as long ago as 1920, when, on behalf of the State of that time – of the Republic – I made a request to the Government of the United States for formal recognition. We mean to see that whatever use is made of our territory will be only that use which is agreed to by an Irish Government in the interests of Ireland and in no other interests; and it is the interests of Ireland to see that our territory is not going to be used as a base of attack upon a neighbouring country.

181

We shall, then, have to defend our territory. There are some who say that that is going to mean money. Of course it is! Freedom always means a certain expenditure of money. If, of course, we were prepared to take the line which, say, Lord Craigavon is taking – I think he said some time ago that he was quite content to allow his defences to be in the hands of the imperial navy – if we were content to allow our defences to rest in the hands of the British Government or the British War Office, then we would not have to pay directly for defence, I suppose, but we would surely be paying indirectly. What we spend on defence now we shall be spending directly. The votes will have to be passed by this House, and not a penny need be voted beyond what this House by its majority may deem to be necessary and proper.

In taking over these ports, then, this Government, at any rate, does not mean to leave them derelict. This Government, at any rate, means to see that they are modernised, if necessary, because these harbours and these ports are obviously points of strategic value. Any state that could easily get them would be glad to get them and to hold them; and it is our duty to our own selves and our own sovereignty to make sure that, when we have them, nobody else will be allowed, except with our permission, to use these harbours. Consequently, although it is not a matter that immediately comes up in connection with this agreement, I am indicating our policy lest there should be any misunderstanding when, for example, an Estimate dealing with defence would be brought forward.

Subsequent Governments will be free to change that policy if they think it unwise, just as this Government can change a policy if it thinks it unwise; but, as I have said on previous occasions and as I have said many times here in the Dáil and in public, I cannot see any responsible Government here that would permit its territory to be used as a base of attack upon Great Britain. It is obvious that to do so would immediately involve us in war with Britain, directly or indirectly; and, having got rid of British interference by peaceful measures now, we certainly would not be wise, and no Irish Government would be wise, in involving itself in a war of that nature. I have always said that, in my view, an independent Ireland would have interests, very many interests, in common with Great Britain. In providing for our defence of our own interests, we would also of necessity be providing to a certain extent for British defence of British interests. I think that the British Government that made this agreement has shown greater wisdom than any previous British Government.

Anybody who would regard this as a one-sided bargain would be making a very big mistake. Britain is undoubtedly going to get from this agreement part of the advantages which I predicted would be hers if the whole of Ireland were an independent state; and, on the day on which the whole of Ireland is recognised as a completely independent state, the full advantages will accrue to Britain. But Britain is getting from this agreement advantages which will probably be greater, relatively, for her than the advantages we are getting for ourselves. It is only agreements giving advantages to both parties that really last. A good agreement is one in which both sides have an interest in its continuance; and the British, no less than we, will have an interest in the continuance of this agreement.

I think it is not necessary for me to say more about this agreement. We are getting the ports unconditionally, and this Government, at any rate, intends to defend them and to see that they are not used by any foreign power that might covet these harbours as a basis of attack either against British trade or against Britain herself.

The next agreement has to deal with finance . . .

In regard to the rest, the dispute [land annuities] is settled for a payment of £10 million. That payment has to be completed by November 30, and one of the Bills which have been introduced here today has reference to the methods by which that money is to be secured and paid. As a consequence of this agreement, the penal duties by means of which the British indirectly got the money which they claim was due to them – roughly £5 million a year – will disappear and also, on our side, the corresponding duties which were put on by way of retaliation. That covers the substance of the second agreement – the financial agreement.

Some may say that this is not a good agreement. I have repeatedly stated my belief that, if we were making agreements on the basis of justice, if sheer equity was to decide these matters, instead of paying money to Britain, whether a big or small sum, the payments should be made the other way. That is still my conviction – that, on the basis of sheer justice, if there was to be a payment on either side, it should be made in the opposite direction. We have agreed to this payment, which represents two years' purchase of the sum which the British were collecting by means of these special duties. We are making this agreement, and we are recommending it to the House. You may, if you like, regard it as ransom money. Look at it as you will, we are making it because we think that it is in the national interest that this settlement should be made.

Now, I have stated, as it appears to us, what sheer justice would suggest; but the matter was not approached from that point of view by the negotiators on the other side, nor, probably, would it be so approached by the British Parliament. Their attitude will be: "Well, we can collect these moneys; why should not we go on doing so?" If there are deputies in the House who think that we must secure what appear to be our rights in justice, well and good; they will have to vote against this agreement and say that this money should not be paid. As I have said, we have agreed to pay it because we think it is in the national interest that the payment should be made and the dispute put aside.

We, no doubt, will be told that it could have been done years ago . . . I say this settlement could not have been made some years ago . . . If this could have been settled, then why was not it done? It was not done because it could not have been done.

Could it have been done earlier, since we came in? I say no, it could not have been done. In this very dispatch of which I have read a portion, you will find mixed up with this question of the financial arrangements certain constitutional questions. The effort was being made to try to force us by means of economic pressure to give way on constitutional questions. We had to resist that, clear all the constitutional questions that we wanted to deal with out of the way, and then we had a field in which constitutional questions were not being drawn across questions of quite a different character. That agreement could not have been made without the sacrifice of constitutional rights before the Constitution was introduced. Since the Constitution was introduced, could it have been made? If it could, I would have known it, because – not merely since the Constitution was introduced but before it – I did my utmost to find out whether it was possible to get the British Government to take the Irish view and to recognise the justice of the Irish case in regard to these annuities.

It has been done now because there has been a concurrence of a number of propitious circumstances. It has been done now because, in the first place, there is not running across it any constitutional question or any inducement to try to bargain by means of these moneys – to bargain for constitutional rights – and, secondly, because, as I have said, there are at the present time a number of concurrent circumstances which enabled it to be done. It has not been done without a hard fight. When negotiators on the one side take the view that money should be paid in one direction and those on the other side take the opposite view, and when the amounts are huge amounts, it is not easy to come to agreement.

One of the circumstances that have made agreement possible is that you have in Britain a Conservative Government which is able to make its will effective, which feels that it has the strength to make its will effective. Anybody who has studied Irish history must have learned the fact, that, if ever there was to be settlement between Ireland and Britain, that settlement would have to come in a time, not when you had a Liberal Government, but when you had a Conservative Government in office; because the Conservative Government, once it convinced its own people that the agreement should be come to, was not likely to be opposed by either Liberal or Labour, who themselves would have advocated such a course long before but would have been unable to carry it out. One of the things, then, that makes this agreement possible is that you have at this moment in England a Conservative Government that can, in Parliament, make its will effective. Another circumstance which makes it possible to have this agreement is that you have in Britain at the present time a Government that is taking broad views of international questions, a Government that does not fail to recognise the importance, from their point of view, of a settlement like this.

I am not going into a number of other circumstances which, fortunately, at this time all concurred to make this agreement possible. One thing more than another that is to be welcomed is this, that it is the first occasion – that I, at any rate, have seen – on which a British Government has taken the wise view, the wise policy, in regard to this country and recognised what I have already mentioned, that a free, independent and friendly Ireland is going to be of much greater value to Britain than an Ireland that Britain tries to keep in subjection.

Just look at the map of Europe today. There was a time when I wished, like a number of other Irishmen, that Ireland was five hundred miles further out in the Atlantic Ocean or, alternatively, was between Britain and the continent. We might, many of us, wish that we were another five hundred miles out in the Atlantic Ocean today as far as European affairs are concerned; but there is one thing that none of us would wish, and that is to exchange the position of the two islands and go between Britain and the continent. Any Irishman who looks at a map must recognise that, from the Irish point of view, once Britain becomes friendly, once there is no interference with Irish affairs, no Irishman will regret that we are on the far side of Britain and not between Britain and Europe at the present time. In these conditions a strong Britain would be a defence, a barrier to attack from the continent. Once we were free and wanted to maintain our freedom, we would be anxious to see that Britain was strong and that Britain was not attacked – through us as the backdoor, at any rate. Consequently I say what I have already said, perhaps, a number of times today, that it is good British policy to have an independent Ireland that is interested in maintaining its own independence; and, because it is interested in maintaining its own independence and that it has not to fear for that independence from Britain, it is interested in seeing a strong Britain as a shield and a barrier between her and the dangers of the continent.

This is nothing new. It is something you can find at any time in statements I have made since 1920. But it is new in this, that it is the first time that a British Government has taken that view of matters; and it is fortunate both for this country and also for Britain that the present British Government does take that view. Perhaps I might say something further. I might say it is a fortunate circumstance also that the present British Prime Minister is the Prime Minister, because there is no doubt that that agreement could not have been made were it not for the fact that he believed in that policy in Britain's interest and that, at critical times, he used all his influence to try to get the difficulties overcome.

If, then, this agreement is possible now, let nobody say it was possible three, or ten, years ago. The fact that it was not made before we came into office is proof, I take it, that our predecessors could not have made it, because the events or the circumstances were not, let us say, propitious. Neither could it have been made by us before the Constitution was through, for the reasons I have given. Although that is not long ago, nevertheless even since then the agreement could not have been made until the proper circumstances and the proper conditions rose. I am glad it has been made. I believe it bodes well for future understanding between two peoples and that that understanding will communicate itself to people who at the present time in this country do not view political affairs and Irish interests in the way we view them.

"THE POLICY OF THE GOVERNMENT
DOES NOT COME AS A SURPRISE"

With the outbreak of the Second World War, and building on the Anglo-Irish Agreement of a year previously, de Valera rose in the Dáil to announce Irish neutrality. The Taoiseach introduced two bills to enact a state of emergency within the State, even though the state was not involved directly in the conflict. The handling of Irish neutrality in the Second World War was the sustained high point of de Valera's political career.

DAIL ÉIREANN, SEPTEMBER 2, 1939

I might be permitted, before I deal with the Amendment to the Constitution Bill, to explain briefly to the House the circumstances in which we find ourselves. For a considerable time past, I am sure, all deputies, like the Government, have been looking anxiously at the European situation and hoping against hope that it was not going to lead to another European war. Until the very last moment there seemed to be a hope, but now that hope appears to be dispelled; and we, who were anxious not to cause any undue anxiety here amongst our own people, put off as long as possible calling the Dáil to deal with the emergency which would arise if such a state of war came into being. Now, our desire not to put members of the House to the inconvenience of coming here unnecessarily, and also the desire not to create any undue public anxiety, has left us with very little time, now that the emergency has come, to give notice of the measures that we think should, in the national interests, come into law during the crisis. We are therefore

188

asking deputies to come here at short notice, and we are asking them to facilitate the Government by giving us these essential measures with all possible speed.

Deputies will notice on the Order Paper that there is a resolution relating to measures of a guillotine character, but, in consultation, we considered that it was more in accord with the general feeling of the House, probably, and more likely to be understood by our people, if we dispensed with such a motion – although there is extreme urgency for the passing of these measures – and if we left it to the good sense of the members of the Dáil and to the co-operation of other parties, which we confidently expect, to facilitate us in getting these measures through.

Now, the policy of the Government, as indicated by the amendment of the Constitution – because it does indicate it indirectly – does not, I am sure, come either upon the members of the House or upon the public as a surprise. Back in February last I stated in a very definite way that it was the aim of Government policy, in case of European war, to keep this country, if at all possible, out of it. We have pursued that policy, and we intend to pursue it. On another occasion, when speaking in the House of that policy, I pointed out how extremely difficult it was going to be. In a sense, it brings up for the government of a nation that proposes to be neutral in a war of this sort problems much more delicate and much more difficult of solution even than the problems that arise for a belligerent.

It is not, as some people appear to think, sufficient for us to indicate our attitude or to express the desire of our people. It is necessary at every step to protect our own interests in that regard, to avoid giving to any of the belligerents any due cause, and proper cause, of complaint. Of course, when you have powerful states in a war of this sort, each trying to utilise whatever advantage it can for itself, the neutral state, if it is a small state, is always open to considerable pressure. I am stating what every one of you knows to be a fact. Therefore I stated, when I was speaking of our policy of neutrality on a former occasion, that it was a policy which could only be pursued if we had a determined people, people who are determined to stand by their own rights, conscious of the fact that they did not wish to injure anybody or to throw their weight, from the belligerent point of view, on the one side or the other.

As I have said, I do not think our policy comes as a surprise to anybody. We, like other peoples, individuals, have, each one of us, our sympathies in struggles of a kind like the present. In fact, as war is a great human tragedy and as wars are initiated usually for no slight reason – there is generally some fundamental cause of sufficient magnitude to make nations resort to the arbitrament of force – it is only natural that, as human beings, we should judge the situation and, having formed a judgement, sympathise with one side or the other. I know that in this country there are sympathies, very strong sympathies, in regard to the present issues, but I do not think that anybody, no matter what his feelings might be, would suggest that the Government policy, the official policy of the State, should be other than what the Government would suggest.

We, of all nations, know what force used by a stronger nation against a weaker one means. We have known what invasion and partition mean; we are not forgetful of our own history, and as long as our own country or any part of it is subject to force, the application of force, by a stronger nation, it is only natural that our people, whatever sympathies they might have in a conflict like the present, should look at their own country first and should accordingly, in looking at their own country, consider what its interests should be and what its interests are.

It is not as representing the sentiments or feelings of our people that the Government stands before you with this policy. It stands before you as the guardian of the interests of our people, and it is to guard these interests as best we can that we are proposing to follow the policy which I indicated as Government policy as far back as February last. I do not think, therefore, it is necessary for me to add anything – in view of the timely notice and in view of the fact that there has been from no part of the country, as far as I have seen, any strong or any definite objection to that policy – except to say that I am sure all reasonable people must realise the difficulty.

I will pass on, then, directly to the measures that are before you. The first measure relates to the amendment of the Constitution. That is a very simple measure, and I hope we will be unanimous, if that is all possible, about it. It arose in this way: when we were considering the powers that it would be necessary to secure for the Government in an emergency such as has arisen, some doubt was expressed by legal officers as to whether "time of war" might not be narrowly interpreted by courts to mean a time in which the State was actually a participant, a belligerent. That narrow interpretation I do not think had occurred to anybody when the Constitution was being considered in the Dáil. I do not know what view a court might take on the matter; but I think you will agree that in circumstances like the present – in which you would have several nations all around you engaged in war, creating conditions of a type here which are altogether abnormal and which could not exist except in a time of such a general war – an amendment of the Constitution, so that that particular meaning will be applicable to it, is in accord with the general idea of the article of the Constitution.

We are therefore extending "time of war" or, if not extending it, we are making it clear that "time of war" should mean a crisis such as the present, provided, when there are hostilities and conflict about us, there is a resolution both by the Dáil and the Seanad, indicating that such an emergency exists – that such a condition exists. You will therefore observe that in that particular measure we are simply resolving a doubt or, if it is not resolving a doubt, if somebody were to hold that legally there is no doubt – that a time of war can only mean a time at which the State is an active participant – we are, under that assumption, extending the meaning to be that which, I think, everybody would reasonably expect it to cover when we were passing the Constitution.

"WE ARE PREPARED TO FEEL ALL OF THE RESPONSIBILITIES THAT ARE IMPOSED ON ULSTER PEOPLE"

The outbreak of war with Germany in 1939 afforded both governments in Ireland the opportunity to emphasise their similarities and differences with the British Government. Both reactions were predictable. Craigavon, as Prime Minister of Northern Ireland, enthusiastically pledged Northern Ireland's support to the allied war effort; while de Valera asserted Ireland's neutrality.

James Craig (1871–1940), the first Viscount Craigavon, had a distinguished political career, and was, next to Carson, the most successful Unionist leader of the century. Craig was a superb military and political organiser, who acted as Carson's deputy until the latter's resignation as leader of Ulster Unionists in February 1921. In 1921 Craig became the First Prime Minister of Northern Ireland, a position he was to hold until his sudden death in 1940.

The onset of war with Germany offered the Unionist government of Northern Ireland the opportunity to demonstrate its fidelity and loyalty to the Crown. Rising in Stormont, on the same day as de Valera spoke to the Dáil, the speech by the Prime Minister contrasts with that of his Southern counterpart.

Craigavon's speech on the war at Stormont also warned that those who did not support the war effort, or who sought to exploit weaknesses at home because of commitments abroad, would be treated severely as the King's enemies and that "there will be nothing of that kind to disturb the public peace".

STORMONT, SEPTEMBER 2, 1939

I rise today in a difficult state of affairs so far as we here are concerned. I would have called the House together earlier, with your permission, had I thought that any good service would be rendered either to Members or to the community; but as will be realised the situation up to a few days ago did not, in my opinion, justify calling the House together, because I felt that it would not be long before some decision was taken one way or the other which would clear the air so far as being able to address Hon. Members is concerned.

We are met now after most exhausting endeavours on the part of Mr Chamberlain to secure peace throughout the world. He admits it himself, I am sure with a very sad heart, that all he did on behalf of the country failed, and, therefore, we here today are in a state of war, and so are prepared with the rest of the United Kingdom and Empire to face all the responsibilities that are imposed upon Ulster people.

There is no slackening in our loyalty. There is no falling off in our determination to place the whole of our resources at the command of the Government in Britain. They have established now a War Cabinet, and I have already communicated with those of them whom I know best to say privately and, I am sure publicly now as well, that anything we can do here, to facilitate them in the terrible times that lie ahead they have only got to let us know and we will do it. In that I feel I have the backing of the whole House.

We are met also with no mean record behind us of what has been done by the Ulster people. During the past month the response to the call for volunteers has amounted to 45,000, while the actual enrollments in the ordinary forces of the Crown have more than doubled, although hitherto Ulster has stood at the very top so far as enlistment for the Army is concerned. That again is a matter of great satisfaction, but much more requires to be done. I am sure the crisis during the next few days will have nerved many of our youth to rally to the colours where they know that not only are they defending their own homes, but the Empire, and where they must know that their own people and women folk must be guarded so far as possible from dread bombing or any other machinery of war . . .

Then I must touch upon another matter. The Government have for some time past been visualising trouble not only from the common enemy, Germany, and her allies but have also been most carefully thinking out plans with regard to the specific dangers in our own area. Orders have been given for the "B" Special Constabulary to be immediately placed upon the basis they were on before they returned to the drill category, that is to say, patrol category. I would like to explain to the "B" Special Constabulary three of the reasons which moved the Government to withdraw them temporarily from the category of patrol men. We discovered that a certain amount of exaggerating was being made out of the fact that our "B" Specials so well patrolled the roads that visitors here on their annual holiday were getting the impression that they were in an armed camp all the time with these men out; that Ulster could not exist without having an armed force going along the roads and lanes of Ulster. We wished, first of all, to give visitors a free run in Ulster without exhibiting the strength which we always have in the background. That is one reason. Another reason was that the harvest was about to come in, and we wanted to release as many men as possible to assist with what will be an important factor in this war – the production of food at home for the people. Then, thirdly, we desired that the men should get more drill, in case, as has happened, we have to turn them out once more to patrol the countryside, especially the Border. Since then there have been some most regrettable incidents, and I have to inform the House that as an additional precaution against sedition and attacks in our midst we took into our care last night forty-five of the IRA and added them to those already in confinement under grave suspicion. There they will remain until the end of the war unless something justifies us in letting them out.

I would like to make a statement with regard to our

194

proposals. We must ensure that we are in complete control, that we are masters of our own house, and not here at the permission of anybody else. We are not here for the citizens to have their lives and property endangered by a lot of cowardly assassins, men who never hesitate to do what they can to destroy the State. Especially at this moment, when the Empire is at war and when every assistance is wanted, nothing should be done to put sand in the wheels of our defence here at home.

There is then the point, who are these men? I can describe them in a sentence. They are the King's enemies. That is the way to describe men who carry on as they did some few hours ago when they dragged the uniform off one of our volunteers going to the front. Are such men not the King's enemies? Can any punishment be too great for them? . . . (Members: No.) I say not, and the Government are determined that whatever precautions are necessary will be taken, and that whatever severity can be dealt out to men of that class this Government is quite powerful enough, thank God, to mete out. It is determined to see that there will be nothing of that kind to disturb the public peace.

I do not often speak like this. This is, as far as I am concerned, my third experience of a great war. I have seen both sides of the picture. I have seen the fighting side, and I have also seen the home side. It is difficult for people at home to realise what war means abroad. Knowing, as I do, how the men abroad day and night look to the home people to keep steadfast and not to allow anything to be given away during their absence, not only do I feel strongly in issuing the solemn warning to the wrongdoers who may crop up in Ulster, but I feel it is necessary to assure those who are boldly going out under the flag of Britain that they will not be neglected or disgraced in their absence.

" . . . ON THE SIDE OF THE ANGLO-AMERICAN ALLIANCE IS RIGHT AND JUSTICE AND ON THE SIDE OF THE AXIS IS EVIL AND INJUSTICE"

In 1941, the Allied position in the Second World War looked increasingly bleak. Most of Europe was overrun by Hitler and his allies James Dillon, vice president of Fine Gael, broke the all-party consensus in Ireland on neutrality.

In July, speaking on the vote for the Department of External Affairs, Dillon challenged the legitimacy of Irish neutrality. The speech was made in the full knowledge that his view was a minority one, and that his views were not representative of the views of the political establishment or of the electorate at large. Through the speech, Dillon asserts the right of the Irish people to maintain their neutral status. Dillon's speech caused consternation among his colleagues, and particularly to his party leader who spoke soon afterwards.

Dillon recognised that his speech put him at odds with his party and resigned soon afterwards. He rejoined Fine Gael in 1953 and became its leader six years later.

DAIL ÉIREANN, JULY 17, 1941

Recently, a well-known Irish political thinker and philosopher wrote the following words:

"Many democrats share the errors of the totalitarians who see in the voice of the State or the leader the very essence of truth and goodness, for on their side they claim that the will of the people is what makes a course of conduct correct, an opinion true – that their decision cannot be questioned."

I adopt those words, and though the Government's present policy of indifferent neutrality is the policy of the majority of our people, is the policy of the legitimate, elected Government of this country and, as I believe, the policy supported by the majority of members of the Party to which I belong, I say that it is not the correct course of conduct. I say that it is not in the true interest, moral or material, of the Irish people. I, perhaps, am at fault in not having said this much before but I confess that I forbore from saying it in the hope that the Government of the country and the majority of my fellow countrymen would come of their own volition to share my view. I think, over and above the references which I made to the activities of the Minister for the Co-ordination of Defence in the United States of America, it is right to say that, in addition to his diplomatic activities, indefinite news of ambiguous speeches made by him in various centres of the United States of America lead me to believe that he set out, as the unanimous views of the Irish people, views to which I do not subscribe and to which I believe a considerable number of our people do not subscribe.

I think it is reasonable and right that on this occasion of the Foreign Affairs debate in this House I should at least state my view and in stating it I do not want to avoid any particle of the truth. I do not think that it would be any service to this country or any service to the friends of this country to leave them under any illusion as to what the true situation is. I believe the majority of our people are in favour of the Government's policy of neutrality. That is a plain, patent fact, to which all responsible men must have regard. My view, however, is this: recognising that no responsible man could conceivably wish to see his country at war, nevertheless, when the choice lies between dishonour and material ruin on the one hand and the risk of war upon the other, terrible as that risk may be, frightful as the consequences may be of facing it, I think a nation with our traditions should face that risk of war and refuse to submit to a blackmail of terror designed to make it sell its honour and stake its whole material future on the vain hope that it may be spared the passing pain of effort now.

I now reassert the sovereign right of the Irish people alone to determine what the foreign policy of this State shall be now and for all time. I reaffirm my conviction that it is the duty of our people and the Government of this country to resist aggression against the sovereignty of this State whence ever it may come, with all the resources at our disposal. But I say that, in the exercise of the sovereign right of the Irish people to determine the foreign policy of the State, we, the Parliament of Ireland, should ascertain precisely what co-operation Great Britain and the United States of America may require to ensure success against the Nazi attempt at world conquest and, as expeditiously as possible, to afford to the United States of America and Great Britain that co-operation to the limit of our resources. I use that word, "limit", deliberately, and I say that the limit of our resources must be deemed by all reasonable men within this country and outside it to preclude the possibility of sending Irish troops abroad. We have neither the means nor the material with which to equip such forces. But I do say that our resources extend to ascertaining what accommodation the United States of America and Great Britain may require within our territory to resist the Nazi aggression against the world and, having ascertained it, I do say that we, the Irish people, should afford that accommodation here and now. I would say to my friends in this House and outside it to be on their guard lest the Soviet intervention in this war should confuse their minds and lest it should give rise to any false sense of security.

There may be those who would say that the threat to Western Europe is now past and is oriented. Let them beware lest what seems a formidable antagonist to the Nazis now might collapse and we would discover the full fury of an unchequered Nazi aggression turned westward to envelop us and all those around us in the course of their campaign. Let those who feel with me that there is only one thing more loathsome than Communism in the world not suffer their minds to be confused by the fact that Soviet Russia is fighting Germany now. Let them ask themselves: if they were being stalked by a man-eating

198

tiger, would they shoot the jaguar that attacked that tiger, or would they not rejoice to see it cripple the aggressor, and give them time and opportunity to prepare their defence? And even though they looked on with equanimity at that jaguar striking down the tiger that sought to destroy them, it would be unnecessary for them to resolve to make a domestic pet of that jaguar when the conflict was over. The fact that Soviet Russia has become locked in deadly conflict with its prototype, Nazi Germany, is a stroke of luck for which Christian civilisation may devoutly thank Providence, but let it create no false sense of security in our minds. The utmost endeavour of all Christian men is requisite if the Nazi threat to Christianity is to be repelled with any casual co-operation that may come our way. I say, Sir, that aid for Great Britain and the United States from this country is called for on spiritual and material grounds. We are fortunate in Ireland that honour and interest coincide, unlike the unhappy countries of Europe, such as Yugoslavia, Holland, Norway, Belgium and Denmark who, finding honour and interest at variance, chose honour and lost all the worldly possessions that they had. That is not our choice . . .

These countries had to make the choice between honour and interest, and they chose honour and they lost all their material goods. This country mercifully finds that its interests and its honour coincide. I say that the honour of this country is involved, because the justification for our existence as a nation is that for 700 years we fought against injustice. We fought and demonstrated our loyalty to the principle of justice before the nations of the world in our resistance to the British imperial claim to make our country a slave country or to thrust upon our people a religion which our people knew to be false. In that fight we sacrificed men, money and material, generation after generation, until we won. That fight was the sheet anchor of resistance in every suffering country in the world, and the beacon of hope to every oppressed people struggling for their liberties from one end of the world to another.

I say today that the German Nazi Axis seeks to enforce on every small nation in Europe the same beastly tyranny that we successfully fought 700 years to prevent the British Empire imposing on this country. I say – and I say it on the authority of Our Holy Father the Pope – that Germany in every small country which she has conquered has sought, not only to establish political domination, but to impose on the conquered peoples an atheist church which derides Christianity and which forbids the people of those States to serve God according to their consciences. I say – and here again I claim the authority of the Holy Father for the statement – that the Nazi domination, in every small State in Europe where it has been established, imposes upon the Christian peoples of those countries the obligation to choose between the Reich and Christ, and that statement is quoted further from the Pastoral Letter from the German Bishops to their own people . . .

Naval and air bases are required in this country by the United States of America and Great Britain at the present time to prevent the Nazi attempt to cut the lifeline between the United States and Britain now. At present we act the part of Pontius Pilate in asking as between the Axis and the Allies, "What is truth?" and washing our hands and calling the world to witness that this is no affair of ours. I say we know, as between these parties, what the truth is – that on the side of the Anglo-American Alliance is right and justice and on the side of the Axis is evil and injustice.

And I say it is our affair, inasmuch as resistance to evil and injustice is the affair of every Christian State and every Christian man in this world. At the present time the issue involved is whether Christianity will pass through the catacombs or survive. I am convinced that, if Nazis prevail in the world today, Christianity will pass through the catacombs and only those with martyrs' fortitude will retain the Faith. It would be well for all of us to ask ourselves the question whether we are sure – each one of us – of martyrs' fortitude; and, if we are not, whether we are prepared to put our faith in jeopardy – because we might lose it if we were called on to suffer the torture and persecution that Catholics in Nazi-dominated countries have been called on to suffer in the last four years. I say that it is not doubt as to the right and wrong of the moral issues in this struggle that deters us from making the right decision now. It is fear of the German blitz that deters us.

No prudent man will minimise that danger: no just man will deride that fear. It is a terrible danger: it is a thing of which every honest public representative must feel deeply apprehensive, when he thinks of bringing that danger upon the people for whom he stands trustee. It is only when he is certain that failure to face that danger now, failure to urge his people to face that danger now, is a lesser evil than the consequences of sinking our heads in the sand and turning our backs upon the evil, that he would be justified in the eyes of God in asking them to face it. Were Germany to win this war, the future of Ireland is as certain as the knowledge we have that we are here today. The Germans, if they win this war, will face our country as the conquerors of the world and, in order to maintain that conquest and dominion over the Continent of Europe and the ocean highways of the world, the first thing they will do is to demand and seize naval and air bases on our South-west coast and western seaboard.

Having seized these bases and established their advanced guards in them for the control of the Atlantic highway, the German General Staff must say to the German Government: "We have our bases on the west coast of Ireland, but the hinterland of those bases must be made safe for us; and there are only two ways of making it safe. You have either to exterminate the Irish people in that hinterland or you have to Nazify the whole population of Ireland." They cannot exterminate our people, and when they attempt to Nazify them, our people will be required to make the choice between the crooked cross of Nazism and the Cross of Christ – and I know the choice our people will make. Let us open our eyes to what that will mean. Our people, in defence of their religion, will be called upon to face a persecution besides which the worst that Oliver Cromwell did in this country will pale into insignificance.

That has been the experience of every Christian country into which the Nazis have found their way. Those who lose their Faith and those who die in defence of their Faith in the course of that persecution will constitute the monument to the leaders amongst us who fail to face the real issue now, and who prefer the illusory hope of safety to the grim duty of facing facts and doing what is right – facing the danger of war while we still have friends to fight beside us, resolved that the day will never dawn when our people will be called upon to face the malignity and might of a Germany, conqueror of the world, face to face with an island standing alone, without friends or hope of help from anywhere.

If Great Britain cannot be guaranteed supplies of food and warlike material from the United States of America she will be defeated by Germany, and the day she falls we fall too. I say that the Atlantic lifeline joining these two champions of democracy and Christian civilisation at the present time is no stronger than its weakest link. British sailors and British ships are bringing England's supplies – and our supply – through German minefields, German air attack and German submarine attack at the present time. A gap is opening in that lifeline. Extending hands between old friends and new friends, we can close that gap. I know that the closing of it, and acting as the bond between the United States of America and the Commonwealth of Nations at the present time, may bring down upon our heads the fury of the Nazi terror. If what I say is right, then let us face that terror, let us say to them: "Do what you can to our bodies and our goods, but you cannot destroy our souls: no one ever has, and Nazi Germany never will". If this course is right, I say that the people of this country are equal to the weight of whatever burden is put upon them in the cause of Right.

If we see our duty and fail to do it now, we seal for ever this nation's claim to be free and independent. If we prove unequal to our duty in this time, we shall stand forth amongst the nations of the world as a nation claiming all the privileges of independence but unequal to its burdens. Citizen and soldier must bear together today the perils of warlike times. There was a time in the history of the world when it was, perhaps, one of the most disagreeable tasks a civilian could discharge to suggest that his country was facing war, because it seemed like asking others to go out and bear the heat and burden of the day while he stayed safely at home. That day is past. The dangers of every individual citizen of this State are as great as, or greater than, those of any soldier serving in the field. Ireland has citizens and soldiers who would do her no discredit if tribulation were to come upon her now. The question I ask myself is: has she leaders equal to the great decisions and the terrible responsibilities of the times in which we find ourselves?

I say most deliberately, I say before God, that I believe the fate of Christianity in the whole world is hanging in the balance. I say that what has borne itself in upon my mind, above all other things, is the profound conviction that, if this terrible doctrine should prevail in on the world, Christianity will go to the catacombs. It is the profound conviction that none amongst us but he who has a martyr's fortitude will keep the faith, if that should happen, that persuades me that it is Ireland's destiny and duty to protect her children from that danger. I am convinced that Ireland's action in this time may prove vital. It is a queer fate for Providence to reserve for us, that we, a small, comparatively weak country, should be fated to fill so critical a part in so unprecedented a time. Why that should be is something which is known only to divine Providence which placed us where we are. I believe that we have an opportunity of fulfilling our high destiny and proving our loyalty and devotion to things higher than material property and political considerations. I profoundly believe that the Irish people are equal to that destiny, if properly led. I share with the Taoiseach the desire to see our people a united people in these times. I should like to see our people, all together, forgetting past differences, recognising the magnitude of the issues now involved and recognising the ability of this country in matters of this kind to play not only one man's part but to be a host in action. I should like to see this small weak country of Ireland, demonstrate, as it has never been demonstrated in the history of the world before, that it is not by bread alone that man must live and that, whatever may have been the material squabbles that precipitated war in the world, to us the only issue of significance is whether Christianity shall survive and whether mankind all over the world will be left the right to render to God the things that are God's and to render to Caesar the things that are Caesar's. I am convinced that that right is in desperate jeopardy. I am convinced that it is given to us to prove its champion. I am convinced that, were we to accept that charge and face that duty, posterity would have it to tell that in the darkest hours of crisis, when dangers seemed heaviest and perils greatest, Ireland, recognising her destiny, faced it without counting the material cost and that, whatever her material losses were, the undying glory of having stood as a nation for great principles and in defence of the higher freedom had secured for her and her people immortality in human history.

If all the struggle that our fathers made and our grandfathers made meant anything, it must have meant that. They could not have made the sacrifices they made for no other purpose than to give us the right to pass trivial legislation in a Parliament of our own. They meant to give this country a soul, in the deep conviction that their children would keep it a living soul and a burning spirit before the nations of the world. Ours is that glorious opportunity; ours is that terrible responsibility. As it presents itself to me, it is a glorious opportunity. I recognise the appalling nature of the responsibility. I have never said anything in my public life which I feel more sincerely or more deeply and I believe our people are equal to their glorious destiny, equal to bear that burden and the awful responsibility and I pray God they may yet find leaders who will be worthy of them in this time of crisis.

"THE IRELAND THAT WE DREAMED OF"

In 1943 Eamon de Valera was at the pinnacle of his political power. He dominated politics in Ireland in a manner unseen before or since in the twentieth century. His policy of neutrality was universally popular and, as the world war swirled around the fledgling State, de Valera was able to deal with any threats, (material, physical or political) with relative success.

De Valera's love of the Irish language has been noted previously. In the latter part of his career its restoration continued to be important to him. De Valera remained consistently focused on the broad philosophy and ambitions that had fuelled his earlier life.

This speech has become renowned for "the romping of sturdy children, the contests of athletic youths and the laughter of comely maidens" but it is a far deeper speech than that. It is totally focused and emphasises the need to move a nation spiritually in one direction. It is also important to place the speech in context. At the height of the Second World War, neutral Ireland's primary interest was on its own preservation.

RADIO BROADCAST, ST PATRICK'S DAY, 1943

Before the present war began I was accustomed on St Patrick's Day to speak to our kinsfolk in foreign lands, particularly those in the United States, and to tell them year by year of the progress being made towards building up the Ireland of their dreams and ours – the Ireland that we believe is destined to play, by its example and its inspiration, a great part as a nation among the nations.

Acutely conscious though we all are of the misery and

desolation in which the greater part of the world is plunged, let us turn aside for a moment to that ideal Ireland that we would have. That Ireland which we dreamed of would be the home of a people who valued material wealth only as the basis of right living, of a people who were satisfied with frugal comfort and devoted their leisure to the things of the spirit – a land whose countryside would be bright with cosy homesteads, whose fields and villages would be joyous with the sounds of industry, with the romping of sturdy children, the contests of athletic youths and the laughter of comely maidens, whose firesides would be forums for the wisdom of serene old age. It would, in a word, be the home of a people living the life that God desires that man should live.

With the tidings that make such an Ireland possible, St Patrick came to our ancestors 1,500 years ago, promising happiness here as well as happiness hereafter. It was the pursuit of such an Ireland that later made our country worthy to be called the Island of Saints and Scholars. It was the idea of such an Ireland, happy, vigorous, spiritual, that fired the imagination of our poets, that made successive generations of patriotic men give their lives to win religious and political liberty, and that will urge men in our own future generations to die, if need be, so that these liberties may be preserved.

One hundred years ago the Young Irelanders, by holding up the vision of such an Ireland before the people, inspired our nation and moved it spiritually as it had hardly been moved since the golden age of Irish civilisation. Fifty years after the Young Irelanders, the founders of the Gaelic League similarly inspired and moved the people of their day, as did later the leaders of the Volunteers. We of this time, if we have the will and the active enthusiasm, have the opportunity to inspire and move our generation in like manner. We can do so by keeping this thought of a noble future for our country constantly before our minds, ever seeking in action to bring that future into being, and ever remembering that it is to our nation as a whole that future must apply.

Thomas Davis, laying down the national programme for his

generation, spoke first of the development of our material resources as he saw them, of the wealth that lay in our harbours, our rivers, our bogs and our mines. Characteristically, however, he passed on to emphasise the still more important development of the resources of the spirit:

"Our young artisans must be familiar with the arts of design and the natural sciences connected with their trade; and so of our farmers; and both should, beside, have that general information which refines and expands the mind, that knowledge of Irish history and statistics that makes it national and those accomplishments and sports which make leisure profitable and home joyous.

Our cities must be stately with sculpture, pictures and buildings, and our fields glorious with peaceful abundance."

"But this is an utopia!" he exclaimed, but when questioned, "Is it?" he answered:

"No: but the practicable (that is, the attainable) object of those who know our resources. To seek it is the solemn, unavoidable duty of every Irishman."

Davis's answer should be our answer also. We are aware that Davis was mistaken in the extent of some of the material resources which he catalogued, but we know, none the less, that our material resources are sufficient for a population much larger than we have at present, if we consider their use with a due appreciation of their value in a right philosophy of life. And we know also that the spiritual resources which Davis asked the nation to cultivate are inexhaustible.

For many the pursuit of the material is a necessity. Man, to express himself fully and to make the best use of the talents God has given him, needs a certain minimum of comfort and leisure. A section of our people have not yet this minimum. They rightly strive to secure it, and it must be our aim and the aim of all who are just and wise to assist in the effort. But many have got more than is required and are free, if they choose, to devote themselves more completely to cultivating the things of the mind, and in particular those which mark us out as a distinct nation.

The first of these latter is the national language. It is for us what no other language can be. It is our very own. It is more than a symbol; it is an essential part of our nationhood. It has been moulded by the thought of a hundred generations of our forebears. In it is stored the accumulated experience of a people, our people, who even before Christianity was brought to them were already cultured and living in a well-ordered society. The Irish language spoken in Ireland today is the direct descendant without break of the language our ancestors spoke in those far-off days.

As a vehicle of three thousand years of our history, the language is for us precious beyond measure. As the bearer to us of a philosophy, of an outlook on life deeply Christian and rich in practical wisdom, the language today is worth far too much to dream of letting it go. To part with it would be to abandon a great part of ourselves, to lose the key of our past, to cut away the roots from the tree. With the language gone we could never aspire again to being more than half a nation.

For my part, I believe that this outstanding mark of our nationhood can be preserved and made forever safe by this generation. I am indeed certain of it, but I know that it cannot be saved without understanding and co-operation and effort and sacrifice. It would be wrong to minimise the difficulties. They are not slight. The task of restoring the language as the everyday speech of our people is a task as great as any nation ever undertook. But it is a noble task. Other nations have succeeded in it, though in their case, when the effort was begun, their national language was probably more widely spoken among their people than is ours with us. As long as the language lives, however, on the lips of the people as their natural speech in any substantial part of this land we are assured of success if – *if* we are in earnest.

It is a task in which the attitude of the individual is what counts most. It is upon the individual citizen, upon you who are listening to me, that the restoration of the language finally depends. The State and public institutions can do much to assist, but if the individual has not the inclination or the will-power to make the serious efforts initially required or to persevere till reasonable fluency is attained, outside aids will be of little use. The individual citizen must desire actively to restore the language and be prepared to take the pains to learn it and to use it, else real progress cannot be made.

Today there is no dearth of books and reading matter and other facilities for those who wish to begin their study or to improve their knowledge. Twenty years of work in the schools has brought some knowledge of the language to hundreds of thousands of our young people. If these make it a practice to read and to speak it to one another, even a little at the beginning, particularly in the case of those living in the same house, they will add to their store continually through conversation until all sense of effort has disappeared and the words and phrases come naturally and correctly as they are needed. Each additional person who speaks the language makes the task of all the others easier. Each one who opposes the language and each one who knowing it fails to use it makes the task of those striving to restore it more difficult. For those who can speak it, to neglect doing so, whenever and wherever it can be understood, is a betrayal of those who gave their lives so that not merely a free but an Irish-speaking nation might be possible. Were all those who now have a knowledge of the language to speak it consistently on all occasions when it could reasonably be spoken, our task would be easy.

Let us all, then, do our part this year. The restoration of the unity of the national territory and the restoration of the language are the greatest of our uncompleted national tasks. Let us devote this year especially to the restoration of the language; let the year be one in which the need for this restoration will be constantly in our thoughts and the language itself as much as possible on our lips.

The physical dangers that threaten, and the need for unceasing vigilance in the matters of defence as well as unremitting attention to the serious day-to-day problems that the war has brought upon us, should not cause us to neglect our duty to the language. Time is running against us in this matter of the language.

We cannot afford to postpone our effort. We should remember also that the more we preserve and develop our individuality and our characteristics as a distinct nation, the more secure will be our freedom and the more valuable our contribution to humanity when this war is over.

Bail ó Dhia oraibh agus bail go gcuire Sé ar an obair atá romhainn. Go gcúmhdai Dia sinn agus gur fiú sinn choíche, mar náisiún, na tiolacaí a thug Pádraig chugainn. Go dtuga an tUilechumhachtadh. A thug slán sinn go dtí seo ón anacháin is ón mí-ádh atá ar oiread sin náisiún eile de bharr an chogaidh seo, scath agus didean dúinn go dtí an deireadh, agus go ndeonaí Sé agus fiú sinn cion uasal a dhéanamh sa saol nua atá romhainn.

"THERE IS A SMALL NATION THAT STOOD ALONE . . .
FOR SEVERAL HUNDRED YEARS AGAINST AGGRESSION"

In his VE address broadcast on May 13, 1945, Churchill had, in the course of a review of the war in Europe, attacked Irish neutrality. Churchill was also angered by de Valera's visit to the German Legation in Dublin to sympathise on the death of Hitler. Churchill later wrote a letter to his son that "it was a speech which, perhaps, I should not have made, but it was made in the heat of the moment. We had just come through the war and I had been looking around at our victories; the idea of Éire sitting at our feet without giving us a hand annoyed me." Churchill's attack ignored the covert support given by Ireland to the Allied side during the war, within the constraints of military neutrality.

In his post-war address, delivered on radio three days later, de Valera reviewed Irish policy throughout the war and emphasised the absence of choice on the issue of neutrality. He stressed the need to be prepared for future calamities, given the uncertain and volatile state of world politics. De Valera then turned to the issues raised by Churchill three days earlier.

RADIO BROADCAST, MAY 16, 1945

. . . Certain newspapers have been very persistent in looking for my answer to Mr Churchill's recent broadcast. I know the kind of answer I am expected to make. I know the answer that first springs to the lips of every man of Irish blood who heard or read that speech, no matter in what circumstances or in what part of the world he found himself.

I know the reply I would have given a quarter of a century

ago. But I have deliberately decided that that is not the reply I shall make tonight. I shall strive not to be guilty of adding any fuel to the flames of hatred and passion which, if continued to be fed, promise to burn up whatever is left by the war of decent human feeling in Europe.

Allowances can be made for Mr Churchill's statement, however unworthy, in the first flush of his victory. No such excuse could be found for me in this quieter atmosphere. There are, however, some things which it is my duty to say, some things which it is essential to say. I shall try to say them as dispassionately as I can.

Mr Churchill makes it clear that, in certain circumstances, he would have violated our neutrality and that he would justify his action by Britain's necessity. It seems strange to me that Mr Churchill does not see that this, if accepted, would mean that Britain's necessity would become a moral code and that when this necessity became sufficiently great, other people's rights were not to count.

It is quite true that other great powers believe in this same code – in their own regard – and have behaved in accordance with it. That is precisely why we have the disastrous succession of wars – World War No. 1 and World War No. 2 – and shall it be World War No. 3?

Surely, Mr Churchill must see that, if his contention be admitted in our regard, a like justification can be framed for similar acts of aggression elsewhere and no small nation adjoining a great power could ever hope to be permitted to go its own way in peace.

It is, indeed, fortunate that Britain's necessity did not reach the point when Mr Churchill would have acted. All credit to him that he successfully resisted the temptation which, I have no doubt, many times assailed him in his difficulties and to which I freely admit many leaders might have easily succumbed. It is, indeed, hard for the strong to be just to the weak, but acting justly always has its rewards.

By resisting his temptation in this instance, Mr Churchill,

instead of adding another horrid chapter to the already bloodstained record of the relations between England and this country, has advanced the cause of international morality an important step – one of the most important, indeed, that can be taken on the road to the establishment of any sure basis for peace.

As far as the peoples of these two islands are concerned, it may, perhaps, mark a fresh beginning towards the realisation of that mutual comprehension to which Mr Churchill has referred and for which he has prayed and for which, I hope, he will not merely pray but work, also, as did his predecessor who will yet, I believe, find the honoured place in British history which is due to him, as certainly he will find it in any fair record of the relations between Britain and ourselves.

That Mr Churchill should be irritated when our neutrality stood in the way of what he thought he vitally needed, I understand, but that he or any thinking person in Britain or elsewhere should fail to see the reason for our neutrality, I find it hard to conceive.

I would like to put a hypothetical question – it is a question I have put to many Englishmen since the last war. Suppose Germany had won the war, had invaded and occupied England, and that after a long lapse of time and many bitter struggles she was finally brought to acquiesce in admitting England's right to freedom, and let England go, but not the whole of England, all but, let us say, the six southern counties.

These six southern counties, those, let us suppose, commanding the entrance to the narrow seas, Germany had singled out and insisted on holding herself with a view to weakening England as a whole and maintaining the security of her own communications through the Straits of Dover.

Let us suppose, further, that after all this had happened Germany was engaged in a great war in which she could show that she was on the side of the freedom of a number of small nations. Would Mr Churchill as an Englishman who believed that his own nation had as good a right to freedom as any other

– not freedom for a part merely, but freedom for the whole –
would he, whilst Germany still maintained the partition of his
country and occupied six counties of it, would he lead this
partitioned England to join with Germany in a crusade? I do not
think Mr Churchill would.

Would he think the people of partitioned England an object
of shame if they stood neutral in such circumstances? I do not
think Mr Churchill would.

Mr Churchill is proud of Britain's stand alone, after France
had fallen and before America entered the war.

Could he not find in his heart the generosity to acknowledge
that there is a small nation that stood alone, not for one year or
two, but for several hundred years against aggression; that
endured spoliations, famines, massacres in endless succession;
that was clubbed many times into insensibility, but that each
time, on returning consciousness, took up the fight anew; a
small nation that could never be got to accept defeat and has
never surrendered her soul?

Mr Churchill is justly proud of his nation's perseverance
against heavy odds. But we in this island are still prouder of our
people's perseverance for freedom through all the centuries. We
of our time have played our part in that perseverance, and we
have pledged ourselves to the dead generations who have
preserved intact for us this glorious heritage, that we too will
strive to be faithful to the end, and pass on this tradition
unblemished.

Many a time in the past there appeared little hope except
that hope to which Mr Churchill referred, that by standing fast a
time would come when, to quote his own words, "the tyrant
would make some ghastly mistake which would alter the whole
balance of the struggle".

I sincerely trust, however, that it is not thus our ultimate
unity and freedom will be achieved, though as a younger man I
confess I prayed even for that, and indeed at times saw no
other.

In latter years I have had a vision of a nobler and better

ending, better for both our people and for the future of mankind. For that I have now been long working. I regret that it is not to this nobler purpose that Mr Churchill is lending his hand rather than, by the abuse of a people who have done him no wrong, trying to find in a crisis like the present excuse for continuing the injustice of the mutilation of our country.

I sincerely hope that Mr Churchill has not deliberately chosen the latter course but, if he has, however regretfully we may say it, we can only say, be it so.

Meanwhile, even as a partitioned small nation, we shall go on and strive to play our part in the world, continuing unswervingly to work for the cause of true freedom and for peace and understanding between all nations.

As a community which has been mercifully spared from all the major sufferings, as well as from the blinding hates and rancours engendered by the present war, we shall endeavour to render thanks to God by playing a Christian part in helping, so far as a small nation can, to bind up some of the gaping wounds of suffering humanity.

"THIS BILL WILL END FOR EVER THIS
COUNTRY'S LONG AND TRAGIC ASSOCIATION
WITH THE BRITISH CROWN"

*John A Costello (1891–1976) was born in Dublin and educated
at O'Connell's Christian Brothers School, University College
Dublin and the King's Inns. He was Attorney General from
1926–32 and elected as TD for the constituency of Dublin
County in 1933. By 1948 he had developed a substantial legal
practice at the Bar.*

*The results of the election of 1948 offered the option of an
alternative government to Fianna Fáil through a coalition of the
opposition parties and some independents. Costello was asked to
head the government because Richard Mulcahy, leader of Fine
Gael, was deemed by other parties to carry too much baggage
from the Civil War. Costello also led the second Inter-Party
Government between 1954–57.*

*At a press conference in September 1948, while in Canada,
Costello announced the Repeal of the External Relations Act, by
which Ireland was part of the British Commonwealth. The
Republic of Ireland was formally inaugurated on Easter Monday
1949.*

*In November 1948, on the second stage of the Republic of
Ireland Bill, Costello set out the reasons for moving to Republic
status.*

DAIL ÉIREANN, NOVEMBER 24, 1948

. . . In moving this motion, Sir, it would be the merest
hypocrisy on my part if I did not give expression in public to

216

the feelings of pride which animate me in being privileged to sponsor this Bill and recommend it to the Dáil for acceptance. Equally, however, it would be quite unworthy if I did not express my feelings of deep humility as I approach the discharge of the duty which I have to fulfil. Those sentiments of humility are genuinely and sincerely felt, and arise from the certain realisation and knowledge that there are on every side of this House people far more worthy, who have merited far more than I have, to fulfil the privilege accorded to me by the turn of events.

This Bill which I am introducing and recommending for acceptance to the House is not a Bill merely to repeal a particular statute which has caused much discussion and considerable controversy. It is a Bill which, when enacted, will have consequences which will mark it as a measure ending an epoch and beginning what I hope will be a new and brighter epoch for the people of this country. This Bill will end, and end forever, in a simple, clear and unequivocal way this country's long and tragic association with the institution of the British Crown and will make it manifest beyond equivocation or subtlety that the national and international status of this country is that of an independent republic. It is necessary for me to state what I believe to be the effect of this Bill as clearly and as emphatically as possible so that there can be no arguments in the future, no misunderstandings, no suggestions that lurking around the political structure of this State there is some remnant or residue of that old institution and that politicians might be able to seize upon that for their own purposes, for the purposes of vote-catching or for the purposes of evoking again the anti-British feeling which has been such fruitful ground on which politicians have played for many years past. While it is necessary for me to make as clear as words can make it what we intend and believe to be the purpose and effect of this Bill, it is equally necessary for me to emphasise with equal clarity and force that this measure is not designed nor was it conceived in any spirit of hostility to the British people or to the institution of the British Crown. Least of all is there any notion of hostility to the person who now occupies the throne in England, who has carried out his duties with efficiency and dignity, whose illness we regret and whose recovery we hope will be speedy.

Again, I want to emphasise that this Bill was not conceived nor is it brought into this House in a mood of flamboyant patriotism or aggressive nationalism, nor in a spirit of irresponsible isolationism nor with any desire or intention in any way to dislocate or interrupt the delicate mechanism of that community of nations known as the Commonwealth of Nations with which, in one shape or another, we have had some association over the last quarter of a century. This Bill, as I want to state – and to restate, if necessary – is a constructive proposal, and not one intended to be destructive or to have any centrifugal effect upon another nation or nations, and particularly those nations that form the Commonwealth of Nations. It is recommended to this Dáil for what it is and what it is intended to be and what I believe it to be; it is recommended as an instrument of domestic peace, of national unity and of international concord and goodwill. We have – and it is hardly necessary for me to say it – had rather too much in the last 25 years of constitutional law and constitutional lawyers. For 25 years, we have had arid, futile and unending discussions as to the nature and character of our constitutional position and our constitutional and international relations with Great Britain, with the other members of the Commonwealth of Nations and with other foreign nations of the comity of nations. It is hoped that this Bill will put an end to these arid and futile discussions, and make our international and constitutional position clear beyond all ambiguity and beyond all argument.

It will be necessary for me in the course of the remarks that I have to make in dealing with this Bill to refer critically to the effect of certain measures that have been passed in the years gone by and to suggest the possible effects and repercussions that they may have had upon our constitutional position. I do not intend in the course of my discussions or observations on this measure to enter upon those discussions or observations in a spirit of argument or to press that this or that view is the correct one. What I hope to do is to show that by reason of the legislation of the past 25 years, we have now reached a position which justifies the enactment of this Bill now before the Dáil. I do sincerely desire that the discussion on this measure will neither lead to nor be led into a competition of claims between this Party or that Party, this person or that person as to the part one or other played or did not play in the national events and policies of the past quarter of a century. While I am desirous that that above all should be avoided, I am equally desirous that my object shall be achieved; and I want to say here at the outset that it is my ambition that that object will be achieved. Anything I have to say cannot be regarded as and is not intended to be a justification or apologia or indictment of any Party and, least of all, a personal justification of my own policies or my own past.

I would like in the course of this discussion if acknowledgement were made and recognition given to all Parties and to all persons who each, in whatever measure, contributed a quota or even a mite towards the common cause in the national advancement. We have had, as I indicated, too many constitutional discussions and too many occasions for these arid constitutional arguments. We have as a consequence been too long occupied, divided and frustrated by fruitless and useless controversy and, therefore, I do not want to make this occasion an occasion of further bickering and further controversy, particularly when this Bill was conceived with the primary purpose, as I shall explain later on, and the compelling motives in my mind and in the minds of my colleagues, of bringing unity here in this country and particularly in this part of our country amongst those sections of our people that have hitherto been divided and of putting an end to the bitterness and personalities which have poisoned the stream of our national life blood during the past 25 years.

In that spirit I approach the task that I have to fulfil, and I do earnestly ask Deputies to follow that headline, which I have set for myself and which I hope and trust I shall follow. I earnestly ask Deputies, in the course of the observations I have to make – which, I am afraid, will have to be rather lengthy – to give me the indulgence of their charity if I should, either by word or phrase, stray beyond the bounds of those limits that I have set myself.

This Bill burns no bridges leading either to national unity or to closer friendship with the people of our neighbouring country, Great Britain. It places no obstacle in the way of the progress which we hope to make towards both those goals. I have said, and I want to repeat it again, because I am addressing here today not merely the audience that is immediately listening to me but to a wider audience, that not merely is this measure intended to be a Bill to promote domestic peace and harmony, but it is a measure designed to achieve and one which we believe will achieve a greater measure of friendship and goodwill than has ever existed in the long and tragic association between Great Britain and Ireland. We want to increase that friendship and that goodwill. This Bill is not a mere expression of nationalistic egoism or isolationism. We are a small nation and we require friends. It is only, as we believe, by goodwill and friendship and fellowship and the recognition of our mutual rights and the appreciation of our reciprocal interest that that measure of goodwill and friendship which we wish to achieve shall be achieved.

Doubtless, there have been in the past few weeks some efforts made to bedevil the situation which we are considering here today. The dying embers of reaction and imperialism sent forth a few flickering flames in an effort to light the fires of turmoil and class hatred and hatred between the two peoples and between sections of our peoples here in Ireland. I am glad to say here today that those efforts have failed; I am glad to say that the fears and apprehensions that were aroused by that poisonous and malicious propaganda can be allayed and be calmed.

It will, I am convinced, when this measure has passed this House, still more when it becomes law, be apparent to the people of this country and to the people in every country that is watching us here now and that has watched us for the last few weeks that as a result of this, this country will be able to take its place, without equivocation, without argument, without subtlety, without having to apologise, explain or discuss as one of the independent nations of the earth, able to do its part and to contribute its quota to the maintenance of peace and the solution of the international problems that face each nation in the world today.

Let me say a few more words about our relations with Great Britain. I believe that as a result of this measure, our relationship with that country will be far closer and far better and will be put upon a better and firmer foundation than it ever has been before. Deputies and those interested will only have to look in retrospect upon the history of this country during the past 25 or 26 years to see that every step made in advance towards the development and the recognition of our national and international sovereignty brought with it, between Great Britain and this country, an additional measure of good feeling and goodwill.

It is a sobering thought that many people who are now in the flower of their manhood and womanhood were not born on the 6th December, 1921, when the Treaty was signed. Many of those do not know anything about the history of the previous years, and the conflicts that took place between this country and Great Britain, but whatever people may think of that Treaty of the 6th December 1921, at least it can be now said in retrospect that it did play its part in bringing about closer relationship and an end of the centuries-old feud between the peoples of these two neighbouring islands.

For ten long years those people who undertook the duty and the task of honouring the signatures to the Treaty walked the via dolorosa of those bitter years, the details of which I do not intend to recall, but at the end of those ten years, when the efforts of the representatives of this country at imperial conferences and international gatherings had borne their fruit, those developments had brought us to the point where we had achieved for this country international recognition as one of the sovereign countries of the world, and we had swept away all the old dead wood of British constitutional theory that lay or appeared to lie in the path of constitutional progress. All those contacts and those controversies that took place both at the imperial conferences and at the international gatherings at which this country was represented, where the efforts of the representatives of this country were directed towards getting complete international recognition for the country and achieving complete freedom for the institutions that were set up under the Treaty, gave their contribution to the goodwill that grew up in spite of all the difficulties and trials of those times between the peoples of these two islands.

After 1932, when the first Government of this State was succeeded by another Government with a different policy, a Government that carried out different Acts, carried out a different policy, as the years went on they too expressed their desire and, be it said, achieved their purpose to some considerable extent of bringing together still more closely the relationship between Great Britain and Ireland and the peoples of these two neighbouring islands. With the Removal of the Oath Act, with the enactment of the Constitution of 1937, with the handing back of the ports, with the recognition of our neutrality during the war, all these things contributed their quota in bringing about the end of those old feuds and bitternesses that divided the peoples of these two islands for centuries.

This measure, in my view, and I recommend it to the Dáil as such, is not merely the logical outcome but the inevitable result of a peaceful political evolution that has gone on here in this country over the past 25 years. During those years we have had close association, some bond of one kind or another, between each of the States and nations forming what is now know as the

Commonwealth of Nations. There has been a recognition that this country of ours is a mother country, a country with a spiritual empire beyond the seas and there has grown up, I believe, from my own experience, and particularly from the experiences which I had in Canada during my visit within the last few months, between those nations and this old nation of ours an abundant goodwill and fellow feeling and an intense desire that we should prosper and go the road that our own people wish to walk.

For reasons which I think are cogent it would be unthinkable for us, by the action which this Bill proposes to take, to go further away from those nations with which we have had such long and, I think, such fruitful association in the past 25 or 26 years. Great Britain, of course, is the dominant partner in that association. Nothing that can be done by this measure will in any way be a retrograde step in our relations with that country. Our people pass freely from here to England. We have trade and commerce of mutual benefit to each other. We have somewhat the same pattern of life, somewhat the same respect for democratic principles and institutions. The English language in our Constitution is recognised as the second official language of this nation. But we have still stronger ties than even those. Our missionary priests, nuns and brothers have gone to England and have brought the faith there, and are giving no inadequate contribution to the spiritual uplift which is so necessary in the atheistic atmosphere of the world today. We have our teachers there, lay and religious; we have our doctors and professional men there; we have our working men and our craftsmen and our girls who have gone over to earn a living there. All these things would, in normal circumstances, bring about and create and necessitate a feeling of fellowship and goodwill between our two countries. There is no reason why that should not continue. There is no reason why we should not get rid of all these causes of friction which have kept us apart for so many years. This Bill gets rid of one cause of friction and leaves only one to be removed, Partition . . .

. . . Why are we doing this? Why are we doing this now? Why are we leaving the Commonwealth of Nations? Why are we breaking the last tenuous link with the Crown? To these people to whom I address myself here today, people of goodwill, people who are entitled to an answer, I have already addressed the words with which I opened my remarks – that so far from having any feelings of hostility towards Great Britain, the British Crown, or the British people, we want to clear away from our past, the past of this country, all obstacles which are a hindrance to the greater and freer development of good relations between our two countries. Many of those people who are asking these questions and bona fide looking for information upon them, do not know anything at all, or practically anything, about the history of this country or its relationship with Great Britain in the years gone by. They know none of the details of the tragic story of British and Irish relationships. I suppose it is true to say that the vast majority of the British people who are looking now at us and wondering why we are doing this, have not the remotest idea or the smallest conception of the wrongs that were inflicted by their own nation upon this country and the people of this country in the centuries gone by. It is because they are asking for information, wanting to be convinced and genuinely anxious to understand our point of view, that I must take a little time in endeavouring to answer the questions to which I have referred.

In answering these questions, it will be necessary for me to say some hard things about the British Crown and the British people, but those who wish to hear or to read my remarks will take them in the context in which they are uttered and the spirit in which I am making them, as I have to recall those past events or to pass in review some of the tragic circumstances or considerations, in order that those people may know and understand why it has been impossible for this country permanently to accept the institution of the Crown as one of our Irish institutions. Again I want to ask those people, the people of goodwill to whom I am addressing myself, not to be misled by the ignorant, ill-formed, malicious and poisonous propaganda that has been spread by some sections of the Press in the last few weeks, nor to let those sections of the Press twist my remarks, turn them into anything in the nature of an endeavour, on my part or on the part of my colleagues or those who support us, to create anti-British feeling or to give another twist to the lion's tail. I want those people to be informed and, being informed, to appreciate and understand and sympathise with our ideals and our aspirations and accept as genuine our efforts towards the promotion of an ever increasing goodwill between our two countries.

This Bill, as I have said at the outset, will close the long and tragic story of the relations between our two countries based upon an acceptance of the institution of the Crown in such a way as to make it certain that there can be no misconception or ambiguity. We hope that, after this Bill is passed, it will open a new era in our relationships and while one tragic chapter is closed a newer and brighter one will be opened in our international record, in the record between Great Britain and this country. During the whole course of that long sustained struggle for political, civil and religious liberty the Irish people never lost the consciousness that they are not and never were a British people, that they were a race, an Irish race with the distinctive nationality, a distinctive language, an ancient culture all their own. It is impossible for a people who for centuries had fought for and been denied those four essential freedoms of which President Roosevelt spoke and of which it is now so popular to speak – Freedom of Speech, Freedom of Worship, Freedom from Fear and Freedom from Want – to associate those ideas, those four freedoms, with the constitutional forms and ideals of the British common law, with the forms and ideas of the British conquerors. Those conquerors persistently refused those freedoms to the Irish people.

As a learned professor has said quite recently, Professor Wheare, Professor of Constitutional Law – I quote him from the *Sunday Times* of October 24, 1948:

"It is difficult for those who regarded the Crown as the badge of servitude to accept it as the badge of freedom."

That phrase summarises our whole attitude. We could never accept, not matter what our views may have been or may be, as Irishmen, the Crown as a badge of freedom. To the minds of a lot of people, of most Irish people – I would almost say, all Irish people, because of our instincts and our tradition and our history, the institution of the Crown has been regarded as a badge of servitude and those instincts can never be eradicated from the tradition and the blood of any Irishman.

I mentioned some of the considerations which bore in upon our people and made it impossible for us to regard the Crown as a badge of freedom. In the course of the remarks that I will make later on, I will have to refer to the symbol of the Crown as it was stated to be in the Statute of Westminster and the symbol of free association, but may I here in this context say this, that those of us who worked in the Imperial Conferences of 1926, 1929 and 1930 to clear away all those real or apparent obstacles to freedom for our Legislature or for this country in its international relations, endeavoured to create the situation where that old instinctive feeling of the Crown being the symbol of servitude would be accepted by our people as the symbol of free association, and that they regarded it as nothing else but a symbol.

Having achieved our purpose of getting it stated in the most solemn way that it was a symbol of freedom, a symbol of association, then our effort was to make the position clear in that way to our own people and so to try to reconcile them, at least for a time, to the institution of the British Crown. But no people can be expected willingly and permanently to accept as part of their political institutions the symbol of the British Crown, when fidelity to the Catholic faith, the faith of the vast majority of our Irish people, was throughout the years regarded as disaffection and disloyalty to the British Crown, when love of country became treason to the British Crown, when every attempt to secure personal rights and national liberty was deemed rebellion against the Crown, when entry into the humble homes of Irishmen, to arrest them as a prelude to their gibbeting or shooting, was demanded in the name of the King. Crown rent, quite rent and rack rents were demanded in the King's name. The evictions carried out during the land war were carried out to enforce the King's writ. The prosecutions against our patriots, against those who fought in the land war, were carried out by His Majesty's attorneys and sentences were passed by His Majesty's judges. Many of us remember during the days of our childhood, not being taught, but having it almost instinctively in our minds and in our blood, that the harp beneath the crown was the symbol of servitude and that the harp without the crown was the symbol of freedom . . .

THE MOTHER AND CHILD CONTROVERSY

After the formation of the first Inter-party Government, headed by John A Costello (Fine Gael), Sean MacBride (Clann na Poblachta) and William Norton (Labour), the new government sent a telegram to the Vatican:

". . . desiring, to repose at the feet of Your Holiness the assurance of our filial loyalty and of our devotion to your August Person, as well as our firm resolve to be guided in all our work by the teaching of Christ, and to strive for the attainment of a social order in Ireland based on Christian principles."

In replacing de Valera, the more liberal coalition felt the need to demonstrate its adherence to Rome. The key Catholic influence on government affairs was Dr John Charles McQuaid, the Archbishop of Dublin and a close personal friend of both Eamon de Valera and John A Costello.

The Minister for Health in the government was Noel Browne, a Trinity educated medical doctor who had been appointed to the government on the first day he took his seat as a Clann na Poblachta TD. In 1950, after successfully dealing with the national scourge of tuberculosis, he tried to re-introduce the Fianna Fáil-initiated Mother and Child scheme, which offered, without a means test, free and voluntary ante- and post-natal care for mothers, and for children up to the age of sixteen.

The Church took the view that the proposed scheme was too radical, that the right to provide healthcare belonged in the first instance to parents rather than the state. The Hierarchy also viewed the proposal as interfering with the rights of the church in education, the rights of the medical profession and of voluntary institutions.

The Hierarchy met with Dr Browne to discuss their objections. The Hierarchy rejected the proposal, and Browne found himself without ally in the government, in any of its parties. He resigned from office on April 12, 1950. The Mother and Child controversy damaged the first Inter- Party Government and it never recovered from its wounds.

The three key government ministers in the affair, Costello, MacBride and Browne, all spoke in the Dáil on the issue in April 1951. The speeches are noteworthy for the bile and bitterness of former colleagues, and for the particular rancour between MacBride and Browne, erstwhile members of the same party. An Taoiseach, John A Costello, spoke first.

"THERE IS NO LIMIT TO THE CAPACITY OF DR BROWNE TO DECEIVE HIMSELF"

DAIL ÉIREANN, APRIL 12, 1951

Throughout the long and agonising months that have just passed, I and three or four of my colleagues gave of our very best, in a sincere desire to help our then colleague, the Minister for Health, and to get him out of the difficulties in which he by his own obstinacy had found himself. Repeatedly I said to him that we were willing and anxious to help him in any possible way and that he could call upon us at any time. The last words I addressed to the Minister for Health as he left his Cabinet colleagues last Friday, after the Government decision had been made, were to ask him to remember that in the last months we had been willing to help him and, as he was going away to consider his decision, I wanted him to know that we still were willing to help him and did not want to turn the corkscrew on him. My attitude during all those frightful months received the thanks embodied in the document read here today by Deputy Dr Browne . . .

I am authorised to give an account as given to me by His Grace the Archbishop and as subsequently confirmed, I believe, to Dr Browne himself by the Most Rev. Secretary to the Irish Hierarchy, Dr Staunton. I do so, not for the purpose of giving any further publicity to matters to which I would very much prefer not to have given any publicity, but merely because I have been attacked, and my colleagues have been attacked, in our integrity and in our public honour, and I am entitled to defend myself and my colleagues. I intend to do so, I hope in all kindliness to my former colleague and in all charity, so far as I can in the circumstances.

I was told by His Grace the Archbishop of Dublin, on October 12, that he had just had, the day before, an incredible interview with the then Minister for Health. I do not wish to wound my former colleague in any way but I must say, in defence of myself and my colleague, that when I am charged with telling him, a few days afterwards, that there was no trouble with the Hierarchy and that he had satisfied them, I am entitled to give the atmosphere in which I received the courteous information as to the troubles and worries of the Hierarchy about this mother and child health scheme. Deputies will remember that Dr Browne has stated that it was his impression that he had satisfied the Hierarchy, or rather, I should say, the Archbishop and two Bishops who were deputed on behalf of the Hierarchy to see him – that he had satisfied them on all points.

May I say, in parentheses, and in the context of a wider issue on this matter, that all this matter was intended to be private and to be adjusted behind closed doors and was never intended to be the subject of public controversy, as it has been made by the former Minister for Health now, and it would have been dealt with in that way had there been any reasonable person, other than the former Minister for Health, engaged in the negotiations at that time. The Hierarchy were anxious that they should treat him in all courtesy and in all kindness. Dr Browne, in his statement today, when referring to that interview, first of all states that he was under the impression, "erroneously as it now appears", that he had satisfied His Grace and Their Lordships in all respects of that scheme. The correspondence which I must read will show the allegation that he made against me, that I had deluded him and tricked him by corroborating the fact, as he said, that he had satisfied His Grace and Their Lordships on all matters . . .

I told Dr Browne that His Grace of Dublin was actuated by nothing but the kindliest motives. I then told him also that the Archbishop had told me that the Irish Hierarchy's interest in this question was, in no remotest possible way, as a matter of politics or as a matter of personal opinion, that their sole interest in this question was as a matter of faith and morals. Nothing else was in question. They were not interested as citizens. They were not interested even as priests, though they as priests and bishops were charged with the duty of safeguarding the faith and morals of the Catholic people of this country. I told Dr Browne that he could rely on His Grace to do everything to settle the matter quietly, and I then offered him my personal help and support and told him that the Archbishop had given me authority to adjust this matter in any way that was possible . . .

I want to say here, and I shall repeat it before I sit down, that the medical profession have been maligned and slandered and libelled in every disreputable way throughout the entire period of this controversy and people outside have got the impression from propaganda that the medical profession have been standing between the people and this scheme. Every time there was any suggestion of an attempt to meet the then Minister for Health, to forget the past and the controversies, the people who said they were willing to come in and consult were the medical profession, and they were turned down every time with contumely by the then Minister. They acted the part which you would expect a noble profession to act in regard to this matter and the only thanks they have got is vilification. I feel it is my duty in this House to pay tribute to these men who have done everything they could to see that a mother-and-child scheme, a sane and legitimate scheme, to use the words used so properly in the bishop's letter, was brought about. I stated my conviction and faith and that I would not belong to any Government for one moment that was in favour of the socialisation of medicine. That was my conviction then and the former Minister for Health knew it, and it is my conviction now . . .

All I have said here now demonstrates the infinite capacity of Dr Browne for self-deception. In an eight-page detailed document he presumes that the fundamental objection is not an objection at all. There is no limit to the capacity of Dr Browne to deceive himself . . .

Deputy Dr Browne made the point that, because the Bishops, when they gave the seven reasons condemning the scheme, spoke of its being opposed to Catholic social teaching, there was nothing in this decision of the Hierarchy at all and that it was not a decision given on a matter of faith and morals. I took the precaution of getting an authoritative interpretation of the expression "Catholic social teaching" and I was informed that it had the same weight as – if not even greater weight than – the expression "Catholic moral teaching". The words used by the Archbishop to me were that it was clear-cut – that it was a clear-cut condemnation of a scheme, which the Bishops detest. The Bishops were solely interested in principles, not in details. As far as this particular scheme is concerned, it was clearly condemned on the grounds of the Catholic moral law; Catholic social teaching, Catholic teaching as applied to society and not restricted to sexual morality or even the laws as applied to the individual . . .

. . . he [the Minister for Health] has put across by propaganda, on the unfortunate people of the country, the idea that they will get something for nothing and that every woman who is going to have a child can go the finest specialist in Dublin and get first-class treatment free of charge, whereas in fact the scheme is based, if it is based on anything, on the dispensary system and making everybody go to the dispensary. Later the former Minister considered letting in the ordinary medical practitioners but no scheme was thought out behind all this. The Bishops say that the scheme is wrong according to the moral law. It is apparent from the Government's decision that this Government has always been, and still is, anxious to provide a scheme which is approved by the Hierarchy and that they will, in that spirit and mood – of which Deputy Dr Browne is quite incapable – of reflection and calm consultation, provide a scheme, which will give what our people require and still respect Catholic social principles . . .

The Minister for External Affairs told me he felt that as he had been responsible for introducing Deputy Dr Browne as a member of the Government and as he felt he had not fulfilled the trust he had reposed in him, it was his duty to ask him to resign. That was not a matter for me, and I felt I ought not either to discuss, argue, persuade or dissuade my colleague in any action he thought fit to take as Leader of his own political Party. I had formed, in my own view, a clear conclusion – and I must say this in justice to Deputy MacBride because of the attacks that have been and that may be made upon him – I had formed in my own mind, having regard to my experience over the last six months and the history of the affairs I have given in the barest outline, the firm conviction that Deputy Dr Browne was not competent or capable to fulfil the duties of the Department of Health. He was incapable of negotiation; he was obstinate at times and vacillating at other times. He was quite incapable of knowing what his decision would be today or, if he made a decision today, it would remain until tomorrow.

It has been said he is inexperienced, but I regret my view is that temperamentally he is unfitted for the post of Cabinet Minister. I say that in public, but I say it in all charity and kindness to a former colleague whose work I appreciate. I regret very much the circumstances which have led to his resignation . . .

Members of my Government have all the one faith. Members of future Governments may have different faiths. My colleagues and I, as a Government, and while we are a Government, have been and always will be prepared to receive representations or complaints from any religious group or organisation in the country. The views of the Church of Ireland, Methodist, Presbyterian or Jewish communities, on any matter affecting them, would receive immediate consideration. One of my first tasks as Taoiseach – I think it was in March, 1948 – was to receive certain complaints from representatives of the Jewish community. I gave on behalf of the Government undertakings which have been fully honoured. That is our attitude and I have no hesitation in saying that we, as a Government, representing a people, the overwhelming majority of whom are of the one faith, who have a special position in the Constitution, when we are given advice or warning by the authoritative people in the Catholic Church, on matters strictly confined to faith and morals, so long as I am here – and I am sure I speak for my colleagues – will give to their directions, given within that scope – and I have no doubt that they do not desire in the slightest to go one fraction of an inch outside the sphere of faith and morals – our complete obedience and allegiance.

There will be suggestions made as to the intervention of the Church authorities in State affairs. That, I'm afraid, is now inevitable. That is the result of the action of Deputy Dr Browne in putting the correspondence into the newspapers this morning. I am not in the least bit afraid of the *Irish Times* or any other newspaper. I, as a Catholic, obey my Church authorities and will continue to do so, in spite of the *Irish Times* or anything else, in spite of the fact that they may take votes from me or my Party, or anything else of that kind.

"I DID HOPE . . . THAT POSSIBLY A LOT OF THE DIFFICULTIES THAT AROSE WERE DUE TO HIS LACK OF EXPERIENCE OR POSSIBLY TO ILL-HEALTH"

Sean MacBride (1904–1988) was born in France, the son of Major John MacBride and Maud Gonne. After early schooling in Paris, he was sent to Mount St Benedict's in Gorey. He joined the Irish Volunteers at a young age and saw active service in the War of Independence. He opposed the Treaty in 1921, served several terms of imprisonment, and was eventually appointed chief of staff of the IRA in 1936. He resigned from that organisation in 1937, after the passage of the new Irish national Constitution. He trained as a barrister, and quickly built both a reputation and a substantial legal practice.

He founded Clann na Poblachta in 1946, and in 1949 he led his party into the first Inter-Party coalition. Clann na Poblachta was severely damaged by the Mother and Child controversy and in the general election of 1951, its representation was reduced to two seats. MacBride lost his own seat in the 1954 election and left Irish politics in 1961. He subsequently focused his energies on human rights, co-founded Amnesty International and was awarded the Nobel Peace Prize in 1974.

Despite being Noel Browne's party leader, MacBride went into the Dáil to support his government colleagues in opposing Dr Browne's policy and approach.

SEAN MACBRIDE, MINISTER FOR EXTERNAL AFFAIRS, APRIL 12, 1950
. . . In the first place, for the purposes of the records of this House, I should like to state what I conceive to be the duty of

the Leader of one of the Parties composing the Government in relation to members of his Party who may be in the Government. I regard it as part of my responsibility, part of the responsibility of the Leader of any Party in the Government, to be in a position at all times to assure the Taoiseach that the member of his Party in the Government are worthy of the confidence of the Government, the Oireachtas and of the people, and that they are capable of discharging their duties effectively. In pursuance of that conception of my duty, I wrote to the Taoiseach on April 10 this letter which, though it has been published already, I shall read here so as to have it on the records of the House:–

"Dear Taoiseach: I enclose a copy of a letter which I have sent by hand tonight to Dr Browne, Minister for Health, requesting him to tender his resignation to you. As the formation of the inter-Party Government is a new concept in our Parliamentary history, it is well that I should set out the considerations that have compelled me to adopt this course.

"I take the view that, as the leader of one of the parties in the Government, it is part of my responsibility to be in a position to assure the Taoiseach at all times that the members of the Party whom I have the honour to lead in the Government are trustworthy of the confidence of the Government, the Oireachtas, and the people, and are capable of discharging their duties effectively. As I can no longer give you this assurance in regard to Dr Browne, for the reasons stated in my letter to him, I deemed it to be the proper course to request him to transmit his resignation to you.

"I am sure that you and the other members of the Government will greatly regret the circumstances which have compelled me to adopt this course. Dr Browne did good work in the Government, for which he deserves full credit, and it is most unfortunate that he should have behaved, in recent times, in a manner which compelled me to take the action I have taken.

"I hope that Dr Browne may benefit by the experience he

236

has gained, and that, at some time in the future, he may again be in a position to render service to the country."

. . . I feel that I owe an apology to this House, to the Government and to the people generally for having failed to handle this situation satisfactorily on my own. I should probably have taken the course I took on April 10, 1951, at a much earlier date. Deputy Dr Browne had done good work for the country in the Department of Health during the first portion of his term of office, and it was largely because I felt that there was a debt of gratitude due to him for the work he had done that I delayed so long in taking the action which I ultimately took. I did hope for a while that possibly a lot of the difficulties that arose were due to his lack of experience, or possibly to ill-health, and that with patience and the passage of time it would have been possible to make him realise his position.

The most serious aspect of the matters that have been disclosed to the House by the Taoiseach are those which relate to what appears to be a clash between the Church and the State. One of the most difficult and important problems of government is the establishment of a proper relationship between the spiritual and the temporal authorities. The science of government involves the task of ensuring a harmonious relationship between Churches on one hand and the civil government on the other. At all times, care should be taken to avoid the creation of a situation which might give the impression that there is a lack of harmony or a lack of co-operation between the Churches and the State. It is, therefore, always a very serious matter that a situation should arise in which the impression is created that a conflict exists between the Government and the Church. From another point of view, too, I think it is also regrettable that a position should ever arise in which the action of the Government, or the action of one of its Ministers, should become the subject of review or of criticism by the Hierarchy. From the point of view of the civil government of the country, it is never desirable that such a situation should arise. In our case in Ireland, there are some additional considerations that make it particularly dangerous that any such situation should arise. In many countries throughout the world, political Parties are based on religious affiliations. That I conceive to be undesirable.

We here in Ireland have avoided the division of Parties. There are Catholics, Protestants and Jews in, I trust, all Parties in this House, and political divisions have never been built upon religious faith. The development of any situation wherein there is a conflict between the Government, between one Party in the State and one of the Churches, or more than one of the Churches, is likely to lead to a situation where Party politics will be based on religious beliefs. That, in my view, would be disastrous. Apart from these general considerations, it is clear that a situation such as the present one is obviously highly damaging to the cause of national unity. This situation has already been, is being and will continue to be exploited by the enemies of this country in order to maintain the division of our national territory.

I would like to make it clear that, in my view, the Government of this country, this Government or any other Government, has a duty to hearken to, and give weight and consideration to, the views put forward by the leaders of any religious denomination recognised by the State, be that denomination Christian or Jewish. I think that it is the duty of the Government to give due weight and consideration to the views which may be put forward by a religious minority, just as it is its duty to give due weight and consideration to the views put forward by the religious leaders of the majority of the people. Those of us in this House who are Catholics, and all of us in the Government who are Catholics are, as such of course, bound to give obedience to the rulings of our Church and of our Hierarchy. But I think that, in any event, it is the duty of a Government to give weight and very careful consideration to the views of the spiritual leaders of any recognised religious group irrespective of the religious views of the particular Government in power.

In this case, we are dealing with the considered views of the leaders of the Catholic Church to which the vast majority of our people belong. These views cannot be ignored and must be given full weight. In my considered view, having been fairly closely associated with the events that have taken place in recent months in connection with this whole matter, I am satisfied, beyond doubt, that the clash which has occurred was completely unnecessary and could have been avoided. It is a clash which is highly damaging to the national interest. I fear that little or no attempt was made by my late colleague to avoid the clash, and I am not even certain that he did not provoke it . . .

I am quite satisfied that, on the basis of that principle, it would have been possible to reach agreement without infringing any of the doctrines of the Catholic Church. The Hierarchy in their last letter set out in the last paragraph thereof the position as they see it:

"Accordingly, the Hierarchy have firm confidence that it will yet be possible, after reflection and calm consultation, for the Government to provide a scheme which, while it affords due facilities for those whom the State, as guardian of the common good, is rightly called upon to assist, will none the less respect in its principles and implementation the traditional life and spirit of our Christian people."

I am quite satisfied that if Deputy Dr Browne had desired to evolve a scheme which conformed to the views expressed by the Hierarchy, such a scheme could have been evolved and would be at least partly in operation by now.

"THE HONESTY OF MY MOTIVES WILL
BE ATTACKED BY ABLE MEN".

Noel Browne (1915–) was educated in England and at Trinity College Dublin, where he qualified as a medical doctor. He joined the newly formed Clann na Poblachta and was elected as a TD for Dublin South-East in the 1948 general election. On his first day in the Dáil, he was appointed Minister for Health.

Browne had initial success in his ministry.

He made tremendous progress in eliminating tuberculosis from Irish life, and established a national blood transfusion service. He then sought to develop a national system of care for mothers and their infants, in the belief that the hierarchy supported his proposal. When it emerged that they were in fact resolutely against it, Browne was left without political or cabinet support.

He resigned from the Government and his party, but stayed involved in active politics for a further thirty years.

DAIL ÉIREANN, APRIL 12, 1951

It is fitting and, I am informed, in accordance with useage, that I should explain to the Dáil very briefly the reasons which led me to resign my position in the Government. I am deeply grieved that I have found myself compelled to take this step.

Since becoming Minister for Health I have striven within the limits of my ability to improve the health services of the country. Some progress has been made but much remains to be done. It is perhaps only human that I should wish to have the honour of continuing the work. However that is not to be. To me the provision of a health scheme for the benefit of the mothers and children of our nation seems to be the very foundation stone of any progressive health service without which much of our efforts in other directions would prove fruitless. It seemed equally important to me that any such scheme to be effective and indeed just should be made available free to all our people who choose of their own free will to use it without the impositions of any form of means test. On this point did I stand firm in my negotiations with the medical profession. On other matters I was willing and, indeed, eager that the profession should from their knowledge and experience play their full part in improving the scheme.

I had been led to believe that my insistence on the exclusion of a means test had the full support of my colleagues in the Government. I now know that it had not. Furthermore, the Hierarchy has informed the Government that they must regard the mother and child scheme proposed by me as opposed to Catholic social teaching. This decision I, as a Catholic, immediately accepted without hesitation. At the same time I do not feel that I could be instrumental in introducing a scheme which would be subject to a means test. Apart from my personal views about a means test I feel that in taking the decision which I have had to take, as a man privileged to hold my high office, there is another principle to which I had to have regard. I have pledged myself to the public and to the Clann na Poblachta Party to introduce a mother and child health scheme which would not embody a means test. Since I could not succeed in fulfilling my promise in this regard I consider it my duty to vacate my office.

While, as I have said, I as a Catholic accept unequivocally and unreservedly the views of the Hierarchy on this matter, I have not been able to accept the manner in which this matter has been dealt with by my former colleagues in the Government . . .

On March 9 I received a letter from His Grace the Archbishop of Dublin. From this letter I was surprised to learn that His Grace might not approve of the scheme, and declared that the objections, which had been raised by him in October, had not been resolved. I was surprised for the simple reason that I had heard nothing further, either from His Grace the Archbishop of Dublin, acting on behalf of the Hierarchy, or from the Taoiseach, acting for the Government, in the four months that had intervened since I had handed the Taoiseach in November my reply to Their Lordships' letter. Following receipt of His Grace's letter, a copy of which was sent by His Grace to the Taoiseach, the latter suggested to me on March 15 that I should take steps at once to consult the Hierarchy regarding their objections to the scheme. I then learned to my distress and amazement that the reply to Their Lordships' letter which I had prepared and sent to the Taoiseach in the previous November had, in fact, never been sent by him. The Taoiseach has given three explanations – two to me and one to the Hierarchy and all differing – as to why he did not forward my letter to the Hierarchy. One reason to me was that he considered the reply ineffective; another was that no covering letter from me was received with it and he did not realise that I wanted it sent to the Hierarchy. In his letter of March 22 the Taoiseach says that he explained to His Grace the Archbishop of Dublin his reasons for not replying to the Hierarchy, and that His Grace conveyed these reasons to the Hierarchy. The third reason for not replying, which appears in the Taoiseach's letter of March 27 to the Hierarchy, was that he and His Grace the Archbishop of Dublin believed it to be more advantageous in the special circumstances of the case to await development.

I told the Taoiseach orally that his failure to forward this reply had placed me in a very embarrassing position and might easily give Their Lordships the impression that I had omitted to give any consideration to their objections and that further I had been guilty of extreme discourtesy in failing to ensure that a reply had been sent to them. I also pointed out that his failure to send this letter had the effect that I remained under the erroneous impression that the objections of the Hierarchy had been fully resolved and that I could proceed with the scheme. I was surprised also to learn from the Taoiseach that he had been in constant communication with His Grace the Archbishop of Dublin on this matter since the receipt of the letter of 10th of October from the Hierarchy, so presumably he was fully aware that Their Lordships' objections were still unresolved. He offered no explanation as to why, in the light of this knowledge, he had failed to keep me informed of the position; had allowed me continuously to refer in public speeches to the scheme as decided and unchanged Government policy, and finally had allowed the scheme to go ahead to the point where it had been advertised at considerable public expense and had been announced to the public, both in these advertisements and by my radio talk. He, furthermore, offered no explanation as to why, being aware of the Hierarchy's objections to the scheme, he continued to allow the Tanaiste, Dr O'Higgins and myself to negotiate with the Medical Association, and why, in the light of this knowledge to which he now confesses, he himself informed the Medical Association that the Government would not agree to the inclusion of a means test.

This conduct on the part of the Taoiseach is open, it seems to me, to only two possible explanations – either that he would not oppose the scheme if agreement were reached with the Medical Association on the means test or that, in the light of his knowledge of the objections still being made by the Hierarchy and withheld from me, he intended that the scheme without a means test must never in fact be implemented . . .

It is a fact noted by many people that in no public speeches did Ministers of the Government other than myself speak in favour of this measure. I regret that for the want of courage on their part they should have allowed the scheme to progress so very far – that they should have failed to keep me informed of the true position in regard to their own attitude and the attitude of others. I have, consequently, been allowed by their silence to commit myself to the country to implement a scheme which certain members of the Government at least did not want, on their own admission, to see implemented and which they were in fact aware could not be implemented.

I trust that the standards manifested in these dealings are not customary in the public life of this or any other democratic nation and I hope that my experience has been exceptional.

I have not, lightly, decided to take the course I have taken. I know the consequences which may follow my action. The honesty of my motives will be attacked by able men; my aims will be called in question; ridicule and doubt will be cast upon the wisdom of my insistence in striving to realise the declared objectives of the Party to which I belonged.

As Minister for Health I was enabled to make some progress in improving the health services of the nation only because I received the generous co-operation of members of all political Parties and of all sections of the community.

I lay down my seal of office content that you – members of this House – and the people who are our masters here, shall judge whether I have striven to honour the trust placed on me.

"I AM DEEPLY HONOURED TO BE YOUR GUEST IN A FREE PARLIAMENT OF A FREE IRELAND"

John Fitzgerald Kennedy (1917–63) was born in Brookline, Massachusetts, and educated at Harvard University. After service in the American Navy during World War II, he entered Congress as a Democrat in 1946, and was elected to the Senate for Massachusetts in 1952. He unsuccessfully contested the 1956 Presidential election, as the Vice-Presidential running mate of the Democratic nominee, Adlai Stevenson. He won the nomination outright in 1960, and beat Republican nominee Richard Nixon by 113,000 votes out of a total vote of 68.8 million. He was the youngest US president ever elected and the first Roman Catholic to hold that office. Two years after his election he paid a visit to Ireland, the first by a serving US President to independent Ireland.

In the course of his four-day visit, Kennedy became the first leader of a foreign state to address a joint sitting of the Oireachtas. For many members of the Oireachtas, who had served since the 1920s, it was a milestone in the growth of the country and particularly of its acceptance as a democracy. It was a brilliant speech, humorous and emotional, serious and deep, and it perfectly caught the mood that surrounded his visit.

Dáil Éireann, June 28, 1963

Mr Speaker, Prime Minister, Members of the Parliament: I am grateful for your welcome and for that of your countrymen.

The 13th day of December, 1862, will be a day long remembered in American history. At Fredericksburg, Virginia, thousands of men fought and died on one of the bloodiest

245

battlefields of the American Civil War. One of the most brilliant stories of that day was written by a band of 1,200 men who went into battle wearing a green sprig in their hats. They bore a proud heritage and a special courage, given to those who had long fought for the cause of freedom. I am referring, of course, to the Irish Brigade. As General Robert E Lee, the great military leader of the Southern Confederate forces, was reported to have said of this group of men after the battle: "The gallant stand which this bold brigade made on the heights of Fredericksburg is well known. Never were men so brave. They ennobled their race by their splendid gallantry on that desperate occasion. Their brilliant, though hopeless, assaults on our lines excited the hearty applause of our officers and soldiers."

Of the 1,200 men who took part in that assault, 280 survived the battle. The Irish Brigade was led into battle on that occasion by Brigadier General Thomas F Meagher, who had participated in the unsuccessful Irish uprising of 1848, was captured by the British and sent in a prison ship to Australia, from whence he finally came to America. In the fall of 1862, after serving with distinction and gallantry in some of the toughest fighting of this most bloody struggle, the Irish Brigade was presented with a new set of flags. In the city ceremony, the city chamberlain gave them the motto "The Union, Our Country, and Ireland Forever." Their old ones having been torn to shreds by bullets in previous battles, Captain Richard McGee took possession of these flags on September 2nd in New York City and arrived with them at the Battle of Fredericksburg and carried them in the battle. Today, in recognition of what these gallant Irishmen and what millions of other Irish have done for my country, and through the generosity of the Fighting 69th, I would like to present one of these flags to the people of Ireland.

As you can see, gentlemen, the battle honours of the Brigade include Fredericksburg, Chancellorsville, Yorktown, Fair Oaks, Gaines Hill, Allen's Farm, Savage's Station, White Oak Bridge, Glendale, Malvern Hills, Antietam, Gettysburg, and Bristoe's Station.

I am deeply honoured to be your guest in the free parliament of a free Ireland. If this nation had achieved its present political and economic stature a century or so ago, my great-grandfather might never have left New Ross, and I might, if fortunate, be sitting down there with you. Of course, if your own President had never left Brooklyn, he might be standing up here instead of me.

This elegant building, as you know, was once the property of the Fitzgerald family, but I have not come here to claim it. Of all the new relations I have discovered on this trip, I regret to say that no one has yet found any link between me and a great Irish patriot, Lord Edward Fitzgerald. Lord Edward, however, did not like to stay here in his family home "because," as he wrote his mother, "Leinster House does not inspire the brightest ideas." That was a long time ago, however. It has also been said by some that a few of the features of this stately mansion served to inspire similar features in the White House in Washington. Whether this is true or not, I know that the White House was designed by James Hoban, a noted Irish-American architect, and I have no doubt that he believed, by incorporating several features of the Dublin style, he would make it more homelike for any President of Irish descent. It was a long wait, but I appreciate his efforts.

There is also an unconfirmed rumour that Hoban was never fully paid for his work on the White House. If this proves to be true, I will speak to our Secretary of the Treasury about it, although I hear this body is not particularly interested in the subject of the revenue.

I am proud to be the first American President to visit Ireland during this term of office, proud to be addressing this distinguished assembly, and proud of the welcome you have given me. My presence and your welcome, however, only symbolise the many and the enduring links which have bound the Irish and the Americans since the earliest days.

Benjamin Franklin, the envoy of the American Revolution, who was also born in Boston, was received by the Irish

Parliament in 1772. It was neither independent nor free from discrimination at the time, but Franklin reported its members "disposed to be friends of America." "By joining our interest with theirs," he said, "a more equitable treatment . . . might be obtained for both nations."

Our interests have been joined ever since. Franklin sent leaflets to Irish freedom fighters. O'Connell was influenced by Washington, and Emmet influenced Lincoln. Irish volunteers played so predominant a role in the American Army that Lord Mountjoy lamented in the British Parliament: "We have lost America through the Irish." John Barry, whose statue was honoured yesterday, and whose sword is in my office, was only one who fought for liberty in America to set an example for liberty in Ireland. Yesterday was the 117th anniversary of the birth of Charles Stewart Parnell – whose grandfather fought under Barry and whose mother was born in America – and who, at the age of 34, was invited to address the American Congress on the cause of Irish freedom. "I have seen since I have been in this country," he said, "so many tokens of the good wishes of the American people toward Ireland . . . ". And today, 83 years later, I can say to you that I have seen in this country so many tokens of good wishes of the Irish people toward America.

And so it is that our two nations, divided by distance, have been united by history. No people ever believed more deeply in the cause of Irish freedom than the people of the United States. And no country contributed more to building my own than your sons and daughters. They came to our shores in a mixture of hope and agony, and I would not underrate the difficulties of their course once they arrived in the United States. They left behind hearts, fields, and a nation yearning to be free. It is no wonder that James Joyce described the Atlantic as a bowl of bitter tears, and an earlier poet wrote: "They are going, going, going, and we cannot bid them stay."

But today this is no longer the country of hunger and famine that those immigrants left behind. It is not rich and its progress is not yet complete, but it is, according to statistics, one of the best-fed countries in the world. Nor is it any longer a country of persecution, political or religious. It is a free country, and that is why any American feels at home.

There are those who regard this history of past strife and exile as better forgotten, but to use the phrase of Yeats: "Let us not casually reduce that great past to a trouble of fools, for we need not feel the bitterness of the past to discover its meaning for the present and the future."

And it is the present and the future of Ireland that today holds so much promise to my nation as well as to yours, and, indeed, to all mankind, for the Ireland of 1963, one of the youngest of nations, and the oldest of civilisations, has discovered that the achievement of nationhood is not an end, but a beginning. In the years since independence, you have undergone a new and peaceful revolution, an economic and industrial revolution, transforming the face of this land, while still holding the old spiritual and cultural values. You have modernised your economy, harnessed your rivers, diversified your industry, liberalised your trade, electrified your farms, accelerated your rate of growth, and improved the living standards of your people.

Other nations of the world in whom Ireland has long invested her people and her children are now investing their capital as well as their vacations here in Ireland. This revolution is not yet over, nor will it be, I am sure, until a fully modern Irish economy fully shares in world prosperity. But prosperity is not enough.

One hundred and eighty-three years ago, Henry Grattan, demanding the more independent Irish Parliament that would always bear his name, denounced those who were satisfied merely by new grants of economic opportunity. "A country," he said, "enlightened as Ireland, chartered as Ireland, armed as Ireland, and injured as Ireland, will not be satisfied with anything less than liberty." And today, I am certain, free Ireland, a full-fledged member of the world community where some are not yet free and where some counsel an acceptance of tyranny

– free Ireland will not be satisfied with anything less than liberty.

I am glad, therefore, that Ireland is moving in the mainstream of current world events. For I sincerely believe that your future is as promising as your past is proud, and that your destiny lies not as a peaceful island in a sea of troubles, but as a maker and shaper of world peace.

For self-determination can no longer mean isolation; and the achievement of national independence today means withdrawal from the old status only to return to the world scene with a new one. New nations can build with their former governing powers the same kind of fruitful relationship that Ireland has established with Great Britain – a relationship founded on equality and mutual interests. And no nation, large or small, can be indifferent to the fate of others, near or far. Modern economics, weapons and communications have made us realise more than ever that we are one human family and this one planet is our home. "The world is large," wrote John Boyle O'Reilly, "The world is large when its weary leagues two loving hearts divide, but the world is small when your enemy is loose on the other side."

The world is even smaller today, though the enemy of John Boyle O'Reilly is no longer a hostile power. Indeed, across the gulfs and barriers that now divide us, we must remember that there are no permanent enemies. Hostility today is a fact, but it not a ruling law. The supreme reality of our time is our indivisibility as children of God and our common vulnerability on this planet.

Some may say that all this means little to Ireland. In an age when "history moves with the tramp of earthquake feet," in an age when a handful of men and nations have the power literally to devastate mankind, in an age when the needs of the developing nations are so large and staggering that even the richest nations often groan with the burden of assistance – in such an age, it may be asked, how can a nation as small as Ireland play much of a role on the world stage?

I would remind those who ask that question, including those

in other small countries, of these words of one of the great orators of the English language:

"All the world owes much to the little 'five feet high' nations. The greatest art of the world was the work of little nations. The most enduring literature of the world came from little nations. The heroic deeds that thrill humanity through generations were the deeds of little nations fighting for their freedom. And, oh, yes, the salvation of mankind came through a little nation."

Ireland has already set an example and a standard for other small nations to follow. This has never been a rich or powerful country, and, yet, since earliest times, its influence on the world has been rich and powerful. No larger nation did more to keep Christianity and Western culture alive in their darkest centuries. No larger nation did more to spark the cause of American independence, and independence, indeed, around the world. And no larger nation has ever provided the world with more literary and artistic genius.

This is an extraordinary country. George Bernard Shaw, speaking as an Irishman, summed up an approach to life: "Other peoples," he said, "see things and say 'Why?' . . . But I dream things that never were – and I say: 'Why not?'"

It is that quality of the Irish, the remarkable combination of hope, confidence and imagination that is needed more than ever today. The problems of the world cannot possibly be solved by sceptics or cynics whose horizons are limited by the obvious realities. We need men who can dream of things that never were, and ask why not. It matters not how small a nation is that seeks world peace and freedom, for, to paraphrase a citizen of my country: "That humblest nation of all the world, when clad in the armour of a righteous cause, is stronger than all the hosts of error."

Ireland is clad in the cause of national and human liberty with peace. To the extent that the peace is disturbed by conflict between the former colonial powers and the new and developing nations, Ireland's role is unique. For every new nation knows that Ireland was the first of the small nations in the twentieth century to win its struggle for independence, and that the Irish have traditionally sent their doctors and technicians and soldiers and priests to help other lands to keep their liberty alive. At the same time, Ireland is part of Europe, associated with the Council of Europe, progressing in the context of Europe, and a prospective member of an expanded European Common Market. Thus Ireland has excellent relations with both the new and the old, the confidence of both sides and an opportunity to act where the actions of greater powers might be looked upon with suspicion.

The central issue of freedom, however, is between those who believe in self-determination and those in the East who would impose upon others the harsh and oppressive Communist system; and here your nation wisely rejects the role of a go-between or a mediator. Ireland pursues an independent course in foreign policy, but it is not neutral between liberty and tyranny and never will be.

For knowing the meaning of foreign domination, Ireland is the example and inspiration to those enduring endless years of oppression. It was fitting and appropriate that this nation played a leading role in censuring the suppression of the Hungarian Revolution, for how many times was Ireland's quest for freedom suppressed only to have that quest renewed by the succeeding generation? Those who suffer beyond that wall I saw on Wednesday in Berlin must not despair of their future. Let them remember the constancy, the faith, the endurance and the final success of the Irish. And let them remember, as I heard sung by your sons and daughters yesterday in Wexford, the words: "The boys of Wexford, who fought with heart and hand, to burst in twain the galling chain and free our native land."

The major forum for your nation's greater role in world affairs is that of protector of the weak and voice of the small, the United Nations. From Cork to the Congo, from Galway to the Gaza Strip, from this legislative assembly to the United Nations, Ireland is sending its most talented men to do the world's most important work – the work of peace. In a sense, this export of talent is in keeping with an historic Irish role. But you no longer go as exiles and emigrants but for the service of your country and, indeed, of all men. Like the Irish missionaries of medieval days, like the Wild Geese after the Battle of the Boyne, you are not content to sit by your fireside while others are in need of your help. Nor are you content with the recollections of the past when you face the responsibilities of the present.

Twenty-six sons of Ireland have died in the Congo; many others have been wounded. I pay tribute to them and to all of you for your commitment and dedication to world order. And their sacrifice reminds us all that we must not falter now.

The United Nations must be fully and fairly financed; its peace-keeping machinery must be strengthened; its institutions must be developed until some day, and perhaps some distant day, a world of law is achieved.

Ireland's influence in the United Nations is far greater than your relative size. You have not hesitated to take the lead on such sensitive issues as the Kashmir dispute, and you sponsored that most vital resolution, adopted by the General Assembly, which opposed the spread of nuclear arms to any nation not now possessing them, urging an international agreement with inspection and control, and I pledge to you that the United States of America will do all in its power to achieve such an agreement and fulfil your resolution.

I speak of these matters today not because Ireland is unaware of its role, but I think it important that you know that we know what you have done, and I speak to remind the other small nations that they, too, can and must help build a world peace. They, too, as we all are, are dependent on the United Nations for security, for an equal chance to be heard, for progress towards a world made safe for diversity. The peace-keeping machinery of the United Nations cannot work without the help of the smaller nations, nations whose forces threaten no one and whose forces can thus help create a world in which no nation is threatened.

Great powers have their responsibilities and their burdens,

but the smaller nations of the world must fulfil their obligations as well. A great Irish poet once wrote: "I believe profoundly in the future of Ireland, that this is an isle of destiny, that that destiny will be glorious, and that when our hour has come we will have something to give to the world."

My friends, Ireland's hour has come. You have something to give to the world, and that is a future of peace with freedom. Thank you.

"WE IN IRELAND HAVE CONSTANTLY
LOOKED ON YOU AS A CHAMPION"

After Kennedy's visit to Ireland, de Valera, as President of Ireland, returned a year later to the United States on a state visit. He addressed a joint session of Congress. His speech ranged over the role that America played in the campaign for Irish independence and his own role in trying to persuade American opinion at that time. For the son of an Irish immigrant to Brooklyn, it was a remarkable return.

JOINT SESSION OF UNITED STATES CONGRESS, MAY 28, 1964

Mr Speaker, Mr President pro tempore of the Senate, Members of the Congress of the United States: my first word to you must be to thank you from my heart for the great privilege you have granted me in permitting me to appear before you and to address you.

I was here some forty-five years ago, and I toured throughout this great country. You may remember that on the 21st January 1919 the national assembly of Ireland – Dáil Éireann – declared Ireland independent and a republic, just as the Second Continental Congress here declared the independence of America.

President Wilson, during the First World War, had put the rights of people to self-determination as a fundamental basis for peace. We in Ireland took advantage of the fact that that principle had been enunciated by the head of this great nation. There was a general election due at the time, and we took advantage of that election to make it clear that the people wanted independence. The elections were held under British law, and therefore there could be no suggestion of any interference in our favour. The results of the elections were such that it would be impossible for anyone to deny what was the status of the nation and what was the form of government that the Irish people desired.

I was sent here some months later – in June of 1919. I have told you that our Declaration of Independence was made on the 21st day of January, 1919. That is our Independence Day, as July 4 is yours.

I was sent here to the United States with a threefold mission. First, to ask for official recognition of the independence and the Republic that had been declared in Ireland in full accordance with the principles of self-determination. I was sent here also to try to float an external loan for the uses of that Republic. And, finally, I was asked to plead with the American people so that, if the Covenant of the League of Nations and the Treaty of Versailles, which were under discussion, were to be ratified, the United States would make it clear that, notwithstanding Article X of that Covenant, the United States was not pledging itself to maintain Ireland as an integral part of British territory.

Some weeks after we had declared our independence – I think it was on March 4 – the House of Representatives here passed a resolution, by something like 216 votes to 41, asking the Peace Conference that was sitting in Paris and passing judgement upon the rights of nations to favourably consider Ireland's right to self-determination. A few months later, on June 6, your Senate here passed a resolution earnestly requesting the American Peace Commissioners, then in Paris, to endeavour to secure that the representatives who had been chosen in Ireland for the purpose, would get a hearing at the Peace Conference in order that they might present Ireland's case.

But the Senate went further. Nearly a year later, when the ratification of the Treaty of Versailles was under discussion, it passed a resolution which was intended to be a reservation to the Treaty, if adopted, reaffirming its adherence to the principle of self-determination and its previous vote of sympathy with the aspirations of the Irish people for a government of their own choice, and went further and expressed the earnest hope that once Ireland had got self-government it would be promptly admitted as a member of the League of Nations.

You know that an account of articles in the Covenant and circumstances of the day the Treaty was not ratified. But the resolutions here in Congress, supported as they were and mirroring as they did the attitude of the American people as a whole, were made manifest by immense demonstrations in all the principal cities throughout the United States. Recognition was given by the mayors of your principal cities, by the governors and legislatures of many of your states, so that Congress here was expressing accurately the will of the American people in regard to Ireland. It is not necessary for me to tell you how heartened our people were by these expressions of sympathy and friendship. We were in a very difficult struggle, facing very great odds. And it was a comfort and an earnest of ultimate success that this great freedom-loving nation of America and its people were behind our efforts.

What was the gratitude of the Irish people was clearly evident to anyone who saw the reception that was given to your late President, President Kennedy. He was welcomed not merely because he was of Irish blood, not merely because of his personal charm and his great qualities of heart and mind, nor even because of the great leadership which he was giving to the world in critical moments; but he was honoured because he was regarded by our people as the symbol of this great nation, because he was the elected President of this great people. In honouring him they felt that they were in some small measure expressing their gratitude to the people of the United States for the aid that had been given to them.

The United States, since the Declaration of Independence, has been looked upon by all freedom-loving peoples as the champion of human liberty, the liberty of nations and the liberty of individuals. We in Ireland have constantly looked to you as such a champion. We all know that the former League of Nations came into being as the result of American initiative – although, as I said, for reasons which seemed good at the time to the American people they did not ratify the Treaty or become members of the League. But the idea came from America, in modern times anyhow. And the successor of the League – the United Nations Organisation – also came into being as the result of American influence. Most thinking people will admit that, if we are to look forward to peace, to anything like a lasting peace in this world, it can only be secured by the working of such an organisation – an organisation that will purposely devote itself to bringing about the rule of law and, where other means have failed, judicial determination of international disputes, and enforcement of peace when that becomes necessary.

Now, you all know that we are far from being at that goal at present. But there is no one who has read the speeches of President Kennedy or the speeches of President Johnson or the speeches and statements of your Secretary of State or the chairman of your Foreign Relations Committee, but must be satisfied that American leaders are thinking at the highest level and that they are facing realistically the complicated situations that confront them and also the social evils that have to be remedied. It is a great comfort to know that a nation like yours is thinking at that level. And we have the hope that, as long as there is thinking at that level and as long as this nation is guided by the Divine Spirit, ultimately the peace and the conditions which we all wish for will be realised.

But freedom and peace are but the foundations. They are the necessary foundations. The United States as a great nation and ours as one of the smaller nations, working in our complementary ways, are endeavouring to build, to secure that these foundations will be well laid. But that is not all, of course. An Irish poet thinking, some 120 years ago, of the role he would wish his nation to play, addressed us in these words:

Oh, Ireland, be it thy high duty
To teach the world the might of moral beauty,
And stamp God's image truly on the struggling soul.

President Kennedy in his address at Amherst College, thinking of the future that he would wish and that he foresaw for America, said he wished an America whose military strength would be matched by its moral strength, the moral strength of its people; its wealth by their wisdom; its power by their purpose – an America that would not be afraid of grace and beauty – in short, he said, an America that would win respect not merely because of its strength but because of its culture. I am sure that is the America that ultimately you would want, as it is the Ireland that we would want. But these things can only be secured by undeviating pursuit of the foundations that I have mentioned and pursuit, ultimately, of the higher ideals that mean the mental life, the full life of the people.

Mr Speaker, I would like to confess, and confess freely, that this is an outstanding day in my own life, to see recognised, as I have here in full, the rights of the Irish people and the independence of the Irish people in a way that was not at all possible forty-five years ago. I have longed to come back and say this to you and, through you, to the people as a whole. I would, indeed, be fully happy today were there not one serious setback that had occurred in these forty-five years. When I was addressing you here in 1919 and 1920, our ancient nation, our ancient Ireland, was undivided. Since then it has been divided by a cruel partition. As my predecessor, Mr Sean T. O'Kelly, when he was addressing you here said, partition is one of our serious problems, but, please God, that too will be solved.

And I salute here, in prospect, the representative of Ireland who may be permitted to address you as I have been permitted, and who will be able with full heart joyfully to announce to you that our severed country has been reunited and that the last source of enmity between the British and Irish peoples has disappeared and that at last we can be truly friends.

And now, Mr Speaker, I would like to renew to you and to

the Members of Congress my thanks for this great privilege – and, of course, to the President of the United States, without whose generous invitation I could not be here. I am deeply grateful. I hope that the close ties which have kept our countries together for centuries will continue into the future and that representatives of Ireland may be able to talk to the American people as close friends, and representatives of the United States to talk to the people of Ireland as their close friends.

May I pray in our own language, the Irish language, that this may be so:

God grant that it be so, and may the Holy Spirit guide the leaders of our two countries, and those of the whole world, on the way of peace and human betterment.

DEATH OF WILLIAM T COSGRAVE

Sean Lemass became leader of Fianna Fáil and Taoiseach after de Valera was elected to the Presidency in 1959. His period as Taoiseach marked the transition from a country with a protected economy looking inwards to one focused more on the external environment and free trade. Lemass's government also included many new ministers, who had not seen active service in the War of Independence or the Civil War and who were to dominate Fianna Fáil for the next three decades.

Lemass's speech on the death of his Civil War adversary, WT Cosgrave, reflected how politics had changed in the Republic since the end of the Civil War, and particularly since the end of the Second World War.

DAIL ÉIREANN, NOVEMBER 17, 1965

The House will have learned with deep regret of the sudden death of Mr William T. Cosgrave. *Ar dheis Dé go raibh a anam.* The Deputies will not need to be reminded of the prominent part played by the late Mr Cosgrave in national affairs from his earliest days – as a member of Dublin Corporation, a founder member of the Irish Volunteers and a participant in the Rising of Easter Week. Elected a member of the first Dáil, he was placed in charge of the Dáil Department of Local Government, which he organised to such good effect that local affairs were soon controlled almost entirely by the Government of the Republic. In 1922 he was called on to assume the leadership of the Government and held that office for ten years. In subsequent years, until he relinquished the leadership of his Party in 1944, he played a prominent and distinguished role in the affairs of the Dáil and of the country.

I have thought it fitting, on this occasion, a Cheann Comhairle, to depart from Parliamentary precedent in order to give the Dáil an opportunity of marking appreciation of the work and influence of the late Mr Cosgrave in the history of the State. For, although William T Cosgrave has left us, the work he has done for Ireland endures. The generosity of his youthful response to the call to serve Ireland, the privations and the sacrifices which he endured so that national freedom might be ours, the capacity he displayed in presiding over the administration while responsibility was his, the grace with which he handed over responsibility when the people so willed, the dignity with which he carried out his duties as Leader of the Opposition and later as a private member of this House, the generosity of spirit with which he lent his hand to the defence of the State in a time of national danger, the readiness with which, even in retirement from active public life, he gave of his counsel in the sphere of national development which was dear to him, and finally, the exemplary character of his long life, these are the elements of a legacy which we in Ireland, and indeed people who value freedom and democracy everywhere, will forever cherish.

I would ask you, Sir, to convey to his son, Deputy Liam Cosgrave, and to the other members of his family, the very sincere sympathy of the Members of Dáil Éireann.

"ULSTER STANDS AT THE CROSSROADS"

Terence O'Neill (1914–1980) was born into an Anglo-Irish family and educated at Eton before joining the Army. Given his background, a political career was obvious and he was elected to Stormont. In 1956 he was appointed Minister for Finance in the Stormont administration, and when Brookeborough resigned as Prime Minister in 1963, he was the natural successor.

O'Neill was never fully trusted by the right wing of Unionism, and this distrust was heightened by the visit of Sean Lemass to Stormont in 1965. As the Civil Rights movement began to gather momentum and media coverage, O'Neill put together a reform package designed to alleviate the tension. It was opposed by William Craig, Minister for Home Affairs, whom O'Neill sacked two days after his broadcast.

In December 1968, O'Neill went on television to announce limited reform measures. Although he received 150,000 letters of support, his own support base was steadily diminishing in the Unionist establishment. Four months later, with the political situation deteriorating rapidly, he resigned as Prime Minister, and was replaced by Chichester-Clarke.

NATIONAL BROADCAST, DECEMBER 9, 1968

Ulster stands at the crossroads. I believe you know me well enough by now to appreciate that I am not a man given to extravagant language. But I must say to you this evening that our conduct over the coming days and weeks will decide our future. And as we face this situation I would be failing in my duty to you as your Prime Minister if I did not put the issues calmly and clearly before you all. These issues are far too serious to be determined behind closed doors or left to noisy minorities. The time has come for the people as a whole to speak in a clear voice.

For more than five years now I have tried to heal some of the deep divisions in our community. I did so because I could not see how an Ulster divided against itself could hope to stand. I made it clear that a Northern Ireland based upon the interest of any one section rather than upon the interest of all could have no long term future.

Throughout the community many people have responded warmly to my words. But if Ulster is to become the happy and united place it could be, there must be the will throughout our province and particularly in Parliament to translate these words into deeds.

In Londonderry and other places recently a minority of agitators, determined to subvert lawful authority, played a part in setting light to highly inflammable material. But the tinder for that fire in the form of grievances, real or imaginary, had been piling up for years.

And so I saw it as our duty to do two things. First, to be firm in the maintenance of law and order and in resisting those elements which seek to profit from any disturbances. Secondly, to ally firmness with fairness and to look at any underlying causes of dissension which were troubling decent and moderate people. As I saw it, if we were not prepared to face up to our problems, we would have to meet mounting pressure both internally, from those who were seeking change, and externally, from British public and parliamentary opinion, which had been deeply disturbed by the events in Londonderry.

That is why it has been my view from the beginning that we should decide – of our own free will and as a responsible Government in command of events – to press on with a continuing programme of change to secure a united and harmonious community. This indeed has been my aim for over five years.

Moreover I knew full well that Britain's financial and other support for Ulster, so laboriously built up, could no longer be guaranteed if we failed to press on with such a programme.

I am aware of course that some foolish people have been saying: "Why should we bow the knee to a Labour Prime Minister? Let's hold out until a Conservative government returns to power and then we need do nothing." My friends, that is a delusion. This letter is from Mr Edward Heath and it tells me – with the full authority of the Shadow Cabinet and the expressed support of my old friend, Sir Alec Douglas-Home – that a reversal of the policies which I have tried to pursue would be every bit as unacceptable to the Conservative Party. If we adopt an attitude of stubborn defiance we will not have a friend left at Westminster.

I make no apology for the financial and economic support we have received from Britain. As a part of the United Kingdom we have always considered this to be our right. But we cannot be a part of the United Kingdom merely when it suits us. And those who talk so glibly about acts of impoverished defiance do not know or care what is at stake. Your job, if you are a worker at Short's or Harland and Wolff; your subsidies, if you are a farmer; your pension, if you are retired – all these aspects of our life and many others depend on support from Britain. Is a freedom to pursue the un-Christian path of communal strife and sectarian bitterness really more important to you than all the benefits of the British Welfare State?

But this is not all. Let me read to you some words from the Government of Ireland Act, 1920 – the Act of the British Parliament on which Ulster's Constitution is founded: "Notwithstanding the establishment of the Parliament of Northern Ireland . . . the supreme authority of the Parliament of the United Kingdom shall remain unaffected and undiminished over all persons, matters and things in (Northern) Ireland and every part thereof."

Because Westminster has trusted us over the years to use the powers of Stormont for the good of all the people of Ulster, a sound custom has grown up that Westminster does not use its supreme authority in fields where we are normally responsible. But Mr Wilson made it absolutely clear to us that if we did not face up to our problems the Westminster Parliament might well decide to act over our heads. Where would our Constitution be then? What shred of self-respect would be left to us? If we allowed others to solve our problems because we had not the guts – let me use a plain word – the guts to face up to them, we would be utterly shamed.

There are, I know, today some so-called loyalists who talk of independence from Britain – who seem to want a kind of Protestant Sinn Féin. These people will not listen when they are told that Ulster's income is £200m a year but that we can spend £300m – only because Britain pays the balance.

Rhodesia, in defying Britain from thousands of miles away, at least has an air force and an army of her own. Where are the Ulster armoured divisions or the Ulster jet planes? They do not exist and we could not afford to buy them. These people are not merely extremists. They are lunatics who would set a course along a road which could only lead at the end into an all-Ireland republic. They are not loyalists but dis-loyalists; disloyal to Britain, disloyal to the constitution, disloyal to the Crown, disloyal – if they are in public life – to the solemn oath they have sworn to Her Majesty the Queen.

But these considerations, important though they are, are not my main concern. What I seek – and I ask for the help and understanding of you all – is a swift end to the growing civil disorder throughout Ulster, for as matters stand today we are on the brink of chaos, where neighbour could be set against neighbour. It is simple-minded to imagine that problems such as these can be solved by repression. I for one am not willing to expose our police force to indefinite insult and injury. Nor am I prepared to see the shopkeepers and traders of Ulster wrecked and looted for the benefit of the rabble. We must tackle root causes if this agitation is to be contained. We must be able to say to the moderates on both sides, come with us into an era of co-operation and leave the extremists to the law. But this I also say to all, Protestant or Roman Catholic, Unionist or Nationalist: disorder must now cease. We are taking the necessary measures to strengthen our police forces. Determined as we are to act with absolute fairness we will also be resolute in restoring respect for the laws of the land.

Some people have suggested that I should call a general election. It would, in my view, be utterly reprehensible to hold an election against a background of bitterness and strike. I have spoken to you in the past about the groundswell of moderate opinion. Its presence was seen three years ago when we fought an election on a manifesto which would stand inspection in any Western democracy and we swept the country on a non-sectarian platform. Those who would sow the wind by having a bitter election now would surely reap the whirlwind.

And now I want to say a word directly to those who have been demonstrating for civil rights. The changes which we have announced are genuine and far-reaching changes and the Government as a whole is committed to them. I would not continue to preside over an administration which would water them down or make them meaningless. You will see when the members of the Londonderry Commission are appointed that we intend to live up to our words that this will be a body to command confidence and respect. You will see that in housing allocations we mean business. You will see that legislation to appoint an ombudsman will be swiftly introduced. Perhaps you are not entirely satisfied: but this is a democracy and I ask you now with all sincerity to call your people off the streets and allow an atmosphere of change to develop. You are Ulstermen yourselves. You know we are all of us stubborn people who will not be pushed too far. I believe that most of you want change, not revolution. Your voice has been heard, and clearly heard. Your duty now is to play your part in taking the heat out of the situation before blood is shed.

But I have a word too, for all those others who see in change a threat to our position in the United Kingdom. I say to them, Unionism, armed with justice, will be a stronger cause than Unionism armed merely with strength. The bully-boy tactics we saw in Armagh are no answer to these grave problems: but they incur for us the contempt of Britain and the world. And such contempt is the greatest threat to Ulster. Let the Government govern and the police take care of law and order.

What in any case, are these changes which we have decided must come? They all amount to this: that in every aspect of our life justice must not only be done but be seen to be done to all sections of the community. There must be evident fairness as between one man and another.

The adoption of such reforms will not, I believe, lose a single seat for those who support the Unionist cause and, indeed, some may be gained. And remember that it is with Stormont that the power of decision rests for maintaining our constitution.

And now a further word to you all. What kind of Ulster do you want? A happy and respected province in good standing with the rest of the United Kingdom? Or a place continually torn apart by riots and demonstrations and regarded by the rest of Britain as a political outcast? As always, in a democracy, the choice is yours. I will accept whatever your verdict may be. If it is your decision that we should live up to the words "Ulster is British", which is part of our creed, then my services will be at your disposal to do what I can. But if you should want a separate inward-looking, selfish and divided Ulster, then you must seek for others to lead you along that road for I cannot and will not do it. Please weigh well all that is at stake and make your voice heard in whatever way you think best so that we may know the views not of the few, but of the many. For this is truly a time of decision and in your silence all that we have built up could be lost. I pray that you will reflect carefully and decide wisely. And I ask all our Christian people, whatever their denomination, to attend their places of worship on Sunday next to pray for the peace and harmony of our country.

268

"THE IRISH GOVERNMENT CAN NO LONGER STAND BY AND SEE INNOCENT PEOPLE INJURED AND PERHAPS WORSE"

Jack Lynch (1917–) was born in Cork City and educated at Christian Brothers School, North Monastery, Cork and The King's Inns, Dublin. After an outstanding Gaelic football and hurling record for his native Cork, with whom he won All Ireland hurling and football championships for six successive years between 1941 and 1946, he was elected to the Dáil for Fianna Fáil at his first attempt in 1948. He joined de Valera's cabinet in 1957, served in various cabinet posts under Lemass, and was elected as leader of Fianna Fáil and Taoiseach after Lemass resigned. He was leader of Fianna Fáil until 1979, serving as Taoiseach 1966–73 and 1973–79.

From 1968 on, the Troubles in Northern Ireland were to dominate his time as Taoiseach. With the situation deteriorating by the day, Lynch made a broadcast on national television outlining government policy on the situation. His broadcast included a call for the involvement for the United Nations in a peace-keeping role in the North, and the announcement of a decision that the Irish Army would establish field hospitals for refugees close to the southern side of the Border.

RTE BROADCAST, AUGUST 13, 1969

It is with deep sadness that you, Irish men and women of goodwill, and I have learned of the tragic events which have been taking place in Derry and elsewhere in the North in recent days. Irishmen in every part of this island have made known their concern at these events. This concern is heightened by the realisation that the spirit of reform and intercommunal co-operation has given way to the forces of sectarianism and prejudice. All people of goodwill must feel saddened and disappointed at this backward turn in events and must be apprehensive for the future.

The Government fully share these feelings and I wish to repeat that we deplore sectarianism and intolerance in all their forms wherever they occur. The Government have been very patient and have acted with great restraint over several months past. While we made our views known to the British Government on a number of occasions, both by direct contact and through our diplomatic representatives in London, we were careful to do nothing that would exacerbate the situation. But it is clear now that the present situation cannot be allowed to continue.

It is evident, also, that the Stormont Government is no longer in control of the situation. Indeed the present situation is the inevitable outcome of the policies pursued for decades by successive Stormont Governments. It is clear, also, that the Irish Government can no longer stand by and see innocent people injured and perhaps worse.

It is obvious that the RUC is no longer accepted as an impartial police force. Neither would the employment of British troops be acceptable nor would they be likely to restore peaceful conditions, certainly not in the long term. The Irish Government have, therefore, requested the British Government to apply immediately to the United Nations for the urgent dispatch of a Peace-keeping Force to the Six Counties of Northern Ireland and have instructed the Irish Permanent Representative to the United Nations to inform the Secretary-General of this request. We have also asked the British Government to see to it that police attacks on the people of Derry should cease immediately.

Very many people have been injured and some of them seriously. We know that many of these do not wish to be treated in Six County hospitals. We have, therefore, directed the Irish Army authorities to have field hospitals established in County Donegal adjacent to Derry and at other points along the Border where they may be necessary.

Recognising, however, that the re-unification of the national territory can provide the only permanent solution for the problem, it is our intention to request the British Government to enter into early negotiations with the Irish Government to review the present constitutional position of the Six Counties of Northern Ireland.

These measures which I have outlined to you seem to the Government to be those most immediately and urgently necessary.

All men and women of goodwill will hope and pray that the present deplorable and distressing situation will not further deteriorate but that it will soon be ended firstly by the granting of full equality of citizenship to every man and woman in the Six County area regardless of class, creed or political persuasion and, eventually, by the restoration of the historic unity of our country.

"COMMUNIQUE AND DECLARATION ON EMPLOYMENT OF TROOPS IN NORTHERN IRELAND"

On August 19, 1969, the British Labour Party government, reacting to the ever worsening situation in the North, decided to deploy troops in Northern Ireland. The communique that was issued announcing the decision reinforced the traditional roles of the Northern Ireland government and of the Westminster parliament. In referring to the "two governments", it quite clearly excludes any role for the Republic, and states that the Border is not an issue. Finally paragraph 7 seeks to define the problem as an economic one, and there is no evident recognition of any other underlying difficulties within the province.

DOWNING STREET, AUGUST 19, 1969

The GOC will assume full command and control of the Ulster Special Constabulary for all purposes including their organisation, deployment, tasks and arms. Their employment by the Northern Ireland Government in riot and crowd control was always envisaged as a purely temporary measure. With the increased deployment of the Army and the assumption by the GOC of operational control of all the security forces, it will be possible for the Special Constabulary to be progressively and rapidly relieved of these temporary duties at his discretion, starting in the cities . . .

The United Kingdom Ministers proposed and the Northern Ireland Ministers readily agreed that two senior civil servants from London should be temporarily stationed with the Northern

Ireland Government in Belfast to represent the increased concern which the United Kingdom Government has necessarily acquired in Northern Ireland affairs through the commitment of the Armed Forces in the present conditions.

1. The United Kingdom Government reaffirm that nothing which has happened in recent weeks in Northern Ireland derogates from the clear pledges made by successive United Kingdom Governments that Northern Ireland should not cease to be a part of the United Kingdom without the consent of the people of Northern Ireland or from the provision in Section 1 of the Ireland Act, 1949, that in no event will Northern Ireland or any part thereof cease to be part of the United Kingdom without the consent of the Parliament of Northern Ireland. The border is not an issue.

2. The United Kingdom Government again affirm that responsibility for affairs in Northern Ireland is entirely a matter of domestic jurisdiction. The United Kingdom Government will take full responsibility for asserting this principle in all international relationships.

3. The United Kingdom Government have ultimate responsibility for the protection of those who live in Northern Ireland when, as in the past week, a breakdown of law and order has occurred. In this spirit, the United Kingdom Government responded to the requests of the Northern Ireland Government for military assistance in Londonderry and Belfast in order to restore law and order. They emphasise again that troops will be withdrawn when law and order has been restored.

4. The Northern Ireland Government have been informed that troops have been provided on a temporary basis in accordance with the United Kingdom's ultimate responsibility. In the context of the commitment of these troops, the Northern Ireland government have reaffirmed their intention to take into the fullest account at all times the views of Her Majesty's Government in the United Kingdom, especially in relation to matters affecting the status of citizens of that part of the United Kingdom and their equal rights and protection under the law.

273

5. The United Kingdom Government have welcomed the decisions of the Northern Ireland Government relating to local government franchise, the revision of local government areas, the allocation of houses, the creation of a Parliamentary Commissioner for Administration in Northern Ireland and machinery to consider citizens' grievances against other public authorities which the Prime Minister reported to the House of Commons at Westminster following his meeting with Northern Ireland Ministers on 21st May as demonstrating the determination of the Northern Ireland Government that there shall be full equality of treatment for all citizens. Both Governments have agreed that it is vital that the momentum of internal reform should be maintained.

6. The two Governments at their meeting at 10 Downing Street today have reaffirmed that in all legislation and executive decisions of Government every citizen of Northern Ireland is entitled to the same equality of treatment and freedom from discrimination as obtains in the rest of the United Kingdom, irrespective of political views or religion. In their further meetings the two Governments will be guided by these mutually accepted principles.

7. Finally, both Governments are determined to take all possible steps to restore normality to the Northern Ireland community so that economic development can proceed at the faster rate which is vital for social stability.

"I WANT TO ASSURE THE HOUSE THAT THESE ARMS HAVE NOT BEEN IMPORTED, HAVE NOT BEEN LANDED IN THIS COUNTRY"

In May 1970, following a tip-off from the Fine Gael leader, Liam Cosgrave, the Taoiseach Jack Lynch sacked Charles Haughey (Minister for Finance) and Neil Blaney (Minister for Agriculture) on suspicion of involvement in importing arms for use by nationalists in Northern Ireland. He also accepted, at the same time, the resignation of Kevin Boland, Minister for Local Government, who left the cabinet in protest at the treatment of his colleagues, and Micheál Ó Moráin, who resigned on health grounds.

Under such circumstances, a government would normally introduce or face a motion of confidence. Lynch, unsure of the support of all of his party in the Dáil, had the issue discussed under a motion appointing Desmond O'Malley as Minister for Justice. Both Blaney and Boland left to form their own separate political parties, while Haughey, who stayed within the party fold, rejoined its front bench in 1975, rejoined the cabinet in 1977 and was elected Taoiseach and leader of Fianna Fáil in 1979.

DAIL ÉIREANN, MAY 6, 1970

Go gcomhaontóidh Dáil Éireann leis an Taoiseach d'ainmniú an Teachta Deasún Ó Máille chun a cheaptha ag an Uachtarán chun bheith ina chomhalta den Rialtas.

I move:

That Dáil Éireann approve the nomination by the Taoiseach of Deputy Desmond J O'Malley for appointment by the President to be a member of the Government.

May I add for the information of the Dáil that, subject to the motion being approved by the House, I propose on his appointment to assign the Department of Justice to Deputy O'Malley.

I should like to state for the information of the Dáil that, having requested the resignation as a member of the Government of Deputy Neil T Blaney, Minister for Agriculture and Fisheries, and Deputy Charles J Haughey, Minister for Finance, as neither would comply with my request, accordingly on my advice the President has today terminated their appointments as members of the Government with effect from the 7th May 1970. On my advice also, the President has today accepted the resignation of Caoimhghín Ó Beoláin, Minister for Local Government and for Social Welfare, as a member of the Government with effect from the same date.

I want to take advantage of this occasion to make a statement on the termination of appointment of the three former members of the Government to which I have just referred. As might be expected, there has been much comment through the news media and otherwise on these terminations of appointment. In at least one case, if not more, there appeared to be an implication that the Minister whose resignation I accepted on Monday last, Micheál Ó Moráin, was involved in some way in the matter with which I now propose to deal. I want to assure the House that that appointment was terminated on health grounds as I have already stated publicly. The Minister was not involved in these matters.

On Monday, 20th April and Tuesday, 21st April, the security forces of the country at my disposal brought me information about an alleged attempt to unlawfully import arms from the continent. Prima facie, these reports involved two members of the Government. I decided to interview the two members of the Government – Deputy Blaney, then Minister for Agriculture and Fisheries and Deputy Haughey, then Minister for Finance. I decided to do this on the following day, Wednesday 22nd April, which was the day of the Budget. In the meantime I ensured

276

that adequate steps were taken to prevent any unauthorised importation of arms. On 22nd April, the day I decided to interview the former Ministers, I received news of the accident to Deputy Haughey and, as a result, I was unable to interview him.

Deputies will remember I informed the House on that day that as a result of that accident Deputy Haughey became concussed and was under medical care in hospital. I contacted his doctor on a number of occasions seeking his permission to interview Deputy Haughey. He told me he was not in a fit condition for interview if the matter I proposed to discuss with him was serious. I told the doctor it was a serious matter and he repeated his opinion that he felt he was not in a position to discuss, certainly at any length, a matter of serious import. However, I ultimately got the doctor's permission and I decided to interview Deputy Haughey in hospital on Wednesday, 29th April. Having made that decision and before I went to the hospital, I then summoned Deputy Blaney to my room and interviewed him, upon which I went to the hospital and interviewed Deputy Haughey.

I told them both I had information which purported to connect them with an alleged attempt to unlawfully import arms, on the basis of which information I felt it was my duty to request their resignations as members of the Government. Each of them denied he instigated in any way the attempted importation of arms. They asked me for time to consider their position. I agreed to do so. In the meantime I authorised the continuation of investigation and I made personal investigations myself, following which I decided to approach the two Ministers again and to repeat my request that they tender to me their resignation as members of the Government. I did so on the basis that I was convinced that not even the slightest suspicion should attach to any member of the Government in a matter of this nature. Having told the Ministers that I wished to have their resignations forthwith, each of them told me he would not give me his resignation until this morning.

I may say that on the question of suspicion Deputy Cosgrave came to me yesterday evening to say he had some information from an anonymous source connecting the two Ministers concerned with this alleged attempt at unlawful importation. Shortly after requesting the resignation of these two Ministers I received the resignation tendered by the Minister for Local Government and Social Welfare, Caoimhghín Ó Beoláin. Not having received the resignations of the other two Ministers, I then informed the President that under the appropriate Article of the Constitution I was requesting him to terminate their appointments as Ministers and advising him to accept the resignation of Caoimhghín Ó Beoláin who had tendered it. As I have already informed the House, he did so.

I want to assure the House that this was the only attempted importation of arms of which I had evidence and with which the two Ministers named were associated. I also want to assure the House that these arms have not been imported, have not been landed in this country, and that the precautions I have taken will ensure they will not be landed.

"THIS COUNTRY IS DRIFTING TOWARDS ANARCHY"

Liam Cosgrave (1920–) was born in Dublin, the son of WT Cosgrave, the first President of the Executive Council. He was educated at Christian Brothers School Synge Street, Castleknock College and the King's Inns. He was first elected to the Dáil in 1943, and was re-elected at every subsequent election until his retirement in 1981. He was Minister for External Affairs in the second Inter-Party Government (1954–57), was elected leader of Fine Gael in 1965, and Taoiseach in 1973–1977. He resigned as leader of Fine Gael after the electoral defeat of the Fine Gael-Labour coalition in 1977.

Given his political pedigree, Cosgrave's belief in law and order as a core party value came as little surprise. When he received a tip-off in relation to the alleged importation of arms, he went directly to Lynch, who then proceeded to act. On May 6, 1970, he recounted the events to the Dail.

DAIL ÉIREANN, MAY 6, 1970

Last night at approximately 8pm I considered it my duty in the national interest to inform the Taoiseach of information I had received and which indicates a situation of such gravity for the nation that it is without parallel in this country since the foundation of the State. By approximately 10 pm two Ministers had been dismissed and a third had resigned. I received information that an attempt had been made involving a number of members of the Government illegally to import a large consignment of arms from the continent for use by an illegal organisation. Arrangements were made under the pretext that this consignment was coming as an official supply of arms to the Army, and that involved making arrangements with the Department of Finance for allowing this consignment through the customs without check at Dublin Airport. My information was that the arrangements involved an Army officer. The affair came to the notice of the Garda authorities and the Garda officer in charge, a senior Garda officer, informed the Commissioner who sought a directive from the Department of Justice in view of a suggestion from an official in the Department of Finance that the Minister for Finance had authorised the passage through the customs of this illegal consignment.

When advice was sought by the Garda no directive was given and when it appeared to the Garda that the situation was not being handled with proper seriousness, a further request for a directive from the Minister for Justice was made. At this stage the matter was notified to the Taoiseach and eventually, after a lot of dithering, the authority from the Department of Finance was dropped.

I understand that because of the linking up of certain Ministers, an Army officer, the brothers of two Ministers, one the brother of the former Minister for Finance and the other the brother of the former Minister for Agriculture and Fisheries, and some of their friends, with these highly dangerous and illegal activities, the question of dismissing the Ministers from the Government arose. No action, however, was taken until the resignation of the Minister for Justice on Monday last. Yesterday when I received a copy of a document on official Garda notepaper which supported the information already at my disposal and which also included some additional names, I decided to put the facts in my possession before the Taoiseach. This particular document says: "A plot to bring in arms from the continent worth £80,000 under the guise of the Department of Defence has been discovered. Those involved are a Captain Kelly, the former Minister for Finance, the former Minister for Agriculture and two associates of the Ministers."

The House will now be aware from the statement the Taoiseach has made and from the brief recital of the information I have given that this is a situation without parallel in this country, that not merely involved here is the security of this State but that those who were drawing public money to serve the nation were, in fact, attempting to undermine it, and that there was a failure to deal with this situation by the Taoiseach . . .

Yesterday at Question Time I said, "Are there going to be other ministerial resignations?" and the Taoiseach said, "I do not know what the Deputy is referring to" and I, as reported in today's *Irish Independent* said, "Is it only the tip of the iceberg?" It was a modest statement.

The situation that has now developed is such that the very security of this State is being threatened. The lives of the people not only in the greatest part of Ireland for which freedom was won at such great price have been put in peril. But, even worse than that, the people, particularly the minority about whom we are so concerned in the Six Counties, have their lives and their welfare put in jeopardy. That is a situation without parallel in the history of this country.

For a considerable time there has been speculation, there have been suggestions, there have been comments from this side of the House that the activities of certain Ministers were such that they were not fit to remain Members of the Government. All during that time the comments that were made by the Taoiseach and by other Ministers were that these were personal attacks on them. I now ask this House and the country to decide who was right and who expressed the real facts of the situation. There was a suggestion made that we were engaged in personal attacks. Not alone, as is now obvious and as it has turned out, were the Ministers concerned unfit to be Ministers but they were engaging in activity undermining the national security and recklessly endangering the lives of our people in the north while continuing to take the people's money. The people of this country can now, tonight, and not for the first time in our history, be grateful to this party for the selfless dedication to the service of the nation . . . that it has discharged without regard to personal interest or party consideration. The position that has now arisen is that this country is in danger of drifting into anarchy. The confidence that has been reposed in this party and the fact that people who were concerned at the trend of events confided this information in me, and in my colleagues through me, indicate that a situation had developed that not merely were those who were paid to serve the people betraying that trust but they were involved in betraying the nation and betraying the welfare of our people.

I want to find out from the Taoiseach tonight – and this House and the country are entitled to find out – what action it is proposed to take against the persons concerned. There is a person who was an Army officer; there are the Ministers or ex-Ministers who have been named; there are the other persons the details of which are available to the Government and to the security service of the Garda and the Army.

This House must be concerned at a situation in which arms were being imported for use by an illegal organisation. It is not necessary to remind the House at this stage that very recently a Garda in the gallant discharge of his duty, serving the public, was murdered; that there have been a series of armed robberies; that, in fact, for some months practically no bank has been safe. This situation is so serious and so grave that it is obvious that this Government, or what is left of them, are not fit to govern.

So far as this situation is concerned, there are these criminal activities but, worse than that, the gravity of the national situation is now emphasised by the fact that the Taoiseach and the Ministers who are left are prepared to cling to power with the support of people whom the Taoiseach considers unfit to hold ministerial office. This is a situation that those whom we commemorated at Arbour Hill today could never have visualised would have happened. I believe the Minister for Labour in a comment today said he went there to pray. We went to pray for them. I am sure that if those who fought and died – and I am privileged to speak from a family tradition that as far back as '98 gave lives in defence of the rights of the Irish people to govern themselves. This party asserted and defended and vindicated the people's rights to ensure that this sovereign authority and it alone would act and work and discharge its responsibility for the people. We are prepared to resume that historic assignment and there is an inescapable obligation on the Taoiseach and his colleagues to resign and to give this country an opportunity of electing a Government of integrity, of honesty, of patriotism, in whom the people and the world can have confidence.

"IRELAND HAS ALWAYS HAD ITS BRITISH LACKEYS"

Neil Blaney (1922–1995) was born in Donegal, the son of Neal Blaney, one of de Valera's colleagues in the founding of Fianna Fáil. Neil Blaney was first elected to the Dail in the by-election caused by the death of his father in 1948, and held the "family" seat in Donegal until his death.

As a member of cabinet from 1957–70, Blaney's views on the North were increasingly out of step with those of his party leaders, and especially Jack Lynch. When confronted by Lynch with the evidence of the alleged importation of arms, and asked to resign, he refused and was sacked. Unlike Haughey, he refused to support Fianna Fáil in the Dail and he was expelled from the party in November 1971.

He went on to establish Independent Fianna Fáil, which had considerable electoral success in the constituencies of Donegal and in the European elections until Blaney's death in 1995.

Dail Éireann, May 8, 1970

I want straightaway to deal with the allegations of gun-running that have been so freely made in so many places during these last few days and to say here before this House that I have run no guns, I have procured no guns, I have paid for no guns, I have provided no money to buy guns and anybody who says otherwise is not telling the truth.

I want also to deal with the much more sinister, far more subtle and blackguardly rumours that are being spread and, indeed, peddled around in various ways, perhaps unwittingly by some but no doubt wittingly and knowingly by others, that I

284

have or had anything to do with subversive organisations in so far as this country is concerned.

To those who say that I have any link with this lousy outfit, Saor Éire, on which perhaps Deputy Cruise O'Brien may be able to enlighten us a little better . . . I want to say that I have nothing but the utmost contempt for that outfit and any association with them would be as repugnant to me as it would be to any other Member of this House. The blackening operation was the suggestion of a tie-up between this organisation and certain Government Ministers who are said to have intervened and used their influence to try to cover up and to allow to escape from this country, as it is said they have escaped, the murderers of Dick Fallon.

These are the sort of things that those who are peddling them should be ashamed of. These are the things that those who unwittingly are merely repeating what others have said should try to retract as fast as they can, because this is not the case, never has been the case, never would be the case in so far as I or any of the people with whom I have associations and friendship are concerned, whether they be north or south.

In regard to my associations, I take a very, very poor view of the manner in which some of my very best friends, some of my associates, some of our best supporters, are being blackguarded and publicly harried at this very time by insinuations and innuendo, by the naming of names, by association of names, to the detriment, no doubt, of those personalities in question. Without any question whatsoever, those associations of names are intended to harm the individuals concerned and any and everybody associated with them. They are intended, perhaps, to try to isolate me from the friends I have and the friends I have made and the organisation to which I have belonged since as long back as I can remember.

Then we come much more close to home and we have brothers being named, not only mine but those of Deputy Haughey, who would be very well able to talk for himself in normal circumstances but who is unable, unfortunately, to be here, not through any lack of wish to be here, but because of the fact that his injuries are such that further damage might be done to him if he were to attempt to do what I know he wants to do in this House, as he has done in the newspapers today, to tell the public, and in particular, the Members of the Dáil, of his not being connected with this whole matter. I want to say in regard to his brothers, whom I know, and whom I am glad to know, and in regard to my own brothers, of whom, lest Deputy Cosgrave does not know, there are five others, that, so far as they are concerned, I know of no connection of theirs with any illegal organisation in this country. They can answer for themselves, are quite well able to do it, and I have no doubt, are doing it, and will do it, thoroughly and properly in due time and, indeed, have already in some cases done so.

I want also to say that my background so far as politics are concerned is one which, perhaps, needs a little restating. I could not but be Fianna Fáil and republican unless I was to renege the heritage of my parents before me. I was born while my late father was under sentence of death. He was again on the run. A few years later, as a child, I was kicked out of the cot I lay in by one of the forces of the then alleged nation, the people who would now decry what republicans stand for and what they stood for. These are the sort of things that at this time come back to me and, added to that, my father, having been condemned, was then lodged and lay for months under sentence in the notorious Davmboe with the gallant men from Kerry and Derry, with whom he was proud to serve and with whom he was prepared to die, and they were Daly, Dan Wright and Sullivan and Larkin from Derry. Those are the associations. This is my background.

We come later then to 1926 and, even at four years of age, even at that young age, I remember, believe it or not, the raids of the irregulars and the special branch of that day. I remember my mother and I, as a child, and others of my family being terrified by these fellows, who were as often drunk as they were sober when they came on these raids, perhaps because, having sold out their republican principles, they had to drown their shame in liquor. I remember it. I shall never forget it. And let nobody in this House or outside ever try to tell me what should be my outlook in so far as the unification of this country is concerned because that is the way I was brought into being. That is the way I was reared. That is the way my thought has been developed. My guidance comes from that source. At this particular time I derive great strength from my past, from my breeding from my father and mother, both of whom have gone to their reward. These things I cannot forget. These things I do not want to trot out, but these things must be said in order that people should fully understand where I stand and how I come to stand there and how I came to be in Fianna Fáil right over the years, working as I did, for I was a child in Fianna Fáil, being kicked by a Blueshirt black and blue on my way from school because I displayed on the lapel of my coat, or jacket, or jersey, or whatever it was, the tricolour that these people would never stand up and give honour to. Well I remember it. I shall never forget it. I try to forgive but never to forget. Let us keep things in mind. I shall keep them in mind, but let us also keep in mind that as those years went on I became part of Fianna Fáil. I could not be otherwise because it was founded with one primary aim of trying to undo the Partition of this land of ours, which has given so much trouble, cost so much pain, and is continuing to do just that, and will continue to do it in lesser or greater measure so long as unity and unification have not been brought about.

I apologise to no one for my views and the views I hold in regard to the re-unification of Ireland, but I do think it is necessary at this particular moment to restate my position. I have been misrepresented, grossly misrepresented, by the architects of Partition both in this House and in Stormont on the question of force. I have never advocated the use of force as a means of bringing about unity of this land – never. Those who say otherwise are liars. What I have said is that we in this part of Ireland cannot stand idly by in these circumstances while the nationalist people of the Six Counties are subjected to murderous assault, as they were last August and, unfortunately and regrettably, it is my opinion that they may well be subjected to the same, or worse, in the not too distant future.

I have no faith in the authority of the British Government and still less in the role that can be played by the British army in preventing bloodshed in the Six Counties. I know from my friends, my personal friends, my very many contacts there, that the Unionist extremists are determined to have what they call the "Ulster Question" finally settled by an all-out assault on the nationalist minority to coerce them and to beat them down into subjection again – this I believe sincerely. The same kind of subjection, I should say, existed until last August when, after many, many years, the people of the Bogside in Derry, later followed by the Falls, by Newry, by Dungannon, by Armagh and Strabane rose up in protest as they had never done before.

Believing, as I do, that violence and, perhaps, bloodshed may be not far away in the Six Counties I charge the leaders of Fine Gael for the disreputable role they have been playing during the past few days to bring down this Government by attempting to provoke a constitutional crisis. They are simply following in the footsteps of their predecessors who sold out in 1925, sold out on the Border question, and handed over almost half a million of our people against those people's expressed wish and against the expressed wish of the majority of all the people of this island, this land, this country of ours, the 32 counties, sold them out and handed them over to the domination of the Orange junta in Stormont, handed them over to discrimination in jobs and housing, about which we all knew but about which others up to recently may not have been aware.

They sold out to injustice and intimidation, to the periodic pogroms that took place in 1921, 1937 and 1969. Ireland has always had its British lackeys; you can pick them out in every generation, those hypocrites, those who for their own ends are always ready to play Britain's game in this country. Listening to the leaders of the two parties here and also on television the other night was enough to nauseate even the strongest of people with honesty in their souls. We heard the posturing about law and order and public security, the same hypocritical tones that come from Paisley and the Orange extremists, the self-righteous concern for the safety of the Irish people; the blank charges thrown about. It did not matter who they hit so long as they did damage.

I want to know – I think it is a fair question – where were these people who are so concerned now last August? Where were they when the people in the Six Counties cried out for help and even for moral support? They were in the same position as they have always been in, trying by every means at their disposal, every trick in the bag, to get whatever selfish, narrow political advantage they could from the grave situation; going up, making sure the Press knew they were coming, that the photographers were around so that they could be photographed and recorded as having been there on conducted tours. This was done and the Deputies and the people of the country know it was done.

I have done what little I could, whatever lay in my power.

I have done whatever I could to help the Irish people in the Six Counties, regardless of their religion because I am not like many here; I have been reared in a mixed community. I know the people of all religions. I have been reared among them, gone to school with them, danced and played with them and I think I know what I am talking about. I have a feeling for all our people, not for any particular section.

I have done what little lay in my power in any way I could to help these people at that time and since because the crisis is not over in the Six Counties. I do not retreat from what I have done to help and encourage our people who were being brutally assaulted in those bad days and, indeed, some other days not so long ago in Belfast. I hope I shall never retreat from that outlook or position.

In regard to the sniping that has been done here at my other colleagues I want to say that the arrogance talked about in regard to Deputy Boland is something that I think Deputy Desmond should not have chosen to mention on this particular day. I listened to Deputy Boland today and I am further impressed by the sincerity of the man who believes in the Republican tradition in which he also was reared. Whatever else may be said about his humility and so on certainly no question of arrogance can be raised in regard to his stand and his forthright speech here today.

In regard to the manner in which another colleague, Deputy Ó Móráin, is concerned I can only say that it comes poorly from his colleagues on the opposite side of the House that he should be vilified as has been done; that it should be said that he was drunk in the Gresham Hotel when in fact he should be applauded for standing up and refusing to bow to the claims that this notorious Sergeant Sullivan was somebody we should be proud of, somebody who should be held up as a model to the young Irish people of today whereas this was the man who proposed, I believe in 1919, to the notorious Tans, the Irregulars of those days, that there should be reprisal shootings and executions and that people from all over the land – innocent or guilty, it did not matter a damn – should be pulled in. I think his proposition was that if one of the forces was lost, 32 of those taken in should be shot.

Credit to the Tans, and God knows it takes something to make me say credit to them and those in charge of them in those days, they did not use his formula. But he got people to use it afterwards, in 1922, and we got the reprisal shootings and we got the 77 people shot down. These are the things we must remember when we talk about Sergeant Sullivan. These are the things we should keep in mind when people are blackguarding Mick Moran who was fully capable that night. I have gone to extreme trouble to make sure that this was so and to nail the lie while the man is still quite ill in hospital. He was fully capable that night and he was doing no more than I, and I think many others, if not all of us here, would do if any dignitary at home or abroad stood up to uphold this particular man of our sad past as a model and example to the young people of Ireland, no matter to what profession they belong.

As regards the idea that there is a split down the middle of Fianna Fáil I want to say that Fianna Fáil is not split; it is not even splintered. I say this as one of the people who is no longer in the Government, who is gone from the Government, who refused to resign from the Government. I want the House to know why. With no disrespect to the Taoiseach or to the Government, and with sadness so far as the President of the country is concerned, I refused to resign because I believe that, by so doing in view of the extremely delicate situation in the Six Counties, I would be aiding, perhaps causing, something that would result in some explosion about which we might be very sorry in the future. If my judgement was wrong, I bow to those who would condemn me. This is why I did not resign at the time I was requested and for no other reason.

To all the newspaper reporters and all those who would write about the manner in which I repudiated our Taoiseach, I want this House, and everybody outside it, to know that it was not a repudiation of him. It was no attempt to denigrate him or take from his authority as the elected leader of the Fianna Fáil Party and as Taoiseach of this country duly elected by a majority of this House which, as displayed again only 48 hours ago, is solidly and completely behind him to see that he continues and carries on as Taoiseach and leader at this critical time, at this difficult time, at a time when those in Opposition would try to make it much more critical then it might otherwise be.

I want the House to be fully aware of that. I want them to know that in going from the Government I go with regret, yes, but I also go with the full knowledge that I believe in the principles of Fianna Fáil as laid down in 1926. I believe above all in the first object of Fianna Fáil, as laid down in our constitution at that time and as enunciated again by the Taoiseach at our recent Ard-Fheis and acclaimed by the thousands there present. Believing as I do, I am as Fianna Fáil today as I was last week, last year or in the past decade.

I want the Opposition to know that they are merely chopping ground with a very poor safety razor blade if they think they will by their tactics here disrupt Fianna Fáil and split that which has stood the test of time, not because it is Fianna Fáil by name but because of the fact, as I am solemnly and completely convinced at this time as, indeed, in many other times, that this is the one party capable of doing what is best for this country. Because of that all of us here right across these benches support the party and the leadership of it. We support the Government members of the party and we are about to support the new members of the Government who are proposed to the House. We will do that when the time comes and whether it be 6 o'clock this evening or 6 o'clock tomorrow morning does not matter.

Having said that, I will leave it to others to give their versions of the split and the crisis – which do not exist on this side of the House. If there is anything riling the Opposition it is – and perhaps this is to be understood – due to their disappointment that there is not actually the split they had hoped for. To the Labour Party I would say in particular: perhaps we have done you a good enough turn by taking you off the headlines as we have done truly and completely in the past few days . . .

However, let me finish by saying there is no question whatever, or no doubt whatever, as to the allegiance of myself and Deputy Charlie Haughey, for whom I speak here this evening, and Deputy Mick Moran who is in hospital – not that that was ever questioned I think, or maybe it was; so much has been said here and so many things have been said in order to confuse – and Deputy Kevin Boland who has spoken for himself.

I am speaking for Deputy Charlie Haughey and myself when I say that there is no question about our allegiance to the leadership of Fianna Fáil, to the members of the Government, and past colleagues, and to the new members who are coming into the Government. So long as there is a Fianna Fáil party standing on their constitution, so long will they have the support of myself, Kevin Boland I am sure, Charlie Haughey and, I hope, those who come after us bearing the same names. The party will have that support in abundance and there will be no doubt about where our allegiance lies because, in my belief, Fianna Fáil and their continuance is synonymous with the advancement of this country and the ultimate bringing about of unity and the betterment of all our people.

"WE REACHED A STATE OF TOTAL DISAGREEMENT WITH THE UNITED KINGDOM GOVERNMENT"

Brian Faulkner (1921–1977) was born in Co. Down and educated at St Columba's College, Dublin. After school he joined the family shirt-making business. At the age of 28 he was elected to Stormont as MP for East Down. He was appointed Government Chief Whip in 1956, Minister for Home Affairs three years later, and Minister for Commerce in 1963. He was perceived to be firmly on the right of the Unionist Party and resigned from government in January 1969 in protest at the establishment of the Cameron Commission to inquire into the causes of violence. When O'Neill resigned as Prime Minister three months later, Faulkner lost the leadership contest by one vote to Chichester-Clark. When Chichester-Clark resigned in March 1971, Faulkner achieved his ambition and beat off the challenge of William Craig to become Prime Minister of Northern Ireland.

In August 1971, Faulkner introduced internment without trial. All of those interned were from the nationalist community, and in the aftermath of its introduction, violence increased and relations between the Catholic community and the Stormont administration descended to an all-time low.

The situation deteriorated further over the winter of 1971 and 1972, particularly after the shooting dead of thirteen civil rights protesters by the Parachute Regiment of the British Army in Derry on January 30 and the subsequent burning of the British Embassy in Dublin in protest. On March 24 1972, and despite previous assurances given by the British Prime Minister, Edward

Heath, the British Government suspended Stormont because of
the refusal of the Northern Ireland Government to give up
responsibility for law and order. The British government
announced the introduction of direct rule of the province for the
first time. Faulkner's speech to Stormont on March 28
demonstrated his complete opposition to the move. It also showed
a recognition that the old order had changed and was unlikely
to return.

STORMONT, MARCH 28, 1972

Mr Speaker, Sir, I propose on this occasion to make a brief statement.

My colleagues and I have made absolutely clear why and how it was that we reached a state of total disagreement with the United Kingdom Government and I do not propose to repeat this today. We have, however, arranged that my own statement, issued later that day by the Cabinet as a whole, should be placed formally on record as a White Paper, of which copies are now being made available to Hon. Members. As for what has followed upon that disagreement, others than we are responsible for it and must answer for it in another place.

I simply want to say this, as we in the present Government meet this House for the last time. For over 50 years the Government and the Parliament of Northern Ireland, and through them the people of Northern Ireland as a whole, have been given devoted service by servants of the Crown. We think of the men of the Royal Ulster Constabulary, of the Ulster Special Constabulary and of the Royal Ulster Constabulary Reserve – all forces, for which Government have answered to this House – and of the sacrifices they have made. In all these forces there have served some of the most splendid, brave and patriotic men the United Kingdom is ever likely to see.

We pay tribute, too, to the Civil Service, which as always worked with loyalty and dedication and which has risen with such cheerful courage to meet the challenges and the dangers of these recent years. And, of course, we have very much in our minds the loyal servants of this House, in great positions and in small, who have sought with total impartiality to serve, irrespective of party, all those all down the years who have been sent here by the people. They know what is in all our minds today – that there is only one authentic voice in any country and that is its elected democratic voice.

Before we adjourn today, I have no doubt that other Right Hon. and Hon. Members may wish to be heard here. We in the Government, however, will have nothing to add as such. We have explained our position. We have taken our stand. We leave our record over the last few days and as a whole to be judged by the country and by posterity.

I conclude with this final word as the government of Ulster is about to pass, temporarily at least, into other hands. I have always been proud to lead the present team in Government, but never so proud as last week. We stood firm and we stood together. When we faced a hard and unpalatable decision no hint of any other interest than the interest of the whole country was heard at the Cabinet table. We did what we believed to be right, for that is the spirit in which Ulster should always be served.

Could I just express the wish and – since I believe in its power – the prayer that we will seek peace, but that it will be peace with justice in our native land? Please God.

"IT IS A DELIBERATE AND CALCULATED ATTEMPT TO USE EVERY DEMOCRATIC AND UNPARLIAMENTARY MEANS FOR THE PURPOSE OF BRINGING DOWN THE WHOLE CONSTITUTION OF NORTHERN IRELAND"

Harold Wilson (1916–1994) was born in Huddersfield and educated at Oxford University where he became a lecturer in economics at the age of 21. He was elected as Labour MP for the Lancashire constituency of Ormskirk in the general election of 1945. He was President of the Board of Trade from 1947–51, and in 1963 succeeded Hugh Gaitskell as leader of the British Labour Party. He was elected Prime Minister a year later, was defeated in the general election of 1970, but returned to power in 1974. In the latter period, he had to deal with a rapidly deteriorating economy, and with increasing difficulties in Northern Ireland. He resigned from the premiership in 1976.

In 1973, the British and Irish governments along with three Northern Ireland political parties (the Unionists led by Brian Faulkner; the SDLP and the Alliance Party) developed the Sunningdale Agreement, which, building on a recently agreed power-sharing executive in Northern Ireland, established a framework within which all-Ireland issues could be discussed – the Council of Ireland.

The Sunningdale Agreement was opposed by the loyalist Ulster Workers' Council who called an all-out strike in opposition to the Executive. It received particularly strong support in the power industry and from loyalist paramilitaries. The strike was extremely effective in disrupting economic and manufacturing activity.

On May 25, Harold Wilson went on British television to give the British government's view of the strike. It is ironic that in spite of his strong rhetoric, many of those who supported the power-sharing

Executive believed that his inability to deal firmly with the strike led to the demise of the Executive four days later.

NATIONAL BROADCAST, MAY 25, 1974

As the holiday begins, Northern Ireland faces the greatest crisis in her history. It is a crisis equally for all of us who live on this side of the water. What we are seeing in Northern Ireland is not just an industrial strike. It has nothing to do with wages. It has nothing to do with jobs – except to imperil jobs.

It is a deliberate and calculated attempt to use every undemocratic and unparliamentary means for the purpose of bringing down the whole constitution of Northern Ireland so as to set up there a sectarian and undemocratic state, from which one-third of the people of Northern Ireland will be excluded. This has not been, at any time over the past few years, a party matter in the House of Commons or in this country at all.

Where the political wildcats of Northern Ireland seek to divide and embitter, all the major parties in Britain have sought to heal and to unite. In the years before 1970, the then Conservative opposition supported the action the Labour government took when we put troops in, in a security role, and issued the Downing Street Declaration about their right to determine their own future.

When Labour was in opposition we supported Mr Heath, Mr Whitelaw and later Mr Francis Pym, first when they suspended the one-sided Stormont parliamentary system which had broken down, then when they devised a new constitution aimed at reconciliation and shared power in Northern Ireland, and again in the initiatives to secure better relations between Ulster and the Irish Republic.

On few constitutional issues in our history have we seen the full government party and the full opposition party voting together for such measures and carrying them with overwhelming majorities.

Agreement was reached by the Northern Ireland Executive in the last few days on arrangements for a new and constructive relationship between North and South. It provides additional reassurance to those in the North who still feared that their way of life would give way to a new all-Ireland system, threatening their religious and political beliefs. There is nothing to fear and they know it.

What has been achieved in Northern Ireland in these last two years provides hope for its future. We are not going to see that set aside by thugs and bullies, behaving as they did in Ballymena last night. We have made it clear as a Government – and we speak for the overwhelming majority of the House of Commons – that we will not negotiate on constitutional or political matters in Northern Ireland with anyone who chooses to operate outside the established political framework; with non-elected self-appointed people who are systematically breaking the law and intimidating the people of Northern Ireland – their fellow citizens and our fellow citizens in the United Kingdom.

We stand by – as our predecessors stood by and still stand by – the decision taken last year that the Northern Ireland Assembly and the Northern Ireland Executive provide the only basis for peace, the only basis for order and good government in Northern Ireland.

Today the law is being set aside. British troops are being hampered in the task which was already daunting and unprecedented within a nation supposed to be enjoying the benefits of peace. Those who are now challenging the constitutional authority are denying the fundamental right of every man and woman – the right to work.

They have decided, without having been elected by a single vote, who shall work in Northern Ireland and who shall not. By their action children are prevented from going to school, essential services are in peril.

The payment of social benefits is reduced to chaos through interference with the methods of payment. By their use of force and intimidation they have condemned hundreds of thousands of workers to involuntary unemployment.

What they do not realise – what I hope they do not realise – is how far they may be imperilling the jobs of Northern Ireland for years to come, and this is a province where unemployment is traditionally one of the greatest social evils.

We recognise that behind the situation lie many genuine and deeply held fears. I have to say that these fears are unfounded, that they are being deliberately fostered by people in search of power . . .

The people on this side of the water, British parents, have seen their sons vilified and spat upon and murdered. British tax-payers have seen the taxes they have poured out almost without regard to cost – £300 million a year this year with the cost of army operations on top of that going into Northern Ireland. They see property being destroyed by evil violence and are asked to pick up the bill for rebuilding it. Yet people who benefit from this now viciously defy Westminster, purporting to act as though they were an elected government – people who spend their lives sponging on Westminster and British democracy and then systematically assault democratic methods. Who do these people think they are?

It is when we see the kind of arrogant undemocratic behaviour now going on that the patience of our citizens, parents, taxpayers, becomes strained . . .

Tonight I ask for an extension of that patience for as long as it is needed. Tonight I ask for the continued support of a long-suffering people in dealing with a situation in which the law is being set aside and essential services are being interrupted. It is out duty as the United Kingdom Parliament and the United Kingdom Government to ensure that minorities are protected, not by the condescension of a group of self-appointed persons operating outside the law, but by those who have been elected to ensure that these things shall be done.

The people of Northern Ireland and their democratically elected Assembly and Executive have the joint duty of seeing this thing through, on the only basis on which true unity can be achieved: democratic elections, constitutional government and the spirit of tolerance and reconciliation. And in doing that they will have the support of the British Government, with our responsibilities in world affairs, for law and order in Northern Ireland. We intend to see it through with them.

"ON MY KNEES, I BEG YOU TO TURN
AWAY FROM VIOLENCE"

Pope John Paul II (1920–), was born in Wadowice, Poland and educated at the University of Krakow, at the Angelicum Institute in Rome and the Catholic University of Lublin, where he gained a doctorate in theology. In 1964, he became Archbishop of Krakow, and three years later was appointed to the College of Cardinals by Pope Paul VI. After the short pontificate of Pope John Paul I, he was elected Pope on October 16, 1978. He is the first non-Italian Pope since 1523. As pontiff, John Paul II immediately adopted an energetic and active approach to his office, and through foreign travel brought the papacy closer to Roman Catholics everywhere.

In 1979 he announced his intention of visiting Ireland to celebrate the centenary of Knock Shrine. His three-day visit at the end of September had a major impact. As a consequence of the tense situation in the North (following the murder of Lord Mountbatten and the killing of eighteen British soldiers at Warrenpoint on the same day), the Pope did not visit Northern Ireland. While celebrating Mass at Drogheda, he made an emotional appeal to those engaged in paramilitary violence to lay down their arms. His appeal was later rejected by the Provisional IRA.

DROGHEDA, OCTOBER 1, 1979

Dear brothers and sisters in Jesus Christ

Having greeted the sod of Ireland today on my arrival in Dublin, I make my first Irish journey to this place, to Drogheda. The cry of centuries sends me here.

301

I arrive as a pilgrim of faith. I arrive also as successor of Peter, to whom Christ has given a particular care for the universal Church. I desire to visit those places in Ireland, in particular, where the power of God and the action of the Holy Spirit have been specially manifested. I seek first those places which carry in themselves the sign of the "beginning", and "beginning" is connected with "firstness", with primacy. Such a place on Irish soil is Armagh, for centuries the Episcopal See of the Primate of Ireland.

The Primate is he who has the first place among the bishops, shepherds of the People of God in this land. This primacy is linked to the "beginning" of the faith, and of the Church in this country. That is to say, it is linked to the heritage of Saint Patrick patron of Ireland.

Hence, I desired to make my first Irish journey a journey towards the "beginning", the place of the primacy. The Church is built in her entirety on the foundation of the Apostles and Prophets, Christ Jesus himself being the chief cornerstone (ref.: Eph. 2:20). But, in each land and nation the Church has her own particular foundation stone. So, it is towards this foundation here in the Primatial See of Armagh that I first direct my pilgrim steps. The See of Armagh is the Primatial See, because it is the See of Saint Patrick. The Archbishop of Armagh is Primate of all Ireland today because he is the Comharba Phadraig, the successor of Saint Patrick, the first Bishop of Armagh.

Standing for the first time on Irish soil, on Armagh soil, the Successor of Peter cannot but recall the first coming here, more than 1,500 years ago, of Saint Patrick.

From his days as a shepherd boy at Slemish right up to his death at Saul, Patrick was a witness to Jesus Christ. Not far from this spot, on the Hill of Slane, it is said that he lit, for the first time in Ireland, the Paschal Fire so that the light of Christ might shine forth on all of Ireland and unite all of its people in the love of the one Jesus Christ.

It gives me great joy to stand here with you today, within

302

sight of Slane, and to proclaim this same Jesus, the Incarnate Word of God, the Saviour of the world. He is the Lord of history, the Light of the world, the Hope of the future of all humanity. In the words of the Easter liturgy, celebrated for the first time in Ireland by Saint Patrick on the hill of Slane, we greet Christ today, he is the Alpha and the Omega, the beginning of all things and their end. All time is his, and all the ages. To him be glory for ever and ever. Lumen Christi Deo Gratias. The Light of Christ Thanks be to God. May the light of Christ, the light of faith continue always to shine out from Ireland. May no darkness ever be able to extinguish it.

That he might be faithful to the end of his life to the light of Christ was Saint Patrick's prayer for himself. That the people of Ireland might remain faithful always to the light of Christ was his constant prayer for the Irish. He wrote in his Confession:

"May God never permit it to happen to me that I should lose his people that he purchased in the utmost parts of the world. I pray to God to give me perseverance and to deign that I be a faithful witness to him to the end of my life for God. From time to time, I came to know him in my youth, the love of God and the fear of him have grown in me and up to now, thanks to the grace of God, I have kept the faith." (Confession 44:58).

"I have kept the faith." That has been the ambition of the Irish down the centuries. Through persecution and through poverty, in famine and in exile, you have kept faith. For many it has meant martyrdom. Here at Drogheda where his relics are honoured, I wish to mention one Irish martyr Saint Oliver Plunkett, at whose canonisation in the Holy Year, 1975, I was happy to assist as Cardinal of Krakow on the invitation of my friend, the late Cardinal Conway.

Saint Oliver Plunkett, Primate of Ireland for 12 years, is for ever an outstanding example of the love of Christ for all men. As bishop, he preached a message of pardon and peace. He was, indeed, the defender of the oppressed and the advocate of justice, but he would never condone violence. For men of violence, his word was the word of the Apostle Peter: "Never pay back one wrong with another" (1Pt 3:9). As a martyr for the faith, he sealed by his death the same message of reconciliation that he had preached during his life. In his heart there was no rancour, for his strength was the love of Jesus, the love of the Good Shepherd who gives his life for his flock. His dying words were words of forgiveness for all his enemies.

Faith and fidelity are the marks of the Church in Ireland, a Church of martyrs, a Church of witnesses, a Church of heroic faith, heroic fidelity. These are the historical signs marking the track of faith on Irish soil. The Gospel and the Church have struck deep roots in the soul of the Irish people.

The See of Armagh, the See of Patrick, is the place to see that track, to feel those roots. It is the place in which to meet, from which to address, those other great and faithful dioceses whose people have suffered so much from the events of the past decade, Down and Connor, Derry, Dromore, Clogher, Kilmore.

During the period and preparation of my visit to Ireland, especially precious to me was the invitation of the Primate of all Ireland that I should visit his cathedral in Armagh. Particularly eloquent, also, was the fact that the invitation of the Primate was taken up and repeated by the representatives of the Church of Ireland, and by leaders, and members of the other Churches, including many from Northern Ireland. For all these invitations, I am particularly grateful.

These invitations are an indication of the fact that the Second Vatican Council is achieving its work and that we are meeting with our fellow Christians of other Churches as people who together confess Jesus Christ as Lord, and who are drawing closer to one another in Him as we search for unity and common witness.

This truly fraternal and ecumenical act on the part of representatives of the Churches is also a testimony that the tragic events taking place in Northern Ireland do not have their source in the fact of belonging to different Churches and Confessions; that this is not – despite what is so often repeated before world opinion – a religious war, a struggle between Catholics and Protestants. On the contrary. Catholics and Protestants, as people who confess Christ taking inspiration from their faith and the Gospel, are seeking to draw closer to one another in unity and peace. When they recall the greatest commandment of Christ, the commandment of love, they cannot behave otherwise.

But Christianity does not command us to close our eyes to difficult human problems. It does not permit us to neglect and refuse to see unjust social or international situations. What Christianity does forbid is to seek solutions to these situations by the ways of hatred, by the murdering of defenceless people, by the methods of terrorism. Let me say more: Christianity understands and recognises the noble and just struggle for justice, but Christianity is decisively opposed to fomenting hatred and to promoting or provoking violence or struggle for the sake of "struggle". The command, "Thou shalt not kill", must be binding on the conscience of humanity, if the terrible tragedy and destiny of Cain is not to be repeated.

For this reason it was fitting for me to come here before going to America, where I hope to address the United Nations Organisation on these same problems of peace and war, justice and human rights. We have decided together, the Cardinal Primate and I, that it would be better for me to come here, to Drogheda, and that it should be from here that I would render homage to the "beginning" of the faith, and to the primacy in your homeland, and from here that I should reflect with all of you before God, before your splendid Christian history, on this most urgent problem, the problem of peace and reconciliation.

We must, above all, clearly realise where the causes of this dramatic struggle are found. We must call by name those systems and ideologies that are responsible for this struggle. We must also reflect whether the ideology of subversion is the true good of your people, for the true good of man. Is it possible to construct the good of individuals and peoples on hatred on war? Is it right to push the young generations into the pit of fratricide? Is it not necessary to seek solutions to our problems by a different way? Does not the fratricidal struggle make it even more urgent for us to seek peaceful solutions with all our energies?

These questions I shall be discussing before the United Nations Assembly in a few days. Here today in this beloved land of Ireland, from which so many before me have departed for America, I wish to discuss them with you.

My message to you today cannot be different from what Saint Patrick and Saint Oliver Plunkett taught you. I preach what they preach, Christ who is the "Prince of Peace" (Is. 9:5), who reconciled us for God and to each other (2 Cor. 5:18), who is the source of all unity.

The Gospel reading of this Mass tells us of Jesus, as "the Good Shepherd" whose one desire is to bring all together in one flock. I come to you in his name, in the name of Jesus Christ, who died in order "to gather into one, the children of God who are scattered abroad" (Jn. 11:52). This is my mission, my message to you: Jesus Christ who is our peace. Christ "is our peace"(Eph. 2.11). And today and forever he repeats to us: "My peace I give to you, my peace I leave with you" (Jn. 14:27). Never before in the history of mankind has peace been so much talked about and so ardently desired as in our day.

The growing interdependence of peoples and nations makes almost everyone subscribe at least in principle to the ideal of universal human brotherhood. Great international institutions debate humanity's peaceful co-existence. Public opinion is growing in consciousness of the absurdity of war as a means to resolve differences. More and more, peace is seen as a necessary condition for fraternal relations among nations, and among peoples.

Peace is more and more clearly seen as the only way to justice: peace is itself the work of justice. And yet again and again one can see how peace is undermined and destroyed. Why is it then that our convictions do not always match our behaviour and our attitudes? Why is it that we do not seem to be able to banish all conflicts from our lives?

Peace is the result of many converging attitudes and realities: it is the product of moral concerns, of ethical principles based on the Gospel message and fortified by it.

I want to mention here in the first place: justice. In his message for the 1971 Day of Peace, my revered predecessor, that Pilgrim for peace, Paul VI said: "True peace must be founded upon justice, upon a sense of the untouchable dignity of man, upon the recognition of an indelible and happy equality between men, upon the basic principle of human brotherhood, that is, of the respect and love due to each man, because he is man."

This same message I affirmed in Mexico and in Poland. I reaffirm it here in Ireland. Every human being has inalienable rights that must be respected. Each human community – ethnic, historical, cultural or religious – has rights which must be respected. Peace is threatened every time one of these rights is violated. The moral law, guardian of human rights, protector of the dignity of man, cannot be set aside by any person or group or by the state itself for any cause, not even for security or in the interests of law and order. The Law of God stands in judgement over all reasons of state.

As long as injustice exists in any of the areas that touch upon the dignity of the human person, be it in the political, social or economic field, be it in the cultural or religious sphere, true peace will not exist. The causes of inequalities must be identified through a courageous and objective evaluation and they must be eliminated so that every person can develop and grow in the full measure of his or her humanity.

Secondly peace cannot be established by violence, peace can never flourish in a climate of terror, intimidation and death. It is Jesus himself who said "All who take the sword will perish by the sword" (Mt. 26:52). This is the word of God, and it commands this generation of violent men to desist from hatred and violence and to repent.

I join my voice today to the voice of Paul VI and my other predecessors, to the voices of your religious leaders, to the voices of all men and women of reason and I proclaim with the conviction of my faith in Christ and with an awareness of my mission that violence is evil, that violence is unacceptable as a solution to problems, that violence is unworthy of men.

Violence is a lie for it goes against the truth of our faith, the truth of our humanity. Violence destroys what it claims to defend: the dignity, the life, the freedom of human beings. Violence is a crime against humanity for it destroys the very fabric of society. I pray with you that the moral sense and Christian conviction of Irish men and women may never become obscured and blunted by the life of violence, so that nobody may ever call murder by any other name than murder, that the spiral of violence may never be given the distinction of unavoidable logic or necessary retaliation. Let us remember that the word remains forever, "All who take the sword will perish by the sword".

There is another word that must be part of the vocabulary of every Christian, especially when barriers of hate and mistrust have been constructed. This is reconciliation: "So if you are offering your gift at the altar, and there remember that your brother has something against you, leave your gift there before the altar and go: be reconciled with your brother and then come out and offer your gift" (Mt. 5:23 – 24).

This command of Jesus is stronger than any barrier that human inadequacy or malice can build. Even when our belief in the fundamental goodness of every human being has been shaken or undermined, even if longer held convictions and attitudes have hardened our hearts, there is one source of power that is stronger than every disappointment, bitterness or ingrained mistrust, and that power is Jesus Christ who brought forgiveness and reconciliation to the world.

I appeal to all who listen to me; to all who are discouraged after the many years of strife, violence and alienation – that they attempt the seemingly impossible to put an end to the intolerable. I pay homage to the many efforts that have been made by countless men and women in Northern Ireland to take the path of reconciliation and peace.

The courage, the patience, the indomitable hope of the men and women of peace have lighted up the darkness of these years of trial. The spirit of Christian forgiveness shown by so many who have suffered in their persons or through their loved ones have given inspiration to multitudes. In the years to come, when the words of hatred and the deeds of violence are forgotten, it is the words of love and the acts of peace and forgiveness which will be remembered. It is these which will inspire the generations to come.

To all of you who are listening I say do not believe in violence; do not support violence. It is not the Christian way. It is not the way of the Catholic Church. Believe in peace and forgiveness and love; for they are of Christ.

Communities who stand together in their acceptance of Jesus's supreme message of love expressed in peace and reconciliation and in their rejection of all violence, constitute an irresistible force for achieving what many have come to accept as impossible and destined to remain so.

Now I wish to speak to all men and women engaged in violence. I appeal to you in language of passionate pleading. On my knees, I beg you to turn away from the path of violence and to return to the way of peace. You may claim to seek justice. I too believe in justice, and I seek justice. But violence only delays the day of justice. Violence destroys my work of justice. Further violence in Ireland will only drag down to ruin the land you claim to love and the values you claim to cherish.

In the name of God I ask you to return to Christ who died so that men might live in forgiveness and peace. He is waiting for you, longing for each one of you to come to him so that he may say to each of you, your sins are forgiven, go in peace.

I appeal to young people who may have become caught up in organisations engaged in violence, to say to you with all the love I have for you, with all the love I have for young people, do not listen to voices which speak the language of hatred, revenge, retaliation. Do not follow any leaders who train you in the ways of inflicting death. Love life, respect life, in yourselves and in others. Give yourselves to the service of life, not the work of death.

Do not think that courage and strength are proved by killing and destruction. The true courage lies in working for peace. The true strength lies in joining with the young men, and women of your generation everywhere in building up a just and human and Christian society, by the ways of peace. Violence is the enemy of justice. Only peace can lead the way to true justice.

My dear young people, if you have been caught up in the ways of violence, even if you have done deeds of violence, come back to Christ whose parting gift to the world was peace. Only when you come back to Christ will you find peace for your troubled consciences and rest for your disturbed souls.

And to you, fathers and mothers, I say: teach your children how to forgive, make your homes places of love and forgiveness, make your streets and neighbourhoods centres of peace and reconciliation. It would be a crime against youth, and their future, to let even one child grow up with nothing but the experience of violence and hate.

Now I wish to speak to all the people in positions of leadership, to all who can influence public opinion, to all members of political parties, and to all who support them, I say to you:

Never think you are betraying your own community by seeking to understand and respect and accept those of a different tradition. You will serve your own tradition best by working for reconciliation with others.

Each of the historical communities in Ireland can only harm itself by seeking to harm the other. Continued violence can only endanger everything that is most precious in the traditions and aspirations of both communities.

Let no one concerned with Ireland have any illusions about the nature and the menace of political violence. The ideology and the methods of violence have become an international problem of the utmost gravity. The longer the violence continues in Ireland, the more the danger will grow that this beloved land could become yet another theatre for international terrorism.

To all who bear political responsibility for the affairs of Ireland, I want to speak with the same urgency and intensity with which I have spoken to the men of violence. Do not cause or condone or tolerate conditions which give excuse or pretext to men of violence.

For those who resort to violence always claim that only violence brings about change. They claim that political action cannot achieve justice. You politicians must prove them to be wrong. You must show that there is a peaceful, political way to justice. You must show that peace achieves the works of justice and violence does not.

I urge you who are called to the noble vocation of politics to have the courage to face up to your responsibility to be leaders in the cause of peace, reconciliation and justice. If politicians do not decide and act for just change then the field is left open to the men of violence. Violence thrives best when there is political vacuum and a refusal of political movement.

Paul VI, writing to Cardinal Conway in March, 1972, said, "Everyone must play his part. Obstacles which stand in the way of justice must be removed, obstacles such as civil inequity, social and political discrimination and misunderstanding between individuals and groups. There must be a mutual and abiding respect for others, for their persons, their rights, and their lawful aspirations." I speak these words of my revered predecessor, my own today.

I came to Drogheda today on a great mission of peace and reconciliation. I come as a pilgrim of peace, Christ's peace. To Catholics, to Protestants my message is peace and love. May no Irish Protestant think that the Pope is an enemy, a danger or a threat. My desire is that instead Protestants would see in me a friend and a brother in Christ. Do not lose trust that this voice of mine may be fruitful, that this voice of mine may be listened to. Let history record that at a difficult moment in the experience of the people of Ireland, the Bishop of Rome set foot in your land, that he was with you and prayed with you for peace and reconciliation, for the victory of justice and love over hatred and violence. Yes, this our witness finally becomes a prayer, a prayer from the heart for peace. For the peoples who live on this earth, peace for all the people of Ireland.

May this fervent prayer for peace penetrate with light on all consciences. Let it purify them and take hold of them. Christ, Prince of Peace: Mary, Mother of Peace; Queen of Ireland, St Patrick, St Oliver, and all the saints of Ireland, I, together with all those gathered here, and with all who join with me, invoke you, watch over Ireland, protect humanity, Amen.

"THE TOTALITY OF RELATIONSHIPS"

Charles Haughey (1925–) was born in Castlebar, Co. Mayo and educated at Christian Brothers School Fairview, University College Dublin and The King's Inns. While at UCD, he met his future wife, Maureen Lemass, daughter of Sean Lemass. After several electoral attempts, he was elected to the Dáil at the 1957 general election.

He was appointed Parliamentary Secretary in 1960 and joined the cabinet as Minister for Justice after the 1961 general election. He also served in the 1960s as Minister for Agriculture and later as Minister for Finance under Jack Lynch. He was sacked by Jack Lynch in 1970 over the alleged importation of arms, and after five years away from the front bench, he returned in 1975. After the 1977 election he was appointed Minister for Health and Social Welfare. He was elected leader of Fianna Fáil and Taoiseach in 1979, led his party in opposition between 1982 and 1987, and served as Taoiseach until his resignation as leader of Fianna Fáil in 1991.

Margaret Thatcher (1925–) was born in Grantham, and studied Chemistry at Oxford before being called to the Bar. She was elected MP for Finchley in 1959, and served as Secretary of State for Education in Heath's administration 1970–74. She was elected leader of the Conservative Party in 1975 and Prime Minister in 1979, a post she held until 1990.

After Haughey's election as Taoiseach, he sought to reinvigorate Anglo-Irish relations. After a series of meetings, Thatcher brought the most powerful British government delegation seen in Dublin since independence to a summit in December 1980. Arising out of that meeting a communiqué was issued. It promised a review of the totality of relationships between the two countries. Unionists were outraged and appalled. Although Thatcher's relationship with Haughey cooled significantly in subsequent years, the summit meeting can be seen as the start of the tortuous process that led to the signing of the Anglo-Irish Agreement in 1985.

DUBLIN CASTLE, DECEMBER 8, 1980

The Taoiseach and the Prime Minister noted with satisfaction the useful exchanges at Ministerial and official level since their last meeting, leading to new and closer co-operation in energy, transport, communications, cross-border economic development and security. They agreed that further improvements in these and other fields should be pursued.

The Taoiseach and the Prime Minister agreed that the economic, social and political interests of the peoples of the United Kingdom of Great Britain and Northern Ireland and the Republic are inextricably linked, but that the full development of these links has been put under strain by division and dissent in Northern Ireland. In that context, they accepted the need to bring forward policies and proposals to achieve peace, reconciliation and stability; and to improve relations between the peoples of the two countries.

They considered that the best prospect of attaining these objectives was the further development of the unique relationship between the two countries.

They accordingly decided to devote their next meeting in London during the coming year to special consideration of the totality of relationships within these islands. For this purpose they have commissioned joint studies, covering a range of issues including possible new institutional structures, citizenship rights, security matters, economic co-operation and measures to encourage mutual understanding.

The Taoiseach and the Prime Minister recalled the statements issued on behalf of their Governments on 4 December about the situation in the H-Blocks and reiterated the hope that the statement made by the Secretary of State for Northern Ireland on 4 December would provide the basis on which the issues could be resolved.

The discussions were regarded by both sides as extremely constructive and significant.

"THE ADDICTION TO THE DRUG OF CHEAP POPULARITY IS CATCHING"

John Kelly (1931–1991) was born in Dublin and educated at Glenstal Abbey, University College, Dublin, Heidelberg and Oxford. After a glittering academic career, he entered the political arena in 1969 as a Fine Gael member of Seanad Éireann. He was elected to the Dáil for Dublin South Central in 1973, and served as Chief Whip and Parliamentary Secretary to the Taoiseach between 1973–1976. In 1976 he was appointed to the position of Attorney General. In the 1981–1982 Fine Gael-Labour minority Coalition administration he was Minister of Trade, Commerce and Tourism. He expressed the desire to stay on the back benches in subsequent administrations, and did not seek re-election in the general election of 1989.

Kelly was one of the best parliamentary speakers in the history of the State. He spoke passionately, clearly and effectively. He was not afraid of attacking policies being pursued by his own side, although he clearly relished attacking his political opponents. At the end of his political career, he favoured the emergence of a left versus right split in Irish politics.

In the 1982–87 period, he criticised, from the back benches, much of that government's economic policy. On the sixtieth anniversary of the Civil War, he spoke of the divisions as he saw them in Irish politics.

DUBLIN, JUNE 21, 1982

Sixty years ago this week the Civil War began. The issues which split the national movement in two did not seem then

316

worth having a civil war to settle; in the retrospect of today they make the war seem a tragic disaster, as though there were really some mí-ádh or jinx on Irish affairs, such as drew from Michael Collins the despairing cry: "Is Ireland never to get a chance?"

It is conventional to lament the "bitterness" which the Civil War left behind it, as though that were its only evil legacy. In fact, considering the terrible deed of taking up arms against the first native Government – the dream of generations, and supported by a clear democratic majority – and considering the terrible things the Government did to put down the rebellion, the degree of enduring bitterness has been very small. What animus can be seen in politics today is more the product of ordinary partisan sentiment – like the enthusiasm for a football team which can drive people to act like hooligans – than a residue of spite left over since before most of us were born.

A far worse, more lasting consequence of the events of 1922 has been the effect on the economic management of the country. The civil war divided the movement in whose original programme economic independence and prosperity had been an important feature, and, having divided it, set the sundered halves in competition with one another for political support.

This did not do much economic damage for as long as old-fashioned financial prudence and rectitude in the State's behalf were practised fairly consistently by both sides. But then standards slipped. We had a 12% wage increase – huge by the measure of the day – in order to win two by-elections in 1964; and we have now been running a current budget deficit since 1971. The deficit was at first fairly insignificant; but it has since increased by huge annual leaps and bounds, reined back only twice in eleven years, by Richie Ryan in 1976, and by John Bruton this year, on both occasions by means of a set of tough budgetary measures.

The unpopularity of this discipline was of course fully exploited by Mr Haughey and Professor O'Donoghue, who told the people there was no need to be "hypnotised by figures", and that another little fix of foreign debt wouldn't do us any harm.

That reckless and wicked style of political competition goes far beyond anything that this party ever attempted. We lost the 1977 election partly, and the 1982 election entirely, because we stopped well short of any such ruthless unscrupulousness, by which the people's future, and their children's – so far as the State's capacity to influence it goes – is hocked off, bit by bit, for party advantage.

But the addiction to the drug of cheap popularity is catching. It would be absurd to pretend that this party never took a decision in Government, or made a promise in Opposition, influenced by anything but sober considerations of the good of the economy. And as long as we are in competition with a large party supported by much the same kind of people as ourselves, aiming at the same floating vote, there will be the danger, in spite of good intentions, of our trying to match their bogus generosity at elections.

Where does this leave the country and this party? I said before that we would do better to decline in advance any coalition with Labour, for so long at least as that party's internal rules and its recent mode of conducting itself make them so difficult to do business with; and for so long as their terms for coalition would include a programme designed to expand the role of the State – the reverse of what the country needs at the present juncture.

We should face the next election alone, with no compromises made with, or hostages given to any other party. I believe the support for Fine Gael and its leader has been growing steadily since 1977, and never faster than in recent months. This spread of support could develop wildfire speed according as disillusionment with the present Taoiseach's regime begins to turn into panic; and a Fine Gael campaign aimed at an overall majority through winning an extra seat in about half the country's constituencies would succeed.

That belief may seem a naive piece of partisan enthusiasm, and it could of course happen that in spite of a successful campaign and the gain of many seats, we were still a few seats short of control. No one can be certain of victory, and I do not think we should practise the vain "We'll be there!" boastfulness of Fianna Fáil which they went in for before their 1981 defeat, and again before their defeat in Dublin West, which had no effect but to deepen their humiliation when they lost. What options would in this event be open to us, assuming a Labour alliance had been ruled out from the start, and assuming that we would also decline the responsibility of running a minority Government depending on day-to-day Labour support or forbearance?

The options would be two. We could, firstly, remain in Opposition, consolidate, and hope for final success the next time round: this option, implying a continuing FF minority Government, dependent entirely on keeping in with and conciliating small numbers of deputies, would leave the country still travelling, but with gathering speed, on the downward slide.

The other option, admittedly not ours to command, is one which up to now, because of civil-war-conditioned instincts, has been unthinkable: an accommodation, a co-operating truce, with the forces from whom forgotten issues sixty years ago divided us, and from whom, if Ireland had been luckier, we need never have been divided.

I have no idea to what extent, if any, the present membership of the Fianna Fáil party would be open to such an idea. On past form, they would most likely treat it with unanimous scorn. At the same time, many of them seem lately genuinely disposed to put the national interest before party considerations, and seem worried by the way the country is moving: these, at least, might look closer now at an option which formerly was not in view at all. They might also reflect that the option must in theory be as easily exercisable this side of a General Election as afterwards.

If their reaction is to damn such a thing out of hand, they ought to reflect that the electorate, in the dangerous conditions of 1982, could easily take a poor view of politicians' intransigence. The Pavlovian reaction of party activists – on either side – does not necessarily represent what ordinary people feel about the prospect of mending the damage caused in 1922; and of freeing the national Government, whether led by us or by FF, from dictation by a minuscule extreme Left.

There are of course deep differences of ethos, of group temperament, between us and our opponents. They are perhaps no greater than would have developed over the years anyway between people who found themselves divided into two separate groups by a quite random distribution, but they are serious enough to provide each side with a set of very negative impressions of the other, which obviously must be an obstacle to co-operation.

To us, the Fianna Fáil character seems shifty and irrational on national issues: begrudging and ungenerous to opponents; crudely arrogant and triumphalist when winning; easily satisfied with what Liam Cosgrave called "verbal patriotism"; constitutionally disinclined to give a straight answer to a straight question. Their caricature of us is equally unlovely: I think I could outline its main features, but hope I can be excused from doing so here.

Parties so long estranged, intellectually petrified into postures of mutual hostility, cannot easily be got to co-operate. The national interest might be best served by such an association; but it does not need to be a merger or fusion. No one now is interested in such a thing, and in this party there would be at least as much resistance to it as in Fianna Fáil. All that it need be is an arrangement – I do not care whether it is called a coalition, a front, a pact, or an alliance – to support a Government chosen from both parties, and determined to put party considerations aside at least until the country's economy is restored to full health, with unemployment and inflation beaten, and the state once more able to pay its way year by year.

Any such large alliance, dominating the Dáil with an initial crushing majority of 140 seats or so, would contain dangers of its own. It could become complacent, self-serving, out-of-touch, even corrupt, monopolising power for the benefit of club members. If it allowed itself to forget the claims of social justice, and to be too closely identified with private enterprise and property at the expense of the needs of less privileged people, it could provoke a polarisation of politics here on class lines, exactly what would suit extreme left-wing ideologies.

If these pitfalls could be avoided, the most probable long-term result would be a continuous rise in support for the democratic Labour Party, as providing the only plausible Opposition and ultimately the only plausible alternative. It is quite likely that within one or two General Elections the Labour Party would advance to 50 seats, and hold at least one seat in every constituency in the country. But as things are going at present, with political rewards being seen to go to the most exigent and strident parts of the Left, the Labour Party seems in real danger of being overtaken on that wing by forces of a somewhat different kind.

Another problem of association between the two large parties would be the construction of a rational Northern policy on which both parties could agree; this is a large question which might be left for another day. For the moment it would be enough if we could look with an open mind at the general idea of an option which, on the basis of the general social and economic outlook of the two parties, would seem obvious and painless in any other Western country, but which here, up to now, the dead hand of 1922 has kept off the table.

"THIS WORDING WOULD NOT EXCLUDE THE POSSIBILITY THAT IN THE FUTURE A LAW COULD BE PASSED PERMITTING ABORTION IN SOME FORM"

Following the visit of Pope John Paul II in 1979, the Pro-Life amendment campaign was launched to place the legal prohibition on abortion into the Irish constitution. This was motivated by the desire of the PLAC to ensure that abortion could not be introduced without a referendum.

Prior to the 1981 general election, PLAC obtained assurances from Garret FitzGerald as leader of Fine Gael and from Charles Haughey, leader of Fianna Fáil, that they would support the introduction of an appropriately-worded amendment. In the following eighteen months, there were a further two general elections, with the minority Fine Gael coalition that had been in power from July 1981 losing power following the rejection of the Budget in January 1982. It was replaced by a minority Fianna Fáil government, which had to go to the country in November 1982, following its loss of a motion of no confidence.

Through this period of political intensity and turmoil, each of the main parties felt vulnerable on the abortion issue. Given the closeness of the electoral contests, and the increased number of marginal five-seat constituencies, neither could afford to lose conservative support. The Fianna Fáil government produced the wording of the proposed constitutional amendment two days before the confidence motion was held. It read:

"The state acknowledges the right to life of the unborn, and with due regard to the equal right to life of the mother, guarantees in its laws to respect and, as far as practicable, by its laws to defend and vindicate that right."

FitzGerald accepted the wording when it initially appeared. After the election, which resulted in a majority Fine Gael-Labour coalition, the Government changed its mind, arguing that the wording was ambiguous, and sought to have a different wording introduced. In the revised wording the Government sought to limit the power of the Supreme Court to introduce abortion, rather than institute a complete constitutional ban on its introduction. The Government's wording simply stated that:

"Nothing in this constitution shall be invoked to invalidate or to deprive of force or effect a provision of the law on the grounds that it prohibits abortion."

The Government's wording was defeated in the Dáil and the Fianna Fáil wording was passed by a two to one majority in a 54% poll on September 7, 1983. Ironically, the wording was used as justification by the Supreme Court in 1992 that abortion was legal in limited cases.

The Pro-Life Amendment debate was one of the most heated political debates in recent decades. The Catholic hierarchy took a stance that was directly opposed to that of FitzGerald's Government and Church-state relations reached a new low. This clash was to be repeated over family planning legislation, and in the divorce referendum in 1986.

On March 30, 1983, the Catholic Hierarchy issued a statement opposing the Government's plans to change the initial wording. It was a key factor in sustaining support for the original wording.

MAYNOOTH, MARCH 30, 1983

Because of their deep concern for the sacredness of human life as created by God in his own image, the vast majority of Irish people and the major political parties are manifestly against the legalisation of abortion. This concern has found expression in a legitimate and commendable aspiration to safeguard the right to life of the unborn child by means of an appropriate amendment to the Constitution.

From the beginning, we have recognised the difficulties

inherent in the task of drafting an appropriate form of amendment. What is being sought is to enshrine in the Constitution the right of the unborn child to life, a right already enjoyed under the Constitution by all citizens. This would ensure that no decision to introduce abortion could be taken without a direct vote of the people.

The new wording proposed by the Minister for Justice does indeed seek to prevent abortion being introduced as a consequence of a judgement by the courts. It has, however, been acknowledged in Dáil Éireann that this wording would not exclude the possibility that in the future a law could be passed permitting abortion in some form, without a direct vote of the people. Experience in other countries shows that this possibility is not as remote as it might seem.

The Constitution is our greatest legal protector in Ireland against violence of the right to life. Surely the most defenceless and voiceless in our midst are entitled to the fullest constitutional protection.

It is our earnest hope that, at the conclusion of the debate, our legislators will put before the people a form of amendment which will give them the opportunity to decide whether or not they wish to give to unborn human life the full constitutional protection already guaranteed to every citizen.

"THE MORAL OBLIGATION, TO PUT NORTHERN IRELAND, ITS PEOPLE, AND THEIR INTERESTS FIRST, IMPOSES ITSELF ALSO . . . ON THOSE IN OTHER LANDS"

Garret FitzGerald (1926–) was born in Dublin and educated at Belvedere College and University College Dublin. After a business and academic career, he was elected to the Dáil in 1969, as TD for Dublin South East. After the 1973 general election, he was appointed to the post of Minister for Foreign Affairs in the new Cosgrave-led Fine Gael-Labour coalition.

After the electoral defeat of that Government in 1977, FitzGerald was elected as leader of Fine Gael, secured a turnaround in the party's fortunes and returned after the June 1981 election as Taoiseach of a minority Fine Gael-Labour coalition. After electoral defeat in 1982, a coalition with Labour resulted in the formation of a majority Fine Gael-Labour coalition that served until its defeat in the February 1987 election.

One of the key policy areas for his last administration was Northern Ireland. FitzGerald established, with the other constitutional nationalist parties, the New Ireland Forum, to examine how a new Ireland might operate. The Forum met regularly for a year. It commissioned and published a series of specialist reports and finally published its own report in 1984.

In 1984, FitzGerald was invited to address a joint session of the United States Congress. In his speech, he outlined the important links between Ireland and the United States (at a time when Irish diplomacy was seen to be increasingly effective in the United States) and also took the opportunity to inform the members of Congress of the work that was ongoing in trying to reach a solution to the problems of Ireland.

WASHINGTON, MARCH 15, 1984

Mr Speaker, Mr Vice-President, distinguished members of the Congress of the United States, with the Irish hospitality for which America is famous, you have been good enough to invite me to address you in the week of St Patrick – Féile Phádraig in the language of the Gael. On behalf of the Irish people, close, as always, in feeling to their American cousins, I thank you for this honour.

This is the second time in eight years you have paid tribute in this way, by hearing from this dais the Head of an Irish Government, in celebration of the friendship and cousinship that binds our two peoples. The tradition is a long one, going back over a century to the year 1880, when you offered a platform to one of the first people from outside of the United States ever permitted to address this Congress, the great Irish leader, Charles Stewart Parnell.

I have said that we are cousins: our countries are linked by a special relationship, not built on mutual calculations of interest, but on human links of kinship and friendship: a unique relationship founded primarily and profoundly on people. The family relationship between us extends to 44 million Irish Americans, but in this week of each year, the whole people of this great nation, our friends for 51 weeks in the year, become our cousins in spirit as we honour together Ireland's national saint.

One of the great characteristics of the American people has always been your pride – your justified pride – in the achievements of the new nation that you have forged over several centuries in the land to which your fore-fathers came from the other continents of the world. That pride has sustained you in many troubles, many trials, many tragedies. It is founded on achievement and is sustained by an abiding faith in your capacity to face any challenge, and by a spirit of generous optimism.

We in Ireland also take pride in our country and in the achievements of our people. We are proud not only of the ancient origins of our race, of the survival of our people through so many struggles and hardships, of the cultural empire we have carved out in literature in the English language complementing our own ancient Gaelic tradition; we are proud also of being a mother country, a people of five million in their own island, but with tens of millions of children scattered throughout the world, keeping fresh the memory of their homeland, most jubilantly on the occasion of this feast of St Patrick.

An ancient nation, we are a modern state. Modern in the sense that the present Irish state took its place in the world community a bare sixty years ago; modern also in the sense that so much of our economic development and specifically our industrialisation, is new, created in recent decades, partly by our own native effort, but also in significant measure by investment from outside our shores. Pre-eminently, this external investment has come from the United States. Allied to the skills and dynamism of our youthful labour force, it has given us a place in the new technology of our European continent that is quite disproportionate to our size.

Our high technology industries – chemicals, electronics and above all, computers, are the source of a dynamism which, even in the absence of export growth in other sectors, last year increased our total manufactured exports by a 14 per cent in the midst of world recession – the highest rate of export increase in Europe. Within twelve years during which two major oil crises have stopped in its tracks world economic growth, we have doubled our share of the world market for manufacturers.

An ancient nation: a modern state, and a youthful people: amongst all the developed countries of the world, Ireland has the youngest population, almost one-third of the electorate being under thirty. Within barely two decades the number of our young people in their twenties has virtually doubled.

There is, of course, another side to all this. Like so many other developed countries we face today a serious employment problem – the more acute because of our young population. The growth of our economy at home, as in so many other countries, has been halted by the recession of recent years – now perhaps coming to an end in response to the American recovery. For many of our people these problems have loomed large, seeming at times indeed to fill the horizon and so dim some of the hopes that the achievements of recent decades had aroused.

And there is another problem, one which constantly overshadows us – and has often touched us directly: the sombre tragedy of Northern Ireland. There is hardly a family on either side of the divided community in the North that has not known insecurity, suffering and all too often, bereavement. This is a fact that must be remembered by all those from outside Northern Ireland who claim to apportion blame or to offer simplistic solutions.

Locked into a corner of our small island, in a piece of territory 100 miles long and sixty miles across, live one-and-a-half million people drawn from two different Irish traditions: the ancient Gaelic, Catholic tradition stretching back through several millennia, and the Protestant tradition of those who settled from Britain in much of the north-eastern corner of our island at the same time as compatriots of theirs were settling on the eastern edge of this great continent.

These two traditions in Northern Ireland have maintained their distinct identities through the centuries. Their loyalties face in two different directions – the forty per cent Catholic nationalist minority looking south towards their kinsmen in the Irish state and the sixty per cent majority looking instead towards Britain, whence their ancestors came four centuries ago.

In passing I cannot help reflecting that here in the United States people from these two separate Irish backgrounds have without difficulty given their allegiance to a common flag and a single Constitution, while on their home ground the clash of their identities has remained undiminished by time. Thus has been created in Northern Ireland one of the most complex political problems in the world today: complex in its intensity and in the apparent irreconcilability of the two traditions within this small piece of territory. But a problem which, nevertheless, is too often viewed from outside in exceedingly simplistic terms: seen by all too many as involving no more than the end of British rule in Northern Ireland.

Would that this were indeed the only problem! Then the British and ourselves could have solved it in agreement long ago. But the real problem at the human level lies in the North itself – in the inter-relationship between the two traditions within that divided community.

Britain, with the responsibility for governing Northern Ireland, has not hitherto addressed this problem with the combination of determination and even-handedness that it requires. Nor has it given to it the priority which, as a great human tragedy, it demands. Britain has, moreover, hitherto seemed often to be preoccupied with the security symptoms of the problem, at the expense of its fundamentally political character.

But can we, for our part, in our Irish State – although we have had neither direct responsibility nor opportunity to solve this problem – truthfully say that we have done all in our power to understand and face the realities of this tragedy? Have we sufficiently tried to reach out with sympathy and understanding to both sides in Northern Ireland?

The answer can only be that not one of us, in Britain or in Ireland, is free of some measure of guilt for what has been happening in Northern Ireland. None of us has a right to seek to shift the whole of the blame on to others. Both the London and Dublin Governments have a duty now to break out of ancient moulds and attitudes and to make the imaginative leap of understanding.

This moral obligation, to put Northern Ireland, its people, and their interests first, imposes itself also, I believe, upon those in other lands, such as this great United States of America, who are concerned, as I know so many of you are concerned, with this problem. It can be fulfilled only by the most resolute support for peace and reconciliation amongst the people of Northern Ireland. It can be fulfilled only by a corresponding rejection of – revulsion against – the very idea of aid by way of money, or by way of weapons, or by way of moral support, to any of those who are engaged in the acts of horrific violence that are corrupting and destroying the life of a whole community. And when I call for rejection of such "moral support", I necessarily include the act of making common cause for any purpose, however speciously well-meaning, with people who advocate, or condone, the use of violence in Ireland for political ends.

Let me tell you, for a few brief moments how the democratically-based political parties of our state have been attempting, in conjunction with the constitutional nationalists of the SDLP Party in the North, led by John Hume, to take our responsibilities in seeking a resolution of this tragic problem. These four parties viz. the two parties in our Government (my own Fine Gael Party and the Labour Party) together with the opposition Fianna Fáil Party, and the SDLP in Northern Ireland, have between them been elected by the votes of ninety per cent of the nationalist people of the island of Ireland and consequently represent seventy per cent of all its inhabitants – nationalist and Unionist. For nine months past, our parties – the parties which aspire to Irish unity achieved by peaceful means – have been working together within the framework of a New Ireland Forum, in search of ways of bringing peace and stability to Northern Ireland and, indeed, to the whole island of Ireland.

Week after week, the Forum has been in session. We four party leaders have already met either in Committee together, or in conjunction with our fellow members in the Forum, no less than sixty-nine times – setting aside our other differences and giving to this work our highest priority.

The Forum has been studying, and hearing personal evidence on, submissions made to us by a wide range of people and groups. These have included many that have been representative of aspects of the Protestant and Unionist tradition of Northern Ireland.

Finally, we have been seeking to find together ways by which political structures could be created in the future that would accommodate not only our own nationalist tradition which aspires to Irish unity achieved peacefully and by agreement, but also that of the Unionist community in Northern Ireland.

It is our hope that we will find common ground amongst our four parties. We hope that this common ground might provide a basis upon which the governments of Britain and Ireland, in conjunction with representatives of both sides of the community in Northern Ireland, could eventually construct a political solution. Such a solution would have to be one that would reconcile the conflicting rights and identities of Unionists and nationalists: one that would render totally irrelevant those who are seeking to impose their tyranny of violence on the people of our island.

What we of the constitutional Irish nationalist tradition are attempting together is unique. It is our hope that it will find a response in Britain. There are indications already that responsible opinion in that neighbouring island has taken note of our initiative and is awaiting its outcome with growing interest. When our task is completed it will in turn be Britain's duty to do as we are doing: to review and revise its approach to the problem.

In thus telling you something of what the constitutional parties of nationalist Ireland are currently engaged upon, and of our hopes of an equally generous response from the British Government and political parties, I am frankly seeking to engage your interest in, and your commitment to, this process, which, we believe, offers a constructive alternative – the only constructive alternative to the violence and terrorism in Northern Ireland.

I believe that you will be glad to hear a message of hope in respect of a problem which many of you must have been tempted to write off as insoluble. We know that in this Congress there are very many people whose affection for Ireland and concern for the welfare of our island and its people are deep and strong. I know that in speaking here today, I am speaking to friends of Ireland. We need the help and encouragement of our friends.

America's voice in the world is a strong one. It is a voice that is listened to. We call it in aid of our efforts, not in support of any narrow sectional interest but in support of a generous attempt to resolve once and for all the conflict of traditional identities in Ireland on a basis that will secure the interests and concerns of both sections of the community in the North – in recognition of the equal validity of the two traditions.

And we ask our friends in the United States that, in the context of any agreement that might emerge from our present efforts, to secure peace and stability in Ireland, they would support in a practical way its implementation.

I have not come to the United States to speak only of this problem, although you will readily understand that it looms foremost in my mind, as it must in the mind of any Irishman who has political responsibilities. We have other common interests to pursue with you, the political leaders of the United States and the European Community, the presidency of which Ireland will be assuming for the third time on July 1st next.

When, in January 1975, Ireland first undertook that presidential responsibility in the Community, your administration invited me as Minister for Foreign Affairs of Ireland to come to Washington to discuss together the common concerns at that time of the United States and the Community. This was, I think, the first full scale consultation between the European Community and the United States in a new process that had been decided upon during the previous year. I was happy on that occasion to be able to play a part in bringing Europe and the United States closer together.

On this visit I shall be engaged once again upon a similar

task – recognising that the common concerns of Europe and the United States are matched also by divergent interests in certain areas of commerce and finance – as also by somewhat different perceptions of the political situation in various parts of the world. It is well that together Europe and America should seek to reconcile these divergent interests and different perceptions, so far as we may be able to do so without doing violence to the legitimate interests, and the principles, of each of the partners in this relationship.

Let me revert for a moment to a festive note appropriate to the joint celebration of St Patrick's Day by our two peoples. I know that we are two days ahead of time and such earliness is perhaps more an American than a European characteristic, exemplified perhaps by your addiction to breakfast television, and, as I have found to my cost, working breakfasts. But I feel that no one in the United States would object if I propose that the celebrations of St Patrick's Day this year be a three-day affair, starting today, and culminating on Saturday – with Sunday as a very necessary day of rest before we all return to our humdrum daily activities next week!

"I STAND BY THE REPUBLIC"

Des O'Malley (1939–) was educated at Crescent College, Limerick, University College Dublin and the Incorporated Law Society. He was elected to the Dáil for Fianna Fáil at his first attempt in the 1968 by-election, caused by the death of his uncle Donagh O'Malley. He was appointed to the Cabinet in 1970 and served in every subsequent Fianna Fáil administration. In the early 1980s, his was a dissident voice within Fianna Fáil, and his differences with its new leader Charles Haughey were well known.

In 1985, the Coalition Government sought to broaden the availability of contraceptives. Fianna Fáil opposed the measure, and a divisive debate ensued.

Des O'Malley spoke in favour of the provisions of the Bill, and abstained on the actual vote. Although he had already lost the party whip, O'Malley was still a member of Fianna Fáil. O'Malley joined with Mary Harney TD in December 1985 and established the Progressive Democrats, which he led until October 1993.

DAIL ÉIREANN, FEBRUARY 20, 1985

. . . The Bill was never very important but it has largely become irrelevant now because issues much greater have raised their heads in relation to far deeper matters than the mere availability of condoms to 18 year olds and over.

I listened to Deputy Noel Treacy speaking this morning.

334

Much of what he said was similar to what quite a number of other Deputies who have spoken in this debate have said, that they have taken the view that as things stand the availability of contraceptives, particularly condoms, in this country is only very limited and that this Bill will change the whole situation radically, that we stand at the crossroads, we are going down the slippery slope to degeneracy and all the rest of it. Do some Deputies and people outside the House think that because the law says something, therefore that is the way things are? . . .

I do not think so, but a feature of our national hypocrisy is that if the law on the Statute Book says that things should be one way, it does not matter it things on the ground are different. As long as the law looks all right we cod ourselves into thinking that something that we do not approve of is not happening. Would it not be more sensible to be realistic and look at what is going on around us and realise that, no matter how strongly we might be opposed in principle or in conscience to contraceptives, we would be better to have a law that will be enforced rather than the present situation? . . .

Difficulties have arisen since the publication of the Bill. In the past ten days or so the most extraordinary and unprecedented extra-parliamentary pressure has been brought to bear on many Members of the House. This is not merely ordinary lobbying. It is far more significant. I regret to have to say that it borders at times almost on the sinister. We have witnessed the public and the private agonies of so many Members of the House who are being asked not to make decisions on this Bill in their own calm and collected judgement but to make them as a result of emotional and at times overwhelming moral pressure. This must constrain their freedom in certain aspects.

Article 6 of the Constitution provides that:

(1) All powers of government, legislative, executive and judicial, derive, under God, from the people, whose right it is to designate the rulers of the State and, in final appeal, to decide

all question of national policy, according to the requirements of the common good.

(2) These powers of government are exercisable only by and on the authority of the organs of State (established by this Constitution.

The essence of this debate is whether this House agrees with that Article and whether it is prepared to stand firm on it. Article 6 is not often quoted because its provisions are taken for granted, but it cannot be taken for granted today because we must declare whether the people are sovereign.

In many respects this debate can be regarded as a sort of watershed in Irish politics. It will have a considerable influence on the whole political institutional, democratic future, not just of these Twenty-six Counties but of the whole island. We must approach the subject very seriously and bearing that in mind, it is right to ask ourselves now what would be the reaction and the effect of this Bill being defeated this evening. I am not interested in the reaction or the effect so far as contraception is concerned because that is no longer relevant. If the Bill is defeated there are two elements on this island who will rejoice to high heaven. They are the Unionists in Northern Ireland and the extremist Roman Catholics in the Republic.

They are a curious alliance, but they are bound together by the vested interest each or them has in the perpetuation of partition. Neither wishes to know the other. Their wish is to keep this island divided. Most of us here realise that the imposition of partition on this island was a grievous wrong, but its deliberate continuation is equally a grievous wrong. No one who wishes that this island, this race and this nation be united again should try to have that division copper-fastened. It does not matter what any of us might like to say to ourselves about what might be the effects of the availability of condoms or anything else, what really matters and what will matter in ten, twenty or thirty years' time is whether the elected representatives of the Irish people decided they wished to underwrite, at least mentally, the concept of partition.

Most of us in the House fervently want to see a thirty-two-county republic on this island. I am not as optimistic as I used to be about that – I think the day is further away than it might otherwise be because of the events of the last ten or fifteen years. I am certain of one thing in relation to partition: we will never see a thirty-two-county republic on this island until first of all we have here a twenty-six-county republic in the part we have jurisdiction over today which is really a republic, practising real republican traditions. Otherwise, we can forget about the possibility of ever succeeding in persuading our fellow Irishmen in the North to join us.

"Republican" is perhaps the most abused word in Ireland today. In practice what does it mean? The newspapers do not have to explain it because there is an immediate preconceived notion of what it is. It consists principally of anglophobia. Mentally, at least, it is an aggressive attitude towards those who do not agree with our views on what the future of this island should be. It consists of turning a blind eye to violence, seeing no immorality, often, in the most awful violence, seeing immorality only in one area, the area with which this Bill deals. Often it is displayed by letting off steam in the fifteen minutes before closing time with some rousing ballad that makes one vaguely feel good and gets one clapped on the back by people who are stupid enough to think that sort of flag-waving is the way to make progress in this island – to go back into your own trenches rather than try to reach out to people whom we need to reach.

One of the most distressing aspects of this debate, inside and outside the House, particularly outside, has been the lack of trust in young people. Young people can hardly be blamed if they look at this House and its Members with a certain cynicism, because they see here a certain hypocrisy. I have had plenty of experience of many Members of this House, and if I were to place my trust anywhere today, before God I would place it in the young people. I would not abuse them or defame them, by implication at least, in the way in which they have been defamed as people who are incapable of making any kind of sound judgement unless it is legislated for them. Even the exercise of their own private consciences must be something that must be legislated for. I have said before that I cannot accept that concept, though I have seen a reverend bishop saying that we can legislate for private morality. I beg to take issue with him.

Technically, of course, he is right. I can think of at least two countries in the world where private morality is legislated for. One is Iran and the other is Pakistan. Private morality is enforced by public flogging every day in Teheran and other cities in Iran. It takes place in Pakistan where they are having an election in three weeks and where every political party has been dissolved except the Government party. One aspect of enforcement of private morality in these countries is the stoning to death of adulteresses. I do not know what happens to adulterers, but adulteresses get stoned to death.

In a democratic republic people should not think in terms of having laws other than those that allow citizens to make their own free choice in so far as these private matters are concerned. That is what I believe a republic should do. It should take account of the reasonable views of all groups, including all minorities, because if we do not take into account the rights of minorities here, can we complain if they are not taken into account in the other part of this island, or anywhere else? The rights of minorities are not taken into account in Iran; the Bahai are murdered at the rate of dozens a week because they will not subscribe to the diktat of Islam. I do not say that will happen here but it is the kind of slippery slope we are on.

The tragedy is that so far as morality, public or private, is concerned the only aspect of it that agitates us is sexual morality or things that have to do with it. Could any other issue get things so worked up here as something like this? Do we not need to remind ourselves that God gave Moses nine other

338

Commandments and the other nine are numbered one through five and seven through ten, as the Americans say . . .

We had last year the Forum report and a tremendous amount was put into it by many Members of this House over an eleven-month period of sustained work. It contains a certain spirit of reconciliation, of openness, a recognition of what needs to be done to show the people in Northern Ireland that they need not fear here for what they call their civil and religious liberties. If this House acts in a particular way this evening, can you ever persuade those people now other than that the Forum report means nothing, that it was a bag of wind, or a lot of words? Is the spirit of it as well as apparently, at times, the letter of it to be cast aside?

I am concerned not just about the Unionists in Northern Ireland. I am concerned also about the position in the context of this debate of the Roman Catholics in Northern Ireland, and I know something about them. I married one of them twenty years ago on this very day, 20th February 1965, and I know a lot of them. I cannot acccept, going on the statements that were so freely made inside and outside this House, that in any country or jurisdiction where there was availability of contraceptives on the lines suggested in this Bill the people would immediately become degenerate. They are not degenerate in Northern Ireland and they have had for very many years full access to any form of contraception they wanted at any time and at any age, in any marital conditions . . .

I took the opportunity over the last weekend to read some of the chapters in JH Whyte's book on *Church and State in Modern Ireland*. To read, perhaps in full for the first time myself, the whole mother and child controversy of 1951, as it was called, is unbelievable. It is incredible that Members of this House and of the Government of the day could be as craven and supine as they were, as we look back on them now. It shows how much the atmosphere has changed. Then one has to ask oneself, "Has the atmosphere changed?" Because when the chips are down is it going to be any different?

It was interesting to read the so-called mother and child scheme. There were ten provisions for women in it relating to ante-natal and post-natal care and care of the children when they were born. One of the provisions was for free dental treatment for pregnant women. The most tremendous objection was taken to that at that time. I recall only a couple of weeks ago, the Minister for Finance reading that out here in the budget speech and there was a howl of laughter all round the House. How could anyone seriously object to something like that? How could anyone seriously object to anything in it, as one looks back on it now? Look at the effect it has had on this island. We have to bear in mind that this is 1985, and whatever excuses one could make for people in 1951, those excuses are not valid today for us.

This whole matter affects me personally and politically. I have thought about it and agonised about it. Quite a number of Deputies have been subjected to a particular type of pressure, but I am possibly unique in that I have been subjected to two enormous pressures, the more general type and a particular political one. They are both like flood tides – neither of them is easy to resist and it is probably more than twice as hard to resist the two of them. But it comes down to certain fundamentals. One has to take into account everything that has been said but one must also act in accordance with one's conscience, not on contraceptives, which is irrelevant now, but on the bigger and deeper issues that I have talked about today.

I cannot avoid acting, in my present situation, where I do not have the protection of the Whip, other than in the way I feel, giving some practical recognition at least to the kind of pressures and the entreaties of my friends for my own good, which I greatly appreciate.

I will conclude by quoting from a letter in the *Irish Times* of 16 February, signed by Fr Dominic Johnson OSB, a monk of Glenstal Abbey where he says:

340

"With respect to Mr O'Malley, he might reflect with profit on the life of St Thomas More, who put his conscience before politics and lost his life for doing so."

The politics of this could be very easy. The politics would be to be one of the lads, the safest way in Ireland. But I do not believe that the interests of this State, or our Constitution and of this Republic, would be served by putting politics before conscience in regard to this. There is a choice of a kind that can only be answered by saying that I stand by the Republic and accordingly I will not oppose this Bill.

"IT IS NOT OFTEN THAT A MAN GETS THE OPPORTUNITY TO DELIVER THE ORATION AT HIS OWN FUNERAL"

Peter Robinson (1948–) was born in Belfast and educated at Castlereagh College. He became the full-time general secretary of Ian Paisley's Democratic Unionist Party in 1975 and following several unsuccessful electoral outings was elected to Castlereagh District Council. In the 1979 General Election, he unseated veteran unionist William Craig, to take the seat for East Belfast. Robinson has been involved in each of the DUP's campaigns to protect the Union in the 1980s and 1990s, and as his profile increased, so too did his electoral support.

Robinson's reaction to the Anglo-Irish agreement was predictable. His speech in the Commons debate displayed the anger and bitterness of the Unionist MPs. In protest at the agreement, all of the Unionist MPs resigned from the Commons and contested the ensuing by-elections as a plebiscite on the Agreement.

HOUSE OF COMMONS, NOVEMBER 26, 1985

This debate provides a unique occasion for Ulster Unionist representatives, because it is not often that a man gets the opportunity to deliver the oration at his own funeral. When the Prime Minister signed the agreement in Hillsborough Castle, she was in reality drafting the obituary of Ulster as we know it in the United Kingdom.

It is important for the House to understand why Ulster Unionists came to that conclusion. We did not reach that conclusion simply because of one document that arrived on 15 November. A long series of events led to that occasion. I am old enough to remember when, in 1969, the Labour Government issued the Downing Street declaration, which said: "the affairs of Northern Ireland are entirely a matter of domestic jurisdiction".

I can recall how our Prime Minister, on 8 December 1980, when in Dublin Castle, signed a communiqué with Charles J Haughey which altered that stance, because the communiqué said that "the totality of relations within these islands" was now a fit subject for discussion between the two Governments. From that moment we had the outworking of the "unique relations" between the Governments of the United Kingdom and the Republic of Ireland. We had joint studies, cross-border co-operation and then the Anglo-Irish Intergovernmental Council, the purpose of which was "to provide the overall framework for intergovernmental consultation . . . on all matters of common interest and concern" – wait for it – "with particular reference to the achievement of peace, reconciliation and stability and the improvement of relations". At that stage, the council had a responsibility to deal with matters of mutual interest and concern. We have moved from that to a new status which, under this institution, is to give the Republic of Ireland – a foreign Government – a direct role in the government of Northern Ireland.

It does not end there, because the agreement announced at Hillsborough Castle is but the tip of the iceberg. I know that the Prime Minister, the Secretary of State and others have been careful to say that there is no other agreement. But, then, we were told that there was no agreement right up until it was signed at Hillsborough Castle. Indeed, some weeks in advance of 15 November, the deputy Prime Minister of the Irish Republic had already had a document printed which he sent to every member of his party. It indicated the full text of the agreement. Incidentally, he said that that agreement was signed by "the Taoiseach and the Prime Minister of Great Britain".

It represents quite a change in our status when the deputy Prime Minister of the Irish Republic recognises that Northern Ireland is not to be one of our Prime Minister's responsibilities.

The document says that the task upon which the conference will embark involves trying to achieve an agreement with our Government on matters such as parades and processions, and putting the UDR out of business. It implies – although we have not yet been told – that the meeting of Ministers will take place in Belfast. It is clearly a framework for further agreements. What other reason could there be for a front cover entitled, "The Republic of Ireland No. 1 Agreement"?

I note that the Hon. Member for Foyle (Mr Hume) is in the Chamber. He has at least been honest with the people of Northern Ireland in saying that the agreement is a process. In the *Irish News* – where else? – he said that it was "a first step". The next day he said that there were to be "progressive stages". Those who had any doubt about where they were to lead were told by him on RTE: "We are not waiting for Irish unity. We are working for it."

I accept that there is no harm in the Hon. Gentleman wanting to work towards that goal, but I wish to ensure that the unionist community in Northern Ireland knows what he and the Republic are working towards. It is clear that this process is intended to take us out of the United Kingdom. Yet the people of Northern Ireland have democratically expressed their wish to stay within it. The agreement is intended to trundle Northern Ireland into a all-Ireland Republic.

The unionist community in Northern Ireland has identified this process. It is not an end in itself, and was never intended to be. It is one step towards a united Ireland. Indeed, the Prime Minister has excused the deal by saying that its laudable aim is to achieve peace, stability, reconciliation and co-operation. That is my aim too. Like some other Hon. Members, I live in Northern Ireland. Our stake and investment are in the Northern Ireland community and, most importantly, our families and constituents live there. It is in our interests to have peace, stability, reconciliation and co-operation. If I felt that they were achievable I would grasp them with a heart and a hand, but not outside the union. That would be too high a price to pay.

The document reminds me of another piece of paper waved by a former Prime Minister. In many ways the words are too similar. That Prime Minister's words were "Peace in our time". Under this agreement, peace, stability, reconciliation and co-operation are not achievable. How can they be achieved by alienating the majority of people in Northern Ireland? It was never intended that there should be peace, stability, reconciliation and co-operation as a result of this agreement. After all, if that had been the intention, the Government would have wanted, above all, to take the elected representatives of the majority community in Northern Ireland along with them . . .

. . . If the document has been intended to do us good, the Prime Minister would have been only too willing to allow the unionist community to be consulted. She would have been only too pleased to take it along with her and to ensure that the representatives of the unionist people in Northern Ireland could have some input to the discussions.

The Government of the Irish Republic were only too happy to give the Hon. Member for Foyle that facility. The Government of the Irish Republic and this Government briefed people all over the world. The Government of the Irish Republic briefed the Secretary of State to the Vatican. The President of the United States was briefed, as were the United Nations and the European Community. But those who were to be affected by the deal were kept in the dark . . .

I ask the Government to scrap this one-sided, anti-unionist deal and to involve unionists in the process of obtaining peace, stability, reconciliation and co-operation in Northern Ireland. As I have said, we would participate with a heart and a half. More than many, I recognise that it is not my duty simply to say, "No, we will not have it." It is my duty and that of other Unionist representatives to say what can be done in a positive way in

Northern Ireland. Before the debate ends, I hope that I shall have had the opportunity to do that.

I want to point out what unionists have done, and are prepared to do within the union . . .

I call upon the Government to consult and not to confront the unionist community. Unionists have been positive. The former Secretary of State for Northern Ireland who laid the Assembly legislation before the House knows very well that it was the unionist community in Northern Ireland that went into the Assembly and that co-operated with the Government. It was the Hon. Member for Foyle and his party who stayed outside and withdrew their consent. Is it the reward for those who co-operate with the Government that an agreement that is ultimately to their destruction should be foisted upon them to the benefit of the Hon. Member for Foyle and his party?

The Northern Ireland unionist parties – the Ulster Unionist party with its document, "The Way Forward" and the Democratic Unionist party with its document, "Ulster – the Future Assured" – put forward positive proposals for peace, stability, reconciliation and co-operation in Northern Ireland.

Even in the Northern Ireland Assembly, with the help of the conciliator, Sir Frederick Catherwood, the parties sat down and reached agreement on a framework that the Government could use in negotiations with the political parties – not only the Unionist parties but the Alliance Party. We have been positive in Northern Ireland.

I say again that we are prepared to remain positive within the United Kingdom. We are prepared to allow the Prime Minister to engage unionists in constructive politics, and if the Prime Minister wishes to call my bluff, I should be only too happy. Do not confront us and put us out of the union with this deal.

The willingness of the unionist community to seek an agreement is undeterred. If the Government want peace and stability in Ulster, I ask them where that can best be achieved? There seems to be a new rule in British politics – if there is a dispute within a house, the way to solve it is to reach an agreement with the two neighbours. It is even more strange when the agreement reached between the two neighbours gives aid and succour to one of the parties to the dispute.

If the Government want peace, stability, reconciliation and co-operation in Northern Ireland, they must recognise that that can be achieved only by the politicians – the elected representatives of the people of Northern Ireland – reaching agreement. They cannot impose reconciliation; they cannot impose peace and stability and they certainly cannot impose such an agreement which strikes at the fundamental principle in which the majority in Northern Ireland believe, and that is the union. That is the strangest of British strategies.

Does the agreement measure up to the Government's test for the sort of proposal that would be acceptable? The former Secretary of State for Northern Ireland brought the 1982 Act before the House on the basis of: "widespread acceptance throughout the community".

He argued passionately that there had to be "cross-community support". Throughout the years there have been homilies from politicians of one party or another about the necessity for consent in Northern Ireland. They told us that Northern Ireland could not be governed without the consent of the minority.

If that is true, I have to tell the Government that they can never govern Northern Ireland without the consent of the majority. Do they have that consent? Have they tried to access whether there is such consent? Will they test whether there is consent? The people of Northern Ireland have the right and entitlement to be consulted about their constitutional future.

Our citizenship of the United Kingdom does not allow the Government to do whatsoever they may wish with Northern Ireland. Our citizenship of the United Kingdom must be on the same basis as applies in any other part of the United Kingdom. If, for whatever reason – be it good or ill – the Government decide that Northern Ireland must be treated differently from the remainder of the United Kingdom, that can be done only if there is consent, and the consent not only of the Government and Parliament, but of the people of Northern Ireland.

It was that principle, enunciated in the House, that resulted in the referendums for Wales and Scotland. Have not the people of Ulster the same right to be consulted as the people of Wales and Scotland? Do they not have the same right to give their approval to any deal that, ultimately, will affect their future and the way that they are governed? I believe that they have that right and that they should be given it. If this House is not prepared to give them that right, it is incumbent upon the elected representatives of Northern Ireland to give them that right.

Right Hon. and Hon. Members criticise me, but I ask them how they would like it if the governance of their people was not directly by this House, but by a structure that allowed a foreign power, at its own behest, to make challenges and to request consultation. The agreement goes even further than that and requires that: "a determined effort is made to resolve the differences" between the two Governments. I doubt whether many Right Hon. and Hon. Members would want that for themselves or their constituents.

The agreement is not merely consultative. The House should not pass this measure believing that it is only a talking shop, in which the Irish Republic can make comments. It is much more than that. I am sure that the Prime Minister will not mind if I divulge certain comments made during our meeting yesterday, when we put the point about consultation to her on two occasions. On the first occasion, she was about to speak when the question was answered by the Secretary of State for Northern Ireland. I asked whether only a consultative role was involved or whether it was more than that. He said, "It is not executive." On the second occasion, the Prime Minister said, "It is what it is in this agreement". What do those who have been more candid say about the agreement? The Prime Minister of the Irish Republic says: "it is more than consultation". The deputy Prime Minister of the Irish Republic says: "the agreement goes beyond the right to consult". John F O'Conner, the dean of the faculty of law at UCC, said: "Whatever the eventual political results, the legal result of the new agreement is that Northern Ireland has now become subject to a status in international law which has no real parallels elsewhere. It never was, nor has it become, a separate entity in international law. It is not a condominium. It is a province of the United Kingdom which for the first time has become subject to the legal right of two sovereign governments to determine how all matters which go to the heart of sovereignty in that area shall in future be determined."

It is not only the unionists – Hon. Members may not like what the dean of the faculty of law said, but if they want to dispute it, they had better do so with him.

It is not only the unionists who believe that the deal is unfair to the unionist community in Northern Ireland. Senator Mary Robinson of the Irish Republic – no relation of mine, I assure the House – rejected the agreement because it went too far. She said: "This is absolutely the most serious moment in the political development of this island since we gained independence." That lady is no unionist – she was one of the signatories to the Forum report. Yet even she says that the agreement goes too far. The *Belfast Telegraph*, never a close friend of the unionist community, said: "Even those who, like this newspaper, can see benefit flowing from closer consultation with Dublin, must draw the line at such institutionalised links between the two countries".

I say again that it is not only the Ulster Unionists and the Democratic Unionists who believe that the deal goes too far. The ordinary citizens of Northern Ireland, never previously involved in politics, were present at the mass demonstration at the city hall in Belfast.

I was born a free citizen of the United Kingdom. I was brought up to respect the Union flag. At my father's knee I was taught the love that I should have for the monarchy, and throughout my life I have put that into practice. I was nurtured on the principle of the greatness of our British heritage. I have taught all that to my children. I now have to tell this House that over the last seventeen cruel years, when Ulster has been confronted by a vicious campaign of terrorism, not one of the unionist community was prepared to allow that campaign to shatter his loyalty to the United Kingdom.

It is not a one-way street. It never has been for Ulster. We cheered with this country during the Falklands campaign. Ulster suffered its losses just as many did on this side of the Irish sea. During the second world war, we made sacrifices, just as many people in this part of the United Kingdom, and we did it without conscription. During the first world war, Ulster gave of its best for Britain. After watching the Ulster Volunteers on the Somme when 5,000 Ulstermen lost their lives at the enemy's hand, a great British general – General Spender – said, "I am not an Ulsterman but there is no one in the world whom I would rather be after seeing the Ulster Volunteers in action." In peace and in war Ulster stood by the kingdom. That has been the way of loyal Ulster.

I never believed that I would see a British Government who were prepared to damage Ulster's position in the United Kingdom. Our resolve has been hardened by the bitter times in past years when a terrorist campaign was aimed at undermining our position in the United Kingdom. There would never have been a Hillsborough Castle agreement if the IRA had not been bombing and shooting. That is a fact of life. Can one blame the people of Northern Ireland for thinking that violence works? It makes the task harder for those of us who chose the way of constitutional politics to tell people not to involve themselves in violence.

I wish that the House had a sense of the deep feeling of anger and betrayal in Northern Ireland. Yesterday, while I was waiting in an ante-room in No. 10 Downing Street before meeting the Prime Minister I saw on the wall a portrait of

Rudyard Kipling, who was a great patriot. I recall the words of his poem "Ulster 1912", which begins:

> "The dark eleventh hour
> Draws on and sees us sold
> To every evil power
> We fought against of old."

Later it states;
> "The blood our fathers split,
> Our love, our toils, our pains,
> Are counted us for guilt,
> And only bind our chains.
> Before an Empire's eyes
> The traitor claims his price.
> What need of further lies?
> We are the sacrifice."

"THIS IS THE FIRST TIME WE HAVE
HAD A REAL FRAMEWORK WITHIN WHICH
TO ADDRESS THE PROBLEM"

John Hume (1937–) was born in Derry and educated at St Columb's College and at Maynooth College. A teacher, he came to prominence during the early days for the Civil Rights movement in Derry and was vice chairman of the Derry Citizens' Action Committee in 1968–1969. In the Stormont election of 1969, he was returned as MP for Foyle, winning a seat from the veteran nationalist leader Eddie McAteer. In 1970, he co-founded the SDLP.

After the collapse of the power-sharing Executive, and failure to win a seat at the Westminster elections of 1974, Hume was elected to the European Parliament in 1979. He became party leader of the SDLP in 1980, in succession to Gerry Fitt.

He courted the Irish American lobby in the 1980s, believing that they had the potential to contribute significantly to the resolution of the problems of Northern Ireland. In 1984, he was one of the driving forces behind the establishment of the new Ireland Forum, and welcomed the signing of the Anglo-Irish Agreement in 1985. The speech below is from that debate and it clearly contrasts with Peter Robinson's view of what had been achieved.

HOUSE OF COMMONS, NOVEMBER 26, 1985

Listening to some of the Hon. Members who have spoken in the debate one could have been forgiven for thinking that we were not discussing a serious problem, but, after listening to the

Hon. Member for Belfast East (Mr Robinson), one should not be in any doubt that we are discussing a serious problem.

I was glad to see a full House at the beginning of the debate. That is the first achievement of the Anglo-Irish conference. It shows that the serious human problem facing the peoples of these islands has at last been given the priority that it deserves. It has been put at the centre of the stage.

I was glad also that a meeting took place at the highest level between the British and the Irish Governments at which a framework for ongoing discussion was set up. In an excellent unionist speech, the Hon. Member for Eastbourne (Mr Gow) told us what we already knew – that he was a committed unionist and that he did not particularly like to associate with the loud-mouthed persons with whom I have to live. We did not learn from him of the problem in Northern Ireland – that we have a deeply divided society. The Hon. Gentleman did not bother to analyse why we have a deeply divided society and the political instability and violence which the agreement seeks to address.

This is the first time that we have had a real framework within which to address the problem. The problem is not just about relationships with Northern Ireland. One need only listen to the speeches of Northern Ireland Members to know that it is about relationships in Ireland and between Ireland and Britain. Those interlocking relationships should be addressed within the framework of the problem. The framework of the problem can only be the framework of the solution, and that is the British-Irish framework. There is no road towards a solution to this problem that does not contain risks. The road that has been chosen by both Governments is the road of maximum consensus and is, therefore, the road of minimum risk. We should welcome that.

Our community has just gone through fifteen years of the most serious violence that it has ever seen. Northern Ireland has a population of 1.5 million people. About 2,500 people have lost their lives in political violence – the equivalent of 86,000 people in Britain. Twenty thousand people have been seriously maimed. When I say "maimed", I mean maimed. That is the equivalent of 750,000 people on this island. About £11 billion worth of damage has been caused to the economies of Ireland – North and South. In 1969, public expenditure by the British Government in subsidy, subvention or whatever one calls it was £74 million: today it is £1.5 billion. Two new prisons have been built and a third is about to be opened – our only growth industry. There are eighteen year olds who have known nothing but violence and armed soldiers on their streets. Young people reach eighteen and then face the highest unemployment we have ever had. Forty-four per cent of the population is under twenty-five.

If that is not a time bomb for the future, what is? If that is not a problem that needs the serious attention of the House and the serious attention that the Prime Ministers of Britain and of the Republic of Ireland have given it in the past eighteen months, what is? Is this not a subject that screams out for political leaders in Northern Ireland to take a good look at themselves, their parties and the leadership that they have given? There is only one clear-cut lesson to be learnt from this tragedy – that our past attitudes have brought us where we are. Unless we agree to take a hard look at our past attitudes, we shall be going nowhere fast and we shall be committing ourselves to the dustbin of history, clutching our respective flagpoles.

We are being given some choices. The agreement gives us no more than an opportunity to begin the process of reconciliation. The choices offered to the people of Northern Ireland are the choices offered by Hon. Members here present. The unionist parties have consistently sought to protect the integrity of their heritage in Ireland – the Protestant heritage – and no one should quarrel with that. A society is richer for its diversity. My quarrel with the unionist parties has been that they have sought to protect their heritage by holding all the power in their own hands and by basing that on sectarian solidarity. That is an exclusive use of power which is inherently violent because it permanently excludes a substantial section of the community from any say in its affairs.

That was spelt out clearly by the Right Hon. Member for Lagan Valley (Mr Molyneaux) when he said that he offered an act of leadership. He was sincere. He said that the majority should assure the minority that they would be made part of society. He tells me that it is an act of leadership to make me and the people I represent part of our society sixty-five years after Northern Ireland was created.

We have been lectured about democracy and the democratic process by Hon. Members from both unionist parties. They are practitioners of the democratic process. I do not want to spend too much time on examples of their practice, but they were the masters of gerrymander. Today their voices are somewhat muted, but they have not changed much.

In Belfast city council not one position on any board has gone to a minority representative. One council has even apologised to the electorate because it made a mistake of appointing a member of the SDLP to one position out of 105 . . .

Hon. Members from both unionist parties have lectured us about democracy. That brings us to the heart of the Irish problem. The sovereignty of this Parliament is the basis of the British system and of the rule of law. The sovereignty of Parliament has been defied only twice in this century – on both occasions by Ulster Unionists.

In 1912 the Ulster Unionists defied the sovereign wish of Parliament to grant home rule. That was only devolution within the United Kingdom. They objected and accepted instead home rule for themselves. That taught them a lesson which they have never forgotten – that if one threatens a British Government or British Parliament and produces crowds in the streets from the Orange lodges the British will back down. Others learnt from that that if one wins by the democratic process the British will back down to their loyalist friends and then they say, "Why not use force instead?" Those two forces are still at the heart of preventing a development in relationships within Ireland. Those who threaten violence are those who use it. The same two forces are opposing the agreement today . . .

The logic of the road down which the unionist leadership is taking its people is inescapable. Unionists once again are prepared to defy the sovereign will of this Parliament. When they come back after their elections and Parliament says that it refuses to back down, what will they do? Where will that lead us? They are going down the UDI road. That is their logic. They say that they are loyal to the United Kingdom. They are the loyalists and they must accept the sovereignty of Her Majesty's Parliament. But they do not.

What would happen if London Members resigned, were re-elected and returned saying that the majority in Greater London wanted to keep the Greater London Council? That would lead to a complete breakdown of parliamentary sovereignty. That is where the unionists are leading us and they must know it.

It is sad in 1985 to meet people who are suspicious of everybody. They are suspicious of London, suspicious of Dublin and suspicious of the rest of the world. Worst of all, they are suspicious of the people with whom they share a little piece of land – their neighbours. It is sad that they never talk of the future except with fear. They talk always of the past. Their thoughts are encapsulated in that marvellous couplet

"To hell with the future and Long live the past
May God in his mercy look down on Belfast".

That is more relevant than the words of Rudyard Kipling.

There has to be a better way. However grand we think we are, we are a small community. We cannot for ever live apart. Those sentiments were expressed in 1938 by Lord Craigavon, one of their own respected leaders. What are we sentencing our people to if we continue to live apart? People are entitled to live apart, but they are not entitled to ask everyone else to pay for it.

The other opposition to the agreement comes from the Provisional IRA and its political surrogates. They murder fellow

Irishmen in the name of Irish unity. They murder members of the UDR and RUC – fellow Irishmen. Those members see themselves as protectors of their heritage, but the Provisional IRA brutally murders UDR and RUC members in the name of uniting the Irish people, the heritage with which we must unite if we are ever to unite Ireland.

The IRA's political wing is full of contradictions. I hope that no one in the House has any sympathy with it. Its members blow up factories, yet complain about unemployment. Its political spokesmen complain about cuts in public expenditure and in the same evening the military wing blows up £2 million of public expenditure in one street. A motion rightly condemns the execution of a young South African poet, but the IRA then shoots in the back of the head a young unemployed man and puts bullets in the head of a young man and his wife in west Belfast. The IRA complains about Diplock courts, yet runs kangaroo courts. What does that offer Ireland?

The Hon. Member for Belfast East (Mr Robinson) asks about Irish unity. In the late 20th century it is nonsense that there should be divisions. If European nations which twice in this century alone have slaughtered one another by the millions can build institutions that allow them to grow together at their own speed, why cannot we do the same? He quoted me in an interview as saying that I was working for Irish unity, but I went on to say that those who think that Irish unity is round the corner are wired to the moon.

The divisions in Ireland go back well beyond partition. Centuries ago the leaders of Irish republicanism said that they wanted to unite Ireland by replacing the name of "Catholic-Protestant dissenter" with the common name of "Irishman". That was in 1795. Thirty years before partition Parnell said that Ireland could never be united or have its freedom until the fears of the Protestant minority in Ireland could be conciliated. This is a deep problem. It will not be solved in a week or in a fortnight. The agreement says that if Ireland is ever to be united it will be united only if those who want it to be united can persuade those who do not want it to be united. Sovereignty has nothing to do with maps but everything to do with people.

The people of Ireland are divided on sovereignty. They will be united only by a process of reconciliation in which both traditions in Ireland can take part and agree. If that happens, it will lead to the only unity that matters – a unity that accepts that the essence of unity is the acceptance of diversity.

Our third choice is the Agreement. For the first time it sets up a framework that addresses the problem of the interlocking relationships between the people of both Irelands. It is the approach of maximum consensus. It is the way of minimum risk. For the first time – this is a positive element in the agreement – it respects the equal validity of both traditions. That is what the Right Hon. and Hon. Members of the Unionist party are complaining about. It is not a concession to me or to the people whom I represent. It is an absolute right to the legitimate expression of our identity and of the people I represent. Nobody can take that from us. The recognition of the equal validity of both traditions removes for the first time every excuse for the use of violence by anybody in Ireland to achieve his objective. A framework for genuine reconciliation is provided. Both sections of our community can take part in it.

Several Hon. Members have said that the SDLP has a double veto on devolution. I have already said several times to them in public, but let me say it again so that they may hear it, that I believe in the partnership between the different sections of the community in Northern Ireland. That is the best way to reconcile our differences. By working together to build our community we shall diminish the prejudices that divide us. The Agreement means that I am prepared to sit down now and determine how we shall administer the affairs of Northern Ireland in a matter that is acceptable to both traditions . . .

The second question that appears to excite people about my party's attitude relates to the security forces and to policing in Northern Ireland. Our position – this is not a policy but a statement of fact that applies to every democratic society – is that law and order are based upon political consensus. Where political consensus is absent there is an Achilles heel. Violent men in Northern Ireland take advantage of that Achilles heel. For the first time the Intergovernmental Conference will address that question. It has committed itself to addressing that question. It has also committed itself to addressing the relationship between the community and the security forces. I want to give every encouragement to the conference to do so at the earliest possible opportunity. If it does so, it will have our fullest co-operation. I want the people whom I represent to play the fullest possible part, as do any citizens in a democratic society, in the process of peace and order. While we await the outcome we shall continue to give our full and unqualified support to the police force in impartially seeking out anybody who commits a crime in Northern Ireland.

What is the alternative to the process of reconciliation and the breaking down of barriers? Why should anybody be afraid of the process of reconciliation? Anybody who is afraid has no confidence in himself or herself. It means that they cannot engage in a process of reconciliation. If they cannot retain mutual respect for their own position as well as for that of somebody else, they have no self-confidence. Therefore, they should not be representatives of the people of Northern Ireland. The only alternative is the old one of hopelessness, tit-for-tat, revenge – the old doctrine of an eye for an eye which has left everybody blind in Northern Ireland.

This is well summed up by a better poet than Kipling, the good, honest voice of the North, Louis MacNeice. Describing the old hopelessness, which is what we are being offered by those who will not take this opportunity, he said:

"Why should I want to go back
To you, Ireland, my Ireland?
The blots on the page are so black
That they cannot be covered with shamrock.
I hate your grandiose airs,
Your sob stuff your laugh and your swagger.

Your assumption that everyone cares
Who is the king of your castle.
Castles are out of date,
The tide flows round the children's fancy,
Put up what flag you like, it is too late
To save your soul with bunting."

It is far too late for the people of Northern Ireland to save their souls with bunting or with flag-waving. We should note that the followers of those who wave flags as though they were the upholders of the standards of those flags paint their colours on kerbstones for people to walk over. In other words, there is no leadership and no integrity in that approach and no respect. The alternative that we are offered is an opportunity which, like others, may fail. It poses great challenges and risk. The challenges are daunting and difficult, but the choices are not. There is no other choice. There is no other road.

THE TALLAGHT STRATEGY

Alan Dukes (1945–) was born in Dublin and educated at Coláiste Mhuire, Dublin and University College Dublin. After university, he worked as an economist for the Irish Farmers Association, headed its Brussels office, and later worked for EC Commissioner Richard Burke. After unsuccessfully contesting the 1979 Euro elections, he won a Dáil seat for Fine Gael at his first attempt in 1981, representing the constituency of Kildare.

Dukes was appointed to Minister of Agriculture on his first day in the Dáil and Minister for Finance when Garret FitzGerald's second Coalition took office in February 1982. He moved to become Minister for Justice in 1985, and after the electoral defeat of that Government, became the leader of Fine Gael on the resignation of Garret FitzGerald.

As leader of the opposition, Dukes faced a Fianna Fáil minority Government led by Charles J Haughey. The policies implemented by Fianna Fáil were broadly similar to those identified as necessary by Fine Gael prior to its departure from office. Recognising the political difficulty for his party, Dukes developed the Tallaght strategy, whereby Fine Gael would effectively support the Government's economic programme. The subsequent turnaround in the national finances brought no electoral glory for Dukes. After a dismal showing by Fine Gael's candidate in the 1990 Presidential election he resigned the leadership of his party, to be replaced by John Bruton.

TALLAGHT CHAMBER OF COMMERCE, SEPTEMBER 2, 1987

The essential task facing us in Ireland today is to find successful and sustainable ways of:

- Expanding employment
- Stimulating economic growth
- Eliminating deprivation in our society
- Removing inequities from our economic and social system.

I am concerned, above all, with the lives and livelihoods of Irish people. I am concerned with finding ways to improve people's lives and to increase their chances of making a livelihood in the economic and social circumstances that surround them.

I want these things for all Irish people – not just for some groups or sectors among them. We live in difficult and challenging times: our response to those difficulties and those challenges must involve all Irish people. It must give everybody the opportunity to participate, both in the effort to find the appropriate responses and solutions and in the fruits of those efforts. I will not accept responses that prevent some of our people from participating in the effort nor will I accept responses that deprive some of them of the results. I cannot accept any course of action which would make those who are already deprived bear the whole burden of the effort required to resolve our problems. Our concern must be with the needy, not the greedy and our action must recognise that, until we can all truly participate both in the resolution of our problems and in the benefits of that resolution, we cannot say that we will succeed.

To deal with the issues I have outlined, we need resources. At the end of the day, we ourselves are the only people who can produce those resources. To face the issues and to resolve our problems, we must be able to use all of the resources which we ourselves produce. The biggest obstacle we now face lies in the pre-emption of current resources which results from high levels of public debt.

The policies required to deal with these issues appear complex. They require us to deal with matters which appear to many people to be very remote from their daily concerns and to have little relevance for them. They are nonetheless real and nonetheless fundamental for all that.

The issues we face raise a variety of problems. They raise

some constitutional problems: they raise problems which arise from the balance of rights enshrined in our laws: but behind all of these problems lies the one fundamental problem of the over-commitment of the resources which we currently produce – the public finance problem. Until we have mastered and overcome this problem, we will be gravely constrained in our efforts to bring about substantial improvements in any of the areas I have mentioned. Those who pretend otherwise or who mistakenly believe otherwise run the risk of doing a grave injustice to the many thousands of Irish people who are unemployed, who are deprived, or who are the victims of inequity in our society. We owe those people too much to run the risk of clouding the real issues which face us in addressing their problems.

What I am saying is, quite simply, that when we strip away all the rhetoric and get down to what really matters in the day to day lives of ordinary people, the resolution of our public finance problems is the essential key to everything that we want to do in the economic and social fields, to everything that we want to do to provide for our people the conditions in which they can live their lives in the way that we believe is right.

In other words, what I want for the Irish people cannot happen until our debt burden is under control.

It is the role of the Government to create the conditions in which all of these issues can be successfully addressed.

It is the role of the Parliamentary Opposition to ensure that the Government does this, to re-direct Government policy where it diverges from the right track, and to oppose Government policy where it is wrong. That is the core of my role as Leader of the Opposition. In specific terms, that means that, when the Government is moving in the right overall direction, I will not oppose the central thrust of its policy. If it is going in the right direction, I do not believe that it should be deviated from its course, or tripped up on macro-economical issues. Specifically, it means that, if in 1988 the Government produces a budget which:

- Opens the way to a reduction in taxes and particularly to a reduction in personal taxes
- Brings about a significant reduction in the current budget deficit below the figure targeted for this year
- Holds out a strategy for real employment expansion in future years
- Does not add to the burden of debt service costs in future years

I will not oppose the general thrust of its policy. No other policy of Opposition will conform to the real needs of Irish people: any other policy of Opposition would amount simply to a cynical exploitation of short-term political opportunities for a political advantage which would inevitably prove to be equally short-lived. I will not play that game, because it would not produce any real or lasting advantage for the Irish people – least of all for those who currently have neither political nor economic advantage.

The reality of Irish life today requires the Opposition to accept responsibility: it also places an obligation on Government to listen. Macro-economic issues are not the only ones that face us. Within the overall framework of macro-economic policy, we must look at questions of detailed implementation. Once the general thrust of economic and budgetary policy has been settled, the next task is to define the specific actions that achieve the overall objectives. This has very specific implications in relation to each of the main categories of public expenditure.

Where the objective of expenditure is economic, it means that the accent must be firmly placed on cost-effectiveness. This in turn means promoting enterprise, efficiency and self-reliance, using public expenditure as a stimulus or as a guide rather than as a remedy for economic weakness. The emphasis on cost-effectiveness is essential: not only does it mean that expenditure programmes designed to assist economic activity must be carefully selected in order to give priority to those that produce the best return, but the implementation of these programmes itself must be carried out in the most cost-effective manner. In particular, this will require an assessment to be made of the comparative advantages of having certain programmes carried out by the private sector rather than the public sector.

Where expenditure has a social objective, the accent must be put on achieving social justice and ensuring that expenditure is clearly and effectively channelled towards those most in need, even at the expense of those in lesser need, and those who can provide for themselves. Here also, there must be a major concern with cost-effectiveness, measured in terms of the effectiveness of programmes in attaining the social objectives which lie behind them. In this connection, it is clear that many of the systems which we now have for measuring need are grossly defective. Many forms of state assistance are currently available almost indiscriminately, while at the same time, many people are denied forms of assistance because of out-dated, inefficient or irrelevant criteria being used to establish need. We need to develop a multi-tier approach to many areas of social expenditure in order to give a graduated response to different levels of need.

The administration of public expenditure must put the accent on efficiency and delivery. Here, however, there is a further layer of choice. We must make clear decisions about our goals and priorities, and concentrate our energies on the most important of those, up to the point where the total of available resources has been committed. After that point, we must be prepared to decide, quite consciously, that no further expenditures can be accommodated.

It is with these principles in mind that I will explore alternatives to Government proposals and explore also the balance in Government proposals as between different expenditure programmes and propose modifications. In order to make such a course of action effective, I am prepared to make specific proposals for alternatives, respecting the requirement that the net effect of any alternative proposals must be to keep expenditure, the current deficit and the borrowing requirement within the overall parameters required by the fundamental financial objectives.

Two more components are essential for effective and constructive Opposition.

First, there must be a forward looking, future dimension to the work of the Opposition. It should articulate its positions in a planning framework that looks ahead for at least five years. There are two main reasons for this. The first of these reasons is that, without such a future horizon, policy proposals can quickly become internally incoherent and inconsistent with overall objectives and constraints. The second reason is that the business of an Opposition is to prepare itself for Government. Without a future planning framework, this essential dimension will be lacking.

The final essential component is a dynamic and a developing view of our society, of the role of Government and of the role of each of the major forces and sectors in our society. My Party will bring forward coherent proposals, plans and responses to deal both with the changes that will be forced on Irish society from the outside and with changes which we ourselves will want to make in order to make our society develop and grow in a way that conforms with our economic and social objectives.

This approach to politics is the right one. It is in marked contrast to the approach adopted by Opposition in the past, particularly in the last five years. I am taking this approach because it is constructive. I am taking it because I believe that it is in the interest of the Irish people. I am taking this approach because I believe that it is the kind of politics which we need and which is relevant to the condition of the Irish people today.

I have been struck by the extraordinarily destructive effect of old-style Opposition over the last five years. An opposition which knows very well the depth of our problems but which encourages every interest group to oppose the government is betraying its political role. An Opposition which acts in a way that makes every step forward more painful than it needs to be is perverting its function. An Opposition which tries, in our times, to say that corrective action is unnecessary is betraying the Irish people.

I will not play the political game which produces the sort of phoney economic analysis which has passed for Opposition in the past. I am in Opposition – I would rather be in Government. But I will not pretend that economic reality has changed just because I now find myself in Opposition.

I have no doubt that we can surmount our economic difficulties. We will do it by adopting the realistic approach which I have set out. We will do it by consciously deciding to work together.

To sum up: it is clear that any real, concerned and compassionate response to the issues facing us requires that our public finance problem be vigorously addressed; I will support the general thrust of budgetary and economic policies designed with this in mind; within that framework, we must give priority to cases and situations of deprivation and real need; this will involve the Opposition, as well as the Government, in making enlightened choices and decisions. That is the way my Party will conduct its business: I challenge the other parties who have accepted the view of the economy which I have proposed and defended for six years to follow my approach.

"MAY I HAVE THE FORTUNE TO PRESIDE OVER AN IRELAND AT A TIME OF EXCITING TRANSFORMATION"

Mary Robinson (1944–) was born in Ballina, Co. Mayo and educated at Mount Anville, Trinity College Dublin and Harvard University. After a brilliant academic career, she was appointed Professor of Constitutional and Criminal Law in TCD at the age of 25. She moved to become Professor of European Community Law in 1976, a post she held until her election as President in 1990.

In tandem with her academic and legal interests, Robinson served as a member of Seanad Éireann, representing Trinity College for twenty years from 1969. She spent nine years in the Labour Party, joining in 1976, and contested two general elections unsuccessfully. She resigned in 1985 over the signing of the Anglo-Irish agreement.

Mary Robinson contested the 1990 Presidential election, supported by the Labour Party and the Workers' Party. Her opponents were Austin Currie (Fine Gael) and Brian Lenihan (Fianna Fáil). After a controversial campaign, Robinson was successful, beating Lenihan on the second count. She is the first woman to hold the office.

In her inauguration speech, Robinson signalled the way that the presidency was to change under her direction, her desire to broaden out its traditional role, her work with local communities and her concern with emigrants.

DUBLIN CASTLE, DECEMBER 3, 1990

Citizens of Ireland, mná na hÉireann agus fir na hÉireann, you have chosen me to represent you and I am humbled by and grateful for your trust.

368

The Ireland I will be representing is a new Ireland, open, tolerant, inclusive. Many of you who voted for me did so without sharing all my views. This, I believe, is a significant signal of change, a sign, however modest, that we have already passed the threshold to a new, pluralist Ireland.

The recent revival of an old concept of the Fifth Province expresses this emerging Ireland of tolerance and empathy. The old Irish term for province is coicead, meaning "fifth"; and yet, as everyone knows, there are only four geographical provinces on this island. So where is the fifth? The Fifth Province is not anywhere here or there, north or south, east or west. It is a place within each of us – that place that is open to the other, that swinging door which allows us to venture out and others to venture in. Ancient legends divide Ireland into four quarters and a "middle", although they differed about the location of this middle or Fifth Province. While Tara was the political centre of Ireland, tradition has it that this Fifth Province acted as a second centre, a necessary balance. If I am a symbol of anything I would like to be a symbol of this reconciling and healing Fifth Province.

My primary role as President will be to represent this state. But the state is not the only model of community with which Irish people can and do identify. Beyond our state there is a vast community of Irish emigrants extending not only across our neighbouring island – which has provided a home away from home for several Irish generations – but also throughout the continents of North America, Australia, and of course Europe itself. There are over seventy million people living on this globe who claim Irish descent. I will be proud to represent them. And I would like to see Áras an Uachtaráin, my official residence, serve – on something of an annual basis – as a place where our emigrant communities could send representatives for a get-together of the extended Irish family abroad.

There is another level of community which I will represent. Not just the national, not just the global, but the local community. Within our state there are a growing number of local and regional communities determined to express their own creativity, identity, heritage and initiative in new and exciting ways. In my travels around Ireland I have found local community groups thriving on a new sense of self-confidence and self-empowerment. Whether it was groups concerned with adult education, employment initiative, women's support, local history and heritage, environmental concern or community culture, one of the most enriching discoveries was to witness the extent of this local empowerment at work.

As President I will seek to the best of my abilities to promote this growing sense of local participatory democracy, this emerging movement of self-development and self-expression which is surfacing more and more at grassroots level. This is the face of modern Ireland.

Ba mhaith liom a rá go bhfuair mé taithneamh agus pléisiúr as an taisteal a rinne mé le míosa anuas ar fuaid na hÉireann. Is fíor álainn agus iontact an tar atá againn, agus is álainn an pobal iad muintir na hÉireann.

Fuair mé teachtaireacht ón bpobal seo agus mé a dul timpeall: "Teastaíonn Uachtarán uainn gur féidir linn bheith bródúil aisti, ach, níos mó ná sin, gur féidir linn bheith bródúil lena chéile – toisc gus Éireannaigh sinn, agus go bhfuil traidisiúin agus cultúr álainn againn."

Is cuid an-tábhachtach don gcultúr sin an Ghaeilge – an teanga bheo – fé má atá á labhairt sa Ghaeltacht agus ag daoine eile ar fuaid na hÉireann.

Tá aistear eile le déanamh anois agam – aistear cultúrtha, leis an saibhreas iontach atá sa teanga Ghaeilge a bhaint amach díom féin.

Ta súil agam go leanfaidh daoine eile mé atá ar mo nós fhéin – beagán as cleachtadh sa Ghaeilge – agus go raghaimíd ar aghaidh le chéile le taithneamh agus pléisiúr a fháil as ár dteanga álainn féin.

The best way we can contribute to a new and integrated Europe of the 1990s is by having a confident sense of our Irishness. Here again we must play to our strengths – take full advantage of our vibrant cultural resources in music, art, drama, literature and film: value the role of our educators, promote and preserve our unique environmental and geographical resources of relatively pollution-free lakes, rivers, landscapes and seas; encourage, and publicly support local initiative projects in aquaculture, forestry, fishing, alternative energy and small-scale technology.

Looking outwards from Ireland, I would like on your behalf to contribute to the international protection and promotion of human rights. One of our greatest natural resources has always been, and still is, our ability to serve as a moral and political conscience in world affairs. We have a long history in providing spiritual, cultural, and social assistance to other countries in need – most notably in Latin America, Africa and other Third World countries. And we can continue to promote these values by taking principal and independent stands on issues of international importance.

As the elected President of this small democratic country I assume office in a vital moment in Europe's history. Ideological boundaries that have separated East from West are withering away at an astounding pace. Eastern countries are seeking to participate as full partners in a restructured and economically buoyant Europe. The stage is set for a new common European home based on respect for human rights, pluralism, tolerance and openness to new ideas. The European Convention on Human Rights – one of the finest achievements of the Council of Europe – is asserting itself as the natural Constitution for the new Europe. These developments have created one of the major challenges for the 1990s.

If it is time, as Joyce's Stephen Dedalus remarked, that the Irish began to forge in the smithy of our souls "the uncreated conscience of our race" – might we not take on the still "uncreated conscience" of the wider international community? Is it not time that the small started believing again that it is beautiful, that the periphery can rise up and speak out on equal terms with the centre, that the most outlying island community of the

European Community really has something "strange and precious" to contribute to the sea-change presently sweeping through the entire continent of Europe? As a native of Ballina, one of the most western towns of the most western province of the most western nation in Europe, I want to say – "the West's awake."

I turn now to another place close to my heart, Northern Ireland. As the elected choice of the people of this part of our island I want to extend the hand of friendship and of love to both communities in the other part. And I want to do this with no hidden agendas, no strings attached. As the person chosen by you to symbolise this Republic and to project our self-image to others, I will seek to encourage mutual understanding and tolerance between all the different communities sharing this island.

In seeking to do this I shall rely to a large extent on symbols. But symbols are what unite and divide people. Symbols give us our identity, our self-image, our way of explaining ourselves to ourselves and to others. Symbols in turn determine the kinds of stories we tell; and the stories we tell determine the kind of history we make and remake. I want Áras an Uachtaráin to be a place where people can tell diverse stories – in the knowledge that there is someone there to listen.

I want this Presidency to promote the telling of stories – stories of celebration through the arts and stories of conscience and of social justice. As a woman, I want women who have felt themselves outside history to be written back into history, in the words of Eavan Boland, "finding a voice where they found a vision."

May God direct me so that my Presidency is one of justice, peace and love. May I have the fortune to preside over an Ireland at a time of exciting transformation when we enter a new Europe where old wounds can be healed, a time when, in the words of Seamus Heaney, "hope and history rhyme." May it be a Presidency where I, the President, can sing to you, citizens of Ireland, the joyous refrain of the 14th century Irish poet as recalled by WB Yeats:

"I am of Ireland . . . come dance with me in Ireland."

Go raibh míle maith agaibh go léir.

"NOTHING CAN STOP THE EVOLUTION OF HUMANITY TOWARDS THE CONDITION OF GREATER AND EVER-EXPANDING FREEDOM"

Nelson Mandela (1918–), President of South Africa, was born in Umtate in the Transkei in Cape Province. He was educated at Fort Hare University College where he met his fellow African National Congress leader Oliver Tambo. Mandela later completed a law degree at Witwatersrand University. He was drawn into the African National Congress in 1942 and became general-secretary of the ANC Youth League in 1947. In 1962 he was jailed for inciting African mineworkers to strike, and sentenced to five years. In 1963 he was charged with membership of a terrorist organisation and with 193 acts of sabotage, found guilty and sentenced to life imprisonment.

In 1990, under mounting world economic and political pressure, the South African President FW De Klerk legalised the ANC and other previously banned organisations. Mandela was released from prison in February 1990. After protracted negotiations, multi-racial elections were held in April 1994, and the ANC won the vast majority of the votes and seats. Mandela was elected President of South Africa.

Six months after his release from prison, Mandela became the fourth foreign leader to address a joint session of the Oireachtas. In his speech Mandela thanked the people of Ireland for the on-going support in their struggle against apartheid, and charted the path ahead.

A Cheann Comhairle, A Thaoisigh, Deputies and Senators, Friends, Ladies and Gentlemen: I must first apologise because I have over the last day or two developed a heavy cold, but the stirring reception we have received both from the Government and the people of Ireland has warmed my heart and every vessel in my body. It is with a feeling of great privilege that we stand here today to address this House. We know that the invitation you extended to us to speak from this podium is one that is rarely extended to a visitor, even one who comes to you as the guest of the head of Government. I thank you most sincerely for the honour you have bestowed on me individually, on our organisation, the African National Congress, as well as the struggling people of South Africa.

We recognise in the possibility you have thus given us the reaffirmation by the Members of this House and the great Irish people whom you represent, of your complete rejection of the apartheid crime against humanity, your support for our endeavours to transform South Africa into a united, democratic, non-racial and non-sexist country, your love and respect for our movement and the millions of peoples it represents. We know that the joy with which you have received us and the respect for our dignity you have demonstrated, come almost as second nature to a people who were themselves victims of colonial rule for centuries.

We know that your desire that the disenfranchised of our country should be heard in this House and throughout Ireland derives from your determination, born of your experience, that our people should, like yourselves, be free to govern themselves and to determine their destiny. The warm feeling that envelopes us as we stand here is therefore but the affinity which belongs to people who have suffered in common and who are tied together by unbreakable bonds of friendship and solidarity.

The very fact there is today an independent Irish state, however long it took to realise the noble goals of the Irish people by bringing it into being, confirms the fact that we too shall become a free people; we too shall have a country which will, as the great Irish patriots said in the proclamation of 1916, cherish all the children of the nation equally.

The outstanding Irish poet, William Butler Yeats, has written that too long a sacrifice can make a stone of the heart. He spoke thus because he could feel within himself the pain of the suffering that Irish men and women of conscience had to endure in centuries of struggle against an unrelenting tyranny. But then he also spoke of love, of the love of these whose warm hearts the oppressors sought to turn to stone, the love of their country and people, and, in the end, the love of humanity itself.

For three-quarters of a century, under the leadership of the ANC, our own people have themselves confronted a racist tyranny which grew more stubborn with each passing day. It had to be our lot that even as we refused to take up arms to save lives, we still had to bury many martyrs who were shot down or tortured to death simply because they dared to cry freedom.

The apartheid system has killed countless numbers, not only in our country but throughout Southern Africa. It has condemned to the gallows some of the best sons of our people. It has imprisoned some and driven others into exile. Even those whose only desire was to live, have had their lives cut short because apartheid means the systematic and conscious deprivation and impoverishment of the black millions.

It could have been that our own hearts turned to stone. It could have been that we inscribed vengeance on our banners of battle and resolved to meet brutality with brutality. But we understood that oppression dehumanises the oppressor as it hurts the oppressed. We understood that to emulate the barbarity of the tyrant would also transform us into savages. We knew that we would sully and degrade our cause if we allowed that it should, at any stage, borrow anything from the practices of the oppressor. We had to refuse that our long sacrifice should make a stone of our hearts.

We are in struggle because we value life and love all humanity. The liberated South Africa we envision is one in which all our people, both black and white, will be one to the other, brother and sister. We see being born a united South African nation of equal compatriots, enriched by the diversity of the colour and culture of the citizens who make up the whole.

This cannot come about until South Africa becomes a democratic country. We, therefore, insist that everybody should have the right to vote without discrimination on any grounds whatsoever. Equally, all adult South Africans should have the right to be elected to all organs of Government without any artificial hindrances being put in their way.

To safeguard the freedom of the individual, we will insist that the democratic constitution should be reinforced with an entrenched bill of rights which should be enforced by an independent and representative Judiciary. At the same time, all our people will be free to form and join any party of their choice within the context of a multi-party political system.

The struggle we are waging is also for the economic transformation of our country. The system to which we are heir was designed and operates for the benefit of the white minority at the expense of the black majority. Clearly the situation cannot be allowed to continue in which millions know nothing but the corrosive ache of hunger, in which countless numbers of children die and are deformed as a result of being afflicted by kwashiorkor and other diseases of poverty. Millions are today without jobs and without land. Nothing awaits them except death from starvation and want.

We must also make this point very clear, that no political settlement in South Africa, however democratic and just, can take hold and survive, if nothing is done radically to improve the standard of living and the quality of life of all our people, and especially the black masses of our country. This will inevitably demand that the economy should achieve significant rates of growth, while it undergoes a process of restructuring and a reallocation of resources to ensure prosperity and equity.

After many years of struggle, during which many in our country and region have paid the supreme sacrifice, it appears that our country is set on the path towards a negotiated political settlement. This is a goal which our movement has pursued throughout the seventy-eight years of its existence. In the past, however hard we knocked at the door of the powers that be in our country, that door remained locked and barred. Inspired by the arrogance of racism, successive white minority regimes held fast to the view that they could, through the use of brute force, maintain the tyranny of white minority domination forever.

But you know this more than we do, that no power on earth, even when it commits the sacrilege of invoking God's blessing for its inhuman cause, as did the apartheid regime, can defeat a people that is determined to liberate itself. Nothing can stop the evolution of humanity towards the condition of greater and ever-expanding freedom. While the voice of an individual can be condemned to silence by death, imprisonment and confinement, the spirit that drives people to seek liberty can never be stilled.

The struggle of our people, so magnificently supported and reinforced by your solidarity actions and those of the rest of the international community, have obliged the South African Government to recognise the validity of these truths. President De Klerk has come to understand that the apartheid system can no longer hold and, at our instance, has accepted that he and his colleagues must enter into dialogue with the genuine representatives of the people to find a peaceful solution to the conflict in our country. We have taken the first steps in this process leading to the situation in which the obstacles to negotiations will be removed.

A good start has indeed been made. Furthermore, we do not doubt the integrity of President De Klerk and his fellow-leaders and are convinced that they are committed to honour all agreements that may be arrived at during the process of negotiations. Despite this, we should not mistake the promise of change for change itself. The reality is that the apartheid system continues. Our country continues to be ruled by a white minority regime. All the fundamental features of the South African racist system remain unchanged. In other words, no profound and irreversible changes have taken place leading to the final abolition of the apartheid system.

In addition, many among our white compatriots are still determined to resist change at all costs. Arms in hand, they are ready to drown the masses of our people in a bloodbath to save the system of white minority rule, assert the permanence of the criminal and insulting ideology of white supremacy and ensure the further entrenchment of white privilege. None can, therefore, guarantee the process of negotiations will soon inevitably lead to the victory of the democratic cause.

It is for these reasons that the struggle against the apartheid system must continue. In regard, we would like to extend our thanks to the Taoiseach, the Government and the people of Ireland for the enormous contributions you have made to the international struggle for the isolation of apartheid South Africa. We salute you for the leadership you have given only recently within the European Community to ensure that pressure against the apartheid system is maintained. We reiterate that we must continue to keep the pressure on until such time as the people of South Africa themselves signal that the time for change has come.

For more than a quarter of a century your country has had one of the most energetic and effective anti-apartheid movements in the world. Irishmen and women have given wholehearted and often sacrificial support for our struggle in the fields of economic, cultural and sports relations. We, therefore, salute your sports people, especially the rugby players, your writers and artists and the Dunnes and other workers. They will not be forgotten by the masses of our people.

We ask that you stay the course with us, we need your support for the democratic perspectives that we represent. We need your support to generate the material resources we need to repatriate and resettle those of our compatriots who were forced into exile and to reintegrate into our communities the political prisoners who will be released. We need financial resources to help us carry out the massive political work among all sectors of our population that has to accompany the process of negotiations. We need resources to reconstruct the ANC which has been an illegal organisation for thirty years. We trust that, as the past, you will stand with us until our common victory is achieved.

In future, we will also need to institute important measures to reconstruct the economy of our country along the lines that we have already indicated. We shall require your co-operation in this as well, so that we build a system of relations that will be of mutual benefit to both our peoples and that will seek to ensure that the conditions are removed when racism can once more impose itself on our people and those of Southern Africa as a whole.

We would also like to take this opportunity to convey to you our thanks for everything you did to secure our release from prison. Even behind the thick prison walls of South Africa's maximum security jails we heard your voices demanding our release. So strong did that call become that we knew that, contrary to the wishes of our jailers, we would return and as you can see, we have returned.

Our reception in this House and outside is a moving indication that the Irish Parliament and people will stay the course with us, recognising that while apartheid remains, while South Africa is unfree, that community of nations and the conscience of the world can never be at peace. This gives us enormous strength and assures us of the certainty of our common victory. That victory will come sooner rather than later. Together we will win.

THE DOWNING STREET DECLARATION

Albert Reynolds (1935–) was born in Roscommon and educated at Summerhill College, Sligo. A successful businessman, he was first elected to the Dáil in 1977, one of the beneficiaries of the landslide Fianna Fáil victory in that election. A key player in the accession of Charles Haughey to the leadership of Fianna Fáil in 1979, Reynolds was appointed Minister for Posts & Telegraphs and Transport and Power in Haughey's first administration. He held front bench positions for Fianna Fáil between 1982 and 1987, and was appointed Minister for Industry and Commerce and later Minister for Finance. In November 1991 he was sacked by Charles Haughey for refusing to vote for him in an internal party vote of confidence. He was elected leader of Fianna Fáil and Taoiseach three months later. After the Fianna Fáil coalition with the Progressive Democrats disintegrated in 1992 over the Beef Tribunal, Fianna Fáil lost seats in the general election. In spite of this, and after drawn-out negotiations, a new Fianna Fáil coalition with Labour was formed. Reynolds resigned as Taoiseach in 1994.

John Major (1943–) was elected to the House of Commons as Conservative MP for Huntingdon in 1979, following a career in banking. He rose rapidly through the ranks of the Tory Party in the 1980s, and served as First Secretary of the Treasury, Foreign Secretary and Chancellor of the Exchequer in Thatcher-led administrations. He was elected leader of the Conservative Party in 1979, following Thatcher's resignation. On his election, he gave fresh impetus to moves to seek a way forward in Northern Ireland.

Major and Reynolds had known each other from European Union Finance Minister meetings. Reynolds had identified the North as a key issue for his time as Taoiseach. There were painstaking negotiations between the two Governments, which ran in parallel with secret meetings between Sinn Féin and the British government and a lengthy discussion process between Gerry Adams, President of Sinn Féin, and John Hume, leader of the SDLP.

The outcome of the governmental negotiations was the Downing Street Declaration, launched in December 1993. It was designed to bring about an end to political violence in the North. Although never endorsed by the IRA or Sinn Féin, it was crucial in the moves to the development of the IRA cease-fire nine months later.

DOWNING STREET, DECEMBER 15, 1993

1. The Taoiseach, Mr Albert Reynolds TD, and the Prime Minister, the Rt Hon. John Major, MP, acknowledge that the most urgent and important issue facing the people of Ireland, North and South, and the British and Irish Governments together, is to remove the causes of conflict, to overcome the legacy of history and to heal the divisions which have resulted, recognising that the absence of a lasting and satisfactory settlement of relationships between the peoples of both islands has contributed to continuing tragedy and suffering. They believe that the development of an agreed framework for peace, which has been discussed between them since early last year, and which is based on a number of key principles articulated by the two Governments over the past twenty years, together with the adaptation of other widely accepted principles, provides the starting point of a peace process designed to culminate in a political settlement.

2. The Taoiseach and the Prime Minister are convinced of the inestimable value to both their peoples, and particularly for the next generation, of healing divisions in Ireland and of ending a conflict which has been so manifestly to the detriment

of all. Both recognise that the ending of divisions can come about only through the agreement and co-operation of the people, North and South, representing both traditions in Ireland. They therefore make a solemn commitment to promote co-operation at all levels on the basis of the fundamental principles, undertakings, obligations under international agreements, to which they have jointly committed themselves, and the guarantees which each Government has given and now reaffirms, including Northern Ireland's statutory constitutional guarantee. It is their aim to foster agreement and reconciliation, leading to a new political framework founded on consent and encompassing arrangements within Northern Ireland, for the whole island, and between these islands.

3. They also consider that the development of Europe will, of itself, require new approaches to serve interests common to both parts of the island of Ireland, and to Ireland, the United Kingdom as partners in the European Union.

4. The Prime Minister, on behalf of the British Government, reaffirms that they will uphold the democratic wish of a greater number of the people of Northern Ireland on the issue of whether they prefer to support the Union or a sovereign united Ireland. On this basis, he reiterates, on behalf of the British Government, that they have no selfish strategic or economic interest in Northern Ireland. Their primary interest is to see peace, stability and reconciliation established by agreement among all the people who inhabit the island, and they will work together with the Irish Government to achieve such an agreement, which will embrace the totality of relationships. The role of the British Government will be to encourage, facilitate and enable the achievement of such agreement over a period through a process of dialogue and co-operation based on full respect for the rights and identities of both traditions in Ireland. They accept that such agreement may, as of right, take the form of agreed structures for the island as a whole, including a united Ireland achieved by peaceful means on the following basis. The British Government agree that it is for the people of the island of

Ireland alone, by agreement between the two parts respectively, to exercise their right of self-determination on the basis of consent, freely and concurrently given, North and South, to bring about a united Ireland, if that is their wish. They reaffirm as a binding obligation that they will, for their part, introduce the necessary legislation to give effect to this, or equally to any measure of agreement on future relationships in Ireland which the people living in Ireland may themselves freely so determine without external impediment. They believe that the people of Britain would wish, in friendship to all sides, to enable the people of Ireland to reach agreement on how they may live together in harmony and in partnership, with respect for their diverse traditions, and with full recognition of the special links and the unique relationship which exist between the peoples of Britain and Ireland.

5. The Taoiseach, on behalf of the Irish Government, considers that the lessons of Irish history, and especially of Northern Ireland, show that stability and well-being will not be found under any political system which is refused allegiance or rejected on grounds of identity by a significant minority of those governed by it. For this reason, it would be wrong to attempt to impose a united Ireland, in the absence of the freely given consent of a majority of the people of Northern Ireland. He accepts, on behalf of the Irish Government, that the democratic right of self-determination by the people of Ireland as a whole must be achieved and exercised with and subject to the agreement and consent of a majority of the people of Northern Ireland and must, consistent with justice and equity, respect the democratic dignity and the civil rights and religious liberties of both communities, including:

- The right of free political thought;
- The right of freedom and expression of religion;
- The right to pursue democratically national and political aspirations;
- The right to seek constitutional change by peaceful and legitimate means;
- The right to live wherever one chooses without hindrance;

• The right to equal opportunity in all social and economic activity, regardless of class, creed, sex or colour.

These would be reflected in any future political and constitutional arrangements emerging from a new and more broadly based agreement.

6. The Taoiseach however recognises the genuine difficulties and barriers to building relationships of trust either within or beyond Northern Ireland, from which both traditions suffer. He will work to create a new era of trust, in which suspicion of the motives or actions of others is removed on the part of either community. He considers that the future of the island depends on the nature of the relationship between the two main traditions that inhabit it. Every effort must be made to build a new sense of trust between those communities. In recognition of the fears of the Unionist community and as a token of his willingness to make a personal contribution to the building up of that necessary trust, the Taoiseach will examine with his colleagues any elements in the democratic life and organisation of the Irish state that can be represented to the Irish Government in the course of political dialogue as a real and substantial threat to their way of life and ethos, or that can be represented as not being fully consistent with a modern democratic and pluralist society, and undertakes to examine any possible ways of removing such obstacles. Such an examination would of course have due regard to the desire to preserve those inherited values that are largely shared throughout the island or that belong to the cultural and historical roots of the people of this island in all their diversity. The Taoiseach hopes that over time a meeting of hearts and minds will develop, which will bring all the people of Ireland together, and will work towards that objective, but he pledges in the meantime that as a result of the efforts that will be made to build mutual confidence no Northern Unionist should ever have to fear in future that this ideal will be pursued either by threat or coercion.

7. Both Governments accept that Irish unity would be

achieved only by those who favour this outcome persuading those who do not, peacefully and without coercion or violence, and that, if in the future a majority of the people of Northern Ireland are so persuaded, both Governments will support and give legislative effect to their wish. But, notwithstanding the solemn affirmation by both Governments in the Anglo-Irish Agreement that any change in the status of Northern Ireland would only come about with the consent of a majority of the people of Northern Ireland, the Taoiseach also recognises the continuing uncertainties and misgivings which dominate so much of Northern Unionist attitudes towards the rest of Ireland. He believes that we stand at a stage of our history when the genuine feelings of all traditions in the North must be recognised and acknowledged. He appeals to both traditions at this time to grasp the opportunity for a fresh start and a new beginning, which could hold such promise for all our lives and the generations to come. He asks the people of Northern Ireland to look on the people of the Republic as friends, who share their grief and shame over all the suffering of the last quarter of a century, and who want to develop the best possible relationship with them, a relationship in which trust and new understanding can flourish and grow. The Taoiseach also acknowledges the presence in the Constitution of the Republic of elements which are deeply resented by Northern Unionists, but which at the same time reflect hopes and ideals which lie deep in the hearts of many Irish men and women North and South. But as we move towards a new era of understanding in which new relationships of trust may grow and bring peace to the island of Ireland, the Taoiseach believes that the time has come to consider together how best the hopes and identities of all can be expressed in more balanced ways, which no longer engender division and the lack of trust to which he has referred. He confirms that, in the event of an overall settlement, the Irish Government will, as part of a balanced constitutional accommodation, put forward and support proposals for change in the Irish Constitution which would fully reflect the principle of consent in Northern Ireland.

8. The Taoiseach recognises the need to engage in dialogue which would address with honesty and integrity the fears of all traditions. But that dialogue, both within the North and between the people and their representatives of both parts of Ireland, must be entered into with an acknowledgement that the future security and welfare of the people of the island will depend on an open, frank and balanced approach to all the problems which for too long have caused division.

9. The British and Irish Governments will seek, along with the Northern Ireland constitutional parties through a process of political dialogue, to create institutions and structures which, while respecting the diversity of the people of Ireland, would enable them to work together in all areas of common interest. This will help over a period to build the trust necessary to end past divisions, leading to an agreed and peaceful future. Such structures would, of course, include institutional recognition of the special links that exist between the peoples of Britain and Ireland as part of the totality of relationships, while taking account of newly forged links with the rest of Europe.

10. The British and Irish Governments reiterate that the achievement of peace must involve a permanent end to the use of, or support for, paramilitary violence. They confirm that, in these circumstances, democratically mandated parties which establish a commitment to exclusively peaceful methods and which have shown that they abide by the democratic process, are free to participate fully in democratic politics and to join in dialogue in due course between the Governments and the political parties on the way ahead.

11. The Irish Government would make their own arrangements within their jurisdiction to enable democratic parties to consult together and share in dialogue about the political future. The Taoiseach's intention is that these arrangements could include the establishment, in consultation with other parties, of a Forum for Peace and Reconciliation to make recommendations on ways in which agreement and trust between both traditions in Ireland can be promoted and established.

12. The Taoiseach and the Prime Minister are determined to build on the fervent wish of both their peoples to see old fears and animosities replaced by a climate of peace. They believe the framework they have set out offers the people of Ireland, North and South, whatever their tradition, the basis to agree that from now on their differences can be negotiated and resolved exclusively by peaceful political means. They appeal to all concerned to grasp the opportunity for a new departure. That step would compromise no position or principle, nor prejudice the future for either community. On the contrary, it would be an incomparable gain for all. It would break decisively the cycle of violence and the intolerable suffering it entails for the people of these islands, particularly for both communities in Northern Ireland. It would allow the process of economic and social co-operation on the island to realise its full potential for prosperity and mutual understanding. It would transform the prospects for building on the progress already made in the Talks process, involving the two Governments and the constitutional parties in Northern Ireland. The Taoiseach and the Prime Minister believe that these arrangements offer an opportunity to lay the foundations for a more peaceful and harmonious future, devoid of the violence and bitter divisions which have scarred the past generation. They commit themselves and their Governments to continue to work together, unremittingly, towards that objective.

"THERE WILL BE A COMPLETE CESSATION
OF MILITARY OPERATIONS"

In August 1994, after extensive behind the scenes negotiations, the IRA Army Council announced a cessation of violence. The Troubles had cost more than 3,000 lives since 1969.

The statement was followed by an insistence from the British government that they would require clarification as to whether the cease-fire was permanent.

The IRA also stated that the solution to the issues of Northern Ireland was to be found in "inclusive negotiations". In the eighteen months after the cease-fire, there were negotiations but no framework within which all-party negotiations could happen was found. This issue was one of many that was to dog the progress of the peace process until the collapse of the cease-fire with a bomb explosion in Canary Wharf in London early in 1996.

DUBLIN, AUGUST 31, 1994

Recognising the potential of the current situation and in order to enhance the democratic peace process and underline our definitive commitment to its success the leadership of Oglaigh na hÉireann have decided that as of midnight, Wednesday, August 31st, there will be a complete cessation of military operations. All our units have been instructed accordingly.

At this historic crossroads the leaderships of Oglaigh na hÉireann salutes and commends our volunteers, and other activists, our supporters and the political prisoners who sustained this struggle, against all odds for the past twenty-five years. Your courage, determination and sacrifices have demonstrated that the spirit of freedom and the desire for peace based on a just and lasting settlement cannot be crushed. We remember all those who have died for Irish freedom and we reiterate our commitment to our republican objectives.

Our struggle has seen many gains and advances made by nationalists and for the democratic position. We believe that an opportunity to secure a just and lasting settlement has been created. We are therefore entering into a new situation in a spirit of determination and confidence, determined that the injustices which created this conflict will be removed and confident in the strength and justice of our struggle to achieve this.

We note that the Downing Street Declaration is not a solution, nor was it presented as such by its authors. A solution will only be found as a result of inclusive negotiations. Others, not least the British government, have a duty to face up to their responsibilities. It is our desire to significantly contribute to the creation of a climate which will encourage this. We urge everyone to approach this new situation with energy, determination and patience.

"THE KEY ISSUE, THROUGHOUT THIS ENTIRE EPISODE, HAS BEEN ACCOUNTABILITY"

Dick Spring (1950–) was born in Tralee, Co. Kerry and educated at the Cistercian College, Roscrea, Trinity College Dublin and the King's Inns. After practising as a barrister, he contested the 1981 election for the constituency of Kerry North, taking the seat held until that election by his father Dan Spring from 1943.

Dick Spring was appointed a Minister of State in the Department of Justice on his first day in the Dáil. One year later he succeeded Michael O'Leary as leader of the Labour Party and at the age of 32, was appointed Tánaiste in FitzGerald's second Coalition of 1982–87. In that position he played a key role in the negotiation of the Anglo-Irish Agreement.

After the defeat of the coalition in 1987, and the adoption by Fine Gael of the Tallaght Strategy, Spring rose to prominence as an extremely effective opposition leader. He achieved notable success in the election of Mary Robinson as President of Ireland in 1990. He was scathing in relation to Fianna Fáil's handling of the beef industry, and his profile on this and other issues led to the doubling of Labour representation at the 1992 General Election. To the surprise of many who had voted for them, Labour formed a coalition with Fianna Fáil, and Spring went back into Government as Tánaiste.

The operation of the 1992–94 Fianna Fáil-Labour Coalition was dominated by the tension between the two party leaders over a number of issues, including the Beef Tribunal.

In Autumn 1994, Reynolds sought to appoint the Attorney General, Harry Whelehan, to the post of President of the High

Court. Labour were uncomfortable with the proposal. Labour were even less keen when it emerged that the handling of the extradition case of Fr Brendan Smyth (involving child sex abuse charges) by the Attorney General's office was seen to be less than effective. Labour walked out of cabinet in protest at the decision to appoint Whelehan. The Fianna Fáil ministers who remained in the Cabinet Room appointed Whelehan to the position.

It also emerged that there was a precedent for such an extradition – that of the Duggan case, which only came to light in the midst of the controversy. As more and more details about the handling of the cases emerged, and as Labour sought vindication for its actions, Reynolds spoke to the Dáil and announced that he regretted the appointment. He also outlined the sequence of events by which he learned of the handling of the affair. Spring's speech on November 16 was on a motion of confidence in theFianna Fáil-Labour administration. At the end of the speech Spring effectively "pulled the plug" on the administration. Later Reynolds announced his resignation when it emerged that in the account of events he had given to the Dáil, it had been inadvertently misled. He was replaced as leader by Bertie Ahern.

Labour then agreed to go back into Government with Fianna Fáil. Just as the final pieces of the jigsaw to renew the Fianna Fáil-Labour partnership were being put in place, Spring learned that the true sequence of events was different from that outlined by Reynolds and his Cabinet colleagues, and announced that he could not lead his party back into Government with Fianna Fáil.

He commenced negotiations which led to the formation of the Rainbow Coalition with Fine Gael and Democratic Left, with John Bruton as Taoiseach. It was the first time in the history of the State that a Government had changed without an election.

DAIL ÉIREANN, NOVEMBER 16, 1994
It is entirely appropriate that I should in this House set out my considered response to the events of recent weeks and

particularly to the events here yesterday and since. This is the correct and appropriate place for those who hold public office and are responsible for decisions of public concern to account for their actions and omissions.

The key issue, throughout this entire episode, has been accountability – the right of the public to secure adequate explanations and the responsibility of the holders of high office to take responsibility for their actions.

At the outset, I have to say that semantic distinctions between responsibility and culpability, however interesting they might be in their own right, do not meet the needs of this case. If this House were to accept that a Minister would never be accountable to the Dáil without direct culpability on his or her part, the principle of accountability would wither away. Without accountability the value of a parliamentary democracy would be fatally undermined.

It is not part of my understanding of the principle of accountability that it only exists in the case of decisions already taken. In the particular horrific case of Father Brendan Smyth, it was a failure to take necessary and urgent decisions that led to a gross breach of responsibility to the public. Are we really to believe that Government or its agents are only accountable in respect of the things they have done, and never in respect of the things they should have done?

Again, I want to make it clear that I did not come into this House to seek an apology to the Labour Party or to me for the political actions of others. Politics is not about bruised egos and I have no interest in seeking either apology or flattery as a substitute for democratic accountability. If an apology is owed to anyone, it is owed to the victims of this priest, and to the parents and family members who have been hurt by his depravity over many years.

Let me also address the question that some seem to be asking – what does the Labour Party want? The question is being asked almost as if it were up to us to decide what others should say, or as if we were looking for some kind of reward for standing over the breach of public responsibility involved and the appointment of Mr Whelehan to the High Court without accountability. Let me answer the question.

What the Labour Party wants is an accounting, a true and fair accounting, and nothing more than that. We were hoping yesterday to hear something that would convince us that it was right to prevent the Attorney General from explaining his actions before publicly promoting him. We were hoping to secure some kind of convincing explanation that the Attorney General's apparent attitude, that everything about this case was handled reasonably, could be reconciled with the actual circumstances of the case, or else an acceptance that the Attorney General's account was plainly wrong and grossly insensitive. We were hoping to hear some sort of admission that a serious error had been made in promoting the Attorney General to a place where he is immune from questioning despite the strongly held convictions of more than a third of the government and that the people had been let down by a reckless and impetuous act. We heard none of those things.

I intend in my contribution to this debate to refer, first, to the issues arising in the handling of the Smyth case in the Office of the Attorney General, and by the former Attorney General himself; second, I intend to deal with the background to the appointment of the Attorney General as President of the High Court; and third, I intend to set out how I will vote on the motion before the House when that vote is taken.

Even before I became aware of certain facts that I intend to deal with later, I have to say, with great regret, that I found the speech of the Taoiseach yesterday extremely disappointing in its failure to recognise that there has to be a higher level of responsibility for the actions of the Government.

In the course of his speech, the Taoiseach, correctly, refused to excuse the failure of the Office of the Attorney General for its handling of the Father Brendan Smyth case. Unfortunately, the Attorney General, in his presentation to Government, did seek to excuse that failure. In effect, he endorsed the handling of the case on entirely spurious and offensive grounds.

Yet even though the Taoiseach apparently now accepts that this matter was handled insensitively, with lack of appropriate urgency, that the delay was totally unacceptable, and that there were gaps and flaws, he knew all of that last Friday, when he apparently accepted the Attorney General's belief that it would be harsh to find fault with the way the case was handled. How else could he have proceeded to appoint Mr Whelehan to the second most senior judicial office?

One has to ask, if the Taoiseach had made yesterday's speech last Thursday, would he still feel comfortable about standing over the actions of last Friday? Alternatively, and this I think goes to the heart of the difficulty, how is it possible to reconcile the entire detailed account of everything that has happened with the assertion, made by the Taoiseach in his speech, that the emergence of the Smyth case did not affect the Attorney General's suitability for high office?

In fact, to an outside observer, it must seem odd that the only difference the Smyth case appeared to make was to increase the urgency of making the appointment.

Even though the Taoiseach purported to account to the House for the events, he at no point addressed the issue of why it was not possible for the Attorney General to similarly account. As is now well known, there is a precedent for such an accounting in the handling of the Fr Ryan extradition case. The Taoiseach barely mentioned this precedent and offers no explanation as to why it was not considered appropriate. He went on to say in his speech that he received no warning of our intention to leave the Cabinet room in the event of the appointment being made, and regarded our withdrawal as nothing more than an expression of dissent from the decision.

That assertion ignores the two letters the Taoiseach received from me, together with the one he sent me, on Thursday last. I circulated copies of those letters with a statement. In the first letter I sent the Taoiseach, I made it clear that:

In the circumstances we have come reluctantly to the view that we cannot support the appointment of the Attorney General as President of the High Court unless and until a satisfactory explanation of these troubling events is offered by the Attorney General, personally or through you in the Dáil, in such a way as to allay the public concern.

In replying to that letter, the Taoiseach said:

. . . in an attempt to meet your concerns, I would propose placing before the Government in the morning the Attorney General's detailed explanation of the Brendan Smyth case, in order to allow any further questions. This is the only appropriate forum in which the Attorney General can be properly questioned. In addition I intend to propose to Government that the Attorney General's explanation be published immediately.

In my further letter, I said to the Taoiseach:

At the very last, I would expect that you would answer questions in the Dáil, in such a way as to allay public concern, before final consideration of any appointment is being made.

That correspondence makes it clear beyond any misunderstanding that we could not accept this appointment prior to proper public accountability.

It is also worth noting that we withdrew from the Cabinet meeting when the Taoiseach terminated discussions of the Attorney General's report and called on the Minister for Justice to propose the appointment of the Attorney General as President of the High Court.

The Taoiseach in his speech said that he understood we were withdrawing only because:

The Government procedures are such that dissenting voices at a Government meeting are not recorded in the Government minutes, whereas members of the Government absenting themselves may be recorded if they so request. It was for this reason that we took the view that, rather than staying at the table, our Labour colleagues were absenting themselves for this decision only, thereby recording their dissent.

In fact, while "Government Procedure Instructions" is an officially protected document, I can assure the House that it contains nothing whatever to this effect.

The Taoiseach also seems to imply by this remark that neither I nor my colleagues need take any accountability for the appointment of the Attorney General, since we were not in the room. Such an argument would clearly fly in the face of collective responsibility. I made it clear on Sunday last that of course we were collectively responsible for that appointment, even though we disagreed fundamentally with it, and that what we had to do was to decide whether that was the right position to be in.

It is further worth noting that if there was any misunderstanding about our intentions, ample opportunity existed to clarify the matter, even after we left the Cabinet room. Instead of doing so, the Taoiseach acted to ensure that the Attorney General became President of the High Court by 6 p.m. that day. It would be hard to see that as anything other than an attempt to present us with a *faît accompli*, even though I accept that the President would not be available on that Saturday or Sunday. All of this brings us back to the central question, to which there is no answer in the Taoiseach's speech – why was it necessary to proceed with the appointment prior to any form of public accountability being available?

In moving to the second part of the remarks I wish to make, let me say at the outset that it is true to say that I had, prior to the Fr Brendan Smyth affair, come to my own conclusion that in the interests of Government cohesion I would have to set aside my reservations about the qualifications of the Attorney General for this post. I never communicated any such view to the Taoiseach and was prepared to do so until certain reforms on which we had reached broad agreement were fully implemented. However, once I became aware of the Fr Brendan Smyth affair, I would not and could not abandon those reservations prior to the exercise of public accountability.

It is however appropriate that I should say something about

the reservations I had. I agreed to the reappointment of the former Attorney General at the time of the negotiations on the formation of the government. I never had any difficulty working with him, and did so on a regular basis, especially for example, in relation to aspects of the Anglo-Irish negotiations in which I am involved.

I have, I think, made it clear that I would not have been at all unhappy to see him promoted to ordinary membership of the High Court at any time that he wished, and that a vacancy existed, always assuming, of course, that the issues with which we are dealing now had been properly accounted for. However, I took the view throughout all my discussions with the Taoiseach – discussions which I initiated well before the end of last year – that the two most senior positions in the Judiciary required appointments which would reflect very high skills and a substantial vision. I felt throughout, and feel still, that at the very least, an Attorney General with no judicial experience should be prepared to "serve an apprenticeship" as an ordinary member of the High Court before aspiring to the presidency. It is worth noting, and it is a point of which I think the Taoiseach is well aware, that the former Attorney General is in fact the first such holder of his office to have been appointed as President of the High Court.

The Taoiseach quoted in his speech Professor Basil Chubb, to justify his assertion that by custom the Attorney General is always offered any vacancy to the High Court that arises during his term of office. However, in the course of preparations for the ethics Bill, my office was supplied with a speaking note prepared for the Taoiseach by the Cabinet Secretary at the time of the appointment of the former Attorney General, in order to assist the Taoiseach in advising the Attorney General of his terms and conditions of employment.

That speaking note makes it unequivocally clear that:

appointment as Attorney General does not imply any commitment whatever, on the Government's part, to subsequent appointment to the next, or any, vacancy on the judicial bench

In fairness to the Taoiseach, I have to say that when I brought this speaking note to his attention, he told me that he had not used it when appointing the former Attorney General, and I believe that. Of course, this speaking note could not be expressed any other way. Our Constitution reserves the right of appointment of members of the Judiciary to the President of Ireland, acting on the advice of the Government. An appointment to the Bench cannot be in the gift of any one person, or be seen as a right by any person.

Any promise or condition of employment which guaranteed an appointment to the Judiciary, thereby pre-empting the free and unfettered decision of the Government in the matter, would clearly have to be null and void. Fortunately, and despite impressions to the contrary, no such conditions of employment exist. It would also be true to say that it was not until very late in my discussions with the Taoiseach about judicial appointments - discussions which I had initiated in the latter part of last year, because of my interest in ensuring that such appointments would receive the maximum consideration – that I was made aware of any promise made by the Taoiseach to the Attorney General in respect of the Presidency of the High Court. At a number of points in our discussions, we sought and received advice from the Attorney General about different options and scenarios that we were considering. It was not until very late indeed in the course of those conversations that I was advised that the Attorney General wanted the office of President of the High Court, and that the Taoiseach had offered it to him. I have often wondered when that request or offer, whichever it was, was in fact made.

Notwithstanding all of that, I had, as I have said, come to the conclusion, prior to the Smyth scandal, that the interests of Government cohesion demanded that I set aside my reservations about the appointment, but I cannot stand over an appointment made in the absence of accountability. I will always believe that the Attorney General himself had an obligation and a duty to answer questions in the public domain prior to any appointment. He chose not to exercise that option, and the Taoiseach and Fianna Fáil members of the Government, despite any misgivings they might have had, chose to support that refusal. I could not.

This brings me to the third part of what I wish to say, and that is to explain how I intend to act and vote in this debate. This has been a good Government, as the Taoiseach said yesterday and again today. I am proud to stand over its record in many respects. We have done much to develop and strengthen the economy, and have established a record of good and careful management. There are signs every day that the strengthening of the economy is reflected in more jobs and greater confidence. At the same time, we have done much to undo the damage inflicted by previous administrations on essential public services. Those who have been housed, or who have found essential health treatments more readily available, or who have seen the major improvements in our education system, or who have been part of the new excitement in the world of arts, music and film, can all testify to that. Those who have benefited from the huge list of reforming legislative measures that have been enacted in the Government's short life will I believe, readily acknowledge that this has been a government that has made a difference.

In no other area of the life of our country has the impact of this government been more profound than in relation to Northern Ireland. From the moment we came into office, the Taoiseach and I committed ourselves to make the movement towards peace and reconciliation the first priority. Nobody can deny that the Taoiseach has been unremitting in his determination to bring people in from the margins on this issue and to persuade those who had previously disdained democratic politics and to give peace a chance. This strategic approach was the bedrock on which the peace process was built, and it is to the Taoiseach's credit that he persevered from beginning to end, with a single-minded determination to achieve the laying aside of arms.

The peace process is not now as fragile as some commentators would have us believe. The decision of the British Government to open preliminary discussions with both Sin Fein and the political representatives of the Loyalist paramilitaries, and to do so in the near future, has given the process added impetus and ensured that there is still room to build, but, of course, political instability in the Republic of Ireland is not a desirable basis on which to proceed. I have always believed that our democracy is strong enough to withstand such temporary difficulties, just as I believe there is no leader in this House who would not be willing to carry on the work started by the Taoiseach, in the spirit in which he started that work, if the necessity arose. That would be nothing less than our bounden duty.

Throughout all this, my own relationship with the Taoiseach has survived a great deal of hard work, carried out together, and a number of disagreements. Whether we are talking about the Structural Funds negotiations, the tax amnesty, the handling of the beef tribunal report, the passports affair or, indeed, other controversies which attracted less publicity, I do not believe that anyone can argue that these issues were approached by us, by me or the Taoiseach, in a spirit that threatened the cohesion of the government. It would never be my wish to do so. I have found the last couple of weeks the most difficult of my political life, and the decisions I have had to make the most painful.

Before outlining those decisions, I must outline the events of the last number of hours.

Early this morning, I was advised that new information has become available to the Taoiseach and his Ministers. This information consisted in broad terms of the following – the Taoiseach referred to this in his address: the new Attorney General had found in his office evidence that a previous case, very similar to the Smyth case, had been handled by the office in a totally different manner to the way in which the Smyth case had been handled. This other case, which had also arisen during the tenure of the previous Attorney General, had involved an ex-monk. It had involved allegations of sexual abuse in another jurisdiction, allegations that related to a period some time ago, and a request for extradition on foot of those allegations.

That previous case had been dealt with in an extremely expeditious way. The issues of law had been teased out very quickly, the matter had been placed in front of the Attorney General very quickly, and the warrant had been endorsed by the Attorney General. In other words, the system worked. There was no breakdown and the "normal" method of operation had resulted in a quick and expeditious extradition. The issues of law referred to as arising for the first time in the Smyth case had in fact been dealt with before.

In addition to being given these facts, I was also informed that the Taoiseach and the Minister for Justice were now satisfied that they had been seriously misled by the explanations of the Attorney in the Smyth case and that there were no grounds for believing that the fault in that case lay in the system in operation in the Attorney General's office. I was informed that both the Taoiseach and the Minister for Justice were prepared to come into the House and to lay out all these facts for the information of the House. The Taoiseach, on foot of this, was prepared to say to the House that he now deeply regretted the decision to appoint the former Attorney General, and the manner in which it was done, and that he now accepted fully that my reservations about this appointment were correct.

On foot of these assurances and undertakings, I indicated that I was prepared to support the government in any vote in the House. In my judgement, this would be necessary in order at the very least to enable this matter to be fully investigated and decisions to be made about the next steps that needed to be taken in view of the former Attorney's misleading explanations about the way in which his office dealt with extradition cases.

However, following all these discussions, I decided to speak to the present Attorney General about these issues, in order to clarify aspects of the case to which I have just referred. I asked the Attorney General if he would inform me when he advised the Taoiseach about these matters. He told me he had done so on Monday – that is to say, before the Taoiseach made his statement to the House yesterday. It was immediately apparent that the Taoiseach should have included this vital information in the statement he made to the House yesterday, if he wished to give a full explanation of all these events. Had he done so, it would have completely altered the thrust of his speech, and had a profound effect on the subsequent debate and questioning.

He described the handling of the Smyth case as the consequence of "a system developed for past conditions failing to cope with present realities", he asserted to the House that he "had asked tough questions" about the system: he said that he regarded the Attorney General's explanations as "a record of system failure, and as something showing the gaps, the flaws, and the liabilities that had to be tackled". None of this, and a great deal more, is possible to reconcile with the new information available to the Taoiseach, but not given to the House yesterday.

Having made this discovery, I went with some of my colleagues to meet the Taoiseach shortly before noon today. I outlined to the Taoiseach what I had discovered and the implications of that discovery.

Before concluding I thank my Government colleagues for their efforts and dedicated work in achieving our objectives outlined in the Programme for Government. I wish them and their families who suffer a lot in the business of politics and public life well for the future. For the reasons I have outlined it will be obvious to the House that neither I nor any of my colleagues can vote confidence in the government at the conclusion of this debate. All my Labour colleagues in Cabinet and all Ministers of State who are members of the Labour Party will resign from their offices before the vote is taken. The House is entitled to nothing less from us.

*John Bruton (1947–) was educated in Clongowes Wood College,
Co. Kildare, University College Dublin and the King's Inns. He
was first elected to the Dáil in 1969, and was a Parliamentary
Secretary in Cosgrave's Fine Gael-Labour Coalition in 1973–77.
After the 1981 election, he was appointed Minister for Finance.
The government collapsed nine months later after the failure of
his budget to win the support of the Dáil. He was Minister for
Trade, Commerce, Tourism and Industry between 1982–86, and
was reappointed Minister for Finance in the government
reshuffle of 1986. He lost the Fine Gael leadership election in
1987, but succeeded to that position in November 1990, on the
resignation of Alan Dukes.*

*Fine Gael lost ground in the 1992 election, and commenced
another period in opposition after Labour went into coalition
with Fianna Fáil. When that government collapsed, Bruton was
appointed Taoiseach, with Labour and Democratic Left's
backing. The first issue to face the new government was the
Framework Document, which sought to facilitate the
development of the peace process in Northern Ireland. In his
speech to the Dáil on his return from the launch of the
document in Belfast, Bruton outlined the thinking behind it.*

DAIL ÉIREANN, FEBRUARY 22, 1995

As the House will be aware, earlier today in Belfast, the
British Prime Minister and I together launched a Joint

Framework Document. The document is a shared understanding between the British and Irish Governments and its purpose is to assist discussion and negotiation involving the Northern Ireland political parties. Copies of the document have been circulated to all members.

At the outset, I wish to put on record my thanks and appreciation to the Tánaiste and his Departmental staff who have negotiated with considerable skill, patience and tenacity to achieve this outcome. It is also appropriate that I pay tribute to my predecessor as Taoiseach, Deputy Albert Reynolds, and his advisors, without whose vision and considerable courage, the peace process, of which this document is an integral part, would not have been possible.

May I again emphasise what this document is: it is a shared understanding between the two governments to assist discussion and negotiation involving the Northern Ireland political parties. Deputies will recall that in 1992, talks involving Northern Ireland political parties came to a halt. It was suggested then that it would be helpful if both governments were to set out their shared view on the broad lines of a possible political accommodation. It was felt that this might give impetus and direction to the process of negotiation.

In response to this suggestion, the British and Irish governments began a painstaking and detailed exercise which has led to the publication to-day of the Joint Framework Document. The Document also draws on the Downing Street Declaration of 15th December, 1993. In a sense, the publication of to-day's document brings together two separate but parallel exercises – the talks process and the peace process are now, formally, one process.

Lasting peace and stability on this island requires that three sets of relationships be addressed: the relationship between the two communities in Northern Ireland, the relationship between both parts of this island, and the relationship between the sovereign governments in Dublin and London.

In the documents published today, the two Governments

have set out their shared view of the points that need to be met if the three relationships are to be satisfactorily accommodated.

May I briefly say what the Framework document is not. It is not a prescription for an unpalatable dose of medicine. It is not a blueprint rigidly to be imposed on the people of Northern Ireland. It is not a cage within which their political leaders will have their dialogue confined. It is not an Irish nationalist agenda. It is not a British agenda. What is it? It is a view, shared by two governments, as to what might most usefully be done to deal with the three, fraught and difficult, sets of relationships.

It represents an assessment by the two governments of what we think might be an agreed outcome from future talks involving the governments and the Northern Ireland political parties. We believe we have got it right. We are open to persuasion by anyone who believes otherwise.

It is now a matter for the people of Northern Ireland, and also for the people in this part of Ireland, and in Britain to study the document, and I recommend that they do so in a constructive and calm way.

No party will regard this document as meeting all their requirements and aspirations. The document represents balance and compromise. If its main elements become the basis for new institutions and political arrangements, I believe that they will ultimately command the widespread support necessary to ensure a fair and effective arrangement for the three sets of relationships to which I have referred.

This document is the contribution of two governments together. It aims at balance between aspirations that are, if put within a traditional absolutist and territorial matrix, basically irreconcilable. But the document does more than just attempt to balance two irreconcilable aspirations. It is the beginning of work towards a wholly new form of expression of traditional aspirations, focusing on individuals and communities rather than on territory. By expressing aspirations in this new way, we hope that the two otherwise irreconcilable sets of aspirations can, in fact, be reconciled.

The Governments will welcome the detailed papers and contributions of political parties, especially in Northern Ireland. We challenge them to seek the same balance, the same rethinking, and the same radical reconciliation that we have sought in our proposals. Let Nationalist parties show how their proposals accommodate Unionist aspirations. Let Unionist parties show how their proposals accommodate Nationalist aspirations. Let both recognise the reality of divisions and the need to bridge them creatively. That is the challenge to both of them. Don't just recite your own fears and aspirations. Tell us how the fear of the other community can be assuaged. Tell us how the other community's aspirations can be given legitimate expression.

And now let me turn to the document itself.

The document is founded on four guiding principles:

(i) the principle of self-determination as set out in the December, 1993 Downing Street Joint Declaration;

(ii) the principle that the consent of the governed is an essential ingredient for stability in any political arrangement;

(iii) the principle that agreement must be pursued and established by exclusively democratic peaceful means without resort to violence or coercion;

(iv) and, finally, the principle that any new political arrangements must be based on full respect for, and protection of the expression of, the rights and identities of both traditions in Ireland and, must in an even-handed way, afford both communities in Northern Ireland parity of esteem, including equality of opportunity.

The document seeks to build such a framework on four main pillars:

- Structures within Northern Ireland.
- North/South institutions.
- East/West structures.
- Constitutional issues.

The Joint Framework Document commends direct dialogue with

the relevant political parties in Northern Ireland to develop new internal political structures. The dialogue is one for the political parties there. The governments confirm that cross-community agreement is an essential requirement for the establishment and successful operation of such structures. While the principles and overall context for such new structures are a recognised concern of both Governments, the structures themselves should be negotiated in direct dialogue involving the relevant political parties in Northern Ireland, who will have to operate them. In a separate document published today, the British Government has unilaterally set out its ideas for structures in Northern Ireland. Neither my predecessor or I felt it appropriate to become involved in the detail of this Document and I do not propose to comment on it.

Moving then to the second pillar, the North/South institutions. We envisage that new institutions should be created to cater adequately for present and future political, social and economic inter-connections on the island of Ireland enabling representatives of the main traditions North and South to enter agreed, dynamic, new, co-operative and constructive relationships.

These institutions should include a North/South body involving Heads of Departments on both sides, duly established and maintained by legislation in both sovereign parliaments. This body would bring together Ministers representing the Irish Government and political heads of departments from the new democratic institutions in Northern Ireland. Its function would be to discharge or to oversee delegated executive, harmonising or consultative functions over a range of matters. In the first instance, the two Governments acting in agreement with the parties will designate these functions. Subsequently, the two administrations North and South may agree to further designations.

It is our intention that the functions for the proposed North/South body would be designated by the two Governments in agreement with the Northern Ireland parties.

Our approach on this, as on all other elements in the Document, is based on the principle of consent. We wish to see a North/South body which will be flexible and dynamic. Its terms of reference, its legal status, and arrangements for its political, legal, administration and financial accountability will be established by legislation in both sovereign parliaments, but again only following the pursuit of agreement with the participants in the Northern Ireland talks process, and only following endorsement by the people of both parts of Ireland voting separately in referendums on the same day. In this process, emphasis will, of course, be placed on making sure that the arrangements are workable and useful. Everybody's views on this will be welcome.

Functions which might be designated to the North/South body would fall into three main categories: consultative, harmonising and executive. The range of functions that might be designated at the outset for executive level action would include sectors involving:

- A natural or physical, cross-border or all-Ireland framework,
- EC programmes and initiatives.
- Marketing and promotion activity abroad.
- Culture and heritage.

Again I emphasise that no function whether executive, harmonising or consultative will be carried out without the agreement of the Northern Ireland representatives on the body. I would also like to make it clear that functions will be designated only where it makes practical common sense. I do not envisage a North/South body with an imposing headquarters. I do not envisage thousands of civil servants working out how all the people on this island might be brought together under some uniform arrangements. The North/South body that I envisage will consist of say, three Ministers from this Government and three Ministers from whatever administration emerges in Northern Ireland, sitting down together from time to time. They will be doing this without in any way diminishing the separate traditions and aspirations. The emphasis will be on practicality and workability.

The third pillar in the Joint Framework Document deals with East/West structures. Both Governments envisage a broadly based agreement which will maintain a standing Anglo-Irish Inter-Governmental Conference chaired by the designated Irish Minister and by the Secretary of State for Northern Ireland with a small supporting permanent secretariat. The Inter-Governmental Conference will have as its main objective the deepening of co-operation between the two Governments, and will provide a continuing institutional expression for the Irish Government's recognised concern and role in relation to Northern Ireland. It will:

• Provide a forum for agreement on bi-lateral matters not covered by other specific arrangements and excluding matters for which responsibility is transferred to new political institutions in Northern Ireland.

• Consider ways of enhancing community identification with policing in Northern Ireland.

• Review the workings of the agreement and promote, support and underwrite the fair and effective operation of all its provisions and the new arrangements established under it.

• Monitor those provisions and where necessary provide a forum for the resolution of disputes and

• Provide a framework for consultation and co-ordination between both Governments and the new North/South institutions.

Let me now deal with the constitutional issues, the fourth and final pillar. The Irish and British Governments are prepared to address them as part of an overall accommodation.

In the case of my Government, I am prepared to introduce and support proposals for change in the Irish Constitution to implement the commitments in this Document and in the Downing Street Joint Declaration. I will return to this point in a moment. In the case of the British Government, their new approach for Northern Ireland, vesting the constitutional future in the people of Northern Ireland, will be enshrined in British constitutional legislation. This will embody the principles and commitments in the Joint Declaration, and in this Framework Document, either by an amendment of the Government of Ireland Act, 1920 or by its replacement by appropriate new legislation and appropriate new provisions entrenched by agreement.

For reasons which I explained here today, I do not propose at this stage to table details of proposed amendments to the Constitution. More time is required for consultation and consideration. The detailed wording of the redrafting of the Constitution is properly a matter for the Government and the Oireachtas, not for negotiation with another government. What I can say is that the principles and immutable political commitments underlying the changes will be:

• To remove any jurisdictional or territorial claim of legal right over the territory of Northern Ireland contrary to the will of the people of Ireland.

• To provide that the creation of a sovereign united Ireland could therefore only occur, in circumstances where a majority of the people of Northern Ireland formally chose to be part of a united Ireland.

• That the existing birthright of everyone born in either jurisdiction in Ireland to be part as of right of the Irish nation would be maintained.

It should also be important to say to unionists that the document contains a recognition by both Governments of the legitimacy of whatever choice is freely exercised by a majority of the people of Northern Ireland with regard to its constitutional status, whether they prefer to continue to support the Union or to opt for a sovereign united Ireland.

In the Framework Document, both Governments also commit themselves to finding a means in their own jurisdictions to protect specified civil, political, social and cultural rights. Obviously, there will be widespread consultation with the relevant political parties. There might also be a covenant enshrining a dedication to mutual respect between the two traditions to the exclusively peaceful resolution of all the differences between them.

So much for the Document itself and for the background developments which lead to it. May I now make some concluding remarks.

The problems which this Document is attempting to deal with are deep-rooted and of long standing. I will not attempt an historical analysis nor do I think it relevant to rehearse the wrongs, the grievances, and the injustices felt on all sides. Much pain has been inflicted, much damage has been done, much trust has been forfeited, and much sorrow has been caused. Those of us who share the island of Ireland have certainly not been enabled to realise our full potential. The tensions between the two communities in Northern Ireland, between the two parts of Ireland and between Britain and Ireland have diminished all of us.

Traditional political structures have not provided solutions to our problems. We must find new and imaginative structures which will provide security to both nationalists and unionists. Paper declarations can only go so far. As long as a significant section of people feel systematically alienated from the structures of government, no one will feel secure. Our proposals today are, I believe, balanced and should provide security for everyone. Security does not come from constitutions or statutes. It comes from knowing that your neighbour, of a different tradition, can feel that same loyalty to the state, and can identify with it on the same terms of equality and esteem, as you do. That's what we want for Northern Ireland.

As we embark on this new phase in our discussions, I am encouraged by a number of things. I am encouraged by the excellent and positive spirit in the Anglo-Irish relationship which has made possible the launching of this Joint Framework Document. I am encouraged that it was possible for my party and for this Government essentially to work with a document inherited from a Fianna Fáil-led Government. I am encouraged by the cessation of violence in Northern Ireland and by the considerable discipline and skill which has been shown in maintaining that cessation on a daily basis.

I welcome the way in which Sinn Féin has embraced the political process and joined with other parties in working the political institutions to which they now have access. I think in particular of their role in the Forum for Peace and Reconciliation where they are making their mark. Senior figures in that party have demonstrated political courage and a sense of openness to new ideas. But perhaps what would most encourage us this year, when we look back fifty years to the end of the Second World War, is that we can see that new and imaginative political institutions made possible the maintenance of peace, and the gradual reconciliation between European States, who had for generations engaged in war as a means of resolving disputes.

I hope that a similarly imaginative and courageous approach on the part of all the political elements on this island and in Britain would achieve the same degree of trust and co-operation. My Government and I are ready to play our part. A successful settlement in Northern Ireland, reconciling different loyalties within the one land area, can provide an Irish and British model for resolving many similar conflicts in the emerging states of central and eastern Europe.

In conclusion, I ask only that all other parties approach the Document, published in Belfast today, in a constructive and calm way. Read it. Think about it. Give us your ideas. But above all, give us your commitment, your faith in the future.

"I BELIEVE IRISH FEMINISTS NOW HAVE THE CONFIDENCE TO DEVELOP THEIR THINKING, SO THAT IT BECOMES TRULY INCLUSIVE"

Finola Bruton (1952–) was born in Castlebar, Co. Mayo and educated locally and at University College Dublin, where she studied Arabic and Politics. After university, she worked as a social worker with unmarried mothers. The wife of John Bruton, she caused political controversy with a speech delivered as an introduction to Hillary Rodham Clinton's meeting with 350 Irish women, as part of the Clinton presidential visit in December 1995.

Mrs Bruton's speech was delivered just one week after the Irish electorate had voted by a margin of 50.2% to 49.8% for the removal of the Constitutional ban on divorce. It received widespread media comment, with many in the feminist movement regretting her depiction of elements of feminism as being divisive. It also got a substantial degree of backing, however, and the level of support generated led many who had been initially very hostile to the speech to tone down their criticisms in further comments.

NATIONAL GALLERY, DUBLIN, DECEMBER 1, 1995

I congratulate and thank Mrs Hillary Rodham Clinton for choosing to set aside time in her all-too-brief visit to Ireland to address this gathering of women.

Mrs Hillary Rodham Clinton is a person of courage. She took on the most difficult domestic policy challenge facing any US administration – health care reform – without hesitation, because she understands how health care issues affect women.

413

This is just part of her search for a public policy response that encompasses a greater sense of community of her search for a philosophy of living, that overcomes what she so well describes as the "sleeping sickness of the soul" which afflicts public discourse in so many countries. That search requires radicalism.

True radicalism is about asking questions. Asking questions especially about those ideas that are most fashionable, most progressive or most politically correct at any given time in history. True feminism is about affirming the uniqueness of women and their contribution to this world. It is also about acknowledging that not all women are the same, either in what they are, or in the choices they make.

The true radical and the true feminist must listen, listen especially to the voices and to the underlying concerns of those who challenge what have now become almost traditional notions in regard to rights and choices.

Now is the time to recognise, in a deeper way, that for every right there is a corresponding obligation, for every choice there is a consequence. Now is the time to recognise that the notion of equality does not necessarily give a natural primacy to a professional career, over other choices a woman may make.

There is a vital place beyond the workplace, many women choose to be there. They should be applauded and acknowledged.

One must recognise, too, that a philosophy which is predicated on success and which provides no consolation for those who fail is not truly universal. We are dealing here with human beings and not raw materials, and as human beings, and as women, we are not only free, independent, strong and courageous but often weak, difficult, lonely and frightened.

A realistic acceptance of the necessity and inevitability of a certain amount of pain in our lives is the first step we can take towards the healing of that pain.

Rights and choices on their own will not banish that pain. Rejection, broken marriages, sudden deaths, natural injustices,

414

mental illness, cannot be prevented by rights or choices. No matter how much education we have, we are dependent on the love and care of those at all times in our lives, and we are shaped and prejudiced by our own attachments and love.

The liberation of women must also be about the liberation of men and fundamentally it must be about the creation of a new society where all citizens must have a share and be given the opportunity to develop their potential.

There has been a certain tendency in the women's movement which seeks to exclude or marginalise men. This line of thinking is not in the long-term interest of women or of society.

In some of our more deprived communities in Ireland and other countries there is already clear evidence of a growing number of young men alienated from society who do not participate in any significant way in the economic and civic life of their community.

In many cases these young men are also excluded from normal family relationships. I believe such a development is fraught with dangers for women, children, the young men themselves and society generally.

As we struggle towards the creation of a new society, we must be aware that a good relationship between men and women is central to the success of any society. We must also be conscious that the values of the marketplace are not the values which are most beneficial to society.

Any undue emphasis on consumer type values and on individualism in relationships is detrimental to the cohesion of society. We only become human in a social context. Without society individual human existence is empty and devoid of meaning.

The primary emphasis, therefore, must be on society and on the values it affirms. Among those values must, of course, be support for individual growth and development. But individual rights must always be anchored by duties and responsibilities to society.

Our Constitution rightly affirms that the family is the

fundamental unit of society. For a family to be successful, values such as consent, commitment and solidarity between the various generations is essential. It is within a family that individuals find the necessary freedom and security to grow and develop as individuals.

A happy family also provides a safe environment for closeness and intimacy, which are essential for the development of well-integrated human beings.

This Government is rightly concerned about the well-being of the family and has recently established a Commission for the Family which will look at the family in all its dimensions and variety, and examine means of supporting families in their various forms.

I strongly support the building of families and, as women and as citizens, I believe we need to affirm that a loving married relationship between a man and a woman is a core value to be recognised, affirmed and supported.

Feminism in Ireland has exacted enormous and lasting achievements to its name and, of course, much remains to be done.

But, as a result of these achievements, I believe Irish feminists now have the confidence to develop their thinking, so that it becomes truly inclusive: inclusive of women in the home; inclusive of children; inclusive of men; inclusive of the positive experiences of all women, whatever their political philosophy, whatever their chosen role in life.

"YOUR ROAD IS OUR ROAD"

Bill Clinton (1946–), 42nd President of the United States, was born in Hope, Arkansas and educated at Georgetown University, Oxford University and Yale University Law School, where he graduated in 1973.

He entered politics soon after graduation, and in 1978 was elected Governor of Arkansas, at the age of 32. In 1991 he commenced his campaign to win the Democratic nomination for the Presidency which he successfully completed in 1992.

In the course of his election campaign, Clinton mentioned his interest in Ireland and specifically, his willingness to appoint a peace envoy. After his election he played a key role in the emerging peace process in Ireland in 1993 and 1994, and supported the efforts of both governments through the Downing Street Declaration.

In November 1995, with peace in Ireland a year old, Clinton paid a visit to both North and South of the country. It was seen by political observers on both sides of the Atlantic as being one of the high points of his years as President.

Clinton became the fifth foreign dignitary to address a joint session of the Houses of the Oireachtas, and his speech, though ranging over topics that are broader than the Irish issue, was built around the need to sustain that peace process.

Dáil Éireann, December 1, 1995

Mr Speaker, Ceann Comhairle . . . Taoiseach, Tánaiste, Members of the Dáil and Seanad, Cathaoirleach of the Seanad, I am honoured to be joined here as all of you know by my wife, members of our Cabinet and members of both parties of the United States Congress . . .

I thank you for the honour of inviting me and I am especially pleased to be here at this moment in your history before the elected representatives of a strong, confident, democratic Ireland, a nation today playing a greater role in world affairs than ever before. We live in a time of immense hope and immense possibility – a time captured, I believe, in the wonderful lines of your poet, Seamus Heaney, when he talked of "the longed-for tidal wave of justice can rise up and hope and history rhyme."

That is the time in which we live. It is the world's good fortune that Ireland has become a force for fulfilling that hope, in redeeming the possibilities of mankind, a force for good far beyond your numbers. And we are all the better for it.

Today I have travelled from the North, where I have seen the difference Ireland's leadership has made for peace there. At the lighting of Belfast's Christmas tree before tens of thousands of people, in the faces of two communities divided by bitter history, we saw the radiance of optimism born, especially among the young of both communities. In the voices of the Shankill and the Falls there was a harmony of new hope and I saw that the people want peace and they will have it.

George Bernard Shaw with his wonderful Irish love of irony said "peace is not only better than war but infinitely more arduous."

Today I thank Prime Minister Bruton, former Prime Minister Reynolds and Deputy Prime Minister Spring and Britain's Prime Minister Major and others, but especially these, for their unfailing dedication to the arduous task of peace.

From the Downing Street Declaration to the historic cease-fire that began fifteen months ago, to Tuesday's announcement of the twin-track initiative which will open a dialogue in which all voices can be heard and all viewpoints can be represented, they have taken great risks without hesitation.

They have chosen a harder role than the comfortable path of

418

pleasant present pieties. But what they have done is right, and the children and grandchildren of this generation of Irish will reap the reward.

Today I renew America's pledge. Your road is our road. We want to walk it together. We will continue our support – political, financial and moral, to those who take risks for peace.

I am proud that our administration was the first to support in the Executive budget sent to the Congress the International Fund for Ireland, because we believe that those on both sides of the Border who have been denied so much for so long should see that their risks are rewarded with the tangible benefits of peace. In another context a long time ago Yeats reminded us that "too long a sacrifice can make a stone of the heart." We must not let the hearts of the young people who yearn for peace turn to stone.

I want to thank you here, not only for the support you have given your leaders working for peace in Northern Ireland, but for the extraordinary work you have done to wage peace over war all around the world.

Almost 1,500 years ago Ireland stood as a lone beacon of civilisation to a continent shrouded in darkness. It has been said, probably without overstatement, that the Irish in that dark period saved civilisation. Certainly, you saved the records of our civilisation, our shared ideas, our shared ideals, our priceless recordings of them.

Now, in our time, when so many nations seek to overcome conflict and barbarism the light still shines out of Ireland. Since 1958, almost forty years now, there has never been a single solitary day that Irish troops did not stand watch for peace on a distant shore – in Lebanon, in Cyprus, in Somalia, in so many other places where more than 41,000 Irish military and police personnel have served over the years as peacekeepers – an immense contribution for a nation whose armed forces today number fewer than 13,000.

I know that during your Presidency of the European Union next year Ireland will help to lead the effort to build security for a stable, strong and free Europe. For all you have done and for your steadfast devotion to peace, I salute the people of Ireland.

Our nation also has a vital stake in a Europe that is stable, strong and free – something which is now in reach for the first time since nation states appeared on the continent of Europe so many centuries ago. We know that such a Europe can never be built as long as conflict pares at the heart of the continent in Bosnia. The fire there threatens the emerging democracies of the region and our allies nearby, and it also breaks our heart and violates our conscience.

That is why now that the parties have committed themselves to peace, we in the United States are determined to help them find the way back from savagery to civility, to end the atrocities and heal the wounds of that terrible war. That is why we are preparing our forces to participate there, not in fighting a war, but in securing a peace rooted in the agreement they have freely made.

Standing here, thinking about the devastation in Bosnia, the long columns of hopeless refugees streaming from their homes, it is impossible not to recall the ravages that were visited on your wonderful country 150 years ago, not by war, of course, but by natural disaster when the crops rotted black in the ground.

Today, the Great Famine is seared in the memory of the Irish nation and all caring peoples. The memory of a million dead and nearly two million more forced into exile – these memories will remain forever vivid to all of us whose heritage is rooted here.

But as an American I repeat what I must say that in that tragedy came the supreme gift of the Irish to the United States – the men, women and children who boarded the coffin ships, with Galway and Mayo emptied, when Kerry and Cork took flight for a life and a spirit that has enormously enriched the life of our country. The regimental banner brought by President Kennedy that hangs in this House reminds us of the nearly 200,000 Irishmen who took up arms in our civil war.

Many of them were barely off the ships when they joined the union forces and they fought and died at Fredricksburg and Chancellorsville and Gettysburg. Theirs was only the first of countless contributions to our nation from those who fled the Famine. But that contribution enabled us to remain a nation and to be here with you today in partnership for peace for your nation and for the peoples who live on this island.

The Irish have been building America ever since – our cities, our industry, our culture, our public life. I am proud that the delegation that is accompanying me here today includes the latest generation of Irish-American leaders in the United States, men and women who remain devoted to increasing our strength and safeguarding our liberty.

In the last century it was often said that the Irish who fled the Great Hunger were searching for caislean oir – castles of gold.

I cannot say that they found those castles of gold in the United States, but I know they built a lot of castles of gold for the United States. In the prosperity and freedom of our nation, we are grateful for what they did and for the deep ties to Ireland that they give us in their sons and daughters. Now we seek to repay that in some small way by being a partner with you for peace. We seek somehow to communicate to every person who lives here that we want for all of your children the right to grow up in an Ireland where this entire island gives every man and woman the right to live up to the fullest of their God-given abilities, and gives people the right to live in equality, freedom and dignity.

That is the tide of history. We must make sure that the tide runs strong here, for no people deserve the brightest future more than the Irish.

God bless you and thank you.

BIBLIOGRAPHY

A Dictionary of Irish Biography, Henry Boylan, Gill and Macmillan, Dublin, 1988.

Ireland 1912–1985, Joseph Lee, Cambridge University Press, 1989.

Ireland Since the Famine, FSL Lyons, Fontana, 1974.

Irish Historical Documents Since 1800, Alan O'Day and John Stevenson (eds), Gill and Macmillan, Dublin, 1992.

Irish Political Documents 1916–1949, Arthur Mitchell and Padraig O Snodaigh (eds), Irish Academic Press, 1985.

Irish Political Documents 1869–1916, Arthur Mitchell and Padraig O Snodaigh (eds), Irish Academic Press, 1989.

James Connolly, Selected Writings, P Beresford Ellis (ed.), Penguin, Harmonsworth, 1973.

Northern Ireland, A Political Directory 1968–1993, WD Flackes and Sydney Elliott, The Blackstaff Press, Belfast, 1994.

Phrases Make History Here, Conor O'Clery, O'Brien Press, Dublin, 1986.

Speeches and Statements by Eamon de Valera, Maurice Moynihan (ed.), Gill and Macmillan, Dublin, 1980.

The Magill Book of Irish Politics, Vincent Browne with Michael Farrell (ed.), Magill Publications, Dublin , 1981.

Twentieth Century Ireland, Nation and State, Dermot Keogh. Gill and Macmillan, Dublin, 1994.

SOURCES

ARTHUR GRIFFITH

"A nation . . . can only maintain self existence and independence by its own power and resources."
Irish Political Documents 1869 – 1916, Arthur Mitchell and Padraig O'Snodaigh (eds). Irish Academic Press, Dublin, 1989.

JAMES CONNOLLY

"Let us Free Ireland"
James Connolly Selected Writings, P Berresford Ellis (ed.). Penguin, 1973.

RUDYARD KIPLING

"Ulster 1912"
The Ulster Crisis, Resistance to Home Rule 1912 – 14, ATQ Stewart, Faber and Faber, London, 1967.

ANDREW BONAR LAW

"Hold the Pass for Empire"
The Unknown Prime Minister, Robert Blake, Eyre & Spottswoode, London, 1955.
The Ulster Covenant
Mitchell & O'Snodaigh, *op. cit.*

JAMES LARKIN

"If they want peace we are prepared to meet them, but if they want war, then war they will have."
The Freeman's Journal, October 6, 1913, Dublin.

EDWARD CARSON

"If you want Ulster, go and take her, or go and win her."
Hansard, February 11, 1914.

HENRY ASQUITH

"The temporary exclusion of Ulster"
Mitchell & O'Snodaigh, *op. cit.*

JOHN REDMOND

"The Interests of Ireland – the whole of Ireland are at stake in this war."

Mitchell & O'Snodaigh, *op. cit.*

PADRAIG PEARSE

"While Ireland holds these graves"

Collected Works of PH Pearse, Phoenix Publishing Company, Dublin, undated.

The 1916 Proclamation

Irish Historical Documents Since 1800, Alan O'Day and John Stevenson (eds) Gill & MacMillan, Dublin, 1992.

JOHN DILLON

"I am proud of these men"

Hansard, May 11, 1916.

ROGER CASEMENT

"In Ireland alone in this twentieth century is loyalty held to be a crime"

Speeches from the Dock, TD, AM and DB O'Sullivan (eds) Gill & MacMillan, Dublin, 1968.

THE LABOUR PARTY

"The Labour Party . . . is prepared to sacrifice party in the interest of the Nation".

Irish Political Documents 1916 – 1949, Arthur Mitchell and Padraig O'Snodaigh (eds). Irish AcademicPress, Dublin, 1985.

ANTI CONSCRIPTION CONFERENCE

"The passing of the Conscription Bill . . . must be viewed as a declaration of war."

Mitchell & O'Snodaigh, *op. cit.*

THE HIERARCHY

The Hierarchy's Statement against conscription

Mitchell & O'Snodaigh, *op. cit.*

THE FIRST DAIL

Message to the Free Nations of the World

Dáil Debates, January 21, 1919.

THE FIRST DAIL

The Democratic Programme

Dáil Debates, January 21, 1919.

S o u r c e s

TERENCE MACSWINEY
"We ask no mercy, and we will make no compromise"
TD, AM and DB O'Sullivan, *op. cit.*

SIR HAMAR GREENWOOD
"I cannot condemn those policemen."
Hansard, November 24, 1920.

ARTHUR GRIFFITH
"It is a treaty honourable to Ireland."
Dáil Éireann, Offical Report on the Debate on the treaty
between Ireland and Great Britain, December 19, 1921.

EAMON DE VALERA
"I am against this treaty because it will not end the centuries of
conflict between the two nations of Great Britain and Ireland."
Dáil Éireann, Offical Report on the Debate on the treaty
between Ireland and Great Britain, December 19, 1921.

MICHAEL COLLINS
"Are we simply going to go on keeping ourselves in slavery
and subjection."
Dáil Éireann, Offical Report on the Debate on the treaty
between Ireland and Great Britain, December 19, 1921.

ERSKINE CHILDERS
"It is the question of what the delegation was entitled to do."
Dáil Éireann, Offical Report on the Debate on the treaty
between Ireland and Great Britain, December 19, 1921.

WINSTON CHURCHILL
"Dreary steeples of Fermanagh and Tyrone"
Hansard, February 16, 1922.

WT COSGRAVE
"The nation . . . will not submit to an armed minority."
Mitchell & O'Snodaigh, *op.cit.*

WB YEATS
"If Southern Ireland is governed by Catholic ideas, and by
Catholic ideas alone, you will never get the North."
Seanad Éireann Debates, June 11, 1925.

EAMON DE VALERA
"The question is . . . whether this oath . . . is really an oath
at all?"

Statements and Speeches by Eamon de Valera 1917 – 1973,
Maurice Moynihan (ed.), Gill & MacMillan, Dublin, 1980.

FIANNA FAIL

"An empty political formula."

Moynihan, *op.cit.*

SEAN T O'KELLY

"I do no propose to hark back to the tragedies of the last five years."

Dáil Debates, August 10, 1927.

SEAN LEMASS

"Fianna Fáil is a slightly constitutional party."

Dáil Debates, March 21, 1928.

JAMES DILLON

"Voting for De Valera"

Dáil Debates, March 9, 1932.

FINE GAEL

The United Ireland Party

The Irish Times, September 9, 1933.

BASIL BROOKE

"Ninety seven per cent of the Roman Catholics of Northern Ireland are disloyal and disruptive."

Mitchell & O'Snodaigh, *op.cit.*

CAHIR HEALY

"The campaign against the employment of Catholics . . . is a grave violation of the rights of the minority."

Northern Ireland Parliament Debates, April 24, 1934.

EAMON DE VALERA

"Today the cynic is our teacher"

Moynihan, *op. cit.*

WT COSGRAVE

"The War in Spain is a War for the victory or defeat of Communism."

Dáil Debates, November 27, 1937.

EAMON DE VALERA

"The ports are handed over unconditionally."

Moynihan, *op. cit.*

426

EAMON DE VALERA

"The policy of the government does not come as a surprise."
Dáil Debates, September 2, 1939.

VISCOUNT CRAIGAVON

"We are prepared to feel all of the responsibilities that are imposed on Ulster people."
Northern Ireland Parliment Debates, September 2, 1939.

JAMES DILLON

". . . on the side of the Anglo-American alliance is right and justice and on the side of the Axis is evil and injustice."
Dáil Debates, July 17, 1941.

EAMON DE VALERA

"The Ireland that we dreamed of."
Moynihan, op.cit.

EAMON DE VALERA

"There is a small nation that stood alone for several hundred years against aggression."
Moynihan, op. cit.

JOHN A COSTELLO

This Bill will end for ever this Country's long and tragic association with the British Crown.
Dáil Debates, November 24, 1948.

JOHN A COSTELLO

"There is no limit to the capacity of Dr. Browne to deceive himself."
Dáil Debates, April 12, 1951.

SEAN MACBRIDE

"I did hope . . . that possibly a lot of the difficulties that arose were due to his lack of experience or possibly to ill-health."
Dáil Debates, April 12, 1951.

DR NOEL BROWNE

"The honesty of my motives will be attacked by able men."
Dáil Debates, April 12, 1951.

JOHN F KENNEDY

"I am deeply honoured to be your guest in a Free Parliament of a Free Ireland."
Dáil Debates, June 28, 1963.

EAMON DE VALERA

"We in Ireland have constantly looked on you as a champion."
Moynihan, *op.cit.*

SEAN LEMASS

Death of William T Cosgrave.
Dáil Debates, November 17, 1965.

TERENCE O'NEILL

"Ulster stands at the crossroads"
The Irish Times, December 10, 1968.

JACK LYNCH

"The Irish government can no longer stand by and see
innocent people injured and perhaps worse."
The Irish Times, August 14, 1969.

THE BRITISH GOVERNMENT

Communique and Declaration on Employment of troops in
Northern Ireland
The Irish Times, August 20, 1969.

Jack Lynch

"I want to assure the house that these arms have not been
imported, have not been landed in this country."
Dáil Debates, May 6, 1970.

LIAM COSGRAVE

"This country is drifting towards anarchy"
Dáil Debates, May 6, 1970.

NEIL BLANEY

"Ireland has always had its British Lackeys"
Dáil Debates, May 6, 1970.

BRIAN FAULKNER

"We reached a state of total disagreement with the United
Kingdom Government"
Northern Ireland Parliament Debates, March 28, 1972.

HAROLD WILSON

"It is a deliberate and calculating attempt . . . for the
purpose of bringing down the whole constitution off
Northern Ireland."
The Irish Times, May 26, 1974.

Sources

POPE JOHN PAUL II
"On my knees, I beg you to turn away from violence"
The Irish Times, October 2, 1979.

CHARLES HAUGHEY & MARGARET THATCHER
"The totality of relationships"
The Irish Times, December 9, 1980.

JOHN KELLY
"The addiction to the drug of cheap popularity is catching"
Belling the Cats, The Collected Speeches of John Kelly, John
Fanagan (ed.), Moytura Press, Dublin, 1992.

THE CATHOLIC HIERARCHY
"The wording would not exclude the possibility that in the
future a law could be passed permitting abortion in some form."
The Irish Times, March 31, 1983.

GARRET FITZGERALD
"The moral obligation, to put Northern Ireland, its people,
and heir interests first, imposes itself also . . . on those in
other lands."
The Irish Times, March 16, 1984.

DES O'MALLEY
"I stand by the Republic"
Dáil Debates, February 20, 1985.

PETER ROBINSON
"It is not often that a man gets the opportunity to deliver the
oration at his own funeral."
Hansard, November 26, 1985.

JOHN HUME
"This is the first time we have had a real framework within
which to address the problem."
Hansard, November 26, 1985.

ALAN DUKES
"The Tallaght Strategy"
Fine Gael, Dublin, undated.

MARY ROBINSON
"May I have the fortune to preside over an Ireland at a time
of exciting transformation."
The Irish Times, December 4, 1990.

NELSON MANDELA

"Nothing can stop the evolution of humanity towards the condition of greater and ever expanding freedom."
Dáil Debates, July 2, 1990.

ALBERT REYNOLDS & JOHN MAJOR

The Downing Street Declaration
The Irish Times, December 16, 1993.

THE PROVISIONAL IRA ARMY COUNCIL

"There will be a complete cessation of military operations."
The *Evening Press*, August 31, 1994.

DICK SPRING

"The key issue, throughout this entire episode, has been accountability."

JOHN BRUTON

"This document . . . is a shared understanding between the two Governments to assist discussion and negotiation."
Dáil debates, February 22, 1995.

FINOLA BRUTON

"I believe Irish feminists now have the confidence to develop their thinking, so that it becomes truly inclusive."
The Irish Times, December 2, 1995

BILL CLINTON

"We live in a time of immense hope and immense possibility."
Dáil Debates, December 1, 1995.